GW00818479

RUSSIAN SOCIETY IN TRANSITION

Russian Society in Transition

Edited by

DR CHRISTOPHER WILLIAMS
Reader in Russian Studies
Department of Politics and European Studies
University of Central Lancashire
Preston

PROFESSOR VLADIMIR CHUPROV
Doctor of Sociological Science
Head of the Sociology of Youth Centre
Institute of Socio-political Research
Moscow

PROFESSOR VLADIMIR STAROVEROV
Doctor of Philosophy
Head of Social Structure and Social Stratification Centre
Institute of Socio-political Research
Moscow

Dartmouth

Aldershot • Brookfield USA • Singapore • Sydney

© Christopher Williams, Vladimir Chuprov, Vladimir Staroverov 1996

All rights reserved. No part of this publication may be reproduced, stored in a retrieval system, or transmitted in any form or by any means, electronic, mechanical, photocopying, recording, or otherwise without the prior permission of Dartmouth Publishing Company Limited.

Published by
Dartmouth Publishing Company Limited
Gower House
Croft Road
Aldershot
Hants GU11 3HR
England

Dartmouth Publishing Company
Old Post Road
Brookfield
Vermont 05036
USA

British Library Cataloguing in Publication Data
Russian society in transition
    1.Social change - Russia (Federation) 2.Russia (Federation)
    - Social conditions 3.Russia (Federation) - Social policy
    I.Williams, Christopher II.Chuprov, Vladimir
    III.Staroverov, Vladimir
    947'.086

Library of Congress Cataloging-in-Publication Data
Library of Congress Catalog Card Number: 96-084475

ISBN 1 85521 748 1

Printed and bound in Great Britain by
Hartnolls Limited, Bodmin, Cornwall

Contents

List of tables and figures

Notes on contributors

Editors

Dr Christopher Williams is Reader in Russian Studies, Department of Politics and European Studies, University of Central Lancashire, Preston, UK and has published numerous articles on Russian history and social policy in scholarly journals in the UK, Ireland and the United States. He is the author of two books on *AIDS in post-Communist Russia and its successor states* (Avebury 1995) and *Young people in post-Communist Russia and Eastern Europe* (co-edited with James Riordan, University of Surrey and Igor Ilynsky, Institute of Youth Studies, Moscow, Dartmouth 1995). He was a visiting Professor at the Institute of Socio-Political Research, Moscow, Russia in March 1994 and September-November 1995 and a visiting Professor in the Department of Sociology, Belarus State University, Minsk, April 1994.

Professor Vladimir Chuprov, Doctor of Sociology is Head of the Sociology of Youth Division of the Institute of Socio-Political Research, Moscow, Russian Federation. He has co-ordinated a 12 region study on Russian youth since 1982 and is the author of over a 100 works for prominent Russian journals, such as *Sociological Research, Soviet Education* and *Socio-Political Science*. His published books include *Student movements in capitalist countries* (Moscow 1972) and *The Social development of the Soviet scientific intelligentsia* (Moscow 1988). Professor Chuprov is the author of a major multi-volume study on the occupational, educational and material position of Russian youth (Moscow 1992-93). His most recent works include: *The position of Russian youth in the new power structures* (Moscow 1993); *Migration patterns among youth: Trends and motivations* (with Mikhail Chernysh, Moscow 1993) and *The Social development of youth: Theoretical and applied aspects* (Moscow 1994).

Professor Vladimir Staroverov, Doctor of Philosophy, has had a very varied career. From 1961-69, he worked as a journalist for the newspapers *Rural Youth* and *Labour* before embarking upon an academic career as Head of the Sociology of the peasantry and Russian agriculture division of the USSR Academy of Sciences in 1971. He was a Deputy chief editor of the journal *Sociological Research* between 1974-82; has been

Vice-President of the All-Russian Society of sociologists and demographers since 1989 and is currently head of the Social structure and Social stratification section of the Institue of Socio-Political Research, Moscow (since 1992). Professor Staroverov is the author of 300 works, including articles for key journals such as *Questions of Economics*, *Economic Sciences* and *Sociological Research*. He is the author of 14 books, the most important of which are: *City and village: Our society today and tomorrow* (Moscow 1972); *Soviet countryside* (Moscow 1977); *Social aspects of the worker-intelligentsia* (Moscow 1977); *The intensification of the socio-economic development of the countryside* (Moscow 1979) and *The evolution of the peasantry of the social countries in the post-war period* (ed. 1984). His most recent publications include *Rebirth of the Russian countryside: Socio-economic trends and problems* (Moscow 1992); *War and Society* (Moscow 1993) and *Russia on the eve of the 21st century* (two volumes, Moscow 1994-95).

Other contributors

Anatolii Dmitriev is a Corresponding Member of the Russian Academy of Sciences, Moscow.

Nikolai Driakhlov is Director of Sociology of Labour Division, Sociology Faculty, Moscow State University, Russia.

Igor Ilynsky is Rector, Institute of Youth Studies, Moscow.

Vilen Ivanov is a Head of the Centre of the Sociology of Inter-ethnic Relations, Institute of Socio-Political Research, Moscow.

Yevgenii Katul'skii is Deputy Minister of Labour, Moscow.

Alexander Khlop'ev is Head of Analytical Centre of Socio-Political information and Deputy Director of the Institute of Socio-Political Research, Moscow and a member of the Russian Academy of Social Sciences.

Professor Solomon Krapivenskii is Deputy Head of the Faculty of Philosophy, Volgograd State University, Volgograd, Russia.

Oksana Kuchmaeva is a PhD Candidate, Moscow Institute of Economics and Statistics, Russia.

Professor Boris Melnikov is Pro-Rector of the University of Komi, Syktyvkar, Komi Autonomous Republic, Russian Federation.

Irena Orlova is Deputy Head, Department of Comparative International Research, Institute of Socio-Political Research, Moscow.

Larisa Romanenko is a Research Associate, Institute of Sociology, Moscow and PhD Candidate, Moscow State University.

Boris Ruchkin is Director, Institute of Youth Studies, Moscow.

Tatiana Rukavishnikov is a Research Associate, Social Dynamics Centre, Institute of Socio-Political Research, Moscow.

Vladimir Rukavishnikov is Head of the Social Dynamics Centre, Institute of Socio-Political Research, Moscow.

Professor Mikhail Rutkevich is a Corresponding Member of the Russian Academy of Sciences and a chief sociologist at the Institute of Socio-Political Research, Moscow.

Andrei Sharonov is President, Russian State Committee on Youth Affairs, Moscow.

Professor Gennadi Zhuravlev is Deputy Head of the Faculty of Sociology and Social Psychology, Moscow Institute of Economics and Statistics, Russia.

Julia Zubok is a Research Associate and PhD candidate in the Sociology of Youth Division of the Institute of Socio-Political Research, Moscow.

Preface and acknowledgements

This collection of essays grew out of a three year link between the University of Central Lancashire, Preston and the Institute for Socio-Political Research, Moscow. During this time Dr. Christopher Williams was a Visiting Professor at the Institute of Socio-Political Research in Moscow on three separate occasions - November 1993, March 1994 and September-November 1995. During the course of these research visits intense debates ensued among Russian and English specialists concerning the impact of the current economic and political reforms on Russian society. The outcome of many of these discussions are contained in the pages of this book.

The editors have made no effort to impose a single set of goals or particular political ideologies on the individual contributors, instead contributions are based on specialist knowledge of a specific topic. As a result what follows is a wide diversity of opinions. This we hope will increase interest in as well as the intrinsic value of this book. It is also based on the firm premise that there are very few existing studies offering distinguished Russian sociologists, demographers, economists and other social scientists the opportunity to make their research findings on trends in Russian society known to a wider audience. We only hope that this practice will continue in future years as we build up closer contact with one another; foster greater trust and increase each other's understanding of the complex process of transition in one of the biggest countries in the world - Russia.

The Editors made the final selection of material and edited all contributions, while Sergei and Yaroslav Sorokopud, Maria Nazarkewych and Christopher Williams translated the various chapters from Russian into English.

We wish to thank all contributors for their co-operation in producing this book, in particular for revising and updating their chapters. Special thanks also go to Mrs Joanne Kirk and Mrs Tracey Wright who prepared this manuscript for publication.

Thanks are due, finally to Dartmouth Publishers for invaluable editorial and technical expertise.

It is hoped that this survey, which is based on the latest sociological and statistical surveys, will enable scholars in the West to gain a greater understanding of the impact of Yeltsin's reforms on Russian society. Russia is currently undergoing a deep systemic crisis. When the communist state collapsed in 1991, it was greeted with cheers of joy. Five years on, many Russians are highly disillusioned with the past and present and extremely pessimistic about the future. They are mainly concerned about the following: falling birth rates and increasing death rates; the Russian family in crisis; antagonistic class relations; the neglect of young people; the low priority given to social policy; growing unemployment; woefully inadequate health care provision; astronomical crime levels; falling standards in education; and finally rising ethnic tension, with the widespread felling that conflict on a Yugoslav scale is a distinct possibility in the near future. In this book, distinguished Russian and English scholars demonstrate that unless greater attention is given to these issues in the lead up to the June 1996 Presidential elections, then Yeltsin may well be forced out of power in 1996. In the long-term this might well have a detrimental effect upon Russia's chance of making a successful transition from communism to liberal democracy by the end of this decade.

Permission to publish

The Editors are grateful to the following authors and publishers:

To Professor Richard Rose, the Centre for the Study of Public Policy, Strathclyde and Paul Lazarsfeld Society, Vienna for permission to cite material from the New Russia Barometer II 1993 and III 1994 surveys.

To Professor Richard Rose for permission to use the material cited in table 12.12 which is taken from 'Getting by without government: Everyday life in Russia', *Daedulus*, Vol. 1, No. 23 (1994), p. 51.

To Dr Christopher Davis of Wolfson College Oxford for permission to use figure 12.1 which is adapted from his chapter entitled 'The organisation and performance of the contemporary Soviet health service', in G.W. Lapidus and G.E. Swanson (eds.), *State and Welfare USA/USSR*, (1988), p. 117.

To Dr Christopher Davis of Wolfson College Oxford for permission to use various tables from 'The health sector in the Soviet and Russian economies; from reform to fragmentation to transition', *The former Soviet Union in transition* (JEC 1993), pp. 855-58, 861.

To Dr Christopher Davis of Wolfson College Oxford for permission to use two tables adapted from 'The health care crisis: The former Soviet Union', *RFE/RL Research Report*, 8 October 1993, pp. 38, 40-41.

To the Editor of *Literaturnaia Gazeta* and the journalist Oleg Moroz for permission to use a cartoon from his article, 'Kto nami budet pravit' 15 iilia 1996 goda?', *Literaturnaia Gazeta* 29 March 1995, p. 11; and finally

To D.S. Mason *Revolution in East-Central Europe*. Copyright (c) 1992 by Westview Press. Reprinted by permission of Westview Press.

Christopher Williams, Preston
Vladimir Chuprov and Vladimir Staroverov, Moscow
March 1996

Abbreviations

AIDS	Acquired Immune Deficiency Syndrome
BASEES	British Association of Slavonic and East European Studies
BR	Birth Rate
CEU	Central European University
CIS	Commonwealth of Independent States
CPD	Congress of People's Deputies
CPRF	Communist Party of the Russian Federation
CPSU	Communist Party of the Soviet Union
CSPP	Centre for the Study of Public Policy, Strathclyde University, Scotland
DPR	Democratic Party of Russia
DR	Death Rate
Duma	Lower House of Russia's Federal Assembly
EBRD	European Bank for Reconstruction and Development
FES	Federal Employment Service
FMS	Federal Migration Service
FSU	Former Soviet Union
GBH	Grievous Bodily Harm
GDP	Gross Domestic Production
GNP	Gross National Product
Goskomstat	State Statistical Committee
ILO	International Labour Organisation
IMF	International Monetary Fund
IMR	Infant Mortality Rate
ISPR	Institute of Socio-Political Research, Moscow
KGB	Committee for State Security
Kolkhozy	State farm(s)
Komsomol	Young Communist League
KRO	Congress of Russian Communities

KVD	Internal Affairs Committee
LDPR	Liberal Democratic Party of Russia
MGAkh	Moscow Chemical and Mechanical Engineering Academy
MGPU	Moscow State Pedagogical University
MGU	Moscow State University
MIC	Military-industrial complex
Minzdrav	Ministry of Public Health
MPhil	Master of Philosophy degree
MPs	Members of Parliament
MPU	Moscow Pedagogical University
MSPU	Moscow State Construction University
MVD	Ministry of Internal Affairs
NATO	North Atlantic Treaty Organisation
OAPs	Old-age Pensioners
OHR	Our Home is Russia
PG	Population Growth
PhD	Doctor of Philosophy degree
PM	Prime Minister
PRES	Party of Unity and Accord
PTU	Technical-vocational establisments
r	rouble
RAN	Russian Academy of Sciences
RDC	Russia's Democratic Choice
REA	Russian Economics Academy
RF	Russian Federation
RFE/RL	Radio Free Europe/Radio Liberty
RSFSR	Russian Soviet Federal Socialist Republic
$	United States Dollars
Smychka	Link (between town and countryside)
Sovkhozy	State farm(s)
SSSR	Union of Soviet Socialist Republics
TB	Tuberculosis
TsSMO	Sociology of Ethnic Relations Centre, Moscow
UB	Unemployment Benefit
UK	United Kingdom
USA	United States of America
USSR	Union of Soviet Socialist Republics
VD	Venereal Disease
VTsIOM	Centre for Public Opinion Research, Moscow
VUZ	Higher education establishment
WHO	World Health Organisation

Introduction

CHRISTOPHER WILLIAMS, VLADIMIR CHUPROV AND
VLADIMIR STAROVEROV

The abortive August 1991 coup d'etat and the collapse of the USSR in December 1991 appeared to put an end to Communist Party rule in Russia. Over the next four years, the one-party state gave way to a multi-party system and centralised planning was replaced by a market economy. However against the backdrop of growing criticism of Yeltsin's economic policy, especially the 'shock therapy', and a number of other problems, namely growing unemployment, falling living standards and rising crime, Russia's second democratic elections took place on 17 December 1995. The main party to gain in the elections to the State Duma, the lower house of Russia's new Federal Assembly was not the Prime Minister Viktor Chernomyrdin's *Our Home is Russia*, which was backed by Yeltsin, but Gennadi Zyuganov's *Communist Party of the Russian Federation* which gained nearly a quarter of the votes. Whilst it would be misleading to read too much into the Communist's victory, their unanticipated success will set the trend for the June 1996 Presidential elections. This book seeks to increase Western understanding of the changes which have swept Russian society over the last four to five years from a largely sociological perspective. We will examine demographic change; the transformation of the social structure; the position of young people; the nature of social policy measures; the extent of unemployment; trends in health care, education, employment and crime; the degree of ethnic conflict and finally the chances of developing a civil society in late 20th century Russia from a Russian rather than Western perspective. The exceptions to this rule are chapters 1 and 12 which are written by a British expert on Russia and chapter 2 which is jointly written by English and Russian academics.

In focusing upon Russian society, it is not the intention of this book to minimise the importance of the process of political democratisation and economic transformation of contemporary Russia. Instead our aim is to show that much of the current literature places too great an emphasis on structural preconditions for democratisation, such as economic liberalisation, and on the bargaining process between defenders of the old regime and reformers and democrats rather than focusing on the impact of these changes upon the populace. The people of Russia are not only *affected by* the policies pursued during the transition to democracy but also *influence* the nature of the latter. The final outcome will depend upon the impact of the state, private sector and individuals in Russia's new market economy of the late 1990s and beyond. What most of the following chapters suggest is that new actors are starting to dominate the policy and decision-making agenda. The dismantled Russian state has failed to step in to protect vulnerable groups in Russian society, such as the young or the elderly, and to guarantee a general education and training, job security, basic health care and so forth. Russia's second democratic elections showed that Yeltsin has failed to consolidate his power and for the moment his government is still looking for a performance legitimacy.

Since the December 1993 elections, Yeltsin's government has faced many problems. There appear to be three possibilities: first, Russia will continue its advance towards the market and democratic reforms, leading to stable economic growth and political success for Yeltsin by 1996; second, we will only see a marginal strengthening of Yeltsin's position, forcing him to adopt aggressive nationalist slogans and relax his macroeconomic policy. Yeltsin might eventually be forced to use authoritarian methods to resolve the acute political and economic crisis. If the second path is chosen, then each and every defeat of the Russian authorities will probably mean a further turning of the 'screw' (*zakrutit' gaiki*). Finally, the people of Russia will vote Yeltsin out of power in 1996 and nominate a new President in the hope that s/he will address the mounting problems facing Russian society.

Up until Easter 1994, Yeltsin seemed to be pursuing the first of these alternatives; however April 1994 marked the start of Russia's U-turn (*povorot*). Yeltsin and Prime Minister Chernomyrdin now proved unwilling to continue with unpopular but necessary measures. This has generated a deep economic recession. On top of this, the bloody military conflict in Chechnya has only served to heighten the level of political tension in Moscow. Does this mean that Russia is moving away from democracy? Is Yeltsin beginning to adopt policies similar to those of his opponents - agrarians, communists and neo-fascists? What might the failure of economic reform, the rise of anti-reform tendencies and a slowing down of the pace of political democratisation mean for Russian society and Yeltsin's image abroad?

The purpose of this monograph, which consists largely of specially commissioned chapters written by Russian specialists, is to trace the impact of the economic recession and political turmoil on contemporary Russian society. Above all, the goal is to assess why the euphoria which greeted the collapse of communism in late 1991 has given rise to feelings of impending disaster in 1996. Part of the explanation lies, as these contributions show, in the fact that trends in demography, education, employment, health care etc. continue to be *subordinated* to Yeltsin's economic and political priorities. Yeltsin has failed time and time again to provide direct solutions to the problems inherent in the sectors of the Russian economy discussed in part III. Instead the Russian state has effectively withdrawn from the policy and decision-making arena. This has produced a stalemate in which the creation of essential legal and institutional frameworks in population policy, education, health care, employment and so forth has been a slow, painful and complex process. On top of this, it is clear that trends in Russian society have not simply been determined by domestic variables, but by global processes. A range of international agencies - IMF, EBRD, World Bank, etc. - are seeking to influence the development of post-communist policy. Bob Deacon has argued that the future of social policy, as one prominent example, will largely be shaped by the struggle between global policy actors and agencies. He goes on to assert that external conflicts over who should determine the nature and direction of social policy have been mirrored by internal struggles in which various internal actors take sides with the external agencies in an attempt to get their policies implemented.[1] While not denying this possibility, this book argues that there are inherent dangers in placing too much emphasis on the role of *global* actors to the detriment of internal forces. Most of the Russian contributors also challenge the widely held Western view that *the intervention of global policy actors in Russia's affairs is a good thing*. They fear too much dependency on the West. According to Stadler[2] dependency can be viewed in a number of ways: first as *dependent modernisation* whereby Russia advances towards a certain 'model of reference' or 'target system' - Western liberal democracy in its parliamentary or Presidential form; second as *asymmetric interdependence* which involves a reliance of the weak (Russia) on the resources of the strong (Western financial institutions) and finally, *dependence* can be defined as a situation in which the stronger system has the power to enforce certain changes on the weaker party and therefore has the capacity to shape the nature of the relationship between the two structures. The key issue which numerous chapters touch upon is the ability of the 'weak' to withstand the 'strong'. Given Russia's collapse, economic recession and high level of political instability - not helped by current rumours concerning Yeltsin's health - Russia is not in a position to resist. She is increasingly dependent upon global policy actors. In the medium to long-term therefore this might distort 'the internal democratic discourse about transformation policies' and have major policy implications well into the next century.[3]

Among the many alternatives open to Russia, there are three main options:

(i)   Russian dependency on the West;
(ii)   extremists of right or left political persuasion take power after the 1996 elections and establish a dictatorship; and/or
(iii)   democracy flourishes in Russia, the rule of law is accepted and the current political inertia and economic stalemate is successfully resolved by the 1996 elections.

In order to throw some light on these possible paths of development *Russian Society in Transition* seeks to explore the social dimensions of Russia's transition.

In Part I, Christopher Williams sets the scene by examining changes in Russia's economic and political system since the collapse of Communism. Vladimir Staroverov and Christopher Williams then offer two perspectives on the role which sociology is playing in improving our understanding, knowledge and awareness of current trends in Russian society.

Part II looks at specific trends in Russia society. In chapter 3, Gennadi Zhuravlev et al. assess demographic trends - the birth and death rate, marriage, divorce and migration patterns - stressing in particular the impending crisis (i.e. that the death rate now exceeds the birth rate and population growth is insufficient for Russia to reproduce herself). In the next chapter, Nikolai Driakhlov looks at the growing conflict between the old and the new in Russia in the 1990s and the impact which this is having on socio-cultural trends.

Chapters 5-7 by Mikhail Rutkevich, Alexander Khlop'ev and Vladimir Staroverov turn our attention to the key issue of the transformation of the social structure - the disintegration of the old communist class system in which workers and peasants were prioritised and the rise of the *nouveau riche* adhering to the virtues of a post-industrial society and materialism. The sources and impact of class conflict as well as the reaction of different sections of society to these trends are outlined using contemporary Russian sociological survey data.

In the next two chapters, the plight of Russian youth is explored. In chapter 8, Vladimir Chuprov and Julia Zubok examine social mobility trends, work patterns and the process of integration in the early-mid 1990s, using longitudinal survey data from 12 regions of the Russian Federation for the period 1990-95; while in chapter 9, Andrei Sharonov and Boris Ruchkin assess the dangers of ignoring young people in the rush for the market and liberal democracy. Particular attention is devoted to the extent of alienation and the rise of anti-social tendencies among young people in Russia today and the impact which this is having on their attitudes towards society, politics and the Yeltsin Administration. The negative impact of economic recession, unemployment, financial instability and *immobolisme* on the standard of living and political orientation of young men and women is fully explored.

Part III then builds upon the aforementioned analysis by focusing on specific aspects of public policy which are designed to offset the adverse effects of the current economic and political crisis on Russian society. In this context, Faina Kosygina and Solomon Krapivenskii survey the general situation with regard to governmental responses and social measures in chapter 10. From chapter 11 onwards the key problems of the day - employment and unemployment (Yevgenii Katul'skii); health care and conditions (Christopher Williams); education (Vladimir Chuprov and Julia Zubok); concerns about law and order (Igor Ilynsky); ethnic conflict (Vilen Ivanov) and difficulties in creating a civil society (Vladimir Rukavishnikov et al.) - are analysed.

A concluding section looks at future trends in the lead up to the June 1996 Presidential elections. The prospects for overcoming current difficulties are assessed. It is argued that the present situation is being further exacerbated by 'globalisation' (a rejection of Russian culture and tradition in favour of Western values) and/or a return to past nationalistic values.

What these essays show is that the impact of the reforms on and the role of social groups in the transition process cannot be ignored if Russia wants to prevent her current crisis from turning into a catastrophe which might ultimately lead to the re-establishment of a new variety of totalitarianism by the start of the 21st century.

Notes

1.   B. Deacon, 'Global policy actors and the shaping of post-communist social policy', in A. de Swaan (ed.), *Social policy beyond borders: The Social question in transnational perspective*, Amsterdam University Press, Amsterdam 1994, pp. 69-91.

2.   A. Stadler, 'Problems of dependant modernization in East-Central Europe: A case for social democratic concern', in: M. Waller et al. (eds.), *Social democracy in post-communist Europe*, Frank Cass, London 1994, pp. 45-46.
3.   Ibid, p. 45.

PART I

BACKGROUND TO THE CURRENT SITUATION

1 Economic reform and political change in Russia, 1991-96

CHRISTOPHER WILLIAMS

Introduction

This chapter seeks to explore the economic and political changes which have swept Russia since the collapse of the USSR in December 1991. The goal is to provide a backdrop against which to examine current developments in Russian society depicted in subsequent chapters.

The economy

The Communist legacy

From the late 1920s to the mid-1980s the Russian economy was based on a system of centralised planning in which production, distribution and exchange were under state ownership and control. The government, under the guidance of the Communist Party, made all the key decisions about investment, consumption, prices and income. The central planning system put in place by Stalin in the 1920s fulfilled two primary functions: firstly, the plan put pressure on the system and acted not only as a tool of co-ordination but also as a means of mobilising resources to achieve specific objectives, such as industrialisation, collectivisation or the defence of the ex-USSR against foreign aggression; and secondly, the plan established a clear set of objectives e.g. priority was given to defence and heavy industry over agriculture or consumer goods. The planner was the person who laid down government policies in the form of plan directives.

In reality, however, few plan targets were met. Hence the standard image in the West of the former USSR was one of 'frequent food shortages, scarce low quality consumer goods, high prices, long queues, inadequate housing etc.'[1] Various attempts were made at fundamental economic reform to rectify these issues during the period 1957-85, ranging from Khrushchev's *Sovnarkhozy* (regional economic councils) reform in the late 1950s which aimed at reducing the concentration of power held by central planners and increasing the ability of managers to make economic decisions for themselves through to the reimposition of central control under Brezhnev (1965-82), but they failed.[2]

Unfortunately, all these economic reforms failed to stem the decline in the Soviet growth rate and the all-pervasive shortages and bottlenecks. Gorbachev sought to change all that. Perestroika was geared towards accelerating growth and modernising the Soviet economy via the reassertion of discipline using the anti-alcohol campaign, technical modernisation, increased East-West trade, greater enterprise independence, decentralisation of decision-making and finally, and perhaps most important of all, Gorbachev sought to replace the obsolete Stalinist command system with a fully functioning market economy.

Although his reforms initially appeared to be successful, by 1988 it was painfully clear that perestroika was producing disappointing results - a large budget deficit, high inflation, rationing, etc. This occurred for three reasons: first, political opposition within the higher echelons of the Communist Party; second, bureaucratic opposition from Ministerial staff and finally because of criticism from enterprise managers due to the uncertainties generated by Gorbachev's reforms. These problems coupled with the general public's fear of mass unemployment and the adverse impact of the market transition on the standard of living meant that by the late 1980s perestroika had effectively ground to a halt.[3] The ensuing economic chaos and failure to deliver sufficient goods at the right time and in the right quantities partly explains why the August 1991 coup d'etat occurred. In any case, by this time, Gorbachev had already slowed down the pace of his reform in order to avoid further economic disruption, on the one hand, and political collapse, on the other. This was too little, too late. He had already sealed his own fate. In December 1991, perestroika was finally put to rest alongside the former Soviet Union (FSU).

This left a legacy of poor economic performance. According to Rutland, by 1990 Russia's GDP was minus 4 per cent in comparison to the previous year; national income was minus 10.1 per cent; industrial output minus 7.8 per cent; consumer goods output minus 4.5 per cent; agricultural output minus 6.9 per cent and capital investment minus 12 per cent. As a consequence, by the end of 1991, the USSR had a budget deficit of 200 billion roubles (20 per cent of GDP) and was close to defaulting on its $58 billion hard currency debt.[4]

The post-Soviet economy

For the last five years or so, Russia has continued its drive towards a market economy via a programme of macroeconomic stabilisation, extensive liberalisation of prices and foreign trade, privatisation of the most productive assets, institutional reforms etc. According to the phasing of economic reform process devised by Fischer and Gelb,

Russia is only in the early stages of market reforms and still has a long way to go.[5]

Throughout the early post-communist period (1992-93), inefficiencies in the economy, all-pervasive shortages and the rapid decline in the standard of living persisted. For example, by June 1992, consumption of basic foodstuffs stood at late 1950s levels and pensioners received benefits two times below the basic wage. All in all, whereas in 1991, 55 per cent of the population lived below the poverty line, by mid-1992 an estimated 90 per cent were said to be in such a position.[6] This was the outcome of declining economic growth and a rising cost of living. Thus the cost of living increased twelve times between March 1991 - March 1992. More specifically, meat prices rose 26 times while that of milk and other dairy products increased 29 times.[7] In industry and other sectors of the Russian economy, production levels plummeted. In the metallurgical industry, for instance, output fell by 18-32 per cent whilst in agriculture the decline was by 32-50 per cent by mid-1992 over 1991.[8] By the end of 1992, the first post-communist year in office, economic destabilisation was widespread. Inflation rose 26 times between December 1991 - December 1992; basic foodstuffs by 100-125 times; butter and sugar by 130-160 times; transport costs by 13-23 times, health care by 20 times, the cost of childcare places by 32 times and so on. These trends compared with a rise in wages of only 10 per cent, not enough to keep pace with inflation.[9] As a result, a staggering 82 per cent of Muscovite families said that they could not cope in 1992, compared to only 20 per cent the year before.[10]

These trends continued on into 1993. Although inflation was starting to fall, wage increases remained minimal at 12 per cent. The plight of pensioners had also worsened, with an estimated 96 per cent living below the poverty line by summer 1993.[11] Furthermore, by October 1993, for example, Russian industrial production was 56.2 per cent of its 1990 level; unemployment stood at 1 million and exports had fallen by 12 per cent while imports declined by 20 per cent. In overall terms, oil production was 64 per cent; coal 78 per cent; meat 49 per cent and bread only 68 per cent of its 1990 level by the end of 1993.[12] As we shall see below, the rapid deterioration in Russia's economic situation was to have a detrimental impact on the results of her first democratic elections to parliament in December 1993.

The situation went from bad to worse in 1994. Yeltsin backed by the likes of Gaidar, Chubais and Fedorov, made a decisive move towards the market up to Easter 1994. This included the following measures: financial stabilisation; the removal of artificial constraints on competition within Russia's internal market; privatisation; clear-cut guarantees on property rights; the introduction of a bankruptcy programme and the transfer of resources from inefficient to efficient sectors of the economy.[13] The goal was stable economic growth. However, under pressure from extremists from the right and left, agrarians, Travkinites and Shakhravites, from April 1994 Yeltsin began a U-turn (*zreiushchii povorot*) in economic policy. This meant a relaxation of macroeconomic policy; great manoeuvring between the various economic and political groupings supporting manufacturing industry; a closure of the external market; the placing of restrictions on competing foreign goods and services and greater targeting of domestic consumers.[14]

As a consequence, by June 1994, industrial production in Russia stood at 74.2 per cent of its 1993 level. This compared to a figure of 93.8 per cent in agriculture; 80.1 per cent in transport and 77 per cent in construction. However, the cost of living was now rising at a lower rate: 7.3 times between January-June 1994 compared to the same period in 1993.[15] By August 1994, this *povorot* began to take effect: real wages fell by at least 50 per cent; the rouble to dollar exchange rate was constantly falling (by a third in mid-October 1994 alone) and a number of other adverse effects were now noticeable: for example, unpaid wages totalled trillions of roubles; industrial output was down by 27 per cent; GNP fell by 17 per cent and 24.8 million Russians were living below the poverty line by October 1994. Thus for most of 1994 Russia suffered from financial instability, especially in its currency, falling production and so on. Nevertheless, although inflation was still high at an estimated 300 per cent in 1994, this was an improvement compared to 509 per cent a year earlier.[16]

Economic indicators for the first half of 1995 suggest that the aforementioned crisis had deepened. Although inflation fell from 18 per cent in January 1995 to around 5 per cent in September 1995, with the forecast for the end of 1995 standing at around 6-7 per cent,[17] the rapid decline in output continued. For instance, between January-June 1995, food production fell on average by 30-40 per cent, with meat production declining by 37 per cent and dairy products by 63 per cent.[18] Furthermore, the cost of living remains high while living standards are falling. According to Premier Chernomyrdin, real incomes fell by 12 per cent between January-October 1995.[19] Official estimates now suggest that 45 million Russians or 30 per cent of the population of the Russian Federation are living below the poverty line. An amazing 43 per cent of this group are in gainful employment.[20] The working population is now having to support a growing number of dependents. For example, the number of poor (*bednye*) rose from 307 per 1,000 population in 1994 to 474 per 1,000 by mid-1995.[21] All the signs are that Russia's economy is still faltering. According to Oleg Cherkopets of the newspaper *Sovetskaia Rossiia*, Russian GDP fell by 4-12 per cent between January-August 1995. Industrial output, like its agricultural counterpart also declined. More specifically output in the construction industry fell by 7 times; machine tools by 6 times; agricultural machinery output by 7-8 times and light industry by 6-7 times over the previous year. This is on top of a budget deficit of 20.9 trillion roubles or 4.5 per cent of GDP in the first half of 1995.[22]

Forecasts for 1996 suggest that overall production in Russia will decline by 7-8 per cent, but in industry the prognosis is bleak at 20 per cent.[23] However, this must be set against inflation estimates of 7-8 per cent per month in 1996, a tremendous improvement on previous years. In order to try and stabilise Russia's economy, the World Bank recently extended an $11 billion loan to Russia over the next three years.[24] One can only hope that this will help smooth out Russia's difficult transition to democracy. However, as economic recovery is not expected for many months to come, it is possible that the current economic crisis will endanger Russia's transition to liberal democracy, as shown by the nationalist and communist victories in the December 1995 parliamentary elections.[25]

As we can see from table 1.1 below the balance sheet in economic terms does not look very good after five years of 'shock therapy'. Most predictions for 1996 suggest a mixed picture: progress in some areas, but continued decline in orders. One leading Russian economist predicts that corruption, crime, economic chaos, reductions in living standards and above all a move away from democracy are very likely in the lead up to the June 1996 Presidential elections.[26]

Table 1.1
Economic trends in Russia, 1990-96

	1990	1991	1992	1993	1994	1995	1996 (est)
Population (millions)	148.2	148.3	148.3	148.0	147.9	148.3	147.9
Population growth	332.9	103.9	-219.8	-750.8	-920.2	-993.0	na
Unemployment (million)	-	-	3.95	4.12	5.3	5.5^a	6.20
GDP (annual % change)	-	-13.0	-19.0	-12.0	-15.0	-2.0	3.0
GDP (per capita)	4.3	8.7	121.5	1091.7	4246.3	na	na
Agricultural output (annual % change)	-	-4.5	-9.0	-4.0	-9.0	na	na
Average wage (in roubles)	303	548	5,995	58,663	216,000	499,500^b	na
Wages (% change over previous year)	15.2	80.9	1,094	978.5	368.0	184.3	na
Exports (value in billion US$)	71.7	50.9	42.4	44.3	48.0	62.3^c	na
Imports (value in billion US$)	71.7	50.9	42.4	44.3	48.0	45.8^c	na
External debt (billion US$)	-	67.0	77.7	83.7	93.4	96.2	98.8
Inflation (in %)	-	92.7	1,353.0	896.0	302.0	140.0	60.0
Industrial output (% change over previous year)	-	-8.0	-18.0	-14.1	-23.7	-13.0	na
Budget deficit (as % of GDP)	1.3	2.9	3.0	5.0	9.9	2.8^d	na

Key:

a	January - August only
b	Up to July 1995 only
c	Up to August 1995
d	January - July 1995 only

Sources: *Rossiia pered vyborom* (Moscow 'Obozrevatel' 1995), p. 25; *Statisticheskoe Obozrenie* No. 9, 1995, pp. 7, 33, 60, 65; *Ekonomika i Zhizn'* No. 41, October 1995, p. 1; *Sevodnya* 27 October 1995, p. 3. *The World in 1996,*

(Economist Group, London 1995), p. 94; IMF, *World Economic Outlook*, May 1995, (IMF, Washington D.C. 1995), pp. 131-32, 178; UN, *Economic Survey of Europe in 1994-1995*, (United Nations, New York/Geneva 1995), pp. 70, 82, 102, *Rossiiskii statisticheskii ezhegodnik 1994*, Moscow, Goskomstat 1994, p. 10, *Rossiia v tsifrakh 1995*, (Moscow, Goskomstat 1995), p. 17, *Ekonomika Rossii, Ianvar' - August 1995g*, (Moscow, Goskomstat Rossii 1995), pp. 85, 121, 134; A.A. Frenkel', *Ekonomika Rossii 1992-1995: Tendentsii, analiz, prognoz*, (Moscow, Finstatinform 1995), pp. 126, 130 and *Finansovaia Gazeta* 22 December 1995, p. 1.

Political change

Russia has an authoritarian political legacy. The Communist Party was very strong and enjoyed supremacy over state bodies in policy-making via the nomenklatura and the principle of democratic centralism. By the time Gorbachev took power in 1985 political inertia was widespread and a major overhaul of the Russian political system was deemed necessary. When Article 6 of the 1977 Constitution, giving the CPSU a leading and guiding role in Soviet society, was abolished in Spring 1990, it became clear that a transition to liberal democracy was not possible without fundamentally undermining the CPSU. But who would replace the CPSU? What type of party system would develop? How much power would be given to the executive, on the one hand, and the legislative, on the other and finally, how would any abuse of political power be controlled? Gorbachev's answer was to create a President.

The origins of Presidential power

Gorbachev was sworn in as President on 15 March 1990 granting him substantial powers - to pass decrees; by-pass the Prime Minister (PM) to nominate the Council of Ministers (or Cabinet); act as head of state; nominate the PM and the Supreme Court Chairman; instigate emergency powers and finally, to dissolve the Supreme Soviet. He was theoretically accountable to the Supreme Soviet and the Congress of People's Deputies (CPD), but in practice dominated these parliamentary bodies. Gorbachev stated that there was no reason to fear a new form of authoritarian rule as several safeguards were already in place: limits on age and tenure of office and the ability of the CPD to remove him if a two-thirds majority decided accordingly.

Ironically, one of Gorbachev's biggest critics was Yeltsin. He accused Gorbachev of being absolutist and authoritarian. Historians, such as Yuri Afanasev, added that the rapid transition to a Presidential system of government was too premature without a new Constitution and might lead to a new personal dictator. Others suggested that even though they could trust Gorbachev, the same might not be true of his successors.

During the second half of the 1980s, it was clear that even though Gorbachev possessed a great deal of power he was unable to exercise it. Thus by mid-1991, according to Lech Walesa, Russia was sailing into the Bermuda Triangle between a weak President, a fractured parliament and an ineffective government.[27]   Gorbachev's political vulnerability was demonstrated by two things: the lack of a popular mandate and his inability to avert the August 1991 coup d'etat. By contrast, Yeltsin represented the aspirations of a people searching for a new Russia without the CPSU.

Yeltsin's Presidency[28]

Despite the political changeover in December 1991, conflicts between the President and the parliament have been evident ever since. For example in April 1992, a parliamentary vote of no confidence was only narrowly defeated. Later on in March 1993, the President was stripped of his emergency powers granted in November 1991 and ordered to act in accordance with the Constitution (i.e. to recognise that the CPD was 'the supreme body of state power' in all questions relating to the Federation while the President was merely the chief official and head of executive authority). Yeltsin responded on 20 March by calling for the legislative to become a 'watch-dog' (i.e. not abandoned but unable to over-rule parliamentary or government decrees). After the April 1993 Referendum granted Yeltsin's request - despite opposition from the Chairman of the Constitutional Court and Vice-President Rutskoi - he was in a position to dissolve and dismantle the CPD in October 1993. During the storming of the 'White House' in the same month, Khasbulatov argued that it was essential for the parliament to act as a counter-balance to Presidential power - via a clear separation of powers - so that not all the power would be in one's person's hands.

The period from August 1991 to the Storming of the 'White House' in 1993 was symbolised by political stalemate. Neither President nor parliament was sufficiently strong to dominate. For Russia this meant few reforms, a loss of law and order and no statehood worthy of her history or traditions. In a speech to the CPD in April 1992 Yeltsin rightly predicted chaos and regional separatism. But not everyone agreed with his solution: a strong executive to preserve the integrity of Russia and a rapid transition to liberal democracy and market reform. For example, a New Russia Barometer survey carried out between June-July 1993 found that 30 per cent out of a sample of 1,975 wanted a strong President; 30 per cent a strong Congress and 21 per cent rule by decree or veto.[29]

Since the CPD was dissolved in September 1993 and a new Constitution was approved by Referendum, a strong Presidency has been created in which Yeltsin is: head of state (Article 80.1); guardian of the Constitution (Article 80.2); able to nominate the PM and the chairmen of the State Bank, Constitutional Court and the Supreme Court; define the direction of domestic and foreign policy; act as head of the Security Council (Article 84); commander in chief (Article 87); organise referendums; dissolve the Duma; sign laws (Article 84) and exercise emergency powers (Article 89).[30] Yeltsin's ability to use these extensive powers depends upon two key factors: the parliament and the political parties.

The Russian Parliament[31]

Russia is the odd man out in the New Europe. She has a short history of parliamentary institutions (i.e. the State Duma of 1906, but the latter exercised no control over the executive because Ministers and members of parliament (MPs) were nominated by and responsible to the Tsar). This weakness was further compounded by the Communist legacy which created a weak judiciary (unable to exercise the rule of law) and a weak parliament (Supreme Soviet) dominated by the CPSU.

Gorbachev sought to build a new system of government based upon a division of powers. Thus the parliament became an arena of political debate. The unanticipated outcome for Gorbachev and Yeltsin after him was also that parliament became a focus of political opposition against the executive. This process occurred in several phases: first, via the creation of the Inter-Regional Group of Deputies (1987-89); second, through the rise of the *soviets* (1989-90); third, the latter culminated in the emergence of the CPDs (1989-90) and finally, the period 1990-91, was marked by growing opposition to the strengthening of executive authority. This eventually led to the ousting of Gorbachev and the collapse of the USSR in December 1991.

The post-communist period can be split into two stages: the first phase (January 1992-September 1993) saw a continuing executive-legislative conflict while the second phase December 1993 to the present day has seen the emergence of a Presidential Republic alongside a new parliament dominated by Yeltsin's opponents. In the bicameral parliament, it is the State Duma (or Lower House) rather than the Council of the Federation (Upper House) which has the greatest powers (to 'approve' the nomination of the PM; proclaim amnesties [hence the embarrassing release of Rutskoi and Khasbulatov]; prepare and adopt laws; oversee the procedure for the election of the President and finally, the Duma has the right to have a vote of confidence in the government).

Although the December 1993 parliamentary elections sent shock waves throughout Russia and the West, it turned out that the new Russian political system was adaptable and flexible enough to survive. Since then, however, Yeltsin has been unable to mobilise sufficient resources or the political will to counteract Duma attempts to block major economic and political decisions, such as the President's nomination for the post of Procurator General; the composition of the Constitutional Court; revisions to the 1994 Federal Budget, etc.[32] This is hardly surprising because only 92 out of the 450 Duma members are supporters of Yeltsin; no one single faction dominates and 56 out of the 172 people elected to the Council of the Federation are opposed to Yeltsin's reform strategy.[33] Such a situation has left Yeltsin little choice but to 'rule by decree'.[34] Rumours in October 1994 of a possible resignation by PM Chernomyrdin plus corruption scandals in the military, before and after Chechnya, as well as a very narrow escape on another vote of no confidence in late October 1994 together with a second no confidence vote in June 1995 indicate that the situation is not improving. This is confirmed by successive VTsIOM polls which suggest that on a rating of one to ten Yeltsin's popularity has fallen from six in October 1991 to around three in March 1995.[35] Can the embryonic political parties break this deadlock?

Russian political parties and party system[36]

The four main functions of political parties are: first, to act as a vehicle for the expression of different interests and values; second, to filter demands and organise them into coherent policies which subsequently form the basis of government programmes;

third, to produce political leaders and finally, to generate the support necessary to govern. Unfortunately, in the case of Russia, they are still too small, fragile and weak to perform many of these essential tasks. Part of the reason for this is that most political parties have similar supporters and party objectives, limited membership and are finding it difficult to identify bases of support.[37]

As a consequence the period 1992-94 was characterised by increased disappointment with the ability of politicians and parties to deliver what the people want - jobs, food, education, law and order. Political apathy is high, especially among young people. One clear indication of this is the declining proportion of the population who vote: 90 per cent in 1989; 74 per cent in 1991; 64 per cent during the April 1993 Referendum, 53 per cent in the December 1993 parliamentary elections and only 15 per cent in the Spring 1994 local elections.[38]   This trend was reversed in the recent 1995 parliamentary elections. Thus although a recent telephone survey of 812 Moscovites found that 31 per cent said they wouldn't vote on 17 December 1995 and 20 per cent were as yet undecided [39], in the end 64 per cent of the Russian electorate voted. Of those failing to vote in the December 1993 parliamentary elections, 6 per cent did so because they did not understand what was going on; 37 per cent because they did not believe politicians' promises; 6 per cent because no party matched their convictions; 7 per cent as a result of disapproval of the current government; 11 per cent no time; 20 per cent no desire and 12 per cent for other reasons.[40]   Similar problems occurred in 1995 too. Thus one Moscow October 1995 survey of 812 potential voters revealed that only 12 per cent had identified a party that represented their interests compared to 48 per cent who said that no such party existed and 40 per cent were undecided with only two months to go.[41]   As table 1.2 below shows this stems from a very low party identity in Russia today:

Table 1.2
Political party identification in Russia, May 1995
n = 3,195

With which party do you identify	Percentage of sample
Yabloko	9.5 per cent
Communist Party	7.5 per cent
Neo-fascists (LDPR)	5.5 per cent
Democratic Party of Russia	5.5 per cent
Party of Unity and Accord	4.5 per cent
Vpered Russia	3.5 per cent
Derzhava (Power)	2.5 per cent
Our Home is Russia	1.5 per cent
None	19.5 per cent
Do not know	24.0 per cent
Refused to answer	16.5 per cent

Source: Adapted from L.A. Sedov, 'Nekotorye kharakteristiki prevybornoi situatsii', *Ekonomicheskie i sotsial'nye peremeny* No. 4, July-August 1995, p. 28.

Thus while in 1992 polls revealed a sense of euphoria after the downfall of Communism, by late 1995 this had given way to a growing realisation that radical economic reform had not created a better society, life or higher living standards. The outcome is increased frustration and dissatisfaction and a lack of interest in politics. Thus those with a strong interest in politics have fallen from 25 per cent in 1989 to as low as 4-5 per cent in 1993-94.[42] This downward trend continues today.

Hence the President, parliament and the political parties in Russia are very weak, the current political situation is highly unstable and the ingredients exist for a possible crisis and breakdown in the near future. Does real salvation lie beyond the old nomenklatura - only 25 per cent of Yeltsin's closest associations were never part of the old elite[43] - in management, the military or other interest-groups, such as the *mafiya*?

Politics outside parliament

Whilst Russia cannot as yet be described as a corporatist state, dominant economic interests might in time influence policy formation. In the past, the military has been influential in Russian politics. Today after several years of economic change, the Army is in crisis, riven with resentment and division. Growing poverty throughout the army ranging from recruits through to officers, together with accusations concerning the bungling of the Chechen hostages crisis in June 1995 and its aftermath in Dagestan in January 1996 not only threatens Russian national security, it also places doubts on the army's reliability. The current corruption scandals are adding insult to injury. However, this is not to say that the military is no longer a force in Russian politics, instead the meteoric rise of Alexandr Lebed demonstrates the opposite.

Some managerial and bureaucratic groups are also opposed to radical economic reform. March-April 1994 surveys indicated, for example, that 22 per cent of respondents blamed foreign governments and 75 per cent foreign organisations and experts for Russia's difficulties.[44] 'Outsider' interest groups, such as the IMF and EBRD, have proved decisive in determining the course of economic or social policy in Russia. But surveys in Russia in June-July 1993 revealed that 64 per cent preferred Russian economists and experts to be in control of their country's economic affairs.[45] There is growing evidence of a fear of outside interference in Russia's domestic affairs - a point emphasised by Vladimir Zhirinovsky's Liberal Democratic Party programme in December 1993 when he argued that Russia was far too *dependent* on the West. This is hardly surprising as by 1994, according to government figures, foreign investment in Russia totalled between US$1.2-$3 billion. In overall terms, 75 per cent of Russia's investors are foreign. As a consequence, by January 1995, 16,063 enterprises in Russia were in foreign hands.[46]

On top of military and corporate opposition to government, large sections of Russian society are disillusioned with the current political leadership. This issue shall be addressed throughout this book so suffice it to say here that when a sample of 2,000 respondents from three Russian cities were asked in May-June 1995 to describe the main problems they were confronted with, the following answers in order of priority were given:

Table 1.3
Key problems facing Russians in May-June 1995

Main Concerns	Response (as per cent of 2,000 sample)		
	Samara (800)	Moscow (800)	Orenburg (400)
High cost of living	46	55	68
Rising crime	36	55	65
Unemployment	22	16	31
Gap between rich and poor	13	20	28
Ethnic conflict	11	14	27
Ecological situation	10	17	23
Migrant question	2	8	7
Inadequate transport system	1	3	8

Source: *Sotsial'no-politicheskaia situatsiia i mezhnatsional'nye otnosheniia v Samare i otsenkakh i predstvalenniakh massovo soznaniia* (Moscow, Institute of Socio-political research 1995), p. 13.

Whilst not attributing blame to any particular person or institution for these problems, summer 1995 surveys demonstrated a lack of faith in the government's ability to resolve the main issues of the day, as table 1.4 below shows:

Table 1.4
Level of trust/distrust in various Russian public institutions, May 1995

Individual/Institution/Organisation	Distrust	Trust
Yeltsin	76 per cent	12 per cent
Parties/movements	67 per cent	7 per cent
Courts	63 per cent	14 per cent
Police	71 per cent	15 per cent
Government	74 per cent	12 per cent
Army	48 per cent	32 per cent
Parliament	72 per cent	12 per cent
Council of Federation	65 per cent	9 per cent
Regional leaders	60 per cent	16 per cent
Lawyers	61 per cent	17 per cent
Trade unions	60 per cent	19 per cent
Church	42 per cent	33 per cent
Enterprise directors	66 per cent	12 per cent
Heads of Banks	74 per cent	6 per cent
Mass media	57 per cent	21 per cent

Source: V.K. Levashov et al., *Kak zhivesh' Rossiia (Rezul'taty sotsiologicheskogo monitoring Mai-Iiun' 1995)* (Moscow 1995), pp. 16, 22.

Surveys covering the period April 1993 to September 1995 show that the ratings of most, though not all of Russia's political elite, had taken a turn for the worse on the eve of the December 1995 parliamentary elections, as table 1.5 demonstrates:

Table 1.5
Ratings of various political figures, April 1993 - September 1995

Political figure	a	b	c	d	e	f
V. Chernomyrdin	11	8	5	5	5	14
A. Lebed	-	-	-	2	2	13
G. Yavlinskii	4	16	9	11	14	12
G. Zyuganov	-	3	5	5	7	11
S. Fedorov	2	3	2	3	6	10
Ye. Gaidar	6	17	8	7	7	8
A. Rutskoi	19	6	7	8	6	7
B. Fedorov	-	1	-	1	4	6
V. Zhirinovskii	2	4	6	5	8	5
B. Yeltsin	19	17	8	9	4	5
N. Ryzhkov	-	-	-	-	-	5
S. Govorukhin	-	-	-	-	-	5
Ye. Pamfilova	-	2	1	1	2	4
B. Nemtsov	1	1	-	-	-	3
Ye. Lakhova	-	-	-	-	2	3
M. Lapshin	-	-	-	-	0.2	3
I. Rybkin	-	-	-	1	2	3
Iu. Luzhkov	-	1	-	1	3	3
S. Shakhrai	10	15	6	5	6	2
A. Tuleev	3	3	1	2	2	2
No one	17	25	29	22	31	25
No answer	39	34	34	39	26	25

Key:

a	April 1993	b	November 1993
c	May 1994	d	November 1994
e	March 1995	f	September 1995

Source: VTsIOM survey results cited by Oleg Savel'ev, 'Chetvertaia chast' rossiiskikh izbiratelei ne goveriaet nikomu iz politikov', *Sevodnya* 19 October 1995, p. 3.

As subsequent chapters will show, the main reason for this is the mounting problems in late 20th century Russia, in particular the series of cleavages based on nationality, class, education and gender; centre-periphery relations; the rural-urban divide; citizenship; the protection of human rights; the organisation of the political process itself and the extent to which citizens of the Russian Federation feel they have a **real say** in political decisions that affect their lives.   These factors made themselves felt in Russia's parliamentary elections of December 1995.

December 1995 Duma election results

On 17 December 1995, Russia's second democratic elections to the Federal Assembly took place.   Russian political scientists talked in terms of either right, left and centre parties or following Yegor Gaidar of parties of the 'return match' (communists and nationalists); the party of power or that representing the Federal bureaucracy and the reformist parties, while yet others simply divided contenders into pro and anti-government groupings.   In terms of economic goals and political orientation, it is possible to categorise those on the *right* as including: Russia's Democratic Choice; Yabloko, Forward Russia and the United Workers Party; those of the *left* meanwhile included the Communist Party of the Russian Federation; Power to the People; *Derzhava* (or Great Power), the Agrarian Party and other-left nationalists and finally, the *centrists* included Our Home is Russia, the Rybkin bloc, Women of Russia and the Congress of Russian Communities.[47] Diagrammatic representations are given in figures 1.1 and 1.2 below.

Out of a possible 100 million voters, 64.3 per cent voted.   The outcome as table 1.6 illustrates was that the Zyuganov's Communist Party received 22.3 per cent of the vote; Zhirinovsky's LDPR got 11.1 per cent; Chernomyrdin's Our Home Is Russia gained 9.7 per cent, Yabloko led by Yavlinsky got 7 per cent and so forth. However, many parties failed to reach the 5 per cent threshold.

According to the newspaper *Pravda*, the distribution of seats to the Duma went as follows: the communists, agrarians and *Power to the People* bloc received 186 seats; Our Home Is Russia, 55 seats; the LDPR, 51 seats, Yabloko 46 seats and other centrists, 11 seats; Russia's Choice, nine seats, other democrats, 8 seats and the Congress of Russian Communities, five seats and finally, independents and other opposition groups gained 79 seats.[48] *Moskovskii Komsomolets* noted that Chernomyrdin's Our Home is Russia party spent $2,709, 451 on its campaign, closely followed by the LDPR with $2,387, 190, then Yabloko with $1,853,253 and finally the communists with more restricted sources of finance and less Western backers spent only $280, 753.[49] However, in the case of the first three parties, such high levels of expenditure did not gain them the most seats. There also appears to have been less correlation than in 1993 between the use of TV-air time and political success. For example, of the four main winners, Our Home is Russia spent seven hours 21 minutes using TV advertisements; the LDPR, five hours, 16 minutes; Yabloko, 53 minutes and the Communists, less than six minutes. Voters seemed less impressed with flashy TV ads and more prone to old fashioned techniques such as marches, canvassing and leaders meeting voters face to face on the campaign trail.[50]

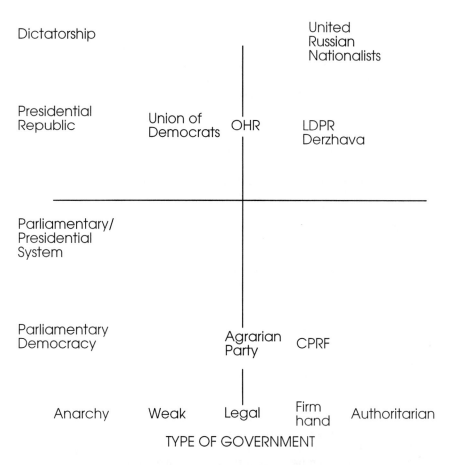

Figure 1.1   **Russia's blocs and factions according to desired governmental and political system**

Key:
CPRF = Communist Party of the Russian Federation
LDPR = Liberal Democratic Party of Russia
OHR = Our Home is Russia

Source: Sergei Popov, 'Rossiiskie partii pered vyborami: Kuda i s kem?' *Vlast'*
              No. 11, 1995, p. 25.

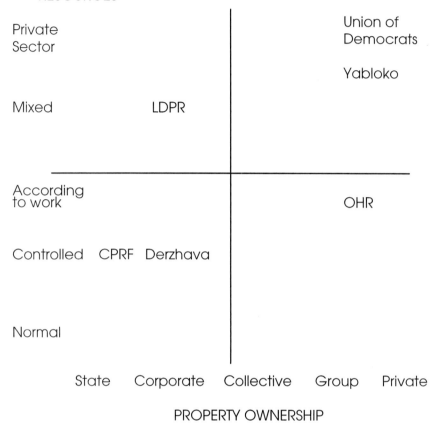

SYSTEM OF
ALLOCATING
RESOURCES

Private
Sector

Union of
Democrats

Yabloko

Mixed   LDPR

According
to work

OHR

Controlled   CPRF   Derzhava

Normal

State   Corporate   Collective   Group   Private

PROPERTY OWNERSHIP

**Figure 1.2   Russia's blocs and factions according to desired system of allocating
resources and property ownership**

Key:
CPRF = Communist Party of the Russian Federation
LDPR = Liberal Democratic Party of Russia
OHR   = Our Home is Russia

Source: Sergei Popov, 'Rossiiskie partii pered vyborami: Kuda i s kem?' *Vlast'*
No. 11, 1995, p. 23.

Table 1.6
The results of the December 1995 parliamentary elections in Russia

Party	Per cent of vote
CPRF	22.3
LDPR	11.1
Our Home is Russia	9.7
Yabloko	7.0

5 per cent threshold

Women of Russia	4.6
KRO	4.3
United Workers Party	4.0
Union of Democrats	3.9
Agrarian Party	3.8
Forward, Russia	2.0
Cedar	1.4
Ivan Rybkin Bloc	1.1
Beer Lovers Party	0.7
PRES	0.4
Stable Russia	0.2
Social Democratic Bloc	0.13

Key:
CPRF = Communist Party of the Russian Federation
KRO = Congress of Russian Communities
LDPR = Liberal Democratic Party of Russia
PRES = Party of Unity and Accord
Cedar = Environmental Group

Source: Igor' Krylov, 'Politicheskaia reklama na televidenii ne povliala na izbiratelei', *Finansovye Izvestiia* No. 4 (238), 18 January 1996, p.6.

In comparison with Russia's first parliamentary elections two years ago, the left gained 6.6 more votes and the centrists 4.7 per cent more. Such gains were largely made at the expense of the right and the independents whose votes were down 4.7 per cent and 5.5 per cent respectively over 1993. Finally, those 'against all' groups also saw their vote declined by 1.1 per cent between 1993-95.[51] Although no overall majority exists, the communists scored an outstanding victory. In general the number of left-wing candidates in the new Duma rose from 176 in 1993 to 267 by 1995 (or by 52 per cent), while the number of centrists fell from 146 to 106 (27 per cent) and the number of right-wing Duma deputies plummeted from 127 to 74 (or 62 per cent).[52] The nature of the losses and gains of the main political parties are illustrated in figure 1.3 below:

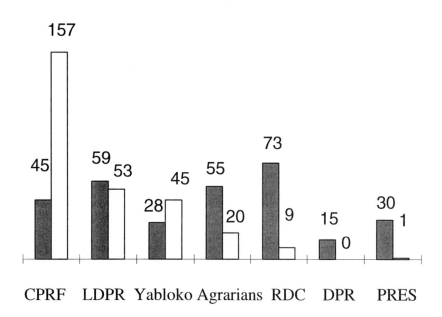

CPRF   LDPR Yabloko Agrarians RDC   DPR   PRES

Figure 1.3   **Winners and losers in Russia's 1995 parliamentary elections (number of seats gained)**

Key:

     = 1993

☐   = 1995

CPRF = Communist Party of the Russian Federation
LDPR = Liberal Democratic Party of Russia
RDC   = Russia's Democratic choice
DPR   = Democratic Party of Russia
PRES = Party of Unity and Accord

Source: Andrei Galiev, 'Seans odnovremennoi igry', *Ekspert* No. 19, 25 December 1995, p. 9.

Taking a representative sample of 1,600 Russian voters, Yuri Levada of VTsIOM looked at who voted for which particular parties. His results in relation to the four main factions in the new 6th Duma are presented in tables 1.7 and 1.8:

Table 1.7
Voting patterns in December 1995 parliamentary elections
according to age and education
Sample n = 1,600

Age group/ educational level	Political Party			
	CPRF	LDPR	Our Home is Russia	Yabloko
Age:				
18 - 24 years	5	10	9	15
25 - 29 years	14	30	29	33
40 - 54 years	32	33	31	28
55 years + older	49	26	31	25
Education:				
Higher	10	4	19	30
Secondary	38	44	53	45
Below Secondary	50	51	28	25

Key:
CPRF = Communist Party of the Russian Federation
LDPR = Liberal Democratic Party of Russia

Source: Yuri Levada, 'Vybory: peizakh posle bitvy i pered nei', *Izvestiia* 11 January 1996, p. 2.

We can see that the Communists drew most of their support from the middle aged voter, with secondary or less education; the LDPR managed to convince more young people, but like the communists had fewer voters with a higher education. Chernomyrdin's Our Home Is Russia had supporters of all ages and education, but it was Yabloko who came out as a 'Catch-all party' attracting the young and old alike as well as those with little through to university-level education (table 1.7). When Levada went on to examine voting patterns according to type of work and place of residence, he discovered that specialists tended to vote for Yabloko and to a lesser extent Our Home is Russia rather than the communists and nationalists; whilst old-age pensioners favoured the communists and workers the LDPR (table 1.8). All parties demonstrated a strong showing in smaller as well as larger towns, but in the villages and provinces, it was Zyuganov's communists and Zhirinovsky's nationalists who dominated.

Table 1.8
**Voting patterns in December 1995 parliamentary elections according
to type of work and area of residence**
Sample n = 1,600

Type of work/ area of residence	CPRF	LDPR	Our Home is Russia	Yabloko
Place of work:				
Enterprise worker	1	2	3	4
Specialist	8	4	15	21
Workers	29	48	23	22
OAP	46	23	32	20
Area of residence:				
Moscow	4	2	7	13
Large town	36	27	45	46
Small town	32	36	28	39
Village	32	37	27	15

Key:
CPRF = Communist Party of the Russian Federation
LDPR = Liberal Democratic Party of Russia
OAP   = Old Age Pensioner

Source: Yuri Levada, 'Vybory: peizakh posle bitvy i pered nei', *Izvestiia* 11
January 1996, p. 2.

A protest vote? Back in December 1993, Boris Yeltsin noted: 'Don't forget the poor. It was they who voted for the Liberal Democratic Party. They weren't for its leader or platform, but against poverty'? Unfortunately Yeltsin failed to take heed of his own advise. Thus when Yuri Levada analysed his sample's motives for voting for particular parties, he found that the large majority who voted communist (90 per cent) or for the LDPR (86 per cent) did so because they did not want to 'suffer' (*terpet'*) any longer. This was especially true of pensioners and the working class.[53] These groups like many others are sick and tired of the current Russian government and its constant failure to meet its promises.

A turbulent period will follow over the next six months in the run up to the June 1996 Presidential elections. Its outcome is far more important than the aforementioned parliamentary elections, but the latter have certainly set the trend. We will not know for several weeks, perhaps months, who will fight for the Presidency. Boris Yeltsin, his health permitting, might stand in order to try and keep his reforms in place. Gennadi Zyuganov, Vladimir Zhirinovsky and Grigory Yavlinsky will certainly attempt to build on gains already made in December 1995. To the possible list of Presidential contenders, we can probably add Viktor Chernomyrdin, Aleksandr Lebed, Vladimir Shumeiko and rumours in January 1996 in Moscow suggested that Mikhail Gorbachev, the former President of the USSR, might make a political comeback.[54]

However we saw earlier that Yeltsin has no secure power base within parliament on which to build. No secure party system which would make his position secure and a new Duma which will probably block his every move. This situation is adversely affecting Russia's transition to liberal democracy and generating concern among Russians. For instance, one *Moscow News* poll of 1,600 people in July 1994 discovered that only 29 per cent thought that Yeltsin should stand for another term (as against 53 per cent who said 'No'); while 25 per cent of respondents wanted a change in government because the Yeltsin Administration was doing 'a poor job'.[55] Since then the level of discontent with his leadership has increased among the general population (see table 1.5). Yeltsin's recent spell in hospital not only fuelled rumours about his health, but also raised the thorny issue of who is running Russia in the mid-1990s.

Despite a doubling of communist party votes since 1993, there is no immediate need for Western concern. Zyuganov's party is a totally different organisation to that of its communist counterpart of the late 1980s. The Communist Party of the Russian Federation is far more social democratic in nature and most importantly of all, Zyuganov demonstrated his more moderate stance by refusing, wisely as it turned out, to ally himself with extremists, such as Zhirinovsky. Although the LDPR suffered a 50 per cent drop in support, thereby losing its place as the largest faction in the Duma to the communists, Zhirinovsky still managed to turn popular concerns about the role of the West in Russia's affairs, about law and order etc. into political gains. Meanwhile, Yavlinsky, a former aid to Gorbachev, kept reformers' dreams alive by ensuring that Yabloko was one of the four main 6th Duma factions. It was the Centrists, in particular Chernomyrdin's Our Home Is Russia, backed by Yeltsin, who suffered the most crushing defeat. In part this represents failures to learn from past mistakes of 1993, but in the main it constitutes a protest vote against unsuccessful economic reforms, an unpopular war in Chechnya, the failure to halt corruption and crime, dissatisfaction about declining living standards and so forth. Given the problems outlined in subsequent chapters, the results of the 1995 parliamentary elections indicate an urgent need to review the pace and direction of current reforms and their negative impact on Russian society.

Finding remedies - closer ties with Europe?

The current economic crisis and political stalemate has also revived questions relating to Russia's future orientation and the goal of **integration** (i.e. the emphasis or lack of it upon the desire to **return to Europe**). Russia has traditionally viewed the West (either in the American or European sense) with suspicion. While this view pre-dates communism, such an attitude was clearly compounded by Cold War rhetoric after 1945. It was not until Gorbachev that, to paraphrase Kipling, the addage 'East is East and West is West, Never the twain shall meet' was gradually eroded.[56] Unfortunately, the current economic recession, resurgent nationalism and the rise of neo-fascist/New-right groupings[57] means that the battle between the **Westerners** (advocating liberal democracy and the virtues of the market economy) and the **Slavophiles** (who stress that Russia and her Slavic neighbours are tied by culture, language and traditions and hence a specifically Russian road to political reform, rather than the one prescribed by the West is the preferable course of action) is far from over.

A Successful transition by the year 2000?

I would now like to end by applying two analyses - those of Dahl and Schmitter - to try and assess Russia's chance of making a successful transition by the year 2000.

Dahl's theory

Robert Dahl in his book **Polyarchy** (1971) identified many procedures and institutions that were required in order to create an effective democracy. He placed particular emphasis upon widespread participation and political competition. Evidence of the former might include secret balloting, universal adult suffrage, regular elections, associational freedoms and executive accountability; while in terms of institutions and competition, this requires numerous political parties, representative institutions (such as legislatures) with policy or decision-making powers and/or an executive accountable to the population (such as US President) or the legislative (UK, Prime Minister). In order for all this to work, the rule of law is essential as it could limit the powers of government, protect civil rights and enable open political activity to take place and the responding organisations to be set up.[58] Although Russia has already established a pluralist political system - there are around 40 major political parties - as we saw earlier they are experiencing a number of difficulties recruiting members; raising money (in a climate of severe depression and hardship); making the giant step from being political spectators (members of a movement) to becoming political actors and finally in making an impact upon the policy and decision-making process. Russia now has a parliament too. But this has merely resulted in an unstable government. Thus the absence of regular elections, well-established political parties and the inability of Russia's parliament to function effectively indicates that some of the main preconditions for liberal democracy as set out by Dahl are still not in place in post-Communist Russia.

Schmitter's Alternative

Using the example of the Mediterranean countries of Greece, Portugal and Spain, all relatively new small democracies which have taken 15-20 years to make the transition from authoritarian rule, Phillip Schmitter and others have argued that there are five, inter-related stages involved in making a political transition from authoritarianism (in this instance of the Communist variety) to liberal democracy, namely:

(i)   persistence of authoritarian rule;
(ii)   demise of authoritarian rule;
(iii)   transition to democracy;

(iv)   consolidation of democracy; and
(v)   persistence of democracy.[59]

This process is shown in figure 1.4 below:

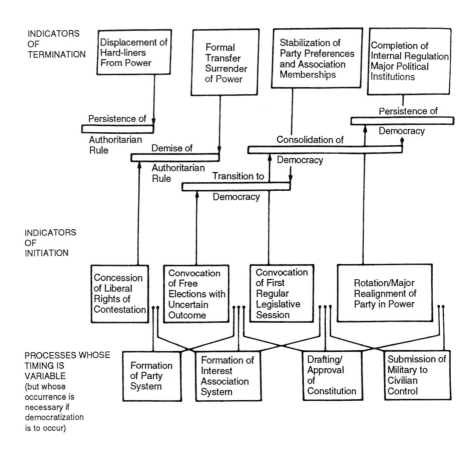

Figure 1.4   Regime change from totalitarian rule to liberal democracy

Source: P. Schmitter, 'The consolidation of political democracy in Southern
            Europe', unpublished manuscript 1988 cited in D.S. Mason, *Revolution in
            East-Central Europe*, (Westview Press, Boulder Colorado 1992), p. 118.

Using this theory we can identify firstly, the *phases* through which countries (such as Russia) pass in moving from the old (totalitarian) to new (liberal-democratic) political order; secondly, it is possible to establish *preconditions* relating to the socio-economic and political circumstances which allow democratisation to take place[60] and finally, we can point to the *causes* behind the formation of given political alliances as well as the historic events (the collapse of Communism in late 1991) which push countries towards or away from democracy (the August 1991 or Autumn 1993 events in Russia for instance).[61]

According to Schmitter's schema, Russia is currently somewhere between iii-iv. It is difficult to say with any certainty just how long it will take her to reach stage v. Schmitter's analysis suggests that this process will take at least 12 years; while Dahl points to the very long-term and talks of the political transition taking *generations*.

Explaining failure: is elite theory useful?

But why have Russia's economic and political reforms not been very successful? It was suggested above that the political power of the nomenklatura elites[62] has not been transferred to other political groups but passed from one part of the old elite (who are now reformed communists under another name - democrats) to another section of the same elite.[63] However, instead of the communist party elites of the past, we now have a plurality of elites - a managerial, bureaucratic, intellectual, old communist party elite etc.

Following Pareto,[64] I would like to argue that the new leaders in the post-communist phase have been recruited largely from within and not from outside the old nomenklatura elite. It is still this political group which is either deciding or influencing governmental policy on the direction and pace of both Russian economic and political reform. Thus if the introduction of specific policies is seen as a threat to the political power of the dominant majority, then little real action is taken. As Michels noted: 'If laws are passed to control the domination of the leaders, it is the laws which gradually weaken, and not the leaders'.[65] This has meant that political power in Russia has become institutionalised. In this sense there has really been the **perpetuation** of old (in a different form) elites not their **replacement** by new ones since the end of 1991. Because a consensus has already been built among these elites, conflict is largely contained and power and influence is exercised by the minority (who share common social origins, desire for prestige, economic interests, institutional positions, loyalties, esprit de corps, unity of purpose etc.). Russian elites today all want the same thing - to maintain the new status-quo, not challenge it.

Conclusions

The inherent danger to the old elite in government in Russia in 1996 is either competition between elites (economic and political) or elite-mass conflict. We have seen above that political power in Russia is unequally distributed and that it is difficult to dislodge elites once they are in power. The key issue in Russia in the 1990s, however, is not only **who** has power but **how** it is used. The new elite must, therefore, be seen to be responsive to the mass if it is to maintain support. Although the gulf between mass demands and elite promises has widened in the last few years, this has not produced major conflict in the public arena. For instance, surveys carried out in Moscow in 1993 and 1994 among samples of 844 and 840 respectively showed that 22 per cent and 24 per cent respectively would join a strike, demonstration or meeting but 78 per cent and 76 per cent of the same samples said they would only occasionally get involved in such activity.[66] In overall terms, the number of Moscovites willing to engage in political protests has fallen from 11 per cent in June 1991 to 9 per cent by the end of 1994.[67] This remains the case despite the fact that by December 1994, 33 per cent of this sample said that the economic situation was better 6-7 years ago and 67 per cent declared that they were faced with severe economic difficulties.[68]

At present then, we have a situation in which there is a fierce political battle between elites. Confronted with the growing prospect of future mass discontent about the direction of economic and political reform in the lead up to the 1996 Presidential elections, the Yeltsin Administration needs to mobilise the people behind its reforms to retain power. However all the signs by early 1996 suggest that this is an impossible task. For example, surveys conducted by the Analytical Centre of the Institute of Socio-Political Research, Moscow revealed that *positive reactions* to reform have remained steady at 6 per cent since August 1992 whereas those possessing a *negative response* to changes since the collapse of communism have increased from 33 per cent in August 1992 to around 40 per cent in January 1995. In overall terms by mid-1995, 58 per cent were against and only 10 per cent in favour of Yeltsin's policies.[69] The results of the recent December 1995 elections and the communist victory means Yeltsin is now under ever greater pressure to act. As the various contributions in this book show, there is a growing feeling of exclusion, a feeling that the government does not care about the people, that the government is powerless to stop the rot. One wonders, therefore, just how much longer the toleration of Ivan Ivanovich and his family will last before he finally decides, like many others living below the poverty line, that enough is enough.[70] Unless Yeltsin addresses many of the problems facing Russian society highlighted in this book or alternatively unless he resorts to force to preserve his political power, as shown during the current Chechen crisis, he may well find himself voted out of power in June 1996.

Notes

1.   M. Matthews, *Poverty in the Soviet Union: the lifestyles of the underprivileged in recent years*, Cambridge University Press, Cambridge 1986, p. 10.

2.   D.A. Dyker, *Restructuring the Soviet Economy*, Routledge, London 1992.

3.   See, for example, M.I. Goldman, *What went wrong with perestroika*, W.W. Norton, New York 1992 and H. Aage, 'Popular attitudes and perestroika', *Soviet Studies* 1991, No. 1, pp. 3-25.

4.   P. Rutland, 'The economy: The rocky road to reform: From plan to market', in: S. White et al. (eds.), *Developments in Russian and post-Soviet politics*, Macmillan,

London 1994, pp. 146-48.

5. S. Fischer and A. Gelb, 'The process of socialist economic transformation', *Journal of Economic perspectives*, Fall 1991, p. 102.

6. G.V. Osipov et al., *Reformirovanie Rossii: Mify i real'nost' (1989-1994)*, Moscow 'Academia' 1994, p. 122.

7. Ibid.

8. Ibid, pp. 133-34.

9. Ibid, p. 165.

10. Ibid, p. 167.

11. Ibid, pp. 248-49.

12. P. Rutland, 'The economy: The rocky road to reform: From plan to market', in: S. White et al. (eds.), *Developments in Russian and post-Soviet politics*, Macmillan, London 1994, pp. 155-56.

13. V. Mau, *Ekonomiko-politicheskie protsessy 1994 goda i Chechenskii krizis*, unpublished Institute for the Economy in Transition report, Moscow, November 1994, pp. 2-3.

14. Ibid, p. 2.

15. G.V. Osipov et al., *Reformirovanie Rossii: Mify i real'nost' (1989-1994)*, Moscow 'Academia' 1994, p. 320.

16. C. Williams, 'Shock therapy and its impact on poverty in Contemporary Russia', Paper presented to the Politics of Social security in East European session of 22nd ECPR workshop, Madrid 17-22 April 1994a and *World in 1995*, Economist Publications, London 1995, pp. 61-62.

17. A. Martynenko, 'Pravitel'stvo vnov' poliubilo 'neotkorretirovannye' reformy', *Interfaks AiF* 16-22 October 1995, p. 11 and *Ekonomika i Zhizn'* No. 41, October 1995, p. 1.

18. G.V. Osipov et al., *Sotsial'naia i sotsial'no-politicheskaia situatsiia v Rossii: Analiz i prognoz (Pervoe polugodie 1995 goda)*, Moscow 'Academia' 1995, p. 13.

19. Cited in *Sovetskaia Rossia* 14 October 1995, p. 11.

20. *Rossiia pered vyborom*, Moscow 'Obozrevatel'' 1995, p. 25 and *Ekonomika i Zhizn'* No. 18, 1995, p. 11.

21. G.V. Osipov et al., *Sotsial'naia i sotsial'no-politicheskaia situatsiia v Rossii: Analiz i prognoz (Pervoe polugodie 1995 goda)*, Moscow 'Academia' 1995, p. 26.

22. *Sovetskaia Rossia* 14 October 1995, pp. 1-2 and *Ekonomika Rossi, Ianvar' - August 1995g*, Moscow 'Goskomstat Rossii' 1995, p. 85.

23. Ibid and *Sevodnya* 19 October 1995, p. 2.

24. A. Martynenko, 'Pravitel'stvo vnov' poliubilo 'neotkorretirovannye' reformy', *Interfaks AiF* 16-22 October 1995, p. 11.

25. D. Daeninckx and P. Drachline, *Jirinovski: Le Russe qui fait trembler le monde:* Collection 'Documents', Le cherche midi editeur, Paris 1994; G. Frazer and G. Lancelle, *Zhirinovskii: The Little Black book*, Penguin, Harmondsworth 1994; V. Kartsev with T. Bludeau, *Zhirinovskii*, Columbia University Press, New York 1995; W. Laqueur, *Black Hundred: The rise of the extreme right in Russia*, Harper Perennial, New York 1994; J. Lester, 'Zhirinovsky's Liberal Democratic

Party: Programme, Leaders and Social base', *Labour Force on Eastern Europe* No. 47, Spring 1994, pp. 17-30; R. Sakwa, 'The Russian elections of December 1993', *Europe-Asia Studies* Vol. 47 (2), 1995, pp. 195-227; C. Williams, 'From the Black Hundreds to Zhirinovsky: The rise of the extreme right in Russia', Renvall Institute of Historical Research, University of Helsinki, Finland, 28 February 1994; M. Wyman et al., 'The Russian elections of December 1993', *Electoral Studies* Vol. 13 (1), September 1994, pp. 254-271.

26.   V. Mau, *Ekonomiko-politicheskie protsessy 1994 goda i Chechenskii krizis*, unpublished Institute for the Economy in Transition report, Moscow, November 1994, pp. 3-8.

27.   Cited in R. Sakwa, *Russian Politics and Society*, Routledge, London 1993, p. 54.

28.   The following discussion draws upon John P. Willerton, 'Yeltsin and the Russian Presidency', in S. White et al. (eds.), *Developments in Russian and post-Soviet politics*, Macmillan, London 1994, pp. 25-57.

29.   R. Rose, I. Boeva and V. Shironin, *How the Russians are coping with transition: New Russia Barometer II*, Studies in Public Policy, No. 228, CSPP, University of Strathcylde 1993, p. 38.

30.   *Konstitutsiia Rossiiskoi Federatsiia*, Moscow 1993.

31.   See, for example, S. Golman, 'The Soviet legislative branch' and T.F. Remington, 'Parliamentary government in the USSR', in R.T. Thuber and D.F. Kelley (eds.), *Perestroika - Era Politics*, M.E. Sharpe, London 1991, pp. 51-75 and 175-205 respectively as well as T.F. Remington, 'Representative power and the Russian State', in S. White et al. (eds.), *Developments in Russian and post-Soviet politics*, Macmillan, London 1994, pp. 57-87.

32.   On these events see *Sevodnya* 26 April 1994; 12 May 1994; 8-10 June 1994.

33.   *Megapolis-ekspress* 5 January 1994 and *Moskovskie novosti* No. 30, 24-31 July 1994, p. 7.

34.   *Moskovskie novosti* No. 30, 24-31 July 1994, p. 7 .

35.   *Ekonomicheskie i sotsial'nye peremeny* VTsIOM Information Bulletin July-August 1995, p. 6.

36.   The following analysis was strongly influenced by R. Sakwa, 'Parties and the multi-party system in Russia', RFE/RL Research Report 30 July 1993, pp. 7-15.

37.   On these issues see Oleg Savel'ev, 'Chetvertaaia chast' rossiiskikh izbiratelei ne goveriaet nikomu iz politikov', *Sevodnya* 19 October 1995, p. 3, *Ekonomicheskie novosti* No. 21, October 1995, pp. 6-7, M.A. Weigle, 'Political participation and party formation in Russia, 1985-92: Institutionalising democracy', *Russian Review* April 1994, p. 259 and R.J. Hill, 'Parties and party system', in S. White et al. (eds.), *Developments in Russian and post-Soviet politics*, Macmillan, London 1994, p. 102.

38.   V. Rukavishnikov et al., 'The dynamics of civil and political society in Russia', paper presented to the XIII World Congress of Sociology, Bielefeld, Germany 18-23 July 1994 and *Finansovaia Gazeta*, 18 January 1996, p. 6.

39.   Cited in *Moskovskaia Pravda* 11 October 1995, p. 1.

40.   R. Rose and C. Haerpfer, *New Russian Barometer III: The Results*, Studies in Public Policy, CSPP, University of Strathclyde 1994, p. 38.

41.   *Ekonomicheskie i sotsial'nye peremeny* VTsIOM Information Bulletin March-April, No. 2, 1994, p. 33.
42.   R. Rose and C. Haerpfer, *New Russian Barometer III: The Results*, Studies in Public Policy, CSPP, University of Strathclyde 1994, p. 35.
43.   *Izvestiia* 18 May 1994, p. 2.
44.   R. Rose and C. Haerpfer, *New Russian Barometer III: The Results*, Studies in Public Policy, CSPP, University of Strathclyde 1994, pp. 19, 33.
45.   R. Rose, I. Boeva and V. Shironin, *How the Russians are coping with transition: New Russia Barometer II*, Studies in Public Policy, No. 228, CSPP, University of Strathcylde 1993, p. 39.
46.   *Moskovskaia Pravda* supplement 11 October 1995, p. 6.
47.   *Izvestiia* 23 December 1995, p. 4.
48.   *Pravda* 28 December 1995, supplement, p. 1.
49.   *Moskovskii Komsomolets* 28 December 1995, p. 1.
50.   *Finansovye Izvestiia* 18 January 1996, p. 6.
51.   A Sobianin and V Sukhovol'skii, 'Demokratam dorovo oblishlis' ambitsii ikh liderov', *Izvestiia* 23 December 1995, p. 4.
52.   Ibid.
53.   Yuri Levada, 'Vybory: peizakh posle bitvy i pered nei', *Izvestiia* 11 January 1996, p. 2.
54.   S Alekseeva, 'Pretendenty: Kto stanet vtorym prezidentom Rossii?', *Rossiiskii Obozrevatel'* No. 1, 1995, pp. 90-98 and *Nezavisimaya Gazeta* 21 December 1995, p. 10.
55.   *Moskovskie Novosti* No. 30, 24-31 July 1994, p. 6.
56.   C. Williams, 'Russian views of European integration: An historical perspective', Conference on the New Europe, University of Nottingham, April 1992.
57.   C. Williams, 'From the Black Hundreds to Zhirinovsky: The rise of the extreme right in Russia', Renvall Institute of Historical Research, University of Helsinki, Finland, 28 February 1994.
58.   R.A. Dahl, *Polyarchy: Participation and Opposition*, New Haven, Yale University Press, 1971.
59.   G. O'Donnell et al., *Transitions from authoritarian rule: Comparative perspectives*, John Hopkins University Press 1986; and P.C. Schmitter with T.L. Karl, 'The conceptual travels of transitologists and consolidologists: How far to the East should they attempt to go?', *Slavic Review* Vol. 3 (1), Spring 1994, pp. 173-85.
60.   Barrington Moore Jr, *Social origins of dictatorship and democracy*, Penguin, Harmondsworth 1967.
61.   E. Baloyra, 'Democratic transition in comparative perspective' in his *Comparing new democracies*, Westview Press, Boulder 1986, pp 9-52.
62.   M. Voslenskii, *Nomenklatura*, Overseas Publications Interchange Ltd, London 1984.
63.   R. Michels, *Political parties*, New York, Free Press, 1915 and G. Mosca, *The ruling class*, New York, McGraw-Hill, 1939.
64.   V. Pareto, *The Mind and Society*, New York, Harcourt-Brace, 1935.
65.   R. Michels, *Political parties*, New York, Free Press, 1915, p. 423.

66.   M.M. Nazarov, *Politicheskie tsennosti i politicheskii protest*, Moscow 1995, p. 31.
67.   Ibid, p. 36.
68.   Ibid, p. 39.
69.   G.V. Osipov et al., *Sotsial'naia i sotsial'no-politicheskaia situatsiia v Rossii: Analiz i prognoz (Pervoe polugodie 1995 goda),* Moscow 'Academia' 1995, pp. 20, 23.
70.   For a poignant example see N. Leonaova's article 'Semeinyi biudzhet: a nu-ka, prozhivi', *Argumenty i fakty* No. 2, 1996, p. 5, which describes the plight of the Ksenii family.

2 Russian sociology: problems and prospects - two perspectives

VLADIMIR STAROVEROV AND CHRISTOPHER WILLIAMS

Introduction

The socio-political problems facing Russia today are immense. The key question explored in this chapter concerns two aspects: firstly, the ability of Russian sociology to become a real, effective instrument of economic reform and political democratisation and secondly, whether or not sociology is in a position to fulfil this role. The first half of this chapter by Christopher Williams looks at Western views of sociology in Russia and the future trends and possibilities; whilst the second half by Vladimir Staroverov presents a Russian view of current trends in sociology and assesses whether or not the difficulties facing the discipline itself as well as its practitioners can be overcome in order to enable sociologists to fulfil their role of interpreting present trends in Russian society in a critical and independent fashion.

A Western perspective

Before looking at the future, it is necessary to consider briefly the developments in Russian sociology in the post-Stalin period.

Since the 1960s, Western sociologists have produced less than a score of works on the state of sociology in Russia. The key works include Fisher;[1] Hollander;[2] Parsons;[3] Simirenko;[4] Matthews and Jones;[5] Ruble;[6] Weinberg[7] or émigrés such as Shlapentokh.[8]

These writings were shaped by two key factors: the Cold War and the rise of Sovietology, on the one hand, and the increased criticism of the latter, in the aftermath of 1968, on the other. However, revisionism in Western sociological writings on Russia has been slower to emerge than has been the case with history.[9] Nevertheless major strides were made in Western analyses of Soviet society. Particularly informative, well researched and ground breaking monographs were published by David Lane, Mervyn Matthews, James Riordan, Murray Yanowitch and others.[10] These works deepened Western understanding of the social dynamics underway in Russia and enabled a generation of scholars to explore the similarities and differences between the USSR and the UK/USA. Although many of these scholars encouraged the development of comparative perspectives, this approach quickly petered out in the late 1970s-early 1980s during the second phase of the Cold War. Part of the reason for this was the tendency in the UK at least, for sociological studies of Russia to be partly tied to Slavic or Soviet Studies. Another aspect was the breakdown of détente which put an end to East-West exchanges of information and ideas.

The impact of Gorbachev

For all our criticism of the Gorbachev experiment, 1985-91, it not only revitalised sociology in Russia, but also led to renewed Western interest in the sociological aspects of a society in transition in the West. For example, Tatiana Zaslavskaya became well-known in Western academic circles, as Gorbachev's adviser on the likely societal impact of perestroika and glasnost. A debate ensued among Russian and Western sociologists over the extent to which Gorbachev's policies constituted a Revolution from above or below. Detailed analyses followed on the role of various social forces working for or against perestroika. Similarly, Western scholars prompted by greater access to our Russian colleagues and sources, began to examine previously uncharted waters - the ills of Russian society: sex, prostitution, abortion, crime, the position of women, AIDS and so forth. Christopher Williams' first book on AIDS in Russia,[11] as well as this book are the product of the tremendous changes which have occurred over the last decade.

From the mid-late 1980s, two tendencies were evident in Soviet sociology. Some, such as Zaslavskaya, allowed sociology to be harnessed in the interests of perestroika. As a consequence, sociology was tarnished. However, others, such as Ryvkina, aware of the weakening of state (totalitarian) control, took advantage by rejecting Marxism-Leninism and sought to gain greater access to the work of Western sociologists.

However, while there was 'new thinking' in some areas - politics, economics, foreign policy - the same trend was slow to emerge among sociologists. At this time, according to Ryvkina, sociologists fell into three broad categories:[12]

(i)   *ideologists*, whose aim it was to retain traditional intellectual boundaries;
(ii)   *pragmatists*, who simply told the authorities what they wanted to hear; and finally,
(iii)   *free-thinkers*, largely younger scholars, who were interested in free inquiry and critical thinking.

To what extent have we made any progress along this continuum from theory to pragmatism and from pragmatism to free thinking? Since 1991, there has been, and still is to a lesser extent, an expansion in the level of sociological enquiry, theoretical advances and closer links between sociology and other disciplines in the former Soviet Union, such as economics, history and politics.[13]

While the new openings in the last decade provided unprecedented opportunities for sociological research, East and West; in the initial stages sociologists seemed to be moving in opposite directions. Thus, at a time when the younger generation of Western sociologists interested in Russia were overcoming the legacy of totalitarianism, some of our Russian counterparts were embracing the ideas of Parsons, Nisbet, Goulder and Abrams and struggling to come to terms with the likes of Weber, Giddens and the French giants, Bourdieu and Touraine.

What comes after communism?

The implications of the collapse of the USSR for the writing and conduct of sociological research in Russia and for sociological research on the ex-USSR in the West have yet to work themselves through. Nevertheless, a shift in perspective is already evident in the pages of the main Russian journal *Sotsiologicheskie issledovaniia* (Sociological Research). Communism's impact on the social sciences has been so deep that it will shape our parameters for some time yet.

However, now that we have moved into the post-communist phase, it is essential that both sides of the iron curtain start to rethink fundamentally the past and develop radically different ways of viewing our respective societies. This has the potential of opening up interesting debates on the meaning of 'social stratification', 'authority', 'state', 'culture', and many of the other themes addressed in this book. The question, as to whether or not we all need to adopt new paradigms or whether Russian sociologists should follow the example of their Western counterparts, will be considered later. For the moment, we would like to examine some areas of sociological research which we think are mutually beneficial and provide Western and Russian sociologists with the opportunity of transforming our understanding of Russian society on the threshold of the 21st century.

Research opportunities

There are a number of issues and concepts which can be used to analyse contemporary Russia. These include: culture, deviance, gender, stratification, ethnicity, authority, education, the family, work, religion, social change and last, but not least, the theory and methods of research. The break-up of the Soviet regime has forced onto the sociological agenda a total rethink of these and other areas of sociological enquiry. We would like to consider a few examples. Our purpose is to raise questions rather than provide definitive answers but in the process we hope to generate debate about the types of issues we should be exploring, preferably together, over the next decade.

Culture

For example, what type of culture exists in Russia today - is it universal in the sense that all societies now share common features? Or are a more diverse set of values and norms developing which are at odds with the West? What happened to traditional values and what if anything has replaced them? Leading on from this, is the related question of the erosion of 'cultural identity' posed by the Westernisation of Russia and the successor states and the impact which this is likely to have on the notions of 'nation' 'identity', 'what it is to be Russian' etc. (see chapters 5 and 16). Many Western books are now including Russian contributors.[14] This would not have been possible without the break down of intellectual and ideological barriers between East and West.

Class

The concept of class is important too. In the West the concept of 'class' is highly controversial, but in Russia it is gathering increased importance as academics and policy-makers rediscover the question of inequalities between social groups (played down in the past but now more widespread following the introduction of a market in the over the last decade). Interesting research is currently underway on the gap between the rich and the poor and on the notion of class consciousness. Key issues such as: Who are the New Russians or the poor? Who belongs to the emerging middle class? What is the link between class and voting patterns, on the one hand and class, citizenship and *narod*, on the other? are now being explored. Furthermore what is the nature of the relationship between classes - is it harmonious or conflictual? what conditions/policies might produce such situations? And finally, how far is Russia's social structure likely to conform to European or American patterns and is this likely to be beneficial or problematic? These issues will be considered in chapters 5-7.

Gender

There are similar opportunities for fruitful research in relation to gender. The *zhenskii vopros* (Woman's Question) has been studied from a variety of angles using numerous disciplines, including sociology, but we now know that the Woman Question is far from solved. How are women responding to change? How do they view the future? Are they interested in politics? What do they think about feminism and finally, how have the economic and political reforms affected their lives?

Ethnicity

But perhaps one of the greatest issues of our times, drawing upon all the above concepts, is that of nation and race. Russia was once dominant, but is no longer. She is now one of many nations and ethnic groups. We are therefore freer to explore the experiences of various ethnic groups, minorities and races across the ex-USSR. This might involve the study of ethnic origins, levels of antagonism, discrimination, racism, the emergence of a national consciousness, the possibility of a future 'melting pot' or else an evaluation of the impact of religion, history, language and culture on Russian, Ukrainian, Georgian and other national identities beyond the year 2000. Some of these issues will be raised in chapter 16.

Political sociology

Finally, we have the notion of power. Here sociology and politics come together. It is time to reject simplistic notions of coercion to consider consent and Russian views of 'authority' and why they 'obey' governments. This means analysing how power is distributed and how its abuse can be controlled. This in turn raises the key question, which was explored in the previous chapter, of what type of 'political system' Russia desires - Presidential, parliamentary or other variety. The key question for us is: will Russia, and indeed sociology, flourish and be able to examine these issues over the next couple of years?

The plight of sociology in Russia

Russian sociologists and historians were among the first academic groups to reject the totalitarian state. But there have been more disadvantages than advantages for sociology and sociologists in Russia over the last decade. Although a number of Western style sociology textbooks are now emerging together with a number of journals - *Sociology, Sociological Research* - newspapers and a forthcoming Sociology encyclopaedia, it is extremely difficult to carry out sociological research in Russia nowadays. Sociologists are poorly paid - academics earn approximately $50-100 (£35-70) per month on average; postgraduates a mere $5 (£3); the price of books is rapidly rising, print runs are small by Russian standards (200-1000 copies) and only government departments and companies can afford them. It is also extremely costly to gather empirical research. Only a small amount of sociological research is 'commissioned' and foreign grants are few and far between. Sociologists are also finding it difficult to remain independent and critical as companies offer them monetary incentives to leave academia. Finally, more and more sociologists in Russia are finding that their research is being expropriated by non-sociologists.

Russian sociologists are themselves divided over how best to resolve the current crisis before it turns to catastrophe. Some are looking to the West for help; others are clinging desperately to the values of the past or urging a rapid return to them and a third group is simply rejecting everything in the confusion, even the more positive trends.

Is recovery possible via convergence?

A comparative perspective might prove to be a powerful tool in helping sociologists - East and West - to examine the validity of past, present and future assumptions, be they of a theoretical or applied kind. These centre upon the uniqueness of Soviet (or communist) experience, on the one hand, and the relevance of Western experience for Russia and the successor states, on the other.

In the past the parameters of sociological research were determined by the ideology of

Marxism-Leninism, but now a variety of theoretical viewpoints prevail i.e. pluralism is possible. Although the 1990s is a time of flux and great uncertainty, Sociology can be utilised to good effect to explain changes currently underway in the class, education, political and social systems of Russia.

But for sociology in Russia to survive into the next century and retain its power as a tool of analysis of social change, everyone must be willing to revise their research strategies, the theories on which they are based, be constructively critical of officialdom and official statistics, open minded, adaptable and flexible and above all bear in mind what type of sociology we want and what type of sociologists we wish to be - ideologists, pragmatists or free-thinkers. The free-thinkers must win over the ideologists and pragmatists if sociology, alongside Russia, is to make a successful transition. If carefully managed, this process should lead to the revitalisation of our discipline.

The ability of sociology and sociologists in Russia to meet the aforementioned challenges will now be analysed from a Russian perspective by Professor Vladimir Staroverov.

A Russian perspective

Russian sociology is currently undergoing a deep-systemic crisis. This crisis is making itself felt in theoretical, conceptual, scientific, organisational, personnel and other senses. However, this does not mean that nothing positive has happened over the last decade. From the mid-1980s onwards, ideological limits on the conduct of sociological research were removed; sociological education underwent major reform and sociological research was conducted by a range of institutions, some new, some old. Of the new variety was the Institute of Socio-Political Research (*Institut Sotsial'no-politicheskikh issledovanii*) of the Russian Academy of Sciences (hereafter simply ISPR). The ISPR has many research laboratories and centres carrying out a variety of research projects. The findings contained in subsequent chapters often emanate from the research of ISPR staff.

Positive indicators

Old and new sociological research centres, institutes and university departments are being reorganised and re-equipped. New study guides are being produced, new textbooks are emerging and the work of classical Western sociologists such as M. Weber, E. Durkheim and R. Aron as well as Russian thinkers such as S. Bulgakov, S. Berdayev, I. Solonevich, I. Il'lin, A. Kondratiev, A. Chayanov and others are either being published in Russian for the first time or re-published. Today, the likes of the *Vestnik MGU* (Moscow State University) sociological Series, *Sociologos* as well as *Sotsiologicheskie issledovaniia*, which celebrated its 20th anniversary recently, and the new *Sotsiologicheskii zhurnal* are all flourishing. In addition, we also have the *Politizdat* series 'A Concise Sociological dictionary' edited by G.V. Osipov, head of the ISPR, together with a four volume reference dictionary on 'Sociology', an ISPR, 'Sociological Encyclopaedia' which is in preparation and so forth. All these works are the product of major sociological, theoretical and applied research over the last decade into not only past and current trends in Russian and Western sociology but also into trends in Russian society. These research outputs are gradually beginning to impact upon the Russian government, parliament, political parties and other influential policy and decision-makers.

Negative indicators

Despite these positive changes, there is no room for complacency. Many research agendas are far from clear, lack flexibility and there is still an on-going struggle between different schools of sociological thought. These problems are not the main reason for the plight of Russian sociology today - the root of the problem is finance.

Financial constraints

There is much interesting research being carried out and in the process of being devised, but financial constraints hamper existing and future research. Even if the money exists it has conditions placed upon it - findings must comply with the government policy or with the wishes of private sponsors. *Partocracy* (rule by the former CPSU) has been replaced by, for the want of another word, *moneyocracy* (research dictated by a financial squeeze on resources). Thus although we now appear to have more sociological journals - their print runs are smaller than the more established *Sotsiologicheskie issledovaniia*. Minor journals are in fact sponsored by the bourgeois-liberal camp in Russian politics which are backed by foreign organisations. This is limiting their degree of independence and certain current trends are reminiscent of Suslov's time when 'Sotsis' was ideologically biased. Similarly, a shortage of money - in the form of the low wages of Russian sociologists - means that the large majority cannot afford the rapidly expanding new works because they are too expensive.   Only government departments and companies are in a position to buy them. This is restricting access to sociological texts to certain sections of society.   Finally, it is proving extremely costly to conduct sociological research, especially of an empirical nature. Everyone could afford to do this work, with major samples in 1975. This is no longer the case 20 years on.

Lack of independence

Such a situation brings in question the nature of certain types of 'commissioned sociological research' under the auspices of government or private agencies. So-called 'sociologists' working in these spheres tend to be unprofessional and far too subjective. Those sociologists who want to be more independent and more critical are finding it more and more difficult to conduct major sociological research in the 1990s. This situation is largely the product of reduced budgets for sociological research, but it is also the product of the radical bourgeois transformation of Russian society.

Information too costly

In line with the virtues of capitalism, obtaining statistics now costs money whereas in the past, they were free of charge to academics. This resulted in a flurry of statistical publications such as '*Narodnoe khozyiastvo SSSR*', '*Narodnoe khozyiastvo RSFSR*', '*SSSR v tsifrikh*', '*RSFSR v tsifrikh*' and so on. In the communist period, they cost 1-3 roubles in most cases, today they cost 15-50,000 roubles, or more than a third of the monthly salary of a scholar in an academic institution. As one publication is insufficient to carry out proper sociological research, this is severely hampering the quality of research outputs. This is not simply true of junior academic staff, it also affects those further up the academic ladder such as those with a BSc degree on 150-160,000 roubles a month, directors of departments/professors on 170,00 roubles and so forth. With rampant inflation a Professor's salary today is worth as much as that of a post-graduate in Soviet times.

On top of this problem is the low print runs of books and other publications. Whereas in the past 10-100,000 copies of statistical handbooks such as '*RSFSR v tsifrikh*' was not uncommon, today a comparabile publication such as '*Rossisskaia Federatsiia v tsifrakh*' rarely goes above 3,000 (as was the case in 1993 and 1994). Essential publications are therefore becoming more scarce and not readily available for consultation by Russian sociologists.

Similarities with the 1930s

Today Russia is becoming more like the 1930s - with impoverishment and the lack of availability of statistical data. This is resulting in an exodus from the profession. The 'brain drain' in sociology is the most acute of all the social sciences.

Facing up to the facts

Nothing is being done to reverse this and the other adverse trends mentioned earlier. Why? Is it that the present government does not wish the real facts to be known? Is the present regime unwilling to face up to its mistakes or to change the error of its ways? Is the current government unwilling to acknowledge that Russia is sliding from crisis into catastrophe?   How long will it be before the people realise that the current transformation has produced nothing but greater polarisation and class conflicts among Russians?

In the meantime impoverishment and the lack of statistics is preventing independent and critical sociologists from making the real situation more widely known to all citizens in Russia today. In this sense, the *free-thinkers*, mentioned above with inquiring and critical minds are not yet flourishing in sufficient numbers. The key problems of the day will never be solved until sociologists are placed in a more secure position and until they are able to conduct all types of research - some supportive of government, others more critical. At the moment, we do not have genuine sociological research in all instances; in some cases findings are **concocted** in favour of the demands of the customer, be they government or the private sector.

The commercialisation of sociology

Commercialisation in its crudest sense is leading to the development of a certain type of apologetic sociologist.[15] Such sociologists are allowing themselves to be corrupted by money and thoughts of wealth. In line with the analysis offered by Christopher Williams they are a combination of the old party *ideologists*, and the *pragmatists*, who simply tell their new employers what they want to hear. This is the new breed of Russians.

The role of foreigners

However, it is not simply domestic customers who are influencing current trends in Russian sociology. Foreign customers are also using better qualified Russian sociologists in the course of their work but there is also a danger here that they will become a 'sociological slave' (*sotsiorab*), which is analogous with the 'literary slave' in the commercialised field of foreign literature. Such programmes of research are not home grown, goals are set abroad and the analysis of any data collected by Russian specialists is also carried out there. It is very disappointing to see highly skilled Russian experts sell themselves because of the pressures brought about by poverty. Many such sociologists regularly rent out their skills to the Americans, English, French or Germans, endlessly producing information like robots. While such research is often funded by foreign grants and as such indirectly sustains Russian sociology, what foreign monies cannot do is guarantee the independence of Russian sociologists.

The possibility of dependency

Western companies and researchers have thus far ignored the possibility of dependency on the West.[16] Westerners employing Russian sociologists can dictate when, where, how and for what reasons they use them and their findings. Although poorly paid, impoverished Russian sociologists are not in a position to resist demands made by their foreign employers, those who have been sucked in know that the price paid is a high one - bias, one-sidedness, ideological inselectivity and so forth.

The need for independent, objective sociological research

But let us make our position clear. We are not against research done 'to order', as demanded by domestic or foreign bodies. This system can be extremely useful not only for the sociologists involved, but also for society as a whole. However, this only applies in cases were the 'commissioned research' is carried out in an objective way, under objective conditions for the benefit of the customer as well as in the interests of society. If such conditions do not occur, then there is a danger that such extensive 'dirty commercialisation' of the sociologists selling his/her labour and results as well as of the discipline of sociology, itself, might not only have major policy implications well into the next century, as sociological data are manipulated by the relevant bodies' own ends, but also undermine the future of Russian sociology, which will become increasingly dominated by badly trained, unprofessional people carrying out 'research' under the guise of 'sociology' and pretending to be 'sociologists'.

Loss of graduates to commerce

Another major problem is that many sociology graduates quickly leave the profession after graduation and enter the business sector. According to Zh.T. Toshchenko out of 34 sociological graduates from the Sociology Faculty of Russian Academy of Sciences in 1992, only one was working as a sociologist. By 1994, out of 64 such graduates, only two were working in a sociological field.[17] The large majority of these graduates - 95 of them - were employed by commercial companies as consultants. Their training may help them in their work, but it is a great loss to the sociology profession.

Amateurism replaces professionalism

The commercialisation of sociological research, in which junior as well as senior sociological personnel are involved, is forcing many to take on tasks for which they are not qualified. This undermines their professionalism and discredits sociology and sociologists in the process, as the activity of these sociologists goes further and further away from their areas of specialism making them more and more amateurish in their behaviour, research and findings. Sadly such practices are widespread in Russia today.

A loss of professional integrity: increased differentiation and polarisation

There is another reason why Russian sociology is in decline and losing its professional integrity. This stems from conflict in the theoretical and conceptual arena. We are currently witnessing the polarisation of sociology in which the *ideologists* and *pragmatists* are fighting it out with the *free-thinkers*. While in a sense this is inevitable, nothing good is coming out of this increased differentiation and polarisation. It is 'pluralism', if we can really call it that, based upon antagonism. It is not a question of a variety of opinions, but of major divisions in Russian society. These social forces cannot agree on two major things: how to get Russian sociology back on its feet and most importantly of all, how to ensure that Russia has a secure, firm future.

Different schools of thought

Modern Russian sociology is polarising into three main streams. These may variously be described as the *globalists*; *Russian rejectionists* and finally, the *pragmatic-rationalists*. It must be realised, however, that this is not the first time that Russian sociology has been traumatised. From the 1930s to the 1960s, sociology was virtually a non-subject. Even after the 1960s, sociologists were divided into two rather crude categories: scientific and non-scientific. This left a very divided group of specialists with no real sense of 'community', except that imposed by officialdom.

Globalists

Since the mid-1980s, the **globalist variety of sociologists** have been trying to encourage increased awareness of international trends, exchange of information and collaborative work. For the globalists, it is not that one system - the USSR and the former socialist countries - gains victory over its adversary - the USA and NATO - rather that nowadays in the post Cold War world it is essential that all sociologists recognise that there are a variety of theoretical and ideological viewpoints with the frontiers of social knowledge constantly changing. Therefore although scholars world-wide need not necessarily abandon their national frontiers and the problems facing their own countries, these difficulties can be interpreted in many ways, using global experiences as a basis for comparison or for resolving particular issues. A good representative of this school of thought is Nikita Pokrovskii.[18]

Rejectionists

The **Russian rejectionists** are going too far in seeking to reject or refute all aspects of Russian culture and tradition. They want to dismiss the value and merits of 5,000 years of Russian Slavic tradition in favour of bowing to the American dream and the ideals of the Western world. This type of Russian sociologist is in favour of centralised capitalism, commercialisation of culture, science and other spheres. According to this school of thought we must fully embrace the values of market and business and put out of our minds any belief in 'Motherland', 'National culture', 'Traditions and customs', spiritual progress, justice and equality. These are all survivals of the past, which are no longer worthy in the present and the future. They are intolerant of the major actors of the past. This refers not simply to supporters of the old regime, but also its opponents in the dissident movement. As Nikita Pokrovskii put it: 'some sociologists refute unconditionally old ways, old awareness, old culture, the old intelligentsia, old borders and so on'.[19] Examples of this brand of sociology can be found in the works of A.G. Zdravomyslov, such as his 'Sociology in Russia'[20] or else in M.S. Komarov's 'Introduction to Sociology'[21] or finally in the SOROS sponsored programme 'The rejuvenation of humanities education'. Such scholars and publications, which are very new, seek to downplay the achievements and history of sociology in the Soviet period. The entire period is written off as worthless without any attempt to assess objectively the merits of individual scholars and works as well as their flaws. It is now a question of seeing sociological trends and publications as falling into one of two categories: 'good', namely most things of the post-communist period, versus the 'bad', that is anything published in the communist period, especially before 1985. The goal is to discredit our socialist experience and exaggerate the benefits of the current tradition and the virtues of capitalism. In this way, some sociologists today are examining trends in the pre-revolutionary period to try and discover antecedents to current trends. A good example is the revival of Positivism or Liberalism as a major trend in Russian sociology today or strict adherence to the basic tenets of post-materialist thinking.

Pragmatic rationalists

Finally, we have the **pragmatic-rationalist** variety of sociologists who like Christopher Williams' *free-thinkers* want greater independence and the right to be critical. They do not see things merely in 'black and white' terms, attacking or blackening the past, especially the Soviet period, merely for the sake of it. While being critical of current trends and the adverse effects of the transition to the market, this school of relatively new and young sociologists, backed by certain older revisionist colleagues, point to the positive developments of the past - free education and health care, cheap housing and transport costs - without ignoring the downside - lack of freedom, restrictions on the practice of religion etc. Pragmatic-rationalist sociologists in trying to retain the best of the old and the new, combine national with international specifics, stressing in particular the peculiarities of the Russian context as well as the pressures brought to bear by the end of the Cold War and the collapse of communism - the risk of becoming a mere appendage of the West. Thus, according to pragmatic-rationalist sociologists in Russia today, two diametrically opposed forces are in play and mutually influencing one another: the legacy of the past as well as the inherent dangers of transition in a period of economic recession and political instability - national disaster.

Although some of these types of schools of sociology are more desirable than others, all types nevertheless increase self awareness within the profession. For sociology to flourish in the future, all sociologists must acknowledge their greatest sin, that of social apologetics (i.e. strict adherence to the basic tenets of Soviet ideology (Marxism-Leninism) in the past). Nobody was value free, everyone was ideological to one degree or another, we are all guilty. It does not serve any purpose for us to differentiate between different categories of sociologists according to their ideology or to expose their moral negligence. If we do not follow this rubric, we will simply continue the retardation of Russian (former Soviet) sociology. In any case, it will not simply be a matter of our criticism of those supportive of the old or new regime, instead it will be a question of whether the *globalists*; *Russian rejectionists* or the *pragmatic-rationalist* variety of sociologists are victorious. The outcome will ultimately depend upon the socio-economic and political context in which they operate.

Globalists or post-materialists are actively borrowing from Western sociological theory. Thus if Westernism gains ground, their cause might win favour. The rejectionists meanwhile, who include not only scholars in Russia but emigrants such as I. Il'in, I. Solonevich, N. Berdyaev and S. and E. Trubetskii, are practising a sort of 'retro-sociology', in that they are seeking to reject many aspects of the old Soviet sociology and replace it with Russian sociology of a different variety, that practiced in the West. Hence Berdyaev's increased popularity in recent times. For similar reasons to the globalists, the rejectionists also have significant numbers of supporters within and outside of Russia. Finally, the pragmatists are not simply devising new sociological approaches, they are also revising past practices. They are approaching current realities, processes and tendencies without looking for analogies in Russia's past or world history. In this sense unlike the *globalists* and *Russian rejectionists*, the *pragmatic-rationalists* do not believe that they have found analogies with experience elsewhere because such analogies between Russia and the West or elsewhere in the globe are not fundamental and deep but superficial. Pragmatic-rationalist sociologists in Russia are therefore particularly interested in the ideas of the likes of M. Weber, G. Zimmel, P. Sorokin and E. Durkheim. Although such theorists are useful if we wish to analyse trends in a stable, well functioning society, they are not easily applied to Russia which is rapidly disintegrating as tradition and modernity conflict with one another (see chapter 4).

The rejection of Marxism was a grave error

The collapse of communism led to a major ideological vacuum. The orthodoxy of Marxism-Leninism had been rejected by a substantial proportion of the population. But, it was also the case that Marxism was sometimes over-simplified, badly represented or simply seen as an ideological alternative to bourgeois theories.[22] In our opinion, the rejection of Marxism was a grave mistake. We should have rejected 'deformed Marxism' of the Soviet variety, not Marxism as such. Sadly, sociology and sociologists in Russia today dismiss out of hand the possible value of Marxism as a means of explaining current trends. It is time for a fundamental reappraisal of the ideas of Marx and Lenin. This is especially important when one considers that the bourgeois revolution in Russia is proceeding apace, with little real alternative to it, or at least a feasible critique. Nowadays, however, *globalists* and *Russian rejectionists*, accept the totalitarian view of Russia's past and in rejecting Marxism they have readily accepted the 'New (capitalist) mentality' - political pluralism and the virtues of the market economy. Nevertheless, the *pragmatic-rationalists* are attempting to devise new concepts and theories. A good example here is Agrafy Tikhonovna who unsuccessfully tried to marry Marxism with post-modernism. However, this will enable the third school of thought to learn from its mistakes in seeking to analyse social processes and tendencies in modern Russia. Representatives of this third school with a left-wing viewpoint include 'Russian scientists with a socialist orientation' set up on 1 October 1994. Unfortunately, they are deprived of the right to publish their findings. It is hardly surprising to find that 'Marxists' or those following 'Marxism' are few and far between among Russian sociologists at present. As sociology becomes increasingly polarised, sociological societies struggle to survive and Russia's links to the near abroad are severed, it is our opinion that we might see a Marxist revival in the not too distant future.

Reduced conflict

There are already signs that the conflict between the various schools of thought mentioned above have started to subside. There were many reasons for this: first, some of the major protagonists left the profession for commercial structures; second, pressures of work and trends in society was leaving less and less time for theoretical debates and discussions and thirdly, and finally, some of the major actors involved have moved to different countries. It is also important to note here that it was globalists and post-modernists as well as nationalists who wanted to retain existing divisions of opinion. But this was gaining less and less approval within the profession for two reasons: firstly, discussions were often very extreme and fierce and secondly, some members of the first two schools started to associate with ruling groups close to the Russian President. This resulted in one group of sociologists branding others because of their politics. Thus V.A. Yadov, Head of the Sociology Institute of the Russian Academy of Sciences once accused one of his colleagues who headed another section of the same Institute of being a Nationalist. Many other political denunciations have followed since. The main reason for such a situation was the growing politicisation of sociologists. As A.G. Zdravomyslov declared:

> 'The condition of sociology after August 1991 and the disintegration of the USSR demonstrated very quickly how research projects and findings were deeply influenced by the researcher's ideology. In sociology, as in the rest of society, one can find evidence of some groups supporting the President and the government and others the opposition. Instead of trying to resolve the country's primary problems - falling living standards, inflation, rising crime, suicide, a falling birth rate and an increasing death rate, ethnic conflict - sociologists simply stood by and blamed politicians for not solving our economic problems or for not preventing certain Republics from breaking ranks from the Russian Federation'.[23]

Tolerating different political standpoints

Political differences are natural. Colleagues should not be criticised by their fellow colleagues simply because they have a different political opinion. If colleagues are criticised, then we are not simply criticising one individual, but the entire collective - all sociologists. Different viewpoints must be tolerated, otherwise we risk returning to the bad practices of the past when the authorities, CPSU, public prosecutors office etc. determined each and every citizen's 'political persuasion'. In this situation where colleagues are trying to discredit each other, we need to distinguish between 'disinterested' and 'interested' categories. In the first category, teaching and research is not done for personal gain, vengeance etc.; but in the second, it is the outcome of attempts to settle scores or discredit the thinking of others for personal reasons. This is grossly dishonest and only serves to undermine the credibility of the profession and its practitioners. A good example here is *Vidok-Bulgarin* concerning the role of spies and informants in sociology which is not written from an objective perspective but from someone with an 'interest' in the outcome.[24] This is demonstrated by the one passage in which the author uses the term 'charlatan' to refer to G.V. Osipov, his former confident and comrade in arms, but at the same time, like a snake, he is trying to ingratiate himself with those in power.

Sociology, sociologists and contemporary Russian politics

Those sociologists supporting the government's reform strategy argue that falling living standards, the growing division of society into different strata, the threat of unemployment and other problems are primarily the result of the transformation process.

By contrast, the rapid decline in output, the collapse of industrial links and political de-stabilisation are the results of democratisation, de-militarisation and the transition to the market. For certain groups of sociologists the roots of these difficulties lay in our totalitarian past; for others, current catastrophic forecasts are used as a means of threatening the population with the aim of uniting them behind anti-reformist forces, thereby preparing the way for the restoration of a authoritarian regime. This point of view is typical of the public statements made by the Institute of Sociology, Russian Academy of Sciences, headed by V.A. Yadov.[25] However, such political allegiances can often back-fire. If sociologists allow themselves to be labelled 'government supporters', they can quickly become discredited if the government loses favour, or declines in popularity. It is far better for Russian sociologists to keep their distance from 'actual politics and politicians' and wherever possible retain an independent, critical perspective.[26]

The Westernisation of Russian sociology

The collapse of Communism has meant that Russian sociology and sociologists have been reintegrated into the New Europe (or even US sociology), so we can now work more closely together. But this can act as a double edged sword. The growing Westernisation of Russian society is setting a new agenda. At the same time, Western access to their colleagues in Russia and elsewhere in the CIS is helping to revise our sociological research agenda. But does closer integration with the West offer Russian sociology its salvation? As stated above, we can both see the merits of closer East-West co-operation, but on balance, we do not see convergence as the solution to the plight of Russian sociology or the ills facing Russian society. Instead we both firmly believe that the recovery of Russian sociology must come from within the profession, from its practitioners and from within Russia itself. This does not prevent us from working closer together to examine the key factors which have led to the collapse of the communist regime and the development of a pluralist political system and/or market economy. During this process, we can learn a great deal from and about each other. However, it is ultimately Russians who must decide their own fate. The rejuvenation of Russian sociology must not come from outside but from within. But what chances are there of this happening?

The self-regeneration of Russian sociology

A number of steps are required in order for Russian sociology to recover its leading role in the diagnosis and remedying of Russia's social ills. These are as follows: firstly, developing the necessary *concepts, theories and methodologies.* These should encapsulate as many fields as possible and a broad range of theories, including Marxism. Marxism should not be dismissed as useless and dogmatic, but viewed as a means of looking at the changing inter-relationship between economics and politics in Russia's current phase of development. We therefore need to reconsider the value of Marx's analysis of Capitalism, in particular his concepts of historical materialism, economic determinism, the nature of social classes, alienation, the relationship between the sub and superstructures, the role of the state and Marx's ideas regarding social change. Although Marx's theories were applied to 19th century capitalism, they can easily be updated using Lenin to assess trends in late 20th century Russia. In addition to Marx, the ideas of M. Kavalevskii, P. Sorokin, M. Weber and R. Dahrendorf might prove particularly illuminating. Secondly, in order to restore the 'broken sociological space' it is necessary to foster greater freedom and a variety of sociological thinking. The first two schools of thought mentioned earlier are in our opinion not in favour of these two steps, but adherents to Marxist sociology as well as so-called 'neutrals' would be willing to take these measures.

Some conclusions: the start of the beginning or the beginning of the end?

One important development is the growing link between Russian sociologists and their colleagues in the near abroad which are now in the process of being resurrected. In the short to medium-term this is likely to result in the regeneration of disintegrated sociological schools in certain parts of the ex-USSR. The Institute of Socio-Political Research in Moscow as well as the All-Russian scientific society of sociologists and demographers are certainly in favour of fostering such links within the former Soviet Union as well as in Asia and Europe. Thus we are in the process of recreating some sense of 'community' among fellow sociologists within and outside of contemporary Russia. However, if we want this 'community of scholars' to become a reality, not fiction, then we must take concrete steps and measures to consolidate our position immediately. This is a relatively easy goal to achieve. It can be rapidly fostered by the writing of joint works on the history of sociology, comparative research within the former USSR on our transformation processes or detailed analyses of similar processes in Europe and Asia. At the same time, it is also essential that we take the necessary steps to help our 'community' flourish by resisting the commercialisation of sociology, restoring a sense of morality and ethics and above all by restoring a belief in ourselves and the value of our research findings. Although sociology has suffered badly in the post-communist period, it need not be lost forever, as it has great potential in helping scholars in the East and West to gain a greater understanding of Russia's process of economic and political reform and its impact on Russian society in the 1990s and beyond.

Notes

1.   G. Fisher, *Science and Politics: The New sociology in the Soviet Union*, Cornell University Press, 1964.

2.   P. Hollander, 'The dilemmas of Soviet sociology', *Problems of Communism*, November-December 1965, pp. 34-46.

3.   T. Parsons, 'An American impression of sociology in the Soviet Union', *American sociological review*, January 1965, pp. 121-125.

4.   A. Simirenko (ed.), *Soviet sociology: Historical antecedents and critical appraisals*, Quadrangle books, Chicago 1966.
5.   M. Matthews and T.A. Jones, *Soviet sociology, 1964-75: A Bibliography*, Praeger, New York 1978.
6.   B. Ruble, *Soviet sociological research establishments*, Kennan Institute for Advanced Russian Studies, Washington D.C. 1978.
7.   E.A. Weinberg, *The Development of sociology in the Soviet Union*, RKP, London 1974.
8.   V. Shlapentokh, *The politics of sociology in the Soviet Union*, Westview Press, Colorado 1987.
9.   S. Smith, 'Writing the History of the Russian Revolution after the fall of Communism', *Europe-Asia Studies*, Vol. 46 (4) 1994, pp. 563-578.
10. D. Lane, *Politics and Society in the USSR*, Weidenfeld & Nicolson, London 1970; D. Lane, *The end of inequality: Stratification under state socialism*, Penguin, Harmondsworth 1971; M. Matthews, *Class and Society in Soviet Russia*, Allen Lane/Penguin Press, London 1972; M. Matthews, *Privilege in the Soviet Union, A study of elite lifestyles under communism*, Allen & Unwin, London 1978; M. Matthews, *Poverty in the Soviet Union: the lifestyles of the underprivileged in recent years*, CUP, Cambridge 1986; J. Riordan (ed.), *Soviet social reality in the mirror of glasnost*, Macmillan/St. Martin's Press, London/New York 1992 and M. Yanowitch, *Social and economic inequality in the USSR*, Martin Robertson, London 1978.
11. C. Williams, *AIDS in post-communist Russia and its successor states*, Avebury, Aldershot 1995.
12. R. Ryvkina, 'Reactionary traditions and revolutionary needs', *Vek XX* and *Mir 3* 1988.
13. Y.N. Davydov, 'Tekhnologiia i biurokratia', *Sotsiologicheskie issledovanniia* No.5, 1988, pp. 116-27; T. Zaslavskaya and R.V. Ryvkina (eds.), *Ekonomicheskaya sotsiologiia i perestroika*, Progress, Moscow 1989.
14. Russians have contributed to more and more Western books such as J. Riordan (ed.), *Soviet social reality in the mirror of glasnost*, Macmillan/St. Martin's Press, London/New York 1992; J. Riordan, C. Williams and I. Ilynsky, *Young people in post-communist Russia and Eastern Europe*, Dartmouth, Aldershot 1995 and others.
15. See, for example, G.V. Osipov, 'Reformirovanie Rossii: Itogi i perspectivy' in the book *Rossiia nakanune XXI veka*, Moscow 1994, p. 34.
16. For more on this see A. Stadler, 'Problems of dependent modernisation in East-Central Europe: A case for social democratic concern', in M. Waller et al. (eds.), *Social democracy in post-communist Europe*, Frank Cass, London 1994, pp. 45-65.
17. 'Rossiiskaia sotsiologicheskaia traditsiia shestidesiatykh godov i sovremennost' ' in *Materialy sipoziuma 23 Marta 1994*, Moscow, Institute of Socio-Political Research 1994, p. 34.
18. N. Pokrovskii, 'Velikii Otkaz: vozvrashchenie v feodalizm s post-modermistckim litsom', *Nezavisimaia Gazeta* 27 September 1994.
19. Ibid.

20. A.G. Zdravomyslov, 'Sotsiologiia v Rossii', *Vestnik Akademii Nauk* 64/9, 1994.
21. M.S. Komarov, *Vvedenie v sotsiologiiu,* Moscow 'Nauka' 1994.
22. See for instance *Voprosy filosofii* 1979, No. 1.
23. A.G. Zdravomyslov, 'Sotsiologiia v Rossii', *Vestnik Akademii Nauk* 64/9, 1994, p. 794.
24. The term *vidok* refers to a French spy/informer and a person without a motherland. His name was used by Pushkin to brand Faddey Bulgarin in this way. See A.S. Pushkin, *Collected Works*, Volume VII Leningrad 1978, pp. 102-03.
25. See A.G. Zdravomyslov, 'Sotsiologiia v Rossii', *Vestnik Akademii Nauk* 64/9, 1994, p. 794.
26. This was the case under perestroika with fatal consequences for the regime and sociology see T. Zaslavskaya, 'Perestroika and sociology', *Social Research* 55 (1-2), 1987a, pp. 267-276; T. Zaslavskaya, 'Rol' sotsiologii v uskorenii razvitiya sovetskogo obshchestva', *Sotsiologicheskie issledovaniia* No. 2, 1987b, pp. 3-15 and T. Zaslavskaya, 'Friends or Foes? Social forces working for or against perestroika' in A. Aganbegyan (ed.), *Perestroika Annual* Futura, London 1988.

PART II

RUSSIAN SOCIETY IN TRANSITION

3 The socio-demographic situation

GENNADI ZHURAVLEV, OKSANA KUCHMAEVA,
BORIS MELNIKOV AND IRENA ORLOVA

In Russia today there is an extremely unfavourable demographic situation. As we can see from table 3.1, the birth rate has declined with each passing year since 1985 from 16.6 per 1,000 population to 9.6 per 1,000 by 1995. In the meantime, the death rate has increased from 11.3 per 1,000 population in 1985 to 15.7 per 1,000 in 1995. The overall difference between the birth rate and death rate has also increased from 5.3 to 6.1 per 1,000 population in the last decade. All in all whereas in 1985, the birth rate exceeded the death rate, ten years later the situation had been reversed. According to V. Khorev, such a difference is best described as an 'abnormal death-rate' (*sverkhsmertnost'*).[1] By September 1995, Russia had a population of 184.4 million, a decline of 100,000 since 1991. Russia's population declined throughout the 1990s, but the rate of natural decrease has become more pronounced in recent years. Thus, as table 3.1 demonstrates the decline in population stood at minus 1.5 in 1992 but had risen to minus 6.2 per 1,000 population by 1995. However, this decrease was partly offset by in-migration which increased from 430,100 in 1993 to 796,400 in 1994.[2] Nevertheless, as the following analysis shows, Russia's population is still decreasing and the number of deaths is exceeding births at a higher rate each year - 15 per cent in 1992 as compared to 64 per cent in 1995. The main reasons for this, according to Vitaly Golovachov of the newspaper *Trud* (Labour), are 'the drastic deterioration in medical services, mass poverty (currently 34 million), a poor diet for tens of millions of people, growing unemployment, stress, anxiety over an uncertain future, alcoholism and so forth'.[3]

If the speed of the decline in the birth rate reduction remains the same, then in 35 years time, the crude birth-rate will be equal (in the cities) to an infinitely small value. The only women who will give birth to children will be those unable to have an abortion for health reasons. In the age-group 30-34 years, this will happen in 15 years and in the age-group 20-29 years, in 25-30 years. Only in the age-group of women younger than

25 years, will this birth rate reduction last for up to 50 years. Meanwhile, if the current rate of increase in the death rate continues, then in a decade the death rate among men will have risen three times, in two decades, the death rate among males will have increased 10-11 times and in 30 years by 20-30 times.

In the 1960s, American specialists estimated that by the year 2000, Russia would have only 28 million left out of a population of 145 million. Similarly several Russian scholars, such as Andreev, Volkov, Antonov and Borisov, talked about the prospect of Russia's depopulation (*depopulatsiia*) by the year 2005.[4] How far will these prognoses become a reality? In order to assess the validity of these claims we would like to make some comments on demographic trends based on the experience of Russia in general and Moscow in particular. Stated bluntly, the demographic situation in the capital is unfavourable, Moscow is in fact marginally ahead of all other territories. To examine this situation in greater detail, we need to look more closely at long-term trends in the birth rate, death rate and life expectancy. We shall examine each in turn.

Table 3.1
Demographic trends in Russia, 1970-95

Year			Russian Federation			Moscow
	Population (millions)	BR	DR	PG	IMR	BR
1970	130.1	14.6	8.7	+5.9	23.0	na
1975	134.7	15.7	9.8	+5.9	23.7	na
1980	139.0	15.9	11.0	+4.9	22.1	na
1985	143.8	16.6	11.3	+5.3	20.7	13.8
1990	148.0	13.4	11.2	+2.2	17.4	10.5
1991	148.5	12.1	11.4	+0.7	17.8	9.2
1992	148.7	10.7	12.2	-1.5	18.0	7.7
1993	148.7	9.4	14.5	-5.1	19.9	7.0
1994	148.4	9.6	15.6	-6.0	19.0	7.6
1995*	188.4	9.5	15.7	-6.2	20.0	na

Key:

* January - September only   na = data not available

BR = Birth rate

DR = Death rate

IMR = Infant mortality rate

PG = Population growth (+) or decline (-)

Source: *Molodezh' Rossii: Vospitanie zhiznesposobnykh pokolenii (Doklad komiteta Rossiiskoi Federatsii po delam molodezhi)*, Moscow 1995, p. 53: *Rossiiskoi Statisticheskii ezhegodnik* 1994 (Moscow, Goskomstat 1994), p. 17.

Birth rate

The main characteristic of Russia's current demographic situation is the acceleration in the reduction in the birth rate since 1987. The situation is such that the current birth rate is inadequate to ensure population reproduction. Family size is getting smaller and smaller. Thus the average family is currently 2.6, with the number of childless marriages on the rise. There are numerous reasons for this - pursuit of a career, no desire to start a family, conflict over whether or not to have children - but the main driving force behind the current position is the deteriorating economic situation and the difficulty in having to care for children once they have entered the world. According to our calculations, the family pattern necessary to reverse Russia's population decline would include: 4 per cent childless families; 10 per cent families with one child; 60 per cent with two children; 10 per cent with up to three children; 14 per cent with four children and 2 per cent with five or more children. However, the actual situation is barely sufficient to permit simple reproduction of the population. According to 1989 census data, the average size of the Moscow family was 3.1 (lower than the national average of 3.2). In 1989, 65 per cent of Moscow families had one child, 31.6 per cent, two children, 2.8 per cent three children, 0.4 per cent four children and only 0.2 per cent five children or more. A further indication of the unfavourable family situation in the country, which is illustrated by the situation in Moscow, is that in 20.6 per cent of families, children are brought up by a single parent (in the majority of cases by their mother).

From 1986 onwards, as table 3.1 shows, the crude birth rate in the Russian Federation fell by 42 per cent but in Moscow, the rate of decline was higher at 51 per cent. This trend can be explained by reference to the time and circumstances under which different generations entered their 'active reproductive age' period. In the case of the birth rate in 1985-88, this period dates back to 1967-69, but in the case of birth rate trends between 1989-93, this factor is not a sufficient explanation. Instead one must point to the fact that women aged 18-20 years were having fewer children in comparison to earlier periods by the end of the perestroika and in the early transition period. For example, in 1985 the number of children born to mothers of reproductive age (i.e. 15-49 years) stood at 52.1 per cent, but by 1990 this figure had fallen to 40.9 per cent and by 1992, it had reached 30.2 per cent. An overall decline of 22.1 per cent. A closer glimpse reveals a further alarming trend, namely that in the age groups 25-29 and 30-34 years, where normally women give birth not to their first but to their second or third child, the birth rate coefficients in the period 1985-92 fell from 98.3 per cent to 58.6 per cent and from 52.8 per cent to 29.4 per cent respectively. This constituted an overall decline of 40.4 per cent in the age group 25-29 years and 44.4 per cent in the case of women aged 30-34 years.

According to one survey conducted in Moscow in 1992, the average family size was 1.5 down by 1.6 since 1989. As regards optimal or desirable family size, opinions differed according to sex. Men wanted a larger family (2.28) than women (0.6). These levels are insufficient for simple reproduction of the existing population. There is little hope at present that this situation will change in the very near future. When asked the question 'How many children all in all are you going to have (including your existing ones)', men answered 1.48 and women 1.40. But the more significant indication of current trends came from women, 83.6 per cent of whom stated in relation to the previous question that **they were not going to have any more children for the foreseeable future.**

Finally, another indicator of the unfavourable situation in the family, is the growing number of children born out of wedlock. In 1985, the number of children born outside of marriage was 10.6 per cent. This has gradually increased ever since to 11.7 per cent in 1989; 13.4 per cent in 1990 and 15.1 per cent in 1991. In 1992, out of 69 children born to mothers under 15 years, only 18 (26.1 per cent) were born into a registered marriage.

Regulating the birth rate

At present there is a deep crisis prevailing in which the birth rate is falling dramatically. Part of the problem here is the high rate of abortion.[5] In Moscow, for instance, in 1992, there were 80 registered abortions per 1,000 women in the reproductive age group 15-49 years. This is only the tip of the iceberg, as many more abortions are performed in private clinics or hospitals without being registered in official statistics. While the number of abortions was 80, the birth rate among the same group of women stood at 30.26 or nearly three times lower.

But abortion is not the only reason for a declining birth rate. Many women are refusing to have children on the grounds that they cannot afford them - prices are too high - and are seeking to prevent children via contraceptive means. Unfortunately, there is a serious deficiency in condoms and other supplies. Such a situation is having an adverse effect on women's health. For example in 60-80 per cent of cases, the causes of women's secondary barrenness is the use of artificial abortions (*iskusstvennyi abort*), and 20-30 per cent of women having such abortions subsequently suffer malfunctions in their child-bearing capabilities. Thus the birth of a child might in theory be delayed until better economic conditions prevail, but in reality, child-birth might never happen at all because women resort to abortion through no fault of their own.

In the present situation the only thing that gives us hope is that many women are still having at least one child. However, if the crisis persists, and for an extended period, even one child families might become less common.

Russia is therefore facing an extremely difficult demographic situation. On average, the birth rate coefficient for women over her lifetime stood at 1.293 in 1991, which is almost two times lower than the level required for population reproduction. The situation has declined still further in the last few years. The consequence of this will be continued population decline and an ageing population. These factors in turn might influence in the size of the working population, labour force mobility, changes in the social sphere and above all put pressure on health care (see chapters 6-7, 11, 12).

Marriage

Together with the decline of the birth rate, especially in large cities, such as Moscow, as well as in the Russian Federation as a whole, the rate of marriage is also falling while the number of divorces are on the increase. These trends are more pronounced in Moscow than in Russia itself (see table 3.2 below). In 1995 there were 72 divorces per 100 marriages compared to only 41 per 100 a decade earlier. All existing data suggest that more and more families are falling apart and less and less families created to replace them. On top of this, the growing number of divorces is leading to an increase in the number of one-parent families.

Table 3.2
Marriage and divorce rate in Russia per 1,000 population, 1985-95

Year	Number of marriages		Number of divorces	
	Russia	**Moscow**	**Russia**	**Moscow**
1985	9.7	10.1	4.0	5.0
1986	9.8	10.2	4.0	4.7
1987	9.9	10.5	4.0	4.6
1988	9.5	10.1	3.9	4.5
1989	9.4	9.7	3.9	4.9
1990	8.9	9.4	4.0	4.5
1991	8.6	8.4	4.0	4.9
1992	7.7	7.6	4.3	4.7
1993	7.5	6.9	4.5	5.1
1994	7.4	na	4.6	na
1995	6.5	na	4.7	na

Source: *Rossiia nakanune XXI veka Vypusk* I (Moscow 1994), p. 102 and *Molodezh' Rossii: Vospitanie zhiznesposobnykh pokolenii (Doklad komiteta Rossiiskoi Federatsii po delam molodezhi)* Moscow 1995, p. 53.

Impact on the family

The Russian family has been in turmoil for a number of decades, as shown by the continued rise in the number of divorces since the late 1960s and early 1970s. This three-fold increase in divorce was not offset by a corresponding increase in the marriage rate, which itself decreased by a third over the same period. Soviet calculations in 1970 suggested that if the death rate remained constant at its 1970 level then, Russia's population would increase by 10 per cent in a few decades. This would lead to an increase from 130 million in 1970 to 148 million by the late 1980s and early 1990s.[6] Although this rate of growth has now been reached, it is highly unlikely, for reasons outlined earlier and below, that this growth will be sustained into the 21st century. Thus although Russian delegates attending the September 1994 Cairo conference on population rejected the use of the term 'depopulation' to describe the current situation in Russia, most of Russia's leading demographers disagree.[7]

The current demographic crisis is having an adverse affect upon the Russian family.

In the early-mid 1990s, every second marriage ended in divorce; many children - 16 per cent - are born out of wedlock; 12 million are said to live in 'social risk families'[8] and government expenditure on schools and kindergardens, children's hospitals, and maternity facilities has been significantly reduced since 1986. For example, in the period 1986-91, expenditure on kindergardens fell by 59 per cent and that on schools by 27 per cent. Similarly, the number of beds in children's hospitals declined 5 times while the number of maternity homes fell by 28 times in the same period.[9] During perestroika nothing was done to reverse the decline in the status of the family.[10] As a result, when the USSR collapsed and Russia went through tremendous turmoil which has intensified in the last few years, the family could not act as a psychological refuge for children under stress. Instead the family itself underwent a period of renewed crisis. It is not in a position to re-socialise youth for the transition to market conditions.

It is important to mention here that more than 30 per cent of divorces today are among young couples. As a consequence by 1994 there were more than 1.5 million single parents in Russia.[11]

The average family size in Russia has declined in the period 1991-94, affected by growing poverty and a lack of prosperity. In this respect, data from the State Statistical committee (*Goskomstat*) show that 30-35 per cent of the population live below the poverty line and a further 10 per cent just above it. Half of those working live below the poverty line. Of this number 17.9 per cent are in a very bad situation; a quarter are described as 'moderately poor'; 16 per cent are said to live in 'relative comfort'; 8 per cent describe themselves as 'prosperous' and 3 per cent as 'rich'.[12]

The material position of Russian families had declined further in 1994-95. For example in February 1994, VTsIOM carried out a survey among 4,000 families in Russia. 0.3 per cent of this sample said their position was 'very good'; 6 per cent 'good'; 51 per cent 'average'; 34 per cent 'bad' and 7 per cent 'very bad'. However by September 1995, a similar survey revealed that 2 per cent had a very good material position, 32 per cent were in a very bad situation and a further 48 per cent lived on the poverty line.[13]

In the international arena the greatest emphasis has been placed on restricting population growth in the developing countries, as a result of fears of 'overpopulation'. But in Russia the reverse is happening, with insufficient population growth to ensure even simple population reproduction in the near future. Certain Russian politicians and scientific specialists have exploited the Malthusian theory of overpopulation to reject the need to introduce an active family policy. They also suggest that as many Western nations do not pursue such a policy, Russia has no need for one either. Nothing could be further from the truth. Russia's depopulation is proceeding twice as fast as elsewhere. Many politicians are simply sitting back, hoping that as prosperity becomes a reality, the birth rate will increase. However as everyone knows, economic recovery is still a long way off. In the meantime many couples are only having one child, two at the most. The motives behind this decision differ according to social group. The 'poor' blame lack of money; the 'rich' insufficient spare time to spend with their children. Either way, some studies suggest that young people today have 0.3-0.5 less of a desire to have a family than their parents.[14] This has led many to conclude that single child families will become more common in Russia by the end of the 20th and into the 21st century. If we are to reverse this trend, we must defend the Russian family now and prevent it from being crushed once and for all.

Death rate

In Russia as a whole, the death rate has exceeded the birth rate since 1992. In Moscow, even in 1989 (for the first time in the history of the city in peacetime), the death rate was 5,000 higher than the birth rate, thereby starting the depopulation of the capital. The general coefficient of natural increase in Moscow in 1989 was already negative at minus 0.6 per cent. The size of Moscow's population fell dramatically from 1992 onwards. In 1991, it was 9.1 million; in 1992, 8.9 million and on 1 January 1993, 8.8 million. The rate of population decline has therefore increased with each passing year. Thus the coefficient of natural increase was minus 6 per cent in 1992 but stood at minus 9.5 per cent in 1993.

By comparison, in the Russian Federation as a whole, population growth was initially positive: plus 5.9 per 1,000 in 1970, plus 4.9 in 1980 and plus 2.2 in 1990. But by 1992 the coefficient was already negative at minus 1.5. This trend has continued ever since: 1993 minus 5.1; 1994 minus 6.0 and finally minus 6.2 in 1995.

Life expectancy

As a consequence of a rising death rate, life expectancy has declined significantly for both men and women. In Moscow's case, the death rate per 1,000 population has risen as follows: 12.0 per cent in 1981-85; 12.1 per cent 1986-90; 12.4 per cent in 1989; 12.8 per cent in 1990 and 12.9 per cent in 1991. This trend is higher than the national average. In certain respects the critical socio-economic situation explains the increasing death rate in both cases. However, whereas in the past mortality was higher for men than women, the level of differentiation is decreasing. Thus in 1992, the crude death rate was 13.6 per cent (for males 6.5 per cent and females 7.1 per cent) but by 1993 it increased to 16.5 per cent (8.4 per cent for men and 8.1 per cent for women). Furthermore, the death rate among the able-bodied working population of both sexes (men aged 16-59 years and women between the ages of 16-54 years) is also on the increase. Thus the combined death rate coefficient for both sexes stood at 4.5 per 1,000 in 1985 but rose to 4.7 in 1991 and 5.6 per 1,000 in 1992.

In overall terms life expectancy fell from a peak of 70 years in 1989 to only 65 years for both sexes in 1994 or from 64 years to 58.9 years for men compared with a decline from 74 years to 71.9 years for women.[15] What is most striking is the growing gap between male and female life expectancy. Unfortunately this trend holds not only for Russia as a whole, but for many of its regions. Part of the reason for this is the present psychological and moral crisis, the crisis of faith, which has hit the elderly particularly badly, but its underlying cause is the deteriorating economic situation, outlined in chapter 1 above, which has had an adverse effect on the evolution and development of the health system. Thus the health service has disintegrated, has fewer staff, medical supplies and equipment. These problems, coupled with a declining food supply and poor nutritional standards, has also exacerbated matters (see chapter 12).

On top of these difficulties is the ageing population. Moscow's population, like that of many other cities and regions, is getting older and older. Current trends indicate that this process will continue for the time being at least. This is partly the product of the rise and fall in the birth rate, but is also caused by the reduction in the number of migrants coming to Moscow from the countryside. It is also highly unlikely that future trends will reverse this process in the short term because those under 14 years only make up 18.8 per cent of Moscow's population, whereas those no longer of able-bodied working age constitute 22.8 per cent.

If we examine the causes of the death rate in more detail, first place is occupied by diseases of the circulatory system. In 1994, 20 per cent died from this cause. In addition, diseases of the respiratory organs are also on the increase, for example, 55 per cent of deaths in 1994 were caused by pneumonia (Tuberculosis is particularly rife). A number of other variables, of lesser significance, but which nevertheless should not be ignored include the rising number of murders and suicides (see chapter 14). What is most worrying in this context for the government and the general public is the rate of increase in both these cases. Murders are up 52 per cent and suicides by 12 per cent. A sad indicator of the current situation is the continued high infant mortality rate (IMR) (i.e. the number of children dying before the age of one year).

Not surprisingly in view of the above, public opinion surveys have revealed a pessimistic picture concerning health status. Moscow residents, according to one late 1993 survey, placed their health status on average at 3.3 where 1 was extremely poor and 5 very good.[16] Unless urgent action is taken to reverse the falling birth rate and reduce the rising death rate from a range of causes, the health status of Muscovites and other citizens of the Russian Federation is likely to deteriorate well below the average indicated by this survey.

Morbidity

This issue will be addressed in greater depth in chapter 12, so we would like to focus on social diseases here. By this term we are referring to the likes of tuberculosis and venereal diseases. Both types of diseases are on the increase in Russia in general, and Moscow in particular. For instance, the number of women who have contracted syphilis has risen from 16.8 per 100,000 women in 1991 to 27.9 per 100,000 by 1992. However, on the whole the illness rate from syphilis is higher among men (14.3 in 1992) than women (12.6). Similarly, with regard to gonorrhoea, the illness rate was 366.8 for Muscovite men and 176 for Muscovite women in 1992. These compared with an overall level in Russia in the same year of 212.1 for men and 132.0 for women. Once again, Moscow's health situation is worse than that of the national average. This trend has continued on into 1993 and 1994.

In overall terms in the last two years, most Muscovites have died from cardiovascular diseases, tumours, injuries and accidents. The group of illness categories alone have steadily accounted for more than 80 per cent of all causes of death in the capital in the period 1988-94. However, not only adults have been affected by these trends. Children have also been badly hit. As table 3.1 shows, the IMR in Russia as a whole initially declined from 23.0 per 1,000 in 1970 to 17.8 in 1991 but thereafter increased each year reaching 20.0 per 1,000 population by 1995. Thus the IMR in Moscow initially decreased from 16.8 in 1990 to 16.0 per 1,000 births in 1992, but since then has increased with each passing year: 16.5 in 1993 and 17.9 per 1,000 births in 1994. At the same time, maternal mortality has also started to increase again from 48.5 per 100,000 live births in 1992 to 57.1 a year later before reaching a staggering 63.5 per 100,000 in 1994. Russian scholars attribute this increase in maternal mortality to female diseases associated with pregnancy, the birth process and the high number of deaths resulting from abortion. The latter is said to constitute around 20 per cent of the total number of female deaths at present.[17]

Given this deterioration in health conditions, it will take Moscow and other cities throughout the Russian Federation many years to escape the current demographic crisis, especially existing high levels of morbidity and mortality. Thus in Moscow alone, the high incidence of respiratory disease accounted for 56.6 per cent of child, 40 per cent of adolescent and 21 per cent of adult morbidity in 1994. This constituted a 20-30 per cent increase on 1992 and a 40 per cent increase on 1993 levels. Part of this situation is attributable to high levels of smoking among both sexes, but the primary agent involved is environmental pollution - especially of the air and soil, due to the detoxification, recycling and burial of waste. Thus recent studies indicate that air pollution with carbon monoxide, nitrogen oxides and other hazardous substances are often 10-12 times the maximum permissible concentrations; while the soil in Moscow is contaminated with heavy metals, such as copper and zinc. Unfortunately, current levels exceed permissible levels by a staggering 200 per cent and 350 per cent respectively. It is hardly surprising, therefore, that the level of respiratory disease in Moscow is high. The same also applies to endocrine-related illness. In 1994 in Moscow, these diseases were twice as high as they had been in 1991. In addition, the frequency of congenital abnormalities is rising, especially among children. Thus among children under the age of 14 years, these diseases stood at 24.5 per 1,000 in 1993, as against a national average of 10.9 per 1,000. In overall terms, the incidence of congenital anomalies in 1994 was 43 per cent higher than in 1991.[18]

In this context, a recent report in the newspaper *Sovetskaia Rossiia* noted how 40-60 per cent of the Russian population are now suffering from protein and vitamin deficiencies.[19]

Finally the position of the young is not much better. A recent *Moskovskii Komsomolets* survey of 500 young people examined their attitudes towards alcohol, drugs and smoking. This research was carried out in association with VTsIOM staff. Researchers found that 60.4 per cent thought it was not very grown up to smoke as opposed to 27.4 per cent who thought smoking was adult-like. However, 5.2 per cent of the sample said they wouldn't mind if their partner smoked; 69.6 per cent were against smoking and 24.2 per cent remained indifferent. Despite these tendencies, Katia Mashkina of *Moskovskii Komsomolets* found 38.6 per cent of this sample smoked and 54.8 per cent drank alcohol once a week. Only 7.8 per cent did not drink, smoke or take drugs compared to 84.6 per cent who smoked, 84 per cent who drank alcohol and 65.4 per cent who took drugs.[20]

To put these problems right will require major finance and other support from the state and a number of civil and other organisations. Nothing is going to be done unless someone acts.

The demographic situation in the countryside and villages

Thus far we have confined our discussion of the demographic crisis to the cities and major urban areas. How, if at all, does the situation differ in the contemporary village?

The process of transformation of the village and its transition to the market economy is taking place under very difficult socio-economic and political conditions. In the period 1991-94, capital investment in the agricultural sector was reduced six times and investments in technology fell three-fold. Many farmers have not been paid for their harvests and there is a great disparity between the prices of industrial goods and agricultural products. This has meant that fewer and fewer farmers have achieved their production targets. Earlier state programmes stressing the need to strengthen the rural infrastructure - the building of houses and roads, the extension of gas and water supplies, communication networks etc. - are now being withdrawn. This is having a considerable impact on living standards in the countryside and aggravating the demographic crisis. Current official statistics indicate that there are 30 million chronically ill people in Russia, but what they do not state is that a significant proportion of these individuals live in the countryside. Thus one newspaper source shows that of the healthy, who constitute about 20 per cent of the population, the large majority live in the bigger towns.[21]

It is difficult to draw concrete conclusions regarding the position in the countryside as the demographic situation is very complicated and often contradictory. We shall use the Republic of Komi as our example to illustrate this point. Over the last three decades Komi has had some periods of rural population growth, and some periods of population decline. In recent times, population decline has become more common. For example, in the period 1988-93, the number of inhabitants of rural regions of the Republic increased by 2.2 per cent, but this was less than the average population expansion which was 24-25 per cent. All in all, the rural population of the Republic declined by 7,900 between 1989-93. This was caused by a series of factors: the reorganisation of workers' settlements in rural areas of Komi between 1991-93; administrative reform and the rural exodus in which more have left the countryside than migrated to it. Thus, in 1989, the difference between in and out-migration was 1,900 but by 1991, it had increased to 2,100. As a result, in Komi, every sixth inhabitant has reached pensionable age. Many areas have also become depopulated. For example, by 1994, Sysol'skii *raion*, situated in the Southern part of Komi, suffered from 80 deserted settlements. Of the 39 still functioning, only 50 people or less lived in each, most of whom were elderly.

A range of push-pull factors have been at work here. On the push side, reduced employment opportunities and the adverse effects of the market reforms. Meanwhile, on the pull side of the equation, we have the socio-economic advantages of an urban over a rural lifestyle, better housing conditions and cultural provision in the city, on top of trading opportunities, better medical services, wages, transport and finally a wider choice of professions and greater chances to improve one's qualifications, work conditions and other situations in the towns. In Komi, the population is getting older, sicker and labour productivity and output are declining rapidly because in the period 1989-93, the working population fell by approximately 8,000 while the number of OAPs rose by 6,500. On the whole, the proportion of the population of Komi of working age is between 50-55 per cent. If the rural infrastructure continues to fragment, then the push factors will gain the upper hand, and the pull of the big city will cause the rural exodus to reach serious levels. This will inevitably place increased strain on the working population left behind. Most of this burden comes from the growing number of people of non-working age. This group has increased from 74.7 for every 100 of working age in 1989 to 80.2 per 100 by 1993.

Besides the impact in economic terms on labour productivity and output, the rural exodus has also caused a gender imbalance. By 1993, men outnumbered women in the Republic of Komi by 8,000. This imbalance is especially acute in the age groups 20-29, 30-39 and 40-49. In these instances for every 100 women, there were 128, 137 and 128 men respectively.

In addition to this problem, mirroring national trends, the crude death rate has exceeded the crude birth rate since 1993. In that year the difference amounted to 1,100 but since then this figure has risen. Given the current situation in the countryside this situation is unlikely to be reversed in the very near future. As the newspaper *Pravda* declared on 10 June 1994: 'at present, the demand is greater for graves than for children's prams'.[22]

Migration

At present Russia is going through a process of major social transformation. This has generated a sharp intensification of the migration processes. In the last few years we have witnessed ethnic migration, repatriation of deported peoples, the homecoming of the Soviet Army from East-Central Europe, various streams of refugees and high levels of emigration, particularly of Jews and Germans. The Gorbachev and then the Yeltsin Administrations were totally unprepared for these new forms of migration in the last decade. The subject of migration is important in a number of respects - socially, politically and economically.

Economic aspects

From an economic point of view, the high rate of immigration to Russia has had negative consequences for the country. Refugees are costing the Russian tax-payer billions of roubles. Such migration is also placing the housing market and welfare state under increased pressure. The employment and labour market situation is also very strained and it will be some time yet before the current economic reforms and political changes begin to have a positive impact. However, even though the immigrants and emigrants differ qualitatively, this need not always be a negative phenomenon. The glowing influx of able-bodied workers might help offset the current demographic crisis in that they could be used to restore and develop neglected parts of the country. This could happen if the migrants are welcomed, accepted and employed. But unfortunately, these prerequisites do not yet exist. Migration of the Russian speaking peoples from 'near abroad' countries involves the loss of engineering, scientific and technical personnel. Emigration on a large scale is also stimulating a decline in production, especially in industry.

From a demographic point of view, migration has influenced the size and structure of the population. Due to the sharp fall of the birth rate and an increase in the death rate, migration is becoming a key factor. The increase in the rate of migration in 1993 was 2.5 times greater than the previous year reaching 430,000 people, the highest level ever reached in the post-war period.

One of the demographic situations specific to Russia at present is the multifarious process currently underway. This involves an influx of people from beyond the borders of the Commonwealth of Independent States (CIS) as well as within CIS borders. With regard to internal migration, the pattern of rural-urban migration has altered. In 1992 for the first time in many years, as well as in 1993, the number of people who moved into rural areas was greater than the number coming to the cities. Although there are a series of push-pull factors influencing this process, the rural exodus was influenced by privatisation of the land, whereas the move to the countryside was prompted by growing unemployment, housing problems, food supply difficulties and the deteriorating ecological situation in the cities. Inter-regional, return migration from the North, Siberia, and the Far East is also gaining momentum. This modification of internal migration patterns will, however, diminish the size of the labour force in these regions and jeopardise their regional economic development. Thus according to Federal Migration Service data, as of 1 January 1994, the population of the North had declined by 37,500 whereas the North Western region had in-migration of 7,400 and that of the Central zone by 113,200. The same was also true of the Volga-Viatka region (26,000), Central-Chernozem (91,800), Volga (131,200), the North Caucasus (143,000), the Urals (41,300) and finally West-Siberia which gained by 26,300 people. By contrast, East-Siberia suffered out-migration of 22,600 and the Far Eastern region lost 101,100 people.[23] On the other hand, the return of these peoples to their former places of residence will increase the level of unemployment in the Russian heartland. Of course, this also works in the opposite direction. According to the Ministry of Internal Affairs (MVD), out of the 102,900 emigrating in 1992, 129,000 were former Moscow residents (or 12.5 per cent). The majority of these were well-qualified specialists. This adversely influences the intellectual and productive potential of the capital. This 'brain drain' represents a serious challenge to Russia's long-term recovery. However, with the development of market relations, the larger cities have started to attract business people, the former unemployed and on the downside the criminal fraternity. This trend has encouraged inter-urban migration from small to larger cities as job and other opportunities arise. Nevertheless, the removal of administrative restrictions on such inter-urban migration might in the short to medium term turn big cities into centres of social tension.

Ethnic aspects

From an ethnic point of view, we are presently witnessing a unique process involving the population redistribution of a sixth of the world's land surface. The share of Russians (in per cent) in the structure of migrants moving into Russia is growing dramatically. Their share has increased as follows: 46 per cent in 1989; 54 per cent in 1990; 57 per cent in 1991; 66 per cent in 1992 and 65 per cent in 1993. Among the total number of 784,000 refugees by 1 April 1995, the percentage of Russians, according to the Federal Migration Service, is very high at 62 per cent. Apart from Russians returning home, the most significant flows of refugees entering Russia, as of 1 April 1995, came from the Republics of the former USSR, which totalled 679,000. Most refugees came from Chechnya or the surrounding areas (104,000) although others originated from Georgia (90,800), Tajikistan (134,046) and Azerbaijan (77,339). Fewer came from the CIS states, such as Belarus (17 people).[24] The policy of ethnic cleansing, which is being practised by most ex-Soviet Republics either overtly or covertly,[25] urges non-native people to return to their titular Republics - mainly Russian speakers to Russia. Forcing Russians out of the social, economic, cultural life or politics in the former Republics has become a routine practice. In the next four to five years, Russia must be prepared to receive even more Russian speakers. According to various forecasts, between 400,000 and 2 to 3 million Russians may be expected in this period.

Political aspects

Finally, as we shall see in chapter 16, from a political point of view, the break-up of the USSR and increased regional separatism since the end of 1991, poses a real danger to Russian sovereignty. The current crisis in Chechnya is viewed in some Russian quarters partly as a response to a situation in which the rights of the titular nationality is given greater priority than general human rights. This is by no means an isolated case and similar conflicts have already arisen or might arise in Tatarstan, Dagestan, Tuva and Northern Ossetia in the not too distant future.

What does the future hold?

This is not the time or place to discuss the economic situation in Russia in great detail, but nevertheless the resolution of current economic difficulties will have a distinct bearing on the present demographic crisis. Let us use Moscow as an illustrative example. In 1993, 40 per cent of the city's population had incomes below the level necessary to survive. The average family income per capita was approximately at the same level as the monthly pension (i.e. 41,675r and 42,142r respectively). The average living wage was 72,751r in December 1993. But, as is well known, Moscow is one of the most expensive cities in Russia, if not the world. How then can the average Muscovite or inhabitants of other cities survive on such a pittance?

The short answer is that most Russian families cannot live on such low wages. As a result the nutritional value of food consumed is being regularly reduced. In 1992, it averaged 2,311 kilocalories per person per day, but fell again in 1993 to 2,141 kilocalories. In addition to this, the number of families registered as needing to improve their housing in the 1990s is stable at around 20 per cent. Recent surveys of Moscow families showed that the large majority of respondents do not foresee an improvement in their living standards in the near future. Thus, in answer to the question 'What do you think will happen in the future to living standards in your family: will they improve, stay the same or worsen?' only 28.8 per cent of Muscovite men believed that conditions will improve. Among women, fewer - 14.9 per cent - shared this view. Such a situation is making itself felt in current birth rate trends - many Russian couples either do not want to have a family or are putting off the decision until the current economic climate improves. However, it is widely believed that the next 2-3 years will not witness a turnaround in the socio-economic situation and with it a reversal of the present demographic downturn.

Any room for optimism?

Despite this possibility, we must resist the temptation to introduce harsh laws to rectify the demographic crisis.[26] If such measures are implemented they are likely to have the reverse rather than the desired effect. This is shown by a survey carried out by Zhuravlev and Kuchmaeva among more than 200 young men and women in Moscow in 1993, only 6 per cent of whom were married.

The majority of boys and girls surveyed (63 per cent and 82 per cent respectively) wanted a family. Only a small proportion of the boys (18 per cent) and girls (11 per cent) said they did not consider a family essential. But we discovered totally opposing attitudes regarding marriage: girls wanted an early marriage; whereas boys planned to get married only after they had achieved their main ambitions, namely financial stability, a career, own apartment etc. Nevertheless, it appears that the majority of this sample accepted the dominant values of society, believing in the sanctity of marriage. But our survey also revealed that there are serious obstacles in the way of marriage, such as low pay. For instance 50 per cent of those surveyed said they would not marry unless they were in a financial position to do so. It was also the case, however, that some respondents viewed marriage as a means of escaping poverty (i.e. they wanted to marry someone wealthy). All in all, we found that it was those boys and girls surveyed, whose parents possess good quality housing, who tended to be the most favourably disposed to starting a family. Finally, those already working in the private business sphere, showed a greater willingness to get married.

Despite the aforementioned stress on pay and housing as factors promoting or hindering marriage, two-thirds of those surveyed placed greatest emphasis on love as the driving factor behind marriage. Love occupied first place overall, whereas only 15-20 per cent of our sample were solely influenced by financial considerations. In this respect, it is important to mention another important finding: that only one in six respondents said they would marry a rich person with low 'moral values'. The primary factors indicated as influencing a young person's decision to get married included: their partner's financial status; sexual compatibility; friends' opinion; viewpoint of parents; partner's nationality and finally, their partner's age. Thus income is not the only priority among all of today's youth, who will help build Russia's future. By comparison, in descending order of priority, the main factors leading to divorce were: spiritual and emotional incompatibility; sexual incompatibility; adultery and finally their partner's poor financial status. Finally, we discovered that a significant proportion of young people in Moscow view 'living together' positively, although others prefer officially registered marriages instead.

In addition to the above, our survey also revealed that the majority intend to get married for the sake of the children - either because they want a family or because they want existing children to have a father. Among those who said that they would be able to raise a child on their own, almost two-thirds claimed that they would like to get married for love or want to find a good friend etc. Furthermore, three-quarters of those surveyed said that they definitely planned to have children. Of this group, more than half wanted two children, but only on the proviso that wages were high enough and housing conditions satisfactory. Not all the news was good. Of the 5 per cent of our youth sample who considered themselves to be rich, most said they would limit their family to only one child, no matter how rich they became. Thus the poor who sometimes cannot afford a child, have one, while the rich, who are in a financial position to have larger families, are planning to have only one child. Although there is some room for optimism, on the basis of this evidence, we can at least expect the birth rate to continue falling for the next couple of years.

In order to encourage the poorer sections of society to have children, the state must step in. It must provide the necessary means for their survival, by providing adequate incomes, educational opportunities and sufficient health care provision. The problem here will not simply be a financial one (i.e. taking appropriate budget measures in these spheres) (see chapters 11-14); it will also be a question of changing public opinion. We discovered during our 1993 Moscow survey that a third of those young people surveyed viewed large families negatively, as a drain on limited state resources, compared to 10 per cent who said large families were a positive feature of Russian society.

Finally, we compared theory with practice regarding family size in Moscow in 1993 and discovered that those who would like to have two to three children, actually have only one to two and those who would like to have one child, at present have no children at all. Thus the value orientations towards marriage and a family and young people's lifestyles have yet to be put into practice. Whether or not desires and reality will ever be matched depends upon housing conditions; spouse's desire to have children; financial situation; spouse's health; parental assistance (financial as well as help with the children), love of children; spouses relationship and his/her age.

Unfortunately, in many young families, conflicts often occur. For this reason, 19 per cent of our sample were going through a divorce, and only 17 per cent were satisfied with their marriage. Among those families who are ready to separate, 2.5 times more lived with their parents and 1.5 times more give their salaries to their parents. It is hardly surprising, therefore, in view of the above, that a high proportion of those undergoing a divorce were totally dissatisfied with housing conditions. Others attributed their divorce to parental pressure or conflict over family responsibilities. This does not mean, however, that parents bear responsibility for their children's divorce, even though Russian youth might attribute blame in this way. Surveys indicate the opposite trend - more and more parents are giving up part of their housing to their children, more and more parents are helping them out financially and finally, more and more parents in Russia today are retiring early to take care of their grandchildren. Sadly, Russia's youth see this as interference in their way of life.

Part of the problem in trying to resolve the demographic crisis is the imbalance between the number of women wanting to get married and the number of eligible men. For example, in Moscow in 1993, there were 8.8 million people. Of this total, 4.8 million were women and 4 million men, leaving a shortage of over three-quarters of a million men.

Conclusion

Above we have demonstrated the extent and nature of Russia's demographic crisis. Current projections suggest that the birth rate is likely to continue falling while the death rate will go on increasing. In relation to the birth rate, there will be an estimated 1.1-1.2 fewer births for every woman by 2005 or 7.6-9.7 per 1,000 births less per 1,000 population, whilst predictions for the death rate are between 15.9-20.2 per 1,000 more deaths per 1,000 population by the year 2005. On the whole, it is believed that Russia's population might fall to between 131.5-138.7 million by the year 2005, a decline of 12.1-19.3 million on 1995 levels.[27] Whether or not this proves to be the case will depend upon the implementation of a new demographic policy which includes measures supporting young families thereby creating favourable conditions in which they want to start a family. This crisis is hitting rural areas particularly badly. Any new policy which is introduced will therefore have to ensure that it takes into account trends in urban and rural areas so that the *smychka* (link) between town and country can be preserved. There is no easy, quick solution available. Only a well-thought out, broad-ranging policy involving some or all of the following measures will suffice: social guarantees for rural and urban inhabitants; decent living conditions; balanced labour market and policy; the introduction of social insurance for the unemployed, especially in rural areas, as well as a minimum wage; special loans for young people and families on favourable terms; expansion of welfare benefits for pregnant women, the disabled and the elderly and finally, better financing for culture, education, health care, communications and road networks. In seeking to resolve the present crisis, we should draw upon our own experience, in particular that of the 1950s and 1960s, and also learn lessons from the West. However, unless we began to address the issues outlined here, in 15-20 years time Russia will find herself in a very difficult position indeed - possessing a declining population, an acute shortage of labour and a population where, according to current projections, life expectancy might fall to 58 years by the year 2005.[28] These factors in turn will have a significant bearing upon our standing in the world.

Notes

1.   V. Khorev, *Demograficheskaya tragediia Rossii*, Moscow 'Paleia' 1994, p. 3.
2.   *Izvestiia* 24 January 1995, p. 1 and Pravda 28 September 1995, p. 2.
3.   *Trud* 20 January 1995, p. 2.
4.   Ye. M. Andreev and A.G. Volkov, *Demograficheskie modeli*, Moscow 1977, p. 70; A.I. Antonov, *Sotsiologiia rozhdaemosti*, Moscow 1980, p. 256 and A.I. Antonov and V.A. Borisov, *Krizis sem'i i puti ego preo doleniia*, Moscow 1990.
5.   On this see C. Williams, 'Abortion and women's health in contemporary Russia' in R. Marsh (ed.), *Women in Russia and the Ukraine*, Cambridge University Press, forthcoming 1996.
6.   A.I. Antonov, 'Depopulatsiia Rossii i problemy sem'i', in the collection *Rossiia nakanune XXI veka*, Moscow 1994, pp. 112-113.
7.   Ibid, p. 110.
8.   *Polozhenie detei v Rossii 1992 god (sotsial'nyi portret)*, Moscow 1993, p. 15.

9. Ibid, pp. 16, 82, 85.
10. For a more detailed discussion see Peter H. Juliver, 'No end of a problem: *Perestroika* for the family', in: Antony Jones, Walter D. Connor and David E. Powell (eds.), *Soviet social problems,* Westview Press, Boulder, Colorado 1991, pp. 194-212 and James Riordan (ed.), *Soviet social reality in the mirror of glasnost* Macmillan/St. Martin's Press, London 1992, Part One.
11. *Molodezh 'Rossii: Vospitanie zhiznesposobnykh pokolenii,* (Doklad komiteta Rossiiskoi Federatsii po delam molodezhi), Moscow 1995, p. 54.
12. A.I. Antonov, 'Depopulatsiia Rossii i problemy sem'i', in the collection *Rossiia nakanune XXI veka,* Moscow 1994, p. 116. For a more detailed discussion of this issue see C. Williams, 'Gaidar's shock therapy and its impact on poverty in Contemporary Russia', Paper presented to the Politics of Social security in Eastern Europe planning session of 22nd ECPR workshop, Madrid 17-22 April 1994.
13. Molodezh' Rossii 1995, p. 54.
14. A.I. Antonov, 'Depopulatsiia Rossii i problemy sem'i', in the collection *Rossiia nakanune XXI veka,* Moscow 1994, n. 1, p. 117.
15. G.V. Osipov, *Sotsial'naia i sotsial'no - politicheskaia situatsiia Rossii: Analiz i prognoz, Pervoe pologudie 1995 goda,* Moscow 'Akademiia' 1995, p. 46.
16. *Rossiia nakanune XXI veka,* Moscow 1994, p. 103.
17. *Sevodnia* 4 May 1995, p. 9.
18. Ibid.
19. *Sovetskaia Rossia* 14 October 1995, p. 3.
20. *Moskovskii Komsomolets* 3 October 1995, p. 4.
21. *Sel'skaya Zhizn'* 13 May 1994, p. 3.
22. *Pravda* 10 June 1994, p. 2.
23. I. Orlova, 'Migratory processes in ex-USSR under conditions of social catalysm', paper presented to the XIII World Congress of Sociology, Bielefeld, Germany 18-23 July 1994.
24. Ibid and *Pravda* 28 September 1995, p. 2.
25. On this, see for example, A. Aasland, 'The Russian population in Latvia: An integrated minority?', *Journal of Communist Studies and Transition Politics,* Vol. 10 (2), June 1994, pp. 233-260.
26. For more on this see A.G. Vishnevskii (ed.), *Evoliutsia sem'i i semeinaia politika v SSSR,* Moscow 1992 and S.I. Golod and A.A. Kletsin, *Sostoianie i perspektivy razvitia sem'i,* Institute of Sociology, Russian Academy of Science, St. Petersburg 1994.
27. I.B. Orlova and Ye.E. Skovortsova, *Demograficheskaia i migratsionnaia situatsiia v Rossii (Sravnitel'nyi analiz),* Moscow, Institute of Socio-Political Research 1994, pp. 19-24.
28. Ibid, p. 23.

4 Tradition versus modernity

NIKOLAI DRIAKHLOV

Introduction

Throughout Russian history, be it the tsarist or Soviet period, there has always been a clash between tradition and modernity. However, this clash has an even greater theoretical and practical significance today. Part of the reason for this is the legacy of the catastrophic consequences of Gorbachev's *perestroika*. The reality of the situation in contemporary Russia, which this and other chapters assess, begs the question what is modernisation? What are its essential elements?

In answer to these questions, some Russian scholars have argued that modernisation means improving the quality of one's life. In order to achieve this goal, economic relations in Russia need to be transformed. This involves technological advances, improvements in the technical aspects of production etc. But so far attempts to do this have ended in disaster. There is now a widespread fear of change. This is hardly surprising because in the past Russia was a superpower (*superderzhavy*) in terms of its history, values, ideals, industrial, scientific and cultural achievements and so forth. Now Russia is a shadow of her former self. She is shapeless and being torn apart by contradictions or cleavages of various types - national, territorial, political, economic and so on. Although there is much talk of modernisation, as indicated by the emphasis upon reform, past as well as present reforms have often had unforeseen consequences. This has created further social deformations, deepening the feeling of crisis in Russian society.

The negative legacy of perestroika

Perestroika tried to address the flaws in Soviet society which had become increasingly obvious since the 1970s. However, Russian and Western politicians and members of the academic community now acknowledge that the contradictions within Gorbachev's reform strategy meant that, as in the past, his leadership could not find solutions to the widespread contradictions inherent in Soviet society by the mid-late 1980s.[1] Evidence of this crisis was spelt out in chapter 1, so it is sufficient to mention here high inflation, the sharp reduction in agricultural and industrial production, unemployment, rising crime, increased morbidity and mortality and a rapid decline in the standard of living in Russia in the last decade or so. The fact that this systemic collapse and general state of chaos has lasted for so long, means that action needs to be taken immediately in order to defend citizens of Russia from politicians' whims and irresponsible experiments. Similarly, politicians must also be held accountable to the Russian people.

Analysing current trends: A theoretical framework

One of the social sciences trying to grapple with these issues is sociology. Although the discipline and its practitioners have been badly hit by the transition, as we saw earlier in chapter 2, this has not stopped Russian sociologists from acknowledging and then trying to interpret the nature of the transformation of Russian society, with all its pros and cons. As a first step towards such an analysis of the changes underway in Russian society, I would like to examine trends in the socio-cultural sphere of Russian society. The basic functions and characteristics of this process are described in table 4.1 below:

Using this schema, it is clear that in order to realise these three principles we must take into account the following factors:

-       the cumulative effect of the historical process on the one hand and the ability of individuals or groups to solve particular socio-cultural problems on the other;

-       current knowledge of traditions, habits, one's role in organisations etc.;

-       the influence of the forces of social inertia, public opinion and the degree of sanctions and incentives acknowledged and adopted by society;

-       the extent to which the rule of law applies, common religious beliefs are held or the potential for self-regulation exists;

-       the degree to which the population has the opportunity to participate in policy and decision-making;

-       the clarity of purpose regarding the need for modernisation and its impact, as well as knowledge concerning the likely negative and positive impact of such a strategy on society;

- the ability of all persons involved to ensure that economic and political changes do not outstrip the modernisation process in the socio-cultural sphere;

- the extent to which democratic institutions exist and are well entrenched, influencing both political culture and trends in the socio-cultural sphere;

- the degree to which individual rights and freedoms are protected during the process of modernisation; and finally,

- it is necessary to examine in a systematic fashion the impact of modernisation on all sections and sectors of society. This might mean using a comparative framework, but we must also ensure that the Russian people are consulted every step of the way.

Table 4.1

Theoretical outline of evolution and development of trends in socio-cultural sphere in Russia

Basic functions	Basic characteristics
1. TRANSMISSION - transmission from the past to the present and the present to the future of the social values, norms, needs, preferences, behaviour patterns and way of life etc.	Degree of autonomy, stability and unity with other spheres of social life and culture
2. SELECTION - evaluation and classification of the inherited values, definition of their place and role in the solution of current problems of society at its present stage of development	Degree of variety of socio-cultural sphere but also element of judicial and normative regulation
3. INNOVATION - renewal of social values and norms but also imposition of certain limits on them. Elaboration of new norms and element of borrowing from other cultures and nations	Degree of innovation (conservatism). Regulation of socio-cultural trends for people's creative development. Also valuable for authority groups.

Understanding Russia's past, present and future

Therefore, in view of what was stated above, one cannot understand where Russian society is going unless we appreciate two things: Russia's past and the factors which determine her present social situation and her place and role in the social process. Thus if society is stable then this tends to encourage innovation and modernisation; by contrast, if society is unstable, then feelings of alienation increase, innovation is less common and the same is also true of modernisation, which tends to be of a limited nature. In this instance, greatest stress is placed upon the selection and transmission of current values. In the long-term this produces stagnation and inertia, as shown by the Brezhnev era, and leads to contradictions which in the end engender a systemic crisis. Although perestroika tried to engender innovation and change, it eventually led to the collapse of the old communist system.

However, the fundamental problems inherent in contemporary Russian society do not simply date back to the mid-1980s, they go much further back in Russia's history to the October 1917 Revolution. This date marks the start of political interference in Russia's *natural process of development*. The Bolsheviks thought that they could modernise Russia by using some abstract theoretical principles. History has, however, proved these theoreticians and politicians wrong. The reason why the socialist experiment failed is because it totally ignored all of the variables outlined above. Starting from 1917, Russia ignored her past historical experience, traditions, habits and regional and national ways of life. In seeking to replace *tradition* with *modernity* Russian society lost all or part of her immense social strength and potential for *rational modernisation*. In a similar vein, current trends risk adding to the uncertainty. Russia has lost her way and does not know in which direction she is going. This view can be illustrated by referring to a recent cartoon in the literary newspaper *Literaturnaia Gazeta* which indicates the possibility that, depending upon circumstances, and the forces for and against change, Russia could either go backwards, forwards or sideways.

As Gennadi Osipov stated recently:

> 'The most important indicator of social crisis which is growing into a national catastrophe is the rapid increase in the level of social tension in our country. The large majority of Russian citizens now realise that the satisfaction of their material, economic, social political, cultural, religious and other vital needs is impossible to fulfil under present conditions. As a result, tension can be felt virtually everywhere. People are becoming increasingly dissatisfied with poor living standards, an inadequate consumer market, a deteriorating environment, the breakdown in the existing system of distribution, growing civil, ethnic and religious conflicts, nationalism, chauvinism, anti-semitism, rising crime and so forth'.[2]

One of the primary factors engendering this situation is the on-going clash between tradition and modernity. Those who are in favour of tradition cite the present political instability as evidence that the transition to a 'new Russia' is not having the desired effect. Critics go on to add that current political difficulties are also engendering significant economic and social problems - population decline, inadequate food supplies, a dramatic fall in production levels, growing unemployment, housing and ecological problems, ethnic conflict etc. Many people are therefore, hardly surprisingly, looking more favourably at the past. For some the past represents the pre-1917 period; for others the communist era. Either way, more and more people are only seeing Russia today in a negative light.

Figure 4.1   Where is Russia going?

Source: Oleg Moroz, 'Kto nami budet pravit' 15 ulia 1996 goda?', *Literaturnaia Gazeta* 29 March 1995, p. 11

Tradition versus modernity

Urgent measures are required to resolve the crisis before Russia is brought to her knees. This situation is leading many scholars to re-examine the three variables outlined in table 4.1 above. Thus they are asking: What values exist and which do we want to transmit from generation to generation? What inherited values need to be selected for Russia to progress to the next stage of her development and finally, many Russian social scientists are asking how can we encourage innovation and the development of new norms and customs? Should we rely upon our own past experience or that of other countries? and finally how can modernisation take place without totally destroying our traditions?

Finding answers to these key questions is far from easy, but in seeking solutions to current ills we must prevent the authorities from abusing their power and also ensure that public officials face up to their mistakes and be held accountable for policy errors, such as the fact that almost 70 per cent of the population live below the poverty line. Here we are not simply talking about students, pensioners and invalids, because 25 per cent of this total includes members of the professions - teachers, doctors, university professors, workers in scientific research institutes and lawyers. No society in the civilised world has paid such a high price for reform. No one is yet in a position to confidently state that modernisation is likely to have a positive effect upon Russia's future course of development. Instead all indicators currently suggest that the process of modernisation undertaken over the last decade has ended in failure causing a major industrial nation and superpower to fall apart.

Ways of achieving modernisation

However, assuming for the sake of argument, that modernisation was a desirable goal, one must ask how is it possible? under what conditions? what are its main characteristics? and finally how far should it go, or to put it another way what are its dimensions? Modernisation is best seen not in national but in global terms. Without arguing that Russia belongs to the same type of social, economic or political system, as its Western counterparts, one has to admit that pressures of a similar nature exist on all systems. These globalisation pressures are forcing countries to converge upon one another.[3] For example, the end of the Cold War and the collapse of communism in late 1991 has led to the triumph of certain liberal democratic values - the market mechanism, a multi-party system, greater freedoms etc. - in Russia. But she still has a long way to go before we see genuine political participation, the rule of law, political stability, economic prosperity etc. But as Meyer notes, we must be careful not to confuse '"modernisation" with Westernisation', as one need not necessarily be the same as the other. Furthermore, one does not automatically lead to the other, although the Gorbachev and Yeltsin Administrations appear to have made such an assumption.[4]

Possible paths of development

In our view when Russia is striving for modernisation and progress, she has three choices: first she can draw on the experience of the West, in the tradition of the Westerners;[5] second, in the Slavophile tradition, she can look to her own history, the wisdom and experience of past generations, and in this sense learn from her own mistakes[6] or finally she can adopt a combination of the two. At the moment, as chapter 1 demonstrates, Russia seems on the one hand to have rejected most of her own traditions, but on the other, she has bowed to international pressure and adhered to Western strategies, but without great success.

Russia is without direction. As figure 4.1 above suggests: she is neither one thing, nor the other. She is a hybrid: our society, like Russia as a whole, is undergoing a crisis of values. However, it will take a long time before old communist values are eliminated and replaced by liberal democratic principles. Many people are highly disillusioned with the past and present, pessimistic about the future and so in essence have lost their vital reference point. Our leaders are interfering in an ad hoc way in society's development. This is placing Russia in 'no man's land'. Retribution for such intervention by ambitious politicians and irresponsible government officials will come sooner or later. In the meantime, however, society is paying a very high price, one that might ultimately be too high as current trends might totally undermine Russia's chance of making a successful transition from communism to liberal democracy. Warning signs of the dangers of failure appeared in the December 1993 parliamentary elections[7] and additional nails in Russia's coffin occurred during the December 1995 parliamentary elections and the same might be true in the June 1996 Presidential elections. Thus far any move away from old traditions to new ones - as epitomised by the drive towards modernisation - has had adverse consequences. No attempt has been made to preserve moral values, advocate humanist principles, improve the quality of life, ensure stability, encourage confidence not uncertainty about the future and so on.

Learning from others

However, one must be careful not to argue that all roads lead to 'Armageddon', or society's ultimate destruction. Modernisation, as the experience of Switzerland, Sweden, Holland, Denmark etc. shows, can have positive outcomes, such as revolutionary changes in the industrial and technological spheres. This process has not been totally painless, but in the long-term it has led to innovations being made. The most extreme case of rapid modernisation is Japan where tremendous progress has occurred in the last few decades. Japan has nevertheless succeeded in preserving many of its traditions - anthems, codes of honour, common vacations, modes of behaviour and above all a sense of collective responsibility for one's actions - while undergoing modernisation. Thus tradition and modernity need not be in conflict, they can in fact complement one other.

By contrast, in the case of Russia, perestroika undermined Russia's traditions - it questioned our history, national values, political culture, national dignity; ignored past achievements (in the fields of space exploration, mathematics, the sciences, computing etc.), undermined our sense of pride and patriotism and above all, squandered our creative and intellectual talents. As a result, we became a people without a history, with no national pride and dignity. This has had a bad effect upon people's morale - increased alienation from one another, from old values, from the authorities and so on, but it has also adversely affected our image abroad - no longer endless queues and constant shortages but growing impoverishment and so forth. As a consequence our recent research shows that 60 per cent of the population are not confident about the future. About the same proportion of people were unable to define their role in society and over three-quarters were concerned about the inability of incompetent politicians to put Russia back on course. All in all, surveys such as these indicate a growing gulf between people and government, on the one hand, and current traditions, history and values and modernisation, on the other.

Correcting the errors of our ways

If we see tradition as representing a series of values which have stood the test of time and which have been transferred from one generation to the next, then what we need is a social class or group capable of performing this role. But sadly under present circumstances it is difficult firstly to identify which traditions should be transmitted and which should not and secondly it is virtually impossible to identify an agent capable of transferring and preserving these values.

What is required, following table 4.1, is a selection of the values which we want to preserve; then we must identify a group capable of transmitting them from generation to generation and finally, we need to devise innovative ways of retaining these social customs, norms and ways of behaving. This might be through older traditional methods, such as religion, or it might involve the use of more modern means, such as the latest communication systems. For the latter to be possible, we need to create the environment in which either traditional or modern value systems, depending upon your perspective, flourish. Either way norms and customs of one kind or another are essential. They determine a person's sense of right and wrong; his/her role in society; attitude to work, social duty, one's relationship to other people, notion of culture and so on. No one is exempt from the influence of tradition and/or modernity. This includes politicians, economists, bankers, managers, administrative workers as well as the man or woman in the street. At different times throughout history, either tradition or modernity has dominated. At present, neither of these notions have gained the upper hand. Before one of these factors becomes the more dominant force, we must ensure that the following principles are guaranteed:

-       equal status for everyone;

-       common goals for all groups and social communities;

-       a realisation that prosperity and success depend upon co-operation not competition with one another; and finally,

-        government and people must work together and support the rule of law,
         preservation of traditions, customs and habits, etc.

These prerequisites are in everyone's interest.   They are essential for the normal
evolution and development of Russian society.   Their implementation, or absence, will
ultimately determine future trends in contemporary Russia.   Taking them into account,
and understanding the need for them, will help us find a solution to the difficult
problems we are currently facing.
    In conclusion, therefore, I would like to argue that due consideration of the above
social forces will enable us to achieve greater harmony in Russia via the preservation of
our history, customs and sense of national pride, on the one hand, while implementing a
strategy of modernisation and innovation in the lead up to the 21st century, on the other.

Notes

1.   On the Russian side see Georgii Shaknazarov, *Tsena svobody: Reformatsiia
         Gorbacheva glazami ego pomoshchnika,* Moscow 1993; Vadim Medvedev, *V
         komande Gorbacheva,* Moscow 1994; A.S. Chernaev, *Shest' let s Gorbachevym,*
         Moscow 1993; V. Sorgin, *Politicheskala istoria sovremennoi Rossii 1985-1994:
         ot Gorbacheva do Yeltsina,* Moscow 1994. and V.A. Krasil'shchikov et al.,
         Modernizatsiia: zarubezhnyi opyt i Rossiia, 'Infomart', Moscow 1994, especially
         pp. 68-114.   For useful Western analyses see for example, Richard Sakwa,
         Gorbachev and His reforms, 1985-1990, Phillip Allan, London 1990; John
         Miller, *Mikhail Gorbachev and the End of Soviet power,* Macmillan, London
         1993.
2.   G.V. Osipov, 'Reformirovannie Rossii: Itogi i perspektivy' in the collection
         Rossiia nakanune XXI veka, Moscow 1994, pp. 19-20.
3.   This notion of convergence is not a new one, see for example Alfred G. Meyer,
         'Theories of convergence', in Chambers Johnson (ed.), *Change in Communist
         Systems,* Stanford University Press, Stanford California 1970, pp. 313-314 and
         Krasil'shchikov et al., 1994 op cit., pp. 6-67.
4.   Ibid, p. 324.
5.   See for example, A. Walicki, *A History of Russian Thought: From the
         Enlightenment to Marxism,* Clarendon Press, Oxford 1980; *The Slavophile
         Controversy: History of a Conservative Utopia in Nineteenth Century Russian
         Thought,* Oxford University Press, Oxford 1975 and his *The controversy over
         Capitalism.   Studies in the Social Philosophy of the Russian Populists,* Oxford
         University Press, Oxford 1969 and S.V. Utechin, *Russian Political Thought: A
         Concise History,* J.M. Dent and Sons Ltd, London 1963.
6.   Ibid.
7.   See *Rossiia pered Vyborom: Sotsiologicheskii analiz obshchestvennogo mneniia
         elektorata* Institut sotsial'no-politicheskikh issledovanii Rossiiskoi Akademii
         Nauk, Moscow 1994, and Sorgin 1994 op cit., pp. 168-82.   Among the most
         pertinent Western analyses are those of M. Wyman et al., 'The Russian elections
         of December 1993', *Electoral Studies* Volume 13 (1), September 1994, pp. 254-

271 and R. Sakwa, 'The Russian elections of December 1993', *Europe-Asia Studies*, Vol. 47 (2), 1995, pp. 195-227.

5 Systemic crisis and Russian society

MIKHAIL RUTKEVICH

Introduction

Today Russia is undergoing a transition from one society to another under unfavourable historical conditions. Russia's state bureaucratic socialism (*gosudarstvenno-biurokraticheskogo sotsializma*) with an economy of the mobilising type, dating back to the 1930s, had, by the end of the 1970s run its course. Russia was no longer able to resist the West and NATO in any military or political sense and at the same time she was unable to put up a fight economically either. Our defence needs dictated that primary attention be devoted to the military-industrial complex and key branches of the national economy, such as energy, transport, engineering and metallurgy. Accelerated industrialisation from the late 1920s, the Second World War and then the space race with the USA in the years of the Cold War restrained the development of Russian agriculture, consumer industries, the service sector and above all led to stagnating living standards. Despite these problems Russia transformed herself from a backward agrarian nation, where half the people in the towns and virtually all in the countryside were illiterate, into a major industrial nation in the post-war period.

The collapse of state bureaucratic socialism

The collapse of state-bureaucratic socialism was engendered not only by its fundamental drawbacks - the neglect of market principles; a monopoly of power in the hands of the party-state bureaucracy, total ideological control - but most of all by its defeat in the Cold War against the West, headed by the USA. It proved impossible to devote equal attention to living standards and the arms race.[1]

This brought the legitimacy of the Soviet regime into question. Legitimacy, according to one British political scientist, refers to the 'acceptance of occupancy of a political office by a particular person or the exercise of power by a person or group in accordance with generally accepted principles and procedures of conferment of authority'.[2] In the case of Russia, this place was occupied by the Communist Party of the Soviet Union (or C.P.S.U. for short). Seymour Martin Lipset in his book *The Political Man* (1963) argued that 'The stability of any democracy depends not only upon economic developments but also on the effectiveness and legitimacy of its political system'.[3] Following Weber, it can be argued that legitimacy or systemic crises occur firstly, when tradition is threatened (e.g. French Revolution of 1789 or the Russian revolutions of 1917); second, when individuals or groups who were not previously politically active, such as the industrial workers in the 19th century and/or colonial elites and peasants in the 20th century, enter into politics then new loyalties have to be maintained or thirdly, if force is used to maintain or obtain power, such as the USSR, Eastern Europe up to 1989 or Central and Latin America today.[4]

The West's policy of the 'containment of communism' developed in the 1940s and continued in each decade thereafter began to bear fruit by the end of the 1980s. The collapse of the Soviet block, that began with the fall of the Berlin Wall and the DDR in 1989, was partly a product of internal contradictions and the failures of communism, but this process was also aided by separatist and nationalist forces, elite competition and successive crises of legitimacy dating back to the 1956 Revolutions in Hungary and Poland. Eventually the systemic crisis spread to Russia, leading to the collapse of the USSR in December 1991 and the emergence of newly independent states since 1992. This left 25 million Russians abroad and many are now returning as refugees or forced migrants to the Russian Federation.

The systemic collapse of the USSR at the end of 1991 has led to a state of crisis not only in economic or political terms but also in psychological terms. The Russian people are traumatised. They have no sense of morality, are pessimistic, politically passive and have no faith in the future.

The role of the West

Russia's national crisis could have taken a much less painful route. Our crisis has been exacerbated by the role of international actors in social and economic policy making. The IMF and numerous other Western advisers have forced changes of a 'shock therapy' nature upon Russia. In reality, this has amounted to shock **without** a therapy. This course of action was based on the erroneous ideas of the Chicago School of Economics and past and present IMF policies towards the Third World. Western advisers assumed that the liberalisation of prices from January 1992 followed by the state playing a less significant role in the regulation of the economy, would automatically, through 'the invisible hand of the market' act as a 'self-tuning system', thereby enabling Russia to totally transform her economy, an economy entrenched for decades, and allow it to be integrated into the world economy. Western advisers also predicted that although inflation might increase in the short term by 3-5 times, a rapid economic recovery would nevertheless occur.

Nothing has proved further from the truth. Russia's economy has been sliding towards the abyss since 1992. Inflation has reached 1000 per cent (and more) per year, savings-bank investors have been robbed of their money, industrial production fell by half in 1994 alone, agricultural production is down by a third and living standards have fallen by half in both 1993 and 1994. In 1994, Russia's GNP was 75 per cent of its 1993 level. Such a deterioration in the quality of life had never previously occurred in peacetime. Such levels even exceed trends during the depression in the USA when production never fell by more than 30 per cent. Even during the more severe periods of World War Two, when a large proportion of our territory was occupied by enemy forces, production only fell by a third.

The current situation is the worst in our history. Such widespread systemic problems might eventually turn into a national catastrophe.

Establishing a system of compulsory advance payment for goods and services but without state credit facilities and with the high lending rates set by commercial banks, brought for the second time (the first dating back to the summer of 1992) a crisis on non-payments in 1993-94 and led to interruptions in production because of breakdowns in the supply system in relation to raw materials, fuel etc. To this we can add the consumer crisis - the Russian consumer cannot afford to pay retailers or other suppliers. In the first quarter of 1994, O. Latsis, a supporter of Gaidar, argued that Russia's economy had hit **rock bottom**: industrial production was down 25 per cent and machine-building output down 50 per cent over the same period in 1993.[5] Without a radical change in the direction of our economic and social policy, it will be impossible to overcome the systemic crisis currently prevailing in Russia.

The social consequences of transition

The adverse impact of the economic recession has made itself felt in the form of radical polarisation and the threat of growing unemployment. *Social polarisation* refers to the process of an increasing gap between rich and poor, both of whom tend to be concentrated at opposite ends of the social spectrum.[6] Polarisation can be measured in a variety of ways, but for the sake of simplicity, I shall use the top 10 per cent and lowest 10 per cent of incomes as my primary indicator. At the outset, however, I would like to note that the income of the wealthy does not include money earned by mafia businessmen or undetermined private income and expenditure on expensive homes, sanatoria, state villas, cars, security or bribes for senior bureaucrats.

Social polarisation

My findings suggest that the rich-poor ratios stood on average at 3-5:1 in the case of Russia and 6-8: 1 in the case of Western social democratic states in 1993. At its widest point, the difference because rich and poor income in Russia was 11:1.[7] Gennadi Osipov goes even further arguing that 20 per cent of Russia's rich owned 43 per cent of the country's wealth by 1994.[8] In March 1992, instead of using the criteria 'minimum necessary for maintaining life' (*prozhitochnyi minimum*), a category into which 80 per cent of the population fell, the Yeltsin government decided to replace this concept with that of 'physiological minimum necessary for survival' (*fiziologicheskogo prozhitochnogo minimum*). The latter presupposes that 60-70 per cent of income is spent on food. Despite this change in terminology, it was still nevertheless the case that by the autumn of 1994, just under 30 per cent of Russia's population fell below the newly defined poverty line. Even the author of this new definition, Ye. Gontmakher, admits that it will only apply for a short period of time, possibly less than a year. However, he was basing this assumption on the fact that price rises would stabilise when this has not occurred.[9]

The rise of the 'New Russians'

On the other side of the coin, the so-called 'New Russians' are tending to accumulate luxury goods which they boast about at home and abroad - the most expensive cars as well as land and property in London and the Mediterranean coast. As distinct from the Party *nomenklatura* of the past,[10] the new elite do not seek to disguise their wealth. They can be observed in any large city, especially Moscow, flaunting their money in hard currency stores, restaurants, night clubs. They have also purchased a great proportion of old peasant *dachas* or else new cottages in the suburbs. On top of this parasitic consumption, the new bourgeoisie have been prime movers in the privatisation process buying the large majority of vouchers, bribing the bureaucracy wherever necessary in order to do so. As the ex-mayor of Moscow Gavriil Popov noted the 'normal' bribe (*normal'naia vziatka*) for 'assistance' (*sodeistvie*) is 10-20 per cent of the overall cost of the deal - substantial income in most cases. It seems that the 'compradore bourgeoisie' (*kompradorskaia burzhaziia*), in the current unstable situation and given high taxation - up to 90 per cent of profits are lost due to the present taxation system - prefers not to invest their capital in Russia's economic recovery. Every month US$1-2 billion goes into foreign bank accounts. This total is many times the figure which the Russian state borrows from the IMF or the credits received from Western governments. Social polarisation is therefore influencing Russia's financial situation in a very negative way.

The decline in the birth rate, increase in the death rate and under-nourishment of the population of the Russian Federation, as shown in chapter 3, has reduced life expectancy to 59 years for men i.e. below the pension age. The future of the nation is being threatened.

Fear of unemployment

Another important social consequence of our deepening social and economic crisis is the threat and fear, perhaps the inevitability, of unemployment. This issue will be addressed in chapter 11, so suffice it to state here that, according to official data, by the beginning of 1994, there were approximately one million jobless in Russia, only two-thirds of whom receive assistance. However, by the autumn of 1994, the previous figure had already risen 1.5 times. Such official statistics ignore the enormous hidden unemployment. When people lose their job, they often fail to register at the labour exchange. Instead they go looking for a job on their own or through friends. But the main issue is the 'half-employed' (*polubezrabotnykh*) namely those who are only employed one to three days per week or those who are laid off for weeks or months. Using ILO calculations for November 1993, there were an estimated 3.6 million unemployed in Russia and a further 4 million were said 'not to be continually employed' (*v rezhim nepol'noi zaniatosti*).[11] This amounts to 10 per cent of the country's active population. By the autumn of 1994, because of the disruption of production in various key enterprises - VPK, ZIL, Urals machine building, various agricultural machine building plants, the textile industry etc. - coupled with their imminent bankruptcy, the previous figure had already exceeded 15 per cent and in a number of Central and Eastern regions of Russia it had reached as high as 30 per cent.

Changes in the social structure

In the next chapter we will explore the impact of the economic recession on Russia's social structure, so I would merely like to point out here that the economic literature accepts the 1930s-80s division of society into the working class, peasantry (largely collective and state farmers) and the intelligentsia. Social divisions are therefore depicted as being connected to property or the nature of the work undertaken. Being somewhat crude (on a formula of 2 + 1), this division was criticised in Russian academic circles as far back as the 1960s, primarily because it did not point out two essential distinctions regarding the intelligentsia, namely: the difference between clerks and specialists according to classification, quality of work etc. on the one hand, and differences between the various branches of the intelligentsia - creative, scientific and so on on the other. This is important because some members of the intelligentsia by virtue of their organisational skills or the importance of their work were able to climb further up the occupational hierarchy thereby moving from the bottom or middle nearer to the top.

Taking into account these theoretical modifications, it is possible to argue that Russian society in the 1990s has preserved the aforementioned social groups despite the outward appearance of the replacement of the old communist *nomenklatura* with a more 'democratic' one. This is not to say that there have not been subtle changes. These have been of the following kind:

(i)   from the 'mafia' (*mafiya* or *tenevikov*) into 'co-operators' (*kooperatorov*) who have become major owners in the field of banking, exchanges, holdings, industrial-financial companies, import-export etc.;

(ii)   there is now a layer of petty-bourgeoisie. In the countryside, they are farmers; in the cities, they are middle ranking salesmen in privately owned shops. There is a form of petty-bourgeois symbiosis in which they move from shop to shop - virtually in shuttles - as if on shopping trips. Some of these petty bourgeois owners are lawyers, doctors, notaries, private tutors/teachers and tailors; and

(iii)   the structure of hired workers has also changed. Here any connection with the means of production and property ownership fundamentally affects their position in society. State shops and service sector enterprises, as a result of privatisation, have become owned not by private individuals but associations with limited liabilities. They independently establish their own sales targets. As a result their income does not only include their salary but also includes a percentage of any profits made.

The majority of large enterprises still belong to the state, but some have become rented or joint-stock companies. The salaries of these workers from 'partly-state' (*polgosudarstvennykh*) enterprises are generally supplemented by income made on shares or profits. However, this factor plays a role only in the gas and oil industries and a few more of the prosperous firms and enterprises which have been transformed into Joint-stock companies.

Unfortunately the majority of enterprises - be they state, rented or joint-stock - are suffering because of growing non-payments. As a result they have not been able to pay employees wages on time. For example, unpaid wages in Russia in the first three-quarters of 1994 are estimated to be run to trillions of roubles. However, those least affected by the unstable economic environment are those employed in private enterprises or joint-stock companies. Here despite high inflation and high taxation, wages remain high. Thus in 1994, whereas the average salary in industry was 167,000r a month; this compared with 2.5 million roubles in private enterprises and 4 million roubles in commercial banks.

The new ruling class

The role of former party, state or *nomenklatura* members in the economic sphere has also changed. In the past their salaries and bonuses were determined by their superiors. After the Communist Party lost its monopoly in 1990 and the major Party controlled departments and Ministries with a great deal of economic clout disappeared, salaries were now set voluntarily. Thus even in unprofitable enterprises, managers, according to mass media reports, are still powerful enough to make their salaries 100 times those of their average employee.[12] One can only imagine how wide the difference is elsewhere in the more profitable enterprises. Furthermore, directors and administrators of enterprises, trusts, plants and firms in the process of being privatised often take a part of their company's shares as 'reward'. Although it is officially prohibited, senior officials in the centre as well as the periphery are combining an administrative role in enterprises with commercial activity elsewhere and dividing any property and share gains accordingly. This is creating a link between the state and private sector. However, once the ground has been prepared, and they have made the money, they quickly move, like 'rats deserting a sinking ship', into an administrative role in the business sector. As a result of this trend the process of convergence of the two groups - the neo-bourgeoisie (*neo-burgzhuazii*) and new nomenklatura (*novaia nomenklatura*) - is proceeding with great speed. This group is becoming a new political and economic ruling class in contemporary Russia.

The basic difference between this class and the working class, clerks, specialists in state and partly-state enterprises, is its well established links with those in key positions of political power. Thus the new emerging *nomenklatura* are often supported by the *comprador bourgeoisie parties* as well as by forces of a socialist and national-patriotic orientation, which formed slowly under the previous authoritarian regime. All of these groups openly emerge during contests for key posts in positions of authority. These range from 'Yabloko' (the Yavlinsky-Boldyrev-Lukin bloc), on the one hand, through to straightforward 'Lobbyists', on the other. Although they do not always agree - therefore economic and business interests do not always coincide - at important moments, such as the storming of the White House in early October 1993 or the December 1993 parliamentary elections, differences were often put aside and these two goals merged.

Conclusion

We have shown above that Russia's future path of development appears to be being directed by the close symbiosis between the new economic and political interests emerging in the 1990s. The new *nomenklatura* is coming from these groups and appears to have experience in one or the other of these fields, if not both. Closer attention will have to be paid in future to the link between changes in the class structure, on the one hand, and the evolution and development of Russia's economic and political system during the transition period, on the other. Research is currently underway on the Presidential administration, government, regional groups, political parties and movements in Russia. The forthcoming results of this work will increase Russian and Western understanding of the complexity of Russia's transition.[13]

Notes

1. *Sovetskaia Rossiia* 18 January 1994, p. 4.
2. G. Roberts, *A Dictionary of Political Science*, Longman, London 1971, p. 113.
3. S.M. Lipset, *The Political Man*, Doubleday, New York 1963.
4. Max Weber, *The Theory of Social & Economic Organisations*, translated by A.M. Henderson and Talcott Parsons, Free Press, Glencoe Illinois 1947, pp. 324-36.
5. *Izvestiia* 16 April 1994, pp. 1-2; *Rossiiskaia Gazeta* 14 April 1994, p. 2.
6. For more on this see M. Rutkevich, 'Sotsial'naia polarizatsiia', *Sotsiologicheskie issledovaniia* 1992, No. 9.
7. These results were reported in the newspaper *Trud* 10 February 1994, p. 2.
8. G.V. Ospiov, 'Reformirovanie Rossii: Itogi i perspektivy' in the collection *Rossiia nakanune XXI veka,* Moscow 1994, p. 10.
9. See B. Khorev, 'Novye mify rezhima', *Pravda* 28 October 1994, pp. 1-2.
10. On this see Mikhail Voslenskii, *Nomenklatura: Gospodstviushchii klass Sovetskogo Soiuza,* Overseas Publications Interchange Ltd, London 1984.
11. *Finansoe Izvestiia* 1994, No. 12, p. 1.
12. See *Sovetskaia Rossiia* 29 October 1994, p. 2.
13. For an interesting Western analysis of the political component see I. McAllister and S. White, 'Democracy, political parties and party formation in post-communist Russia', *Party Politics*, Vol. 1 (1), 1995, pp. 49-72.

6 The transformation of the social structure

ALEXANDER KHLOP'EV

Introduction

Structural changes in the economy, social sphere, politics, spiritual life and international relations are currently taking place in Russia. Ongoing radical changes have largely been accompanied by a destructive process involving the whole of society. Such destruction is always a painful process. In our case this has led to a rapid decline in production, living standards and a decline in respect for moral values and law and order. Depending upon the combination of objective and subjective factors together with other internal factors as well as external ones, Russia's crisis might be either short lived or of longer duration. At present the conflict between old and new values is causing great instability. Therefore, the key questions are: will the system's transformation lead to catastrophe? or can Russia overcome the crisis? In order for constructive rather than destructive variables to gain ground, Russia must tread a tightrope between the past and present - borrowing some things from the past while also allowing the strengthening and establishment of new values to take place. After all, a transformed social system requires sufficient stability in order to sustain itself.

Stages in the transformation of Russia's social structure

Society's transition from one system to a different one has necessitated not just the formation but transformation of Russia's social structure. As figure 6.1 below shows there are numerous stages in this process, each of which carries its own distinctive features:

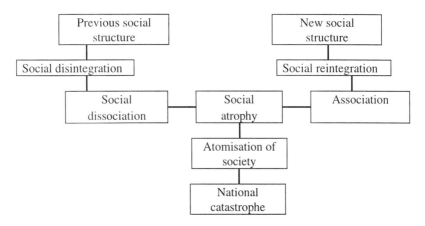

Figure 6.1   Stages in the transformation of Russia's social structure during the period of transition

Source: V.I. Staroverov et al. *Rossiia nakanune XXI veka vypusk II* ('Nauchnia kniga', Moscow 1995), p. 197.

A tentative theoretical framework

It might be useful initially to clarify some of the terms used.   The term *previous condition of the structure* (*Predshesvuiushchee sostoianie struktury*) as the name suggests refers to earlier distinctions between the various strata in Russian society - social classes and groups - the roles they played and extent to which they were integrated into society.[1]   However, as a result of changes in the economy, the scientific and technical revolution, the emergence of mafia businessmen, a new political elite and the collapse of the old economic and political system, the previous social structure is in crisis.

Social Disintegration

As a result of the failure of earlier reform experiments ranging from the more modest changes under Khrushchev and Brezhnev to the radical reforms under Gorbachev, Russian society in recent years has undergone systemic transformation. This has led to social disintegration (*sotsial'naia dezintegratsiia*) in some cases but to social dissociation (*sotsial'naia dissotsiatsiia*) in the large majority of instances. This is hardly surprising given that systemic collapse has led to declining living standards and life expectancy as well as fewer jobs and a shorter working week for many Russians. These factors have culminated in greater geographical mobility and also affected social mobility patterns in the process. All in all, Russia is undergoing a transition from collectivism to individualism. The *social disintegration* stage has already begun.

By contrast, *social integration* (*sotsial'naia integratsiia*) is characterised by the presence of well-regulated and non-conflictual relations between individuals, groups and other components of the social system. These goals are achieved on the basis of either perceived mutual benefits or similar interests, purposes and values. Integration and differentiation are the essence of a stable, developing society.

What is happening in the transition period? The process of social integration has been gradually replaced by social disintegration. This has partly occurred as a consequence of systemic crisis, but in the main it has resulted from the absence of well-thought out ideas about the purpose of the transformation, on the one hand, and how it could be carefully managed, on the other. The general public thought that change would be for the better but instead we have witnessed the beginning of the decay of the social structure, the decline of solidarity, the rise of conflict, especially between individuals, and an overall feeling of a loss of self-identity. In this sense the rising degree of *social dissociation* is beginning to strike at Russia's heart. Thus at present there is a narrow gap between *dissociation* and *disintegration* or the dismemberment of Russia's social organism. If this happens, there will be a national catastrophe. The new system's present inability to cope with transformation - which is hardly surprising as the old one could not even cope with Gorbachev's reforms which were much milder - and the resulting instability can best be described as social atrophy (*sotsial'naia entropiia*). This refers to the process of the wearing away of the old social structure without putting something solid in its place. Thus the future shape and development of Russia's social structure is unknown, and a number of different outcomes are possible depending upon whether the existing socio-economic problems are resolved.

Social dissociation is an extreme stage of this process and involves the final destruction of all connections within society which eventually leads to the complete breakdown of the possibility of social integration. This phase leads to the 'atomisation of society' (*atomizatsiia obshchestva*). Politicians and society's overall inability to solve the crisis leads to more and more chaos in all spheres of life. Ultimately this reduces the possibility of social integration and results in a national disaster.

Social reintegration

By contrast, if the authorities had a clearer idea of what the aims of transformation were and if they also possessed the means to achieve their goals, then this could have a positive outcome for Russia. For this to happen, the Russian people would need to start forging new connections, thereby recreating the process of *social association* (*sotsial'naia assotsiatsiia*) in society. Overcoming the alienation or atomisation of the people will be an extremely difficult task. It would necessitate the creation of a new economic system capable of meeting the material needs of the population. However, if this goal was achieved, even if this meant increasing the level of social differentiation, then it would allow a process of *social reintegration* (*sotsial'naia reintegratsiia*) to begin.

Further strengthening of the economy and the social infrastructure, the devotion of greater attention to education and culture and an improvement in living standards, will encourage Russia's democratisation process. These changes will led to the formation of social ideals, norms and values and stabilise Russia's new social structure.

The transformation of Russia's social structure, the speed of this development and the final outcome will be determined by the nature of the transition itself as well as the role and impact of the numerous objective and subjective variables mentioned above. Historically, the task and responsibility of both the authorities and society as a whole has been to solve the country's problems together. But is this still the case? Are society and polity working against each other in the 1990s?

The crisis in the social sphere

Change in the socio-economic and political system during the transition period has led to the breakdown of old norms and their replacement with new ones. The introduction of the market economy has led to the creation of new commercial and financial structures, new social structures, a wide range of political parties, new subcultures and a new ideology, or lack of it, depending upon one's viewpoint.

Failure to prevent a social shock

Of all of the above changes, the most significant outcome of the 'shock therapy' strategy has been the rapid rise in the number of poor and unemployed and with it growing inequality. President Yeltsin vowed that he would prevent Russia from suffering from a severe 'social shock' while his reforms were being implemented. However although the 1993 Constitution sets the length of the working day, guarantees a minimum wage, protection for the unemployed, mothers and children and vows to ensure that people have food and shelter,[2] continued economic difficulties have reduced the level of social protection offered by the state and seen not only a massive deterioration in the standard of living but also less support being offered for the needy.[3]

Family and education lack priority

Obviously Yeltsin's government, by introducing the changes encapsulated in the 1993 Constitution, is starting to acknowledge that the transition is having an adverse effect upon Russian society. However, little has been done to curb the decline of the family and other agencies of socialisation. This has meant that Russian citizens today are getting less and less instruction about modes of social practice, the acquisition of social qualities and features and finally, less and less information on how to master social experience and on how to realise their goals in life by applying themselves to everything they do.[4]

The main precondition for effective socialisation is the education system, which is vital to everyone's upbringing. Unfortunately the education system has been badly hit during transition and is a low priority sector, despite a 1991 decree promising the reverse.[5] Teachers, like many other groups in society, have suffered badly as a consequence of hyper-inflation. The gulf between their wages and those of the industrial workers has increased each year. In 1992, for instance, teachers received 756 roubles while industrial workers earned 2,567 roubles.[6] Strikes were narrowly averted in April-May 1992 but the subsequent introduction of a single tariff scale (*edinaia tarifnaia setka*), in the Autumn of 1992 which included 18 scales for education staff ranging from 1,800 roubles at the bottom to 18,126 roubles at the top, caused further conflict among different teaching staff, increased teachers' feeling of neglect and alienation and above all failed to boast morale causing many to leave the profession. These problems, when coupled with the appalling conditions in schools,[7] have done little to improve the quality of the present younger generation's education or to preserve Russia's future intellectual potential (see chapter 13 for more detailed discussions). Finally, the lack of socialisation makes Russian youth more susceptible to outside influences, such as Western mass-culture, as well as undesirable internal influences, namely the various underground subcultures.

Life expectancy and demographic situation deteriorating

In recent years, Russia has assigned lower importance to the preservation and the quality of life. Thus life expectancy fell twice in 1993 and is now around 66 years on average. In 1994, nearly 2 million people passed away, which is 20 per cent more than the previous year. In addition, 14 per cent less were born in 1994 than in 1993.[8] The results of government research into the plight of young families in Russia in 1993 revealed that 44.7 per cent had a 'dismal' existence and were not thinking of bringing a child into the world while a further 28.7 per cent were faced with 'difficult times'.[9] In addition to these problems, degradation of the environment and declining nutrition is posing a serious threat to the nation's health as is the tendency not to exercise - partly because sports and leisure facilities are being cut back. All in all, the decline in the quality of medical services available has led to a serious decline in health status and conditions. Thus is due to reduced access to prophylactic measures, medical treatment and rehabilitation for the majority of Russians.

Class and ethnic conflict

There has also been a growth in the level of tension between classes, groups and strata as well as between individuals and families. These tensions, under present circumstances, are assuming nationalistic, ideological or criminal proportions. Russian surveys also demonstrate that tension between ethnic groupings is rising. There is a growing tendency for respondents' to state that they are willing to defend their ethnic group against others by using force if necessary.

Such conflict is, however, not limited to different nationalities. Sociological surveys indicate that there is also tension in the labour sphere between employees and employers, as well as between buyers and sellers, share owners and financiers and so on. On the whole, though, living standards are still regarded as an issue of greater concern than crime. Nevertheless, surveys regularly show that the high crime rate troubles every second Russian. During three years of reform, the number of people afraid that their child might eventually become addicted to drugs has risen from 18.3 per cent in 1992 to 27.9 per cent by 1994. Fear of their children becoming alcoholics has gone up from 19.3 per cent to 29.4 per cent over the same period. Finally, regarding the prospects of their children becoming a criminal, 20 per cent of those surveyed thought this a distinct possibility in 1992 but this figure had almost doubled by 1994 to 39.6 per cent. A very alarming trend.

Negative attitudes towards reform

The aforementioned levels of social tension are often channelled towards increased dissatisfaction with the on-going reform strategy. Recent Russian surveys suggest that as many as four-fifths of the Russian population think that the reforms have yet to produce something of value. The majority see the reform as having only negative consequences. For example, data collected in May 1994 showed that 22.3 per cent of those surveyed had no faith in the present government, with 50 per cent of those surveyed showing a lack of trust in the President, government and the police (*militsia*). Only 2.9 per cent of the respondents' stated that they were completely satisfied with the present political system, as compared to 48.2 per cent who thought that it should be radically changed. The latter figure roughly corresponds to those willing to defend their interests at all costs - 44.3 per cent in 1992 rising to 45.3 per cent in 1994. 13.1 per cent of the May 1994 sample declared 'if necessary, I'll use a gun' while a further 10.5 per cent showed a willingness to engage in strikes and protests. The latter figure has virtually doubled since 1992, when only 5.9 per cent were prepared to strike. State Statistical Committee (*Goskomstat*) data show that more and more people are acting upon their concerns. Thus the number of strikes (*zabastovki*) was 10.3 times higher in the first quarter of 1994, compared to the same period the previous year.[10]

Greater attention clearly needs to be paid to the decline in the role of the organs of social control, on the one hand, while higher priority should be given to health care, education, youth and so forth, on the other, before it is too late and the antagonisms which are currently developing become too firmly entrenched. Sadly, there are already signs that class and ethnic conflict plus the economy's destruction, are having an adverse effect upon the evolution and development of Russia's political system and social structure. The former was addressed in chapter 1, I would, therefore, like to focus here on the growing tendency towards social dissociation.

The social dissociation of Russian society

As is well known, *dissociation* is a chemical term which refers to the breaking down of a molecule into smaller molecules or atoms or if used in its psychological sense dissociation refers to a state of temporary loosening of control over consciousness, in which the unconscious complexes take control of the personality. In extreme cases this amounts to a splitting of a personality. In the physical or chemical processes the factors which cause break up include changes in temperature, light etc.[11]

However, this term has not simply been used in relation to the natural sciences. The term *dissociation* was widely utilised by the German sociologist Ferdinand Tönnies, who argued that society and social relationships are the products of will, of which natural or essential will (community) and rational will (an association) are the main two types. Tönnies was therefore making a distinction between community, on the one hand, and society, on the other.[12] Leopold Von Weise also considered *dissociation* to be a characteristic of the *social integration process*. In this sense the term embraced such stages as separation and conflict; whereas association, according to Von Weise, referred to the process of rapprochement, imitation, adjustment and unity. Howard Becker introduced the more appropriate notion of 'sociation' (*sotsiatsiia*) which refers to the mutually active interaction between three types of activity - personality, social relations and culture. The transition from dissociation to sociation, according to Becker, occurs during a shift from competition to co-operation.[13]

In the crisis conditions of present day Russia, the social structure has been thrown into turmoil and transformed beyond belief. *Dissociation* is occurring on a very broad scale - people have become increasingly isolated from the social system. Society has broken into smaller parts. There has been a break firstly, at a *horizontal* level - within classes and groups and secondly, at a *vertical* level between various strata. Nowadays, the situation is characterised not by **inter-class** (*mezhklassovye*) or **inter-group** movement (*mezhgruppovye*) but rather by changing **inter-layer relations** (*mezhsloevye*), mainly between the rich minority and the impoverished majority.

Survey results

In recent surveys, which have tried to investigate these changes, we utilised a range of indicators which are relatively constant as means of measurement. These included, for example, refrigerators or the cost of a car which were correlated with private incomes each time at regular survey intervals. In addition to these quantitative variables we also utilised qualitative indicators such as self-evaluation by our sample of their place and position in society. Some of our results are presented in table 6.1 below.

We can see from this table that nearly a fifth of our sample are living below the poverty line; nearly half on the poverty line and just over a quarter slightly above the poverty line. Less than 5 per cent of our sample were in a relatively comfortable position and only just under 2 per cent could be described as wealthy enough 'not to want for anything'.

A comparison with official figures

The upper classes

Our findings need to be put in context by comparing them with official data.[14] According to State Statistical Committee data for the first quarter of 1994, there were 1.2 million people (or less than 1 per cent of the population) who could best be described as extremely wealthy (their monthly income at this time was US$25,000 or 50 million roubles and more a month). The next group, whose income was in the 2-3 million roubles range, totalled 5.6 million (or 3.4-3.6 per cent of the population). Finally, according to official statistics, the 'rich' amounted to the 9 million people with an income of more than 500,000 roubles a month (or 5-6 per cent of the population). All in all, after two years of radical reform, there are 16 million people rich people living in

Russia today. In our May 1994 survey, the 'rich' represented 6.3 per cent of our sample, which is very close to the national average of 10.8 per cent (assuming a population of 148 million).[15]

Table 6.1
Respondents' answer to the question 'Which of the following categories describes your monetary position most accurately?'*
(Answers are given as a per cent of those surveyed)
(n = 1,375)

Question	Per cent
'I have enough to live on and do not want for anything'	1.6
'We can easily afford a refrigerator or a TV set, but we cannot afford to buy a car'	4.7
'We have enough money to buy essential food and clothes, however we have to delay buying major items'	28.9
'We only have enough money to buy food'	45.1
'We don't have enough money to buy food and are constantly in debt'	19.8

Note * This survey was carried out in May 1994 by the Analytical Centre of the Institute of Socio-Political Research, Russian Academy of Sciences, Moscow under the author's direction as part of the project investigating 'Russian lifestyles 1992-94'. The representative sample of 1,375 people came from Moscow, Krasnodar, Krasnoyarsk, Primorskaia, the Republics of Karelia, Tatarstan and Udmurtia, as well as Voronezh, Kursk, Saratov and Svedlovsk Oblasts.

Middle class

Official state statistics estimate that 44-51 million people (27-28 per cent of the population) belong to the 'middle class'. Their income at present is around 60-500,000 roubles a month. These results tally with our May 1994 survey which showed that group III stood at 28.9 per cent.

Poor and extremely poor

The 'poor', according to State Statistical committee data, make up 44.5 million people (27-28 per cent of the population). Their income is as low as 30-60,000 roubles per month. Finally, in this category, we also have the extremely poor who constitute 52 million people (33-34 per cent of the population). They have incomes of less than 30,000 roubles per month, not enough to survive on. This group taken together, made up 65 per cent of our May 1994 sample, as compared to 60-62 per cent in official surveys. This tiny difference is largely accounted for by our respondents' self-evaluation of which social class category they fall into.

Other aspects of social class

Having established the various categories existing in Russian society today, we went on to use our May 1994 survey as a basis for taking a closer look at various aspects of social class during the transition phase. One key aspect chosen was the respondents' own subjective perception of their position in society. The results of this research are presented in table 6.2 below:

Table 6.2
Respondents' answer to the question: 'What is your present material position?'
(May 1994)
(Answers as a per cent of those surveyed and according to social group)
(n = 1,375)

	a	b	c	d	e
Average among sample	1.6	4.7	28.9	45.1	19.8
Workers	0.7	2.8	23.5	49.2	23.8
Peasants	-	6.7	45.2	36.3	11.8
Engineering-technical workers	-	3.2	32.3	46.8	17.7
Clerks	-	2.8	28.6	52.8	15.8
Non-producing intelligentsia	3.7	5.5	38.5	39.4	15.4
Owners	42.7	25.0	48.3	15.0	-
Students	-	11.1	34.8	26.1	28.0
Pensioners	-	0.9	17.1	56.3	25.7

Key:

a   I have enough to live on and do not want for anything
b   I have sufficient money to buy the majority of goods, including consumer durables
c   I have enough money to purchase essential goods and services, including food
d   I have only enough money to buy food
e   I have insufficient money and am frequently in debt

It is clear from this table that the financial position of each social group was a major area of concern. In general, we can conclude that the category with sufficient money to live comfortably on included the 'owners' - 41.7 per cent - whereas those with insufficient income included students (28 per cent), pensioners (25.7 per cent) and workers (23.8 per cent). Such subjective evaluations of our respondents' own material position reveal a keen appreciation of the current changes underway in Russia and their possible impact upon the social structure.

However, these changes have not only been brought about by changes within classes; they are also influenced by variables beyond the control of individuals and   social groups, such as the running down or closure of enterprises or their de-nationalisation. In addition to these factors, the introduction of the market has led to the privatisation of state property, the creation of different kinds of small and joint ventures, joint-stock companies and so forth. Thus where people are employed has also proved decisive, as table 6.3 below demonstrates:

Table 6.3
Respondents' answer to the question: 'What is your current material situation?'
(May 1994)
(Answers as a per cent of those surveyed and according to place of employment)
(n = 1,375)

	a	b	c	d	e
Average among sample	1.6	4.7	28.9	45.1	19.8
State enterprise	1.3	3.3	27.9	47.7	19.8
Joint-stock company	0.7	1.7	24.1	49.2	19.9
Limited liability company	3.8	14.5	32.7	32.8	9.2
Leased enterprise	5.9	10.0	42.6	30.9	10.6
Small joint enterprise	7.1	14.2	47.6	26.2	4.9

Key:

a   I have enough to live on and do not want for anything
b   I have sufficient money to buy the majority of goods, including consumer durables
c   I have enough money to purchase essential goods and services, including food
d   I have only enough money to buy food
e   I have insufficient money and am frequently in debt

It is evident from the above table that the threshold between the three upper groups of respondents' and the two lower ones is accounted for by the extent to which new forms of economic activity have developed (in this case we should also include state enterprises and joint stock companies as many of the latter were former state enterprises under a more 'modern name'). Those working for leased enterprises or small joint enterprises were the best off, with 7.1 per cent and 5.9 per cent of these companies' employees, covered by our survey, having enough money to live comfortably. By comparison those working in state sector enterprises were the worst off - 27.9 per cent of this category, covered in our survey, had enough to buy essential goods; 47.7 per cent only enough to buy food and 19.8 per cent had inadequate income levels forcing them into debt.

Having discussed official and personal viewpoints concerning social class as well as various aspects of the material position of numerous social groups in the early stages of Russia's transition, we went on to analyse our May 1994 respondents' subjective views of their social class position. The results are shown in table 6.4 overleaf.

Table 6.4

Respondents' answer to the question: 'In what social class would you place yourself?' (May 1994)

(Answers as a per cent of those surveyed)

(n = 1,375)

Subjective assessment of social class position	Per cent
Upper class	0.6
Middle class	38.9
Lower class	44.3
Difficult to say	16.2

Thus when respondents' looked at their material prosperity, income and compared their position with that of others in various regions of Russia in May 1994, the large majority - 44.3 per cent - placed themselves in the 'lower class' (*nizshii klass*); which was closely followed by a perception of being part of the 'middle class' (*srednii klass*). This included 38.9 per cent of our respondents'. The next group was a high proportion of undecided - 16.2 per cent - and then finally only 0.6 per cent of the sample thought they might be in or belong to the 'upper class' (*vyshii klass*).

Having looked at our sample's subjective view of their social class, we then asked them about their income level. These results are displayed in table 6.5 below which suggests that there was a correlation between income level and social class.

Table 6.5

Respondents' answer to the question: 'What is your material position? (May 1994) (Answers as a per cent of those surveyed and according to Respondents' perception of their own social class membership)

(n = 1,375)

Subjective social class position	a	b	c	d	e
Average among sample	1.6	4.7	28.9	45.1	19.8
Upper class	25.0	12.5	62.5	-	-
Middle class	2.6	7.3	49.7	35.5	4.9
Lower class	0.8	0.5	11.2	53.2	34.3
Difficult to say	0.4	9.4	26.0	47.5	16.7

Key:

a   I have enough to live on and do not want for anything

b   I have sufficient money to buy the majority of goods, including consumer durables

c   I have enough money to purchase essential goods and services, including food

d   I have only enough money to buy food

e   I have insufficient money and am frequently in debt

Thus the greater the respondents' income, the more likely he or she thought they were 'upper class', while the lower the respondent's income, the more they thought that they came from the 'lower class'. For example, 25 per cent of our sample who had enough to live on and did not want for anything said they came from the 'upper class'; while 34.3 per cent of those with insufficient income who found they were frequently in debt said they were of 'working class' origins.

Finally, we compared our sample's theoretical and actual social class positions. The evidence presented in table 6.6 below suggests that their subjective perception does not match their real position in the status hierarchy. However, there was a subtle difference between social groups. Only 'owners' did not place themselves in a lower social class. What is the most revealing finding of our survey is the fact that the large majority of workers and engineers together with pensioners viewed their present socio-economic situation as 'humiliating' (*unizitel'nyi*). Somewhat surprisingly a high proportion of clerks, peasants, non-producing intelligentsia and students were generally satisfied with their present position. Therefore today, there is no class or social group, with the exception of representatives of the emerging bourgeoisie, which is not deeply divided.

Table 6.6
Respondents' 'Class' distribution according to the 'social class situation' index
(as a percentage of the number surveyed from the corresponding social group)

	a	b	c	d	e	f	g	h
Middle Class	29.5	35.5	28.4	50.0	42.5	45.9	58.7	73.3
Lower Class	55.6	52.4	49.1	42.1	37.0	29.4	23.9	3.3

Key:
a   Workers
b   Engineering-technical workers
c   Pensioners
d   Clerks
e   Peasants
f   Non-producing intelligentsia
g   Students
h   Owners

Conclusion

By examining the factors which might determine the process of social dissociation, we have shown that at present the transformation of Russian society during the period of transition is generating deep social divisions. Such a situation is having an adverse effect upon people's attitudes towards their jobs and fellow employees as well as their bosses and others in a similar social situation. The process of collapse and disintegration of various branches of industry, collectives, establishments and organisations, is forcing people to migrate. This is influencing patterns of geographical and social mobility. Thus a worker becomes a 'commuter'; a clerk a 'shop-keeper' and a member of the intelligentsia a 'street-vendor'. In overall terms, we have demonstrated that the present system of social stratification is disintegrating and bears no resemblance to its earlier Soviet counterpart. The authorities have not yet realised the consequence of society's atomisation, of its transformation into something shapeless and structureless. To prevent any further social dissociation, social dispersion of group and class solidarity and the loss of an individual's feeling of social identification, it is necessary to start averting the impact of the destructive processes which have begun to take hold. One step in the right direction would be to give social policy measures higher priority and also to pay closer attention to ways and means of developing the social association process in Russia (see chapter 10).

Notes

1.   In the Soviet period, there were three groups in Russian society, the working-class, peasantry and the intelligentsia whose position was determined by their relationship to the means of production. Each of these groups, was officially declared to be in a non-antagonistic relationship because society was deemed to be 'classless' in the Western sense of the word, as class was traditionally defined in terms of ownership of private property and this had been abolished by the October Revolution. However, this is not to say that differences between social classes did not exist - as shown by the varying provision of social amenities or differences in the degree of educational opportunity between town and countryside - rather, I would like to suggest that the scientific and technical revolution significantly reduced such differences by drawing together different types of work through the fusion of mental and physical labour.

2.   See *Konstitutsiia Rossiiskoi Federatsii: Priniata vsenarodnym golosovaniem 12 dekabria 1993g*, Moscow, 'Iuridicheskaia literatura' 1993.

3.   See *Rossiiskaya Gazeta* 25 February 1994.

4.   *Slovar' prikladnoi sotsiologii*, Minsk, 'Universitetskoe' 1984, pp. 157-60.

5.   The relevant decree was 'Concerning top priority measures to develop the education system of the Russian Federation', dated 11 July 1991 - Editors.

6.   *Uchitel'skaia gazeta* No. 16, 13 May 1992, p. 2.

7.   In 1993, for example, 19 billion roubles were required to carry out school repairs but only 5.4 billion had been allocated and in the same year Russia was ranked bottom in terms of its education budget (with 2-3 per cent) while the UK came fourth with 11.4 per cent and the USA top with 13.7 per cent, *Uchitel'skaia gazeta* No. 30, 30 August 1993, p. 1 and No. 31, 31 August 1993, p. 6.

8.   *Argumenty i fakty* No. 52 1993 and No. 52, 1994.

9.   *Perspektivy razvitiia molodoi sem'i (dannye edinovremennogo obsledovaniia)*, Moscow, Goskomstat, Rossiisskoi Federatsii 1993.

10.   *Rossiiskaia Gazeta* 25 August 1994.

11.   *Fizicheskii entsiklopedicheskii slovar'*, Moscow 'Sovetskaia Entsiklopediia', 1984, p. 168.

12.   F. Tönnies, *Community and Society*, translated and introduced by Charles P. Loomis, Michigan State University Press, Michigan 1957, pp. 33-40, 42-44, 46-48, 64-69, 75-78.

13.   *Sovremennaia zapadnaia sotsiologiia: slovar'*, Moscow 'Politzdat' 1990, pp. 29-30, 53-54, 345-47.

14.   The following discussion is based on an article in *Argumenty i Fakty* No. 24, 1994.

15.   This national average consists of the 16 million rich divided by a population total of 148 million giving us a figure of just under 11 per cent.

7 Antagonisms in Russian society

VLADIMIR STAROVEROV

Introduction

The present economic reforms being carried out in Russia including the privatisation of public property, the decline of the planned economy, the transition to market relations etc. have fundamentally altered the social system. New social classes are appearing with their own particular needs and interests. The style and way of life and the social character of traditional Russian communities are all radically changing. Previous influential groups in society have virtually ceased to exist. This means that new groups with different roles and greater significance are emerging to replace them.

In order to understand what is going on in our society and to be able to assess the effectiveness of policy and decision-making by government, we need to be well-informed about changes in Russia's social structure. These changes hold the key. Unfortunately many government figures as well as the general public are not well-informed, or else the information which they do possess is not used constructively. Does this reflect ignorance or something more sinister - a deliberate desire to conceal the truth? With respect to the first proposition many Russian specialists argue that it is extremely difficult to know what is happening as the pace and direction of change is far too rapid. It will therefore take a long time before the full impact of current changes on the class structure are known. As a result, data on this aspect is often incomplete. By contrast, arguments in favour of the second of these scenarios centre around the direct link between economic policy and social changes, which is seen as a major ideological issue. Because of the latter, there is always a risk that data and other information will be distorted. Hence, information, for example, on the adverse effect of policy changes on the level of class conflict might be concealed because its disclosure is undesirable. In both these cases, however, analysts, usually sociologists, have a certain theoretical model and empirical approach in mind. These theories may be home grown or borrowed from the West. In this chapter, I would like to tell you about the research of one branch of the Institute of Socio-Political Research (*Institut sotsial'no-politicheskikh issledovanii*) in Moscow, namely the Department of Social Structure and Stratification, of which I am head.

Concepts, theory and practice

Our approach to the issue of social class and antagonisms in Russian society proceeds from the assumption that the social structure is based upon material and economic criteria as well as other factors such as cultural, psychological and spiritual status and so on. The first two of these criteria help to build the social organism - classes, social groups, strata and other aspects of the social community; whereas the other criteria, represent certain parts of the social organism. Thus determining the social structure of a society is a complex matter involving hundreds, perhaps thousands, of elements. If we under-estimate the complexity of the issue at hand, we risk only gaining a partial grasp of the problem and the nature of the changes currently underway. Furthermore, such an ill-thought out, half-hearted approach, could lead to errors in policy responses to particular social structure changes, for instance in the field of social policy, which would have further negative knock-on effects.

We also proceeded from the assumption that changes in the social structure can have negative (i.e. destructive) and positive (i.e. system stability) features. The time when each appears and which is dominant, depends upon which period of social development we are talking about. The collapse of the USSR and the current government's policy of reform combine both these aspects at one and the same time. The former destroyed the old social structure whereas the latter has fundamentally altered the nature of social classes in Russia as well as the relationship between and within social groups. Some Russian scholars are even going so far as to argue that it is no longer possible to speak of 'social classes' in any significant sense, as performing a key role in society. Classes may have been crucial in the early capitalist era, but it is no longer meaningful to speak of them in the same way in the post-industrial society phase. This chapter will evaluate the validity of this assertion and suggest instead that in the case of Russia, social classes, despite their constantly changing characteristics, remain important. The main reason for this is that events under Communism did not allow classes to flourish in any real sense, so they are now being recreated during the transition period. As a result, we are witnessing greater class antagonism in Russia today. We can measure this conflict by examining the attitude of various social classes towards each other, property, work, the distribution of resources, ideology and so forth.

Harmony versus conflict

In the past, Russia and other former socialist bloc countries have looked at class in a particular way - in terms of harmony and the lack of antagonism. The old communist regimes tried to govern on the basis of this assumption. Events in 1989 throughout East-Central Europe and throughout the Gorbachev era in Russia exposed this view as false.

Since 1991 in Russia, we have made a quantum leap to a new stage in our development - away from 'harmony' towards 'antagonism'. If Trotsky were still alive he would refer to the present situation as being part of an on-going 'Permanent Revolution', in this case of social relations. There are two possible types of transformation: the first is characterised by the destruction of antagonistic relations in society; while the second involves restructuring the subjective aspects of antagonism or the resurgence of conflict.

The nature of the changes in Russia's social structure

The current changes in Russia's social structure are of the second variety described above - the restructuring or reform of social class structures. This is partly the legacy of the 1988-91 period in which Russia set about trying to build a capitalist society in a former socialist country. It is well known that in all capitalist societies, social conflict takes place. However, capitalism is a novelty in Russia. Today's reformers are using capitalist goals to achieve their aims - privilege and reward. But they have gone too far, too soon. Reformers have been too impatient and the costs have been high. For example in April 1994, A.I. Ivanenko, deputy chairman of *Goskomimyshestva* (the State Property Committee of Russia) declared: 'By the end of 1994, Russia will have moved from being a pseudo-socialist country to being a fully fledged capitalist one. This will mark one of the greatest achievements in the world'. Compare this with Khrushchev's naive statement during the 1950s that 'We will achieve communism in 20 years'. Both statements are unrealistic. Khrushchev tried and failed, will the current reformers suffer the same fate? or is it more accurate to describe those instigating change at present as 'pseudo-reformers' who came to power on the crest of a wave of socialist slogans - 'Developed socialism', 'Eradicate privileges', 'Provide real social justice' etc.? Since then, these former socialists, have formed a government which is bourgeois to the core. How the leopards change their spots!

The social revolution

The reformers realised that they had very little time to implement a social revolution. The foundations for change were laid largely by Gorbachev's perestroika which was unstable and very fragile. Russia set about on a course to reform in the shortest possible time. The key question was how to achieve it without destroying the existing system? Part of the reason why Gorbachev failed was his successes abroad and his failures at home - he largely ignored the mounting internal problems. Unfortunately, this questioned the leading role of the Party - culminating in the attempt to reverse the process of reform during the August 1991 coup d'etat[1] but in any case Russia was beyond redemption at this stage and so promises were made to the people, by Yeltsin and others, which subsequently were not honoured. To add insult to injury Russia had to go cap in hand to the West from 1992 onwards in order to keep the country afloat. The West in an attempt to prevent another Cold War, on the one hand, and to prevent a geopolitical situation of Yugoslav dimensions, on the other, applied greater pressure on Russia. Like Gorbachev before him, Yeltsin was forced to bow to international pressure - exerted by the IMF, EBRD, World Bank, G7 etc. - and give priority to Russia's external relations not growing internal difficulties. As a consequence, we may have created a new type of economic system - market as opposed to planned - but we have yet to create our own social base. More and more Russians believe that their country is on the wrong course. Thus in one May-June 1995 survey on 'How Russians live', 61 per cent of the 1,431 respondents surveyed believed Russia was on the wrong road compared to only 15 per cent who said we were on the right road. Of those in the 'wrong course' category, 71 per cent were middle-aged adults, 74 per cent peasants, 72 per cent were 'poor', 47 per cent were on social security, 48 per cent were entrepreneurs, 28 per cent students, 23 per cent young people, 23 per cent had a higher education and 25 per cent were housewives.[2] On the whole, by mid-1995, 58 per cent of those had a negative view of current reforms compared to only 10 per cent who held a positive attitude. 12 per cent remained indifferent and 20 per cent were unable to draw any firm conclusions on the question '*Kuda idet Rossiia*'?[3] Socialist values therefore still predominate in the mentality of many Russians, and reformers are trying to stamp them out using authoritarian methods. Unless we build a proper social base for the current reforms, the reform will inevitably end in failure.

Privatisation[4]

One main aspect of the current transition is the privatisation of state property. Privatisation refers to the transfer of ownership of particular assets from state into private hands. The number of state-owned enterprises is constantly falling. In 1991, for example, 96 per cent industrial enterprises were state-owned. By 1992, the year when privatisation officially began, this figure had fallen to 87 and by the beginning of 1994, only a fifth of them were left - 18. By 1 January 1995 112,625 enterprises had been privatised. They produce 47 per cent of our country's industrial output and are worth 2,357,611 million roubles.[5] The two areas most affected by privatisation have been trade and transport. Private property as an objective is high on the reformers agenda. The main reason for this, so the argument goes, is that the introduction of private property leads to prosperity, and a better quality of life for all citizens. However, this conclusion is drawn on the basis of the experience of capitalist countries of the industrialised West. This strategy might not work in Russia's case for two main reasons: firstly, it does not take into account the specifics of Russia and second, and perhaps most important of all, it does not take the interests of the people into account. Hence, privatisation might exacerbate an already tense situation, leading to the polarisation of social groupings, increased, conflict, producing a 'social explosion' (*sotsial'nyi vzryv*). Our data indicate that this process started back in 1993 but has yet to reach the outburst stage. However, there are already signs of decay - labour productivity and output levels are dropping. For instance, between January 1991 and January 1994, industrial output fell by 51.1 per cent, and food-stuffs declined even more by 64 per cent.[6] One recent survey in May-June 1995 indicated that the number of people against privatisation was more than two times greater than those in favour - 36 per cent as against 16 per cent.[7] This was only to be expected, but Russia faces a major problem as a consequence - a rising number of dependants but a diminishing working population able to take the burden.

Working population versus dependants

Although this trend is emerging in the mid-1990s, the first signs of this tendency go as far back as the mid-1950s. What is important now is the differing nature of the same phenomenon. During the first quarter of this century, prior to the rise of Stalin, the rising number of dependants and the decline in the working population was a consequence of world war, revolution and civil war which caused the birth rate to fall and the death rate to increase. Russia was also faced by an ageing population. By comparison, during the Brezhnev era (1965-82), when less attention was devoted to full employment, the number of so-called 'drones' started to grow. This was due to two things: an increasing birth-rate between 1975-85 and a higher proportion of women entering the workforce. As a whole, participation rates in industry were very high - 87 per cent in 1970 rising to 94 per cent in the second half of the 1980s. Today, as a result of the transition, those who were formerly very economically active have now become dependants. According to *Goskomstat* (the State Statistical Committee) data, participation rates in industry were already down to 83 per cent in 1993 (i.e. close to 1970 levels). Therefore, Russia is taking two steps backwards, not one step forwards - Russians are becoming increasingly apathetic, especially as regards work. The outlook is bleak, as the situation appears to be worse than initially expected. There are fewer people who are economically active, and a higher proportion of parasitic dependants. Current statistical data suggest that 72 million out of a possible 86 million able-bodied men were employed, more than third of whom worked in the private sector. Surveys estimate that more than half of these people are 'con-men', speculators, swindlers and other parasites, who are merely registered as employees of commercial and private enterprises.[8]

What about the dependants? Some, such as pensioners, have done their bit for society in the past, but others, such as children and teenagers, are our future active/working population. Unfortunately under present conditions both are struggling. Pensioners are among the poorest group in society, whilst the number of jobless, homeless and down and out children and teenagers, who can be seen openly begging on the streets in any major Russian city, are growing.

Unemployed and down and outs

The official number of unemployed in Russia is 900,000 to one million people. But in reality, 14 million people did not have jobs in Russia in 1993. This compares with an estimated total of 12.9 million for the USSR as a whole in 1989, a quarter of which lived in Russia.[9] Those most affected by a loss of job are mothers with large families and the 111 different types of invalids. Others have simply become beggars, tramps and the social dregs of society. We questioned a sample of vagrants (*bomzhi*) in Vologda and Moscow to explore the reasons for their plight. We concluded that it was the result of the following factors:

(i)   ill-considered housing reforms, which forced the most needy - old people, children, alcoholics, the mentally-ill - to become victims of swindlers, racketeers etc., who took possession of their housing;

(ii)   the rejection of old, well-established principles, such as that of egalitarianism; and

(iii)   loss of job and related security - housing provided by firms - through no fault of their own.

We must not neglect such groups, although society's view of them is sometimes hostile. Thus one All-Union Public Opinion Centre (VTsIOM) survey carried out in 1989 among a sample of 2,696 discovered that 10 per cent of those surveyed wanted to rid society of tramps, the homeless and the so-called 'social dregs' and a further 23 per cent said they must be isolated from society.[10] However, if we resort to such action the risks are high. For example the *Great white Brothers*, a religious cult established in the Ukraine in 1990, whose membership numbers 200,000, draws many of its recruits from those without homes and jobs. Similar cults are now emerging in Russia too. The number of tramps has tripled in the last few years. In 1994, there were more than one million in Russia alone.[11] This is just the tip of the iceberg. It is impossible to be precise because the network of organisations responsible for the poor and needy has virtually collapsed because of a lack of state funding and frequent reorganisations of its work. It has yet to be replaced by an up and running new system which cares for the poor, mentally ill, tramps, homeless, alcoholics etc. Nevertheless, there is hope. Among respondents in the aforementioned VTsIOM 1990 survey, 46 per cent wanted to help the down and outs in Russia.[12]

The number of unemployed is growing as the number of refugees coming into Russia increases. As a result of the collapse of the USSR, the large majority of newly independent states have become increasingly nationalistic. *Russophobia* has developed and conflicts have already broken out. Russia has been forced to accept 2 million refugees. There is a distinct possibility that this total will increase to 4-6 million in the very near future. Moreover, there are hundreds of thousands of refugees from Afghanistan, Somalia, India, Turkey and other developing countries, 100-150,000 of whom have settled in Moscow.[13] This flow is expected to become greater as the West places stricter rules on emigration for Russians seeking residence abroad. The number of illegals is unknown, but some Russian commercial firms are exploiting this situation by inviting inhabitants of the aforementioned countries who enter legally as 'tourists' but then become illegal residents once their visas expire. These refugees are stretching Russian resources to the limit and making the employment situation acute. According to Federal Employment Service data, there were 978,800 people not involved in any kind of work at the beginning of 1994, but only 713,900 were registered as unemployed. Who is supporting the missing quarter of a million and more?

Of the unemployed - in reality said to be as high as 14 million - over half want to work, but do not have the opportunity to do so. There is increasing apathy and laziness. Of the 14 million jobless, 2 million have no desire to work. They see themselves as the 'forgotten'. No-one cares about them. Part of the reason for the large discrepancy between official (one million) and unofficial (fourteen million) figures on unemployment is the tendency for the jobless not to register themselves at labour exchanges. Instead they search for jobs themselves through family, friends and other contacts. However, since February 1994, the number of bankruptcies has risen dramatically. This has forced more people onto the dole queue. Those who were previously employed in state enterprises are virtually being condemned to the ranks of the long-term unemployed. Hence searching for a non-existent job is more of a reality these days and the situation will remain hopeless for the large majority of jobless Russians for the foreseeable future. Thus the growing number of dependants relying on a smaller proportion of able-bodied workers looks set to continue well into the 1990s.

The rich get richer and the poor get poorer: distribution of the population according to income

In the past, as part of Russian egalitarianism, wages and incomes tended to be equalised deliberately by the CPSU. The state closely regulated incomes and the difference between groups was marginal. According to Kryshtanovskaya, the minimum monthly income was 80 roubles and the maximum set at around 1,200 roubles on average. That makes a difference of 15:1 between the richest and poorest sections of society, ignoring the *nomenklatura*.[14] Today the situation has changed dramatically. According to a recent *Moskovskii Komsomolets* article, the average wage in Russia fell from $25 a month in December 1989 to $10 in November 1991 before rising to $30 in November 1992 and then to $90 in November 1993. Average wages reached a peak of $100 in January 1994 and have fluctuated widely ever since. By March 1995, average wages had fallen back to around $80 a month.[15] The minimum wage now stands at 50,000 roubles (approximately $12) per month, with those working for foreign companies earning more than those working for their Russian counterparts, as table 7.1 shows.

Table 7.1
Monthly wages in foreign and Russian companies compared
March - June 1995 (in US $ dollars)

Job	Foreign firm	Russian firm
Executive Director	3000-5000	2000-3000
Financial Director	2000-3000	1500-3000
Chief Accountant	500-2000	500-2000
Marketing & Advertising	700-1500	500-1000
Lawyer	1000-3000	700-2000
Sales Manager	1200-2500	600-1000
Public Relations	700-1500	400-900
Office Administrator	500-700	500-700
Programmer	500-1000	400-500
Engineer	500-1000	250-500
Translator/Interpreter	500-1000	500-700
Personal Assistant	400-800	250-300
Driver	300-800	300-400
Chambermaid	200-300	100-250

Source: Unistaff survey cited in *Moskovskii Komsomolets* 10 August 1995, p. 6.

It is clear that on average, Russians earn 50 per cent less when they are employed by Russian firms. Of course what this table does not take into account is those without jobs or those on state pensions. Thus by the end of 1994, 61 per cent of OAPs were living below the poverty line, while the President of 'Russkii Dom Selenga' earned an astonishing $35,000 a month.[16]

According to *Goskomstat* data the Geni coefficient of income concentration for the Russian Federation was as follows: 0.327 in 1992; 0.346 in December 1993 and 0.352 by January 1994. The specific differentiation according to different income groups was as in table 7.2 below:

Table 7.2
Distribution of population by average incomes

Monthly income (in thousands of roubles)	December 1993 a	b	January 1994 a	b	August 1995 a	b
up to 10,000	0.3	0.2	0.4	0.3	0.0	0.0
10,100-20,000	4.2	2.8	5.6	3.7	0.0	0.0
20,100-30,000	10.2	6.9	12.4	8.3	0.1	0.0
30,100-40,000	14.0	9.4	15.8	10.7	0.1	0.0
40,100-50,000	15.1	10.1	16.3	11.0	3.6	2.4
50,100-60,000	14.5	9.8	15.2	10.2	3.6	2.4
60,100-70,000	13.2	8.9	13.4	9.0	3.6	2.4
70,100-80,000	11.7	7.9	11.3	7.7	3.6	2.4
80,100-90,000	10.1	6.8	9.6	6.5	3.6	2.4
90,100-100,000	8.6	5.8	8.1	5.4	3.6	2.4
100,100-120,000	13.4	9.1	12.3	8.3	9.3	6.3
120,100-140,000	9.6	6.5	8.5	5.7	9.3	6.3
140,100-160,000	6.8	4.6	5.9	4.0	13.5	9.1
160,100-180,000	4.9	3.3	4.1	2.8	13.5	9.1
180,100-200,000	3.6	2.4	2.9	2.9	13.5	9.1
More than 200,000	8.2	5.5	6.5	4.4	121.7	82.2

Key:
a   Million population
b   in percentage

Sources: *Sotsial'no-ekonomicheskoe polozhenie Rossii: Operativnaia informatsiia*, (Moscow, Goskomstat 1994), and *Statisticheskoe obozrenie* No. 9, 1995, p. 59.

This table demonstrates that an increasing proportion of the population is being paid wages below the minimum of 51,400 roubles a month. This amounted to 34 per cent or one in three Russians in January 1994. The situation had deteriorated over the previous year when the minimum wage stood at 4,275 roubles and 1 in 12 Russians were living on salaries below the minimum.[17] However, it should be borne in mind that inflation rates in 1994 were greater than 1993 meaning an overall decline in minimum wage levels in real terms by 11 per cent. In 1995 the gap between rich and poor was more substantial and the proportion of the well-to-do in the population was gradually increasing. The highest incomes of the rich have exceeded those of the poor by several thousands in the last three years with the proportion of the population on higher salaries accelerating as rapidly in 1995.

Another alarming trend is the growing proportion of the people falling below the poverty line, as shown by the data contained in table 7.3 below which illustrates that although the number of people with minimum wages has remained the same in January 1994 as compared to January 1993, more and more people are starving and using their meagre incomes to purchase basic foodstuffs - a rise from 14.5 per cent of the population in early 1993 to nearly 18 per cent a year later. Generally speaking the greater the amount spent on foodstuffs, the lower the income; whereas those in a more prosperous position are able to afford some luxury goods, such as consumer durables. This assertion is supported by the evidence presented in the previous chapter (see table 6.1). It is also essential to remember that in a country the size of Russia, there are tremendous regional variations in incomes. These range from 18-20,000 roubles a month up to as high as 117-119,000 roubles per month. In overall terms by August 1995, 28 per cent of the Russian population were receiving incomes below the minimum wage. Their number in real terms constituted 4.2 million.

Table 7.3
Proportion of the population with incomes lower than minimum wage

Month and Year	Minimum wage	
	a	b
January 1993	52.8	35.5
January 1994	52.6	35.4
August 1995	42.2	28.0

Key:
a   million people
b   as percentage of entire population

Source: *Sotsial'no-ekonomicheskoe polozhenie Rossii: Operativnaia informatsiia* (Moscow, Goskomstat 1994) and *Statisticheskoe obozrenie* No. 9, 1995, p. 63.

Rich versus poor

Russia's social structure is undergoing tremendous change - this process is so profound that reform is not an adequate enough term to capture the nature of the changes, instead it is preferable to use the term transformation. By the beginning of 1995, as a result of the changes since 1991, Russia had a very thin layer of rich people at 2.5 - 3 per cent (although officially said to be much more substantial at 30-35 per cent) together with a significant number of poor people - 60-70 per cent. Those very close to the poverty line are estimated to total 20-25 per cent of the population. A further 7 per cent are said to be relatively well off.

It is best to describe these people using the term group or strata rather than class as they have not yet began to act in their own interests and in a unified way. Even the use of the terms 'rich' and 'poor' obscure more than they reveal. Take, for example, the categories 'rich' (*bogatch*) or 'extremely rich' (*sverkhbogachi*): if we examine them more closely they include officials, bureaucrats, patriotic multi-millionaires, leading racketeers, drug barons and Russian democrats with Western leanings who use their position for personal gain. In this context, according to Kryshtanovskaya, one 1992 survey which asked who are the richest people in Russia, came up with 72 names. Among them were V.V. Zhirinovskii, B. Yeltsin, A. Yakovlev, M. Gorbachev, A.I. Vol'skii etc. - all politicians; K. Zatulin - a businessman; M. Khodorskii - an entrepreneur and A. Karpov - a chess player.[18] A 'New Millionaires' survey of 1992-93 discovered that rich people in Moscow tended to be married, aged 35 years old, with higher education, usually including a higher degree, natives of Moscow and of intelligentsia background. Some 'millionaire-nomenklaturists' also had CPSU, Komsomol or KGB connections or backgrounds.[19] All this is acknowledged by government officials as the norm. As one sceptical *Rossiisskii Vestnik* journalist put it in late October 1993: 'Society must rid itself of the illusion that Russia is made up of loyal Leninists. This was never the case. Power corrupts, but the people are being conned by slogans'.[20] This is as true today as it was then. The only difference is that in the meantime, the rich have got richer, and the poor, poorer.

Similarly, we must be careful when we use the term 'poor' with all the connotations that has as indicating the lower strata in society. However, while this category includes some parasites, it also includes a great number of others - committed, hard-working members of the working class, peasantry and the intelligentsia, including scientists, who through no fault of their own have fallen on hard times.

Thus concepts and theories are one thing, reality another. We need to learn to be more precise with the terms we use, we need to look deeper beyond the terms themselves and above all we need to remember that the current situation is a very fluid one, forever changing.

Nevertheless, it is possible on the basis of the aforementioned analysis to draw a number of tentative conclusions. These are:

(i)   the class structure of modern Russia resembles that of early Capitalism;
(ii)   we now have an amorphous class structure as a result of extremely well developed internal social differentiation;
(iii)   extensive processes of lumpenisation of representatives of the exploited and exploiting groups is taking place;
(iv)   a process of criminalisation of the exploited and exploiting classes has begun (see below);
(v)   there is now increased social mobility, which in the Soviet period was more

restricted; and
(vi)   All the above characteristics can be observed in Russia today.

If the heterogeneous character of the bourgeoisie reflects different origins then the increasing homogeneity of the Russian working-class, peasantry and the intelligentsia has a great deal to do with the ideological and political nature of the current reforms which have lead to an economic crisis in Russia.

The first consequence of these processes is the 'lumpenisation' of the population (*liumpenizatsiia naseleniia*). The majority is at risk of being affected in a similar way. In the absence of laws and 'normal market' relations, qualified workers and experienced specialists are losing their jobs and farmers are going bankrupt. They are being replaced by businessmen. On the whole this has meant downward mobility for the former lumpen proletariat and upward mobility for the new Russians. Both types of social mobility are intensifying, but a more rapid decline has occurred among workers and a speedier climb amongst those at the top. The key variable missing here is the influence of criminality (*prestupnost'*). This variable can help all groups climb the social ladder. Thus criminal elements from all sections of society, able through privatisation, to purchase or sell land and property can shift social classes as a result of extremely high incomes.   This is best termed 'criminal social mobility' (*sotsial'noi mobil'nost' kriminal'nogo tipa*).

Class conflict between capital and labour: them versus us

According to Chubais, the features of a classical capitalist social structure are becoming more and more evident in Russia. This is especially true of property relations. Two opposing classes are forming: those who sell their labour and those who own it i.e. a proletariat and a capital class in the old Marxist sense. Class conflict between these two groups has occurred from the early to mid-1990s. This conflict has arisen for several reasons: fewer jobs because of reduced production - 24.9 per cent down in the first quarter of 1995 compared to the same period in 1993 - the rate of which is increasing every month.   Manufacturing industry and its workforce have suffered most. The negative impact of economic restructuring is denied. This was confirmed by Professor A.Ia. Livshits, a Presidential adviser, who declared in early July 1994 that: 'Despite the transition to market relations, we have not been able to halt the rate of decline in production.   However, this is normal in any country undergoing economic transformation.   Even in more advantaged nations, such as the USA, changes in capacity, as a result of changes in demand - to the tune of 20-25 per cent - are not unknown.   The economy starts to recover when the order books fill up again, but no country works at 100 per cent capacity. That is not natural'.[21]

In Russia's case, though, the fall in production has been spectacular and much higher than predicted - a decline by 60 per cent in the last few years. True Soviet industry may not have worked at full capacity in the past, despite propaganda to the contrary, but it was much higher than present levels. The present government has done very little - half-hearted, ill-thought out industrial reforms - to halt this decline even though some branches of industry, most notably textiles, agriculture, machine-building, construction etc. are vital. Such a mishandling of industry, which resulted from the lack of clear guidance and initiative on the part of the government, has meant that Yeltsin and his advisers have been unwilling to confront the administrative and financial problems arising in industry. As a result, the number of industrial enterprise closures is gradually increasing - 6 per cent in 1992, 12 per cent in 1993, 30 per cent in the first half of 1994. In March 1994 alone, 4,800 enterprises closed. This resulted in the loss of a staggering 24 million man-hours or 16 per cent of formal working time. The dramatic increase in such phenomena is shown in table 7.4 below:

Table 7.4
Enterprise stoppages or closures in Russia, January 1993 - March 1994

Time period	Enterprise stoppages	Enterprise closures	Losses	
			a	b
January 1993	2,811	389	8,539	8.8
February 1993	2,441	195	5,979	8.6
March 1993	2,541	157	6,612	7.3
January 1994	3,789	641	20,198	18.6
February 1994	4,280	428	21,814	18.0
March 1994	480	329	24,189	16.0

Key:
a   thousand days per head
b   percentage of formal working time

Source: *Rossiia nakanune XXI veka vypusk I* (Moscow 1994), p. 35.

Privatisation of industry despite its negative impact is not being halted, but rather is being stepped up.[22] The plan is to privatise seven out every 10 industrial/technological enterprises. If this succeeds, only 15-20 per cent of industry will not be in private hands. By 1993, according to Peter Rutland, about 40 per cent of firms had been privatised.[23] As one might expect this is not being greeted enthusiastically. More and more workers are showing a willingness to strike, as table 7.5 below illustrates.

Thus the number of enterprises involved in strikes initially increased from 260 in 1990 to 6,273 in 1992 but eventually fell to 514 by 1994. Over the same four years the number of workers on strike rose from 99,500 to 1.55 million. This situation is having an adverse effect upon economic performance, as the days lost through strikes nearly quadrupled from 207,740 in 1990 to 755,066 in 1994. Most workers were either fighting for better wages and working conditions, or where closures were inevitable, for as much redundancy pay as possible. Unfortunately, most workers were being sacked or laid off without pay - in 1994 twice as many as the year before. Under these circumstances, it is hardly surprising to find that most workers went on strike - 81,822 by March 1994 compared to 12,319 in December 1993, nearly a 700 per cent increase -

for fear of losing their jobs. Surveys show that 80 per cent of working people live in constant fear of this happening to them in the not too distant future. In 1994, over 50 per cent of workers stated that fear of unemployment was their major concern, 1.5 times more than in 1993. Moreover, instead of the socialist competition of the past, each worker is now competing with his fellow workmates in order to keep his job. This is increasing the level of conflict on the shop floor and throughout the factory. As a result more and more people are putting themselves first. Thus the notion of 'I'm all right jack' is now commonplace - clearly individualism has now replaced the collective ideology of former times. Such a view is not restricted just to industry, it has permeated all of Russian society. However, although most of those surveyed realised that closures and stoppages were associated with Russia's 'shock therapy' strategy, they put the blame firmly in the hands of the government - thus the strike movement, as it was under Gorbachev, is acquiring a political edge.

Table 7.5
Willingness to strike and level of strike activity in Russia, 1990-94

Time period	a	b	c	d
1990	260	99.5	2.1	207,740
1991	1,755	237.7	9.7	2,314,845
1992	6,273	357.6	5.3	1,894,446
1993	264	120.2	2.0	236,016
1994	514	155.3	4.9	755,066

Key:

a   Number of enterprises taking part in strike activity
b   Number of workers on strike
c   Number of days on average of each strike
d   Days lost through strike

Source: *Rossiia v tsifrakh 1995*, (Goskomstat, Moscow 1995), p. 58.

A second feature has also emerged from surveys, that is, strikes are not simply used as a means to criticise government policy, they are also part of the class conflict between capital and labour over the failure of privatisation to deliver what was expected - an improvement in living and working conditions as well as job security. Thus one 1993 survey indicated that only 17 per cent of those interviewed said they would personally gain from privatisation, compared to 28 per cent who said they would lose out.[24] The situation since then has worsened, thus the number losing will have increased, probably at the expense of the small percentage of capitalists benefiting - set at 74 per cent in July 1993 - from such industrial reorganisation.[25] Of course people are not satisfied with this situation. Workers are particularly unhappy about the fact that the redistribution of wages, social goods and profits tend to be made by enterprise managers and other holders of senior posts. In overall terms, privatisation has resulted in 17 per cent more workers living below the poverty in 1994 compared to 1993. Meanwhile, the wage gap between the 10 per cent well-off shareholders, managers and captains of Russian industry and the 10 per cent not so well paid workers on the shop floor increased 27 times over the same period. Every worker below management level is finding that they are sliding further and further down the wage scale in comparison to the pre-reform period. Thus, scientific and maintenance personnel have slipped from third place in previous wage levels to twelfth after the reform whilst transport staff have benefited climbing from fourth in the pre-reform period to sixth place afterwards. In an attempt to survive, the growing number of low-paid workers, are taking on second, third and fourth jobs where they can find them. This is increasing the length of the working day to an astonishing 20 hours in some cases. This does little to improve the quality of our products and make them competitive in our own domestic market, let alone abroad, but such excessive working hours provides a compelling reason for declining life expectancy in Russia today. Such a poor quality of life is not restricted to the masses, it is also true of the professional classes. For example, professors and post-doctoral staff frequently work as watchmen or porters to supplement their meagre wages. All in all, two-fifths of academics describe their material position as 'bad'. Hence, the 'shock therapy' is hitting all occupational groups irrespective of the origins of their social class.

The introduction of the market and capitalist philosophy in Russia has made labour one of the cheapest factors of production in Russia today (see table 7.1). In pre-perestroika days, wages were set by the state in accordance with its goals - plan fulfilment, importance of branch of industry etc. However from September 1986 Gorbachev introduced measures to overhaul the old wage system which sought to curtail wage levelling and to tie wages to profitability and productivity.[26] This was to be implemented between 1987-90 branch by branch and firm by firm. This decree also gave enterprises a variety of options for adjusting job rates and awarding bonuses to encourage efficiency and higher productivity. But in the late 1980s as perestroika went into crisis, attempts were made to impede wage increases both by administrative means and punitive taxes on wage rises.[27] However, although the growth in earnings decelerated slightly by mid-1989, wages were still not totally under state control.[28] Until the collapse of the USSR at the end of 1991, Gorbachev struggled to curb wage increases not related to a corresponding rise in productivity. In effect, the more profitable enterprises were subsidising the unprofitable ones. Over the last few years as the state sector has declined and the private sector has expanded the extent of its economy activity, most of the profits earned have not been used to award well-deserved pay rises, but to keep management and shareholders happy, with one exception. When profits fall, workers are sacked or their wages severely curtailed. Under these circumstances it is hardly surprising that Russian economic growth is declining and labour productivity is low. Most workers find themselves being paid wages below the minimum and struggling to keep themselves and their families afloat. They have little incentive to work harder, except perhaps in an attempt to keep their jobs at a time of high unemployment. Finally low wages and high prices are failing to stimulate consumption and savings. The Russian economy is therefore on a downward spiral.

Finally, the tendency of factory managers and bosses of other firms to abandon the pre-perestroika principle of providing their workforce with various inducements - health care, education, pioneer camps, sanatoria etc. - has also been a major bone of contention.

Unfortunately workers are at present powerless to change the situation. Even those workers who were privileged under the privatisation programme to become worker owners, are not co-owners in any real sense of the word because it is the employer not the employee who has ultimate control over goods and services. It is the employer not the 'worker owners' who sets output targets, prices, wages, sales, investment, finds buyers etc. Although, bosses should be blamed for any resulting failures, it is only the workers themselves who carry the can - they suffer wage cuts, stoppages, closures and ultimately the loss of their jobs.

All the aforementioned factors are causing class conflict between capital and labour to increase in Russia in the 1990s.

The criminalisation of the Russian business sector[29]

The transformation of Russia's economy and social structure has only occurred at great social cost. The government's attempts to make the process less painful have proved fruitless. One of the key features of the market reforms of the last decade has been the emergence of the private sector and a range of private businesses. Unfortunately, the state did not take steps to prevent the latter from exposure to criminal elements. Similarly, following the principle 'whatever is not prohibited legally is permissible', capitalists and criminals have found common ground - survival and maximising profits. As a result by 1995, the state only has a few legal bases to defend private businesses from criminal infiltration and the mentality, morality and values of Russian society have now become more susceptible to criminal behaviour.

The need for Russian businesses to survive and make as much money as they can in the process means that many corporate groups have established links with criminals or used criminal methods to achieve their objectives. They have taken advantage of the legislative chaos - the rewards for breaking the law and making a profit are at present greater than the penalties for infringement. As a consequence law breaking rather than law abiding has become the norm in the Russian business sector. Businesses break the law in a number of ways: in setting prices, in relation to the quality of goods and services, when trying to beat competitors, in endangering people's health and the environment and so forth.

Research carried out on the managers and directors of private firms and joint-stock companies in the Moscow region in the winter of 1993-94 has revealed some startling facts. 30 per cent of the starting capital in the private sector was of criminal origin while 51 per cent of sales operations had similar ties. It is widely believed that privatisation was partly financed in a similar vein making the overall link between the private sector and criminals quite substantial.[30] Criminal activity has grown from an interest in street kiosks to practically all types and aspects of business activity. Criminals are involved in drugs, prostitution, money laundering and the arms trade. This image of Russia is causing serious concern to the outside world, representatives of foreign countries as well as the average Russian citizen. This is one of the reasons why a Federal Bureau of Investigation (FBI) office was set up in Russia in May 1994.

Numerous surveys have demonstrated that most Russians are very worried about rising crime (see chapter 14). The most serious aspect of this is the Russian *mafiya* which is paralysing our businesses yet the state does nothing. Research carried out on the managers and directors of private firms and joint-stock companies in the Moscow region in the winter of 1993-94 showed that 38 per cent of them had already suffered physical violence, while 85 per cent of respondents and their families had received threats. Nearly a quarter (24 per cent) of business wanted something done about organised crime and criticised the government for its lack of a concerted response. Businessmen pointed out that taxes were not being paid in many instances. They estimated that somewhere between 8-50 per cent of monthly profits in the private sector were escaping taxation. Managers and directors did not only blame the government, they also criticised the police and the courts for failing to take a firmer stand.[31] All in all, our surveys suggest that official figures - which put extortion or rackets at only 5-7 per cent of all crime - grossly underestimate the real extent of the problem. Criminal activity is all an important issue in relation to social structure. Russian criminals seek to imitate their Western counterparts because as everyone knows being 'rich' is a symbol of success in capitalist society. In Russian society, some people are achieving this goal via criminal activity. It seems, at least in theory, that 'crime does pay'. Organised crime is not only possible because of the weak state response, it is also being facilitated by widespread migration - criminals are free to travel wherever they want, because bribery is common and there is no international co-operation in clamping down on the problem, especially in relation to criminals from the Caucasus and Central Asia. In summary therefore the transformation of Russia from a socialist to capitalist society has produced more and more chaos and crime, especially of the organised variety. This is affecting all areas of society and distorting the social structure. The state seems reluctant to step in for two reasons: either because it can't cope with the extent of the problem due to resource constraints or, as the more cynical view would have it, the state does not want to intervene because some of the regimes supporters are from the criminal fraternity. Therefore, the latter are more or less free to do what they wish.

The growing social gap between town and countryside

In the past, there was a *smychka* (link) between the city and the village, but the transition of recent years has begun to take its toll on this link. Thus in recent surveys village residents stated: 'Earlier, we would give to the city and the city would give to us, but this no longer applies'. Why? Agriculture and with it the village has been destroyed by the current reforms. By 1993, 66 per cent of Russia's 13,022 *kolkhozy* had been subject to shifts in ownership. Of this number, 551 had become associations of peasant farms; 2,495 joint-stock companies, and 976 co-operatives. The rest stayed as they were. Meanwhile, of the 19,061 *sovkhozy*, 8,378 (or 44 per cent) had undergone transformation. Of this number, 393 had become associations of peasant farms; 3,149 joint-stock companies, 749 agricultural co-operatives and 4,087 stayed the same.[32] This has merely added to the chaos and made an already difficult situation much worse. For example, between 1984-94, the production of tractors fell 2.8 times; combines by 3.4 times, ploughs three times; seeders, cultivators and movers 6 times and so on. Furthermore, the price of agricultural machinery increased by hundreds then thousands of times, the income of farmers is much much lower and the state is failing to pay them for produce: by the beginning of June 1994, for instance, the state owed farmers 7 billion roubles for agricultural goods and services supplied.[33] Agricultural specialists estimate that it will take at least two generations to recover from the devastation caused by Gorbachev and Yeltsin's reforms.

As agriculture goes into decline, so production levels fall. Between January-June 1994, a third of agricultural machinery plants were not operating and the remaining two-thirds were on a reduced working week. As a result of this and other problems highlighted above, the production of machines for harvesting flax and rice and for mineral fertilisers has ceased. There has been a three-fold decrease in the production of phosphorous raw materials since 1988. The soil is deteriorating in many rural areas - 20 million hectares of grain and 15 million hectares of feed - because it has not been fertilised. Arable land is also badly hit. Future harvests will be way down on previous years. For example, in 1993, grain harvests were down to 125-130 million tons, but future projections suggest a grain harvest of 80-80 million tons in 1996 which is comparable with the 1961-65 period. However we had 27-29 million less people to feed then. It looks as if agriculture will become the Achilles heel of the Russian economy once again, forcing Russia to become more dependent on the West for food and other products, just as Khrushchev did in the early 1960s having previously tried to feed the population bread made out of a mixture of grain and corn (see table 1.1).

Other changes are also underway in the agricultural sector of the economy.[34] The most important of these is the collapse of the agro-industrial complexes. Many *kolkhozy* and *sovkhozy* are in danger of extinction. Conflict between different peasants is now common, as they fight to keep their land and jobs. The old collective farms, largely the product of Stalinist collectivisation, are now being broken up into smaller units in an attempt to make them more family based and more productive. Thus capitalist methods are being used in the countryside too, with similar consequences: class conflict.

Farmers have become a small cog in the democratic wheel of reform. They are at the mercy of the state. The speed with which farmers are becoming bankrupt is increasing. In the past farmers were more fortunate. Those who were operating prior to perestroika received favourable credits and gained when grain prices went up. But from perestroika onwards, state subsidies for agriculture were withdrawn, the extension of credit exacted a high price and the state often did not pay the peasants for grain sold. The way in which conditions in agriculture have changed in the last decade can be illustrated by a simple example: in 1991, the average farm could buy three to four tractors; in 1992, the number had fallen to two; in 1993 to one but by 1994 farmers could not even buy a wheel let alone the tractor. A combination of decades of neglect and yet another agricultural reform is having an adverse effect upon the countryside, as we saw in chapter 3. People are becoming less caring - many rural inhabitants have turned to stealing *kolkhozy* and *sovkhozy* property or else they turn up for work drunk saying 'I don't care'. If expelled, the alcoholic takes his share of the goods causing further chaos. This, on top of crop-rotations, reorganisation, a lack of money and the failure to maintain the social infrastructure of the village - thus kindergartens, clubs and schools are closing - is resulting in a continued rural exodus. The state has issued many decrees on agriculture in the last two years, but few have been implemented, instead democrats have launched a full-scale attack on agriculture for supposedly adhering to collectivist and socialist principles.

Conclusion

The aforementioned analysis shows that Russia's reforms over the last decade have totally transformed her social structure. Where there was once harmony there is now widespread class conflict between different social groups as well as between town and country dwellers. Far from allowing Russia to advance, the reproduction of capitalist relations, is ripping havoc. In the name of progress, great crimes are being committed.

Notes

1. On these issues see V. Sorgin, *Politicheskaia istoria sovremennoi Rossii,* Moscow, 1994.
2. V.K. Levashov et al., *Kak zhivesh' Rossiia?* Moscow 1995, pp. 8-9.
3. Ibid p. 10.
4. On this see A.S. Bum, 'Sotsial'nye aspekty privatizatsii', in T.I. Zaslavskaia (ed.), *Kuda idet Rossiia: Al'ternativy obshchestvennogo razvitiia,* Moscow, 'Aspekt Press' 1995, pp. 120-32.
5. T. Popova, 'Privatizatsiia i investitsii v Rossii: istoriia nesoupladenii', *Moskovskaia Pravda,* 11 October 1995, supplement, p. 3.
6. *Rossiia nakanune XXI veka,* Moscow 1994, p. 26.
7. V.K. Levashov et al., *Kak zhivesh' Rossiia?* Moscow 1995, p. 12.
8. Ibid, p. 27.
9. Ibid.
10. *Obshchestvennoe mnenie v tsifrakh* No. 2, 1990.
11. *Rossiia nakanune XXI veka,* Moscow 1994, p. 28.
12. *Obshchestvennoe mnenie v tsifrakh* No. 2, 1990.
13. *Rossiia nakanune XXI veka,* Moscow 1994, p. 28.
14. Olga Kryshtanovskaya, 'Rich and poor in post-communist Russia', *Journal of Communist Studies and Transition Politics,* Volume 10 (1), March 1994, p. 3.
15. *Moskovskii Komsomolets,* 10 August 1995, p. 6.
16. *Rossiia pered vyborom,* Moscow *'obozrevatel'* 1995, p. 41 and *Moskovskii Komsomolets* 10 August 1995, p. 6.
17. Ibid, p. 5.
18. Ibid, p. 12.
19. Ibid.
20. T. Reshetnikova, 'Kakuiu pobedu my prazdnuek', *Rossisskii Vestnik* 23 October 1993.
21. Cited in *Pravda* 4 June 1994.
22. For a more detailed discussion see Iu.V. Beletskii, 'Tendentsii promyshlennogo razvitiia Rossii' in T.I. Zaslavskaia (ed.), *Kuda idet Rossiia?* Moscow 'Aspekt Press' 1995, pp. 94-99 and S. Fortescue, 'Privatisation of large-scale industry', in A. Saikal and W Maley (eds.), *Russia in search of its future,* Cambridge University Press, Cambridge 1995, pp. 85-101.
23. P. Rutland, 'The economy: The rocky road to reform: From plan to market', in: S. White et al. (eds.), *Developments in Russian and post-Soviet politics,* Macmillan:

London 1994, p. 160.

24.   *Ekonomicheskie i sotsial'nye peremeny: monitoring obshchestvennogo mneniye* 1993, No. 5, p. 23.

25.   Ibid.

26.   *Izvestiia* 26 September 1986. For a more detailed discussion see J.G. Chapman, 'Gorbachev's wage reform', *Soviet Economy* Volume 4 (4), October-December 1988, pp. 338-65.

27.   *Pravda* 28 January 1990.

28.   *Komsomol'skaia Pravda* 1 May 1990, p. 1.

29.   This section of the chapter draws on the work of my colleague Professor K.V. Andreeva who carried out research on the managers of private firms and joint-stock companies in the Moscow region in the winter of 1993-94.

30.   On the link between privatisation and criminals see S. Handelman, *Comrade criminal: The theft of the Second Russian Revolution*, Michael Joseph, London 1994, pp. 112-13, 189, 224, 232, 263.

31.   On the difficulties for law enforcers in general and this field in particular see Handelman ibid.

32.   R.F. Miller, 'Reforming Russian agriculture: Privatisation in comparative perspective', in A. Saikal and W. Maley (eds.), *Russia in search of its future,* Cambridge University Press, Cambridge 1995, pp. 73-74.

33.   *Sel'skaia Zhizn'* 10 June 1994.

34.   For a useful overview here see Miller 1995 op cit., pp. 66-84.

8 Youth and social change

VLADIMIR CHUPROV AND JULIA ZUBOK

Introduction

This chapter draws on our on-going project concerning 'The social development of youth'. This research has been carried out in 12 regions of the Russian Federation since 1982. We have described the methodical and theoretical framework underpinning this research elsewhere,[1] here we would like to look at empirical data collected between 1990-94. In 1990, we surveyed 10,412 young people aged between 15-29 years and then in 1994, we interviewed 2,612 young people in the same age group. This research was co-ordinated by Professor Chuprov of the Sociology of Youth Division of the Russian Academy of Sciences, who was assisted by Julia Zubok, a Research Associate and a doctoral candidate in Sociology. We also co-operated with other scholarly institutions and social scientists in Moscow, St. Petersburg and other cities of Russia. Our work addresses many aspects of the social status and development of youth, in particular the prospects of young people's integration into the new Russian society of the 1990s.[2]

Stages in youth transition

As Coles argues it is possible to interpret changes in the position of youth in terms of a series of transitions:

(i)   from school to work;
(ii)   from childhood to adulthood and
(iii)   from dependency (upon parents and family) to independence.[3]

By and large, we shall only deal with the first of these three processes here by focusing on several spheres: work, education, social mobility and social communication.

However, we shall also touch of the third aspect of transition when we discuss the material position of Russian youth today.

It is also important to appreciate that on top of the three aforementioned types of transition, there is a fourth one in Russia's case, namely that she is undergoing a total transformation of her economic and political systems as well as her society. Young people in Russia, like society as a whole, are undergoing a crisis of values. However, it will take a long time before their old communist values are eliminated and replaced by ones based on the principles of liberal democracy. The fact that young people are highly disillusioned with the past and present, pessimistic about the future[4] and so in essence have lost their vital reference point, is likely to have an impact firstly upon Russia's chance of making a successful transition from communism to liberal democracy and secondly upon developments on a more global scale. The preliminary results of some of our research, which combines an analysis of Russian statistical data and sociological surveys with interviews among young Russian workers, peasants, white-collar employees, academics, businessmen, students and school pupils throughout 12 regions of the Russian Federation, show what the end of Communism and the transition to a new type of society has meant for young people. This chapter deals with youth and work, education, social mobility and social communication while the following chapter by Sharonov and Ruchkin deals with the socio-political attitudes of and anti-social tendencies among Russian youth in the 1990s.

The importance of youth

Young people will be an essential element in the rebuilding of Russian society. Their active participation in this process is vital. If they are excluded, our transition will be incomplete and only partial transformation will be possible. However, if young people are made part of the transition, have a say in it and are sufficiently motivated to participate - by no means an easy task as Sharonov and Ruchkin demonstrate in chapter 9 - then Russian youth has a greater chance of becoming integrated into society and Russia in turn is more likely, *inter alia*, to make a successful transition.

The most significant change brought about by the collapse of communism is in the economic situation of youth. Today young people have greater freedom and more choice. But despite this, the real possibility of them finding a job are slim. This stems from the process of economic restructuring - the closure of factories etc. - but the transition to the market, as we shall see in greater depth in chapter 12, has led to a total rethink on the part of youth regarding their future career - former very prestigious jobs are now less well thought of because they are poorly paid. Employment in the state sector is now severely limited, instead young people are moving into the business and commercial sector. Unfortunately for the large majority of young people their material position has worsened and their standard of living has declined dramatically. These trends are having a negative impact on the social structure in so far as tension among youth is a reflection of widespread class conflict among different groups in contemporary Russian society. Our surveys between 1990-92 and 1992-94 show that the changes that have taken place under and after communism are making themselves felt among the younger generation.

Rejecting old and building new value systems

As one might expect, some of the former ideological beliefs have been rejected in more recent years. These include collectivism, respect for individuals and human life, duty to society etc. They have been replaced by a youth culture oriented towards capitalism and a consumer society based upon materialist values. The transition to the market over the last decade has had different influences upon different types of youth activities. We shall now consider a few examples.

Attitudes towards work

Nearly one-third (32.5 per cent) of our 1994 sample considered work as the only means to achieve other goals. This compared with 27.5 per cent in 1990. For 4.4 per cent work is essential. We discovered that two-thirds of young people worked in state structures, but over the last few years there had been a gradual decline in youth employment in the state sector. However, there has been a considerable increase in the number of youth opportunities in the private sector during the same period. In 1994, as a consequence, one in five young people work and one in ten earn extra money by being employed in co-operatives or joint-stock companies. This group made up 27.5 per cent of those surveyed in 1994, compared to less than 5 per cent who were working in the private sector among our (1990) sample. Fewer young people want to work in the state sector in the future - there has been a two-fold decrease overall between 1990-94.

Career prospects

As regards career prospects, 37.7 per cent of young people want to set up their own private business, 35.1 per cent to work for foreign companies, 26.2 per cent to be employed in joint-ventures and 17.8 per cent to work in privately owned companies in 1994. Many young people in Russia have been quick to adapt to the new climate by adopting capitalist values (see chapter 13 for a more detailed discussion).

Education and training opportunities

This issue shall be discussed in greater detail in chapter 13, so suffice it to say here that the ability of young people to grasp the opportunities open to them has very much depended upon their *level of qualifications*. In 1990, only one in three (28.4 per cent) young people worked in areas related to their specialism, however by 1994, this figure had increased to one in two (51.5 per cent). The prospect of better opportunities and job satisfaction has prompted many young people to seek higher qualifications: in 1990, 30.5 per cent valued qualifications but four years later this number had increased slightly to 34 per cent. The ability to achieve higher qualifications was very much dependent upon educational facilities and training opportunities. But occupational training is rapidly shrinking. Thus our 1990 sample was adversely affected by the fact that between 1985-90, those graduating from vocational schools and other training institutions fell from one million to 335,000 or by 64.5 per cent. At the same time, the number of university and college graduates fell by 75,900.

Of those with qualifications, not all young people were fortunate enough to be employed in jobs directly related to their specialisms. More than 50 per cent of young workers and specialists between 1990-94 had jobs that required lower or different skills. Even though more and more young people in Russia have pride in their profession (17.9 per cent in 1990 as against 22.5 per cent in 1994), fewer are getting job satisfaction. Thus in 1994, we found that 30.5 per cent of our sample of 2,612 were indifferent to their work and 5.6 per cent were reluctant to talk about work to their closest friends and family. There is not a single European country that is characterised by such low youth occupational status.

Despite this situation, many young people (31.4 per cent) in 1994 were in no hurry to change their profession. Titles remain important in a time of great uncertainty. Nevertheless, although young people in post-communist Russia want to improve their chances of getting a better job via higher qualifications, 31.2 per cent fewer in 1994 over 1990 had the possibility of doing so. Furthermore, over this four year period, only 25 per cent of Russian young people linked education to social advancement and only 10 per cent linked education to a career. Less than 15 per cent would like to continue education after school or undertake vocational training. The exception here were young people from provincial towns because good grades at school gave them the opportunity to go to university and college, thereby facilitating their move to the big cities.

Better pay and promotion

As for other goals associated with work - 45.4 per cent wanted a higher salary, 48.2 per cent promotion and 51 per cent employment in the business sector in 1994. Older work values are therefore gradually being replaced by newer capitalist ones. But there is one glimmer of hope: whereas in 1990, wages were young people's highest priority in relation to work, by 1994, they have begun to give greater priority to good working relations with their employer, on the one hand, and protection against dismissal, on the other. On the whole, our survey data suggest that the majority of young people (80 per cent) remain upwardly mobile until the age of 30 years.

Management opportunities

By 1992, 2.8 per cent of young people occupied managerial positions. The large majority of these were shop floor managers, brigade leaders or shop managers. Half of the young people we surveyed between 1990-94 said they had no opportunity to influence decision-making. More specifically only 10 per cent participated in decisions regarding bonus distribution, 3.6 per cent in debates concerning housing, 3 per cent in discussions on the distribution of vacancies in kindergardens and 3.8 per cent in talks about openings in sanatoria and rest homes. Of these groups, only 22 per cent felt their opinion had any impact. New blood needs to be introduced in Russian management in a practical as well as theoretical sense (in the teaching of management courses) in order for the rejuvenation of our management skills and knowledge to take place and for old values to be rejected. But this is not yet happening. Unless this occurs soon the consequences may be detrimental to Russian youth in general as well as the nation as a whole.

Although more young people believed that they had a greater influence in their primary work groups (75.9 per cent believed this to be the case in 1990), our research shows that the alienation of Russian youth from the institutions of power has been occurring for sometime but its full effects are being felt in the 1990s. This reluctance to let young people into the corridors of power stems from suspicion about youth in the minds of adult policy and decision-makers and from Russia's tendency in the past to be a gerontocracy. This approach is having a negative impact because such exclusion in later life turns into accusations of there being 'no justice at the top' and also a feeling that 'the authorities cannot be trusted'.

Youth unemployment

Above we talked about those in work, but there are an estimated one million young people in Russia today (3.5 per cent) who neither work or study. One-third of this total may be referred to as the unemployed. This issue will be addressed in greater depth in chapter 11.

Labour productivity

As far as the economy is concerned, labour productivity of the young is significantly lower than that of other age groups. This is concomitant with their low salaries, as we shall now see.

Incomes

On average, young people's wages in Russia rose by 9 per cent in 1990 and 13.4 per cent in 1994. In both cases this was well below the rate of inflation. Even in so-called middle-income groups (50-100,000 roubles), which made up 33.9 per cent of the population, many still lived below the poverty line. In overall terms, 82.4 per cent of young people today have an income below the poverty line or just equivalent to the minimum wage. Concern about declining standards of living showed up time and time again in our surveys: For instance, 11.2 per cent of our 1994 sample stated that their incomes were too low to feed and clothe them and 65 per cent said they were totally dissatisfied with their present condition. Mirroring trends among adults, there is also a growing disparity between 'rich' and 'poor' young people. By comparison to the previous situation, those young people in the high income group, that is those able to buy everything they needed except an apartment or cottage, increased by 10 per cent between 1990-94. Finally, we have also begun to witness the emergence of a small, but fast-growing group of rich young people (0.5 per cent), who have everything.

Dependency upon family

The number of young people reliant on parental support has increased from 81 per cent in 1990 to 88 per cent in 1994. Today fewer young people prefer other ways of solving their financial difficulties. For example, while 39 per cent planned to change to a better paid job to solve their problems in 1990, only 24.3 per cent planned to do so in 1994. The same goes for earning extra money. In 1990, 30 per cent adopted this tactic, compared to only 13.6 per cent in 1994. Although these trends might have something to do with the self-motivation of young people over time, a more plausible explanation is the deteriorating economic situation in Russia today: thus whereas 24.5 per cent of our 1990 sample anticipated a wage increase, only 13 per cent of our 1994 respondents' thought this likely. To try and alleviate the financial pressures, young people are searching for new methods: in 1994, for instance, 14.2 per cent planned to become involved in business, 7.6 per cent wanted to go abroad and 4.7 per cent said they would get involved in strike activity. The most alarming tendency, but a completely understandable one, is that there has been a 40 per cent increase between 1990-94 in the proportion of young people surveyed willing to engage in illegal activity to solve money and other worries. All in all, 62.6 per cent by 1994 argued that nowadays there was no such thing as 'honest' and 'dishonest' ways of earning money, just 'easy' or 'difficult' ways of making money. Nevertheless around about half (51.2 per cent) said they were unwilling to get involved in business and in overall terms, business and commerce occupy eighth place in comparison to their contemporaries. Our findings suggest that the primary reasons are the lack of opportunity (only 19.2 per cent thought a job in business was a possibility) and the fact that some young people are psychologically unprepared for such a role at present. We also found that some youngsters who have worked in businesses, subsequently became disillusioned. Thus if in 1990, a job in business and commerce was the main motive for one in two young people, by 1994 only one in three (35.5 per cent) had the same goal. Less and less people are willing to gamble and take chances: in 1994, only 26.5 per cent were willing to change and take risks, that is 11.3 per cent lower than in 1990. In conditions of economic and political instability, 50 per cent of young people prefer the status-quo.

Youth consumption patterns, 1990-94

The consumer orientation of young people has changed very little. The first four places are occupied by the need to improve living conditions, obtain clothing, food and other essential items. Only the possibility of solving such difficulties was rated lower in 1994 than 1990. The purchase of consumer durables (furniture, a fridge, a TV) as well as buying a car and building a dacha have slid to last place in the hierarchy of youth material needs because of their unavailability. Growing dissatisfaction with levels of consumption has started to have an adverse effect in youth circles as shown by the emergence of 'subcultural violence' (*subkul'tury nasiliia*). In a context in which our power structures are corrupt, young people quickly become accustomed to the type of behaviour practised by yuppies, prestige groups and young people in high places in society. Sadly in seeking to emulate the behaviour of these 'new Russians' many young people are turning to crime. Deviant behaviour is now seen as the alternative to honest work when trying to achieve prosperity in Russia today. Until this situation is reversed, Russian society will not emerge from its crisis.

Education

In this area significant changes have taken place. Knowledge is still viewed as important by 33.9 per cent of Russian youth. The number of young people who considered knowledge exclusively as a means of reaching certain goals has risen slightly from 38.9 per cent in 1990 to 44.1 per cent in 1994. However, the proportion of young people dissatisfied with their education remained unchanged at around a third (32.9 per cent) throughout the same period. Similarly those eager to improve their education level has also remained constant at 14.7 per cent between 1990-94. The value of an elite education has however increased while more mass forms of training are declining in importance. Education abroad and paid forms of training have moved up to first place in 1994, whereas there is now less emphasis on technical education (down from 9.8 per cent in 1990 to 4.7 per cent in 1994) and on economics (10.1 per cent to 4 per cent over the same period). Part of the reason for this is the declining state of Russia's education system, but the primary reason is the fact that education was free in 1990 but fee-paying by 1994. In overall terms, there is less interest in technical subjects (down by 37.6 per cent in the last four years), social studies (down from 40.5 per cent in 1990 to 29.2 per cent in 1994), literature, music and the arts (from 66.4 per cent to 52.5 per cent), but a greater stress on business studies (36.7 per cent to 53 per cent) and agricultural subjects (19.6 per cent to 24.6 per cent). Interest in physics, mathematics, dentistry, biology and medicine as professions remains largely unchanged. Since the collapse of communism, technical studies, which occupied first place as far as prestige was concerned in 1990, have now been overtaken by business, economics and computer science. Although this is largely the consequence of the transition, the continuing chaos in education is exacerbating matters. Our education system, as chapter 13 shows, is in urgent need of reform.

Social communication

Here we are concerned with evaluating the factors promoting and/or preventing social maturity. The usual indicators here are age on receiving a passport, finishing school, earning your first wage etc. Of all of these variables, young people in Russia rate wages (up from 6.4 per cent in 1990 to 16 per cent in 1994), a permanent job (from 8.1 per cent to 24.8 per cent) and starting their own family (up from 7.7 per cent in 1990 to 14.9 per cent by 1994) as the most important measurements of maturity. In terms of Coles' schema, jobs and economic independence are crucial factors signalling the tradition from teenage years to adulthood. However, the transition to market conditions has complicated matters in comparison to the past. Whereas under communism, students were paid grants to study and then went on to get jobs, nowadays they have to work and study at the same time as one activity helps to finance the other. This is causing confusion and conflicts about what roles young people should perform in society - student or wage earner?

The introduction of the market is also forcing Russian youth to reconsider its relationship to others - in 1990, for instance, their duty to society was primary, but by 1994, they were thinking more about themselves and their material needs. Over the same four year period, work has virtually replaced friends and family as the driving force in young people's lives. However, Russian youth still values the need to be cultured, on the one hand, and to be able to communicate with others, on the other. These factors alongside a good upbringing, high qualifications, being good at one's profession, having a good salary, being in excellent health and finally being viewed as honest, hard working and reliable were all rated highly by young people, especially in relation to one's capacity to perform any task to high standards.

Attitudes towards the family

Greater emphasis on spiritual closeness, rights and personal security are becoming increasingly common today as is the depoliticisation of youth in contemporary Russia. Interest in politics has fallen from third place in young people's hierarchy of values in 1990 to eleventh by 1994. By contrast, whereas in 1990, the first three places in the same hierarchy were occupied by brother and sister, mother and spouse or partner, by 1994 the situation had changed. Although in general, the large majority of young people identify with their parents and family (66 per cent), want to keep their lives private (80.1 per cent) and to a lesser extent rely on friends and peer groups, young people's relationship to their family was showing signs of strain. Thus 72.3 per cent of our 1990 sample said their parents were 'good' but only 54.3 per cent declared the same in 1994. Parents are now accused of not understanding their children and many young people also stated that their parents were far too 'conservative' in their views. This is part of an overall decline in the family over the last decade.

Such tension is also making itself felt in young families. In 1990, for example, 27.6 per cent of young couples were satisfied with their marriages, but four years later this figure had fallen to 20 per cent. The number who thought that a split was inevitable had doubled. Dissatisfaction about the future has also manifest itself in debates surrounding family planning.[5] By 1994, the number of young couples wishing to have three children had halved (to 8.8 per cent) and those who planned to have two children had declined one and a half times to 50.7 per cent of those surveyed.

Lack of interest in politics

We mentioned earlier that young people in Russia today are indifferent to all forms of socio-political activity. When we interviewed many young people we discovered that:

(i)   72.1 per cent said that there was no point in turning to deputies (in the parliament) because they are not at all interested in the problems of the Russian people;
(ii)   73.2 per cent declared that today everything in life has become worthless;
(iii)   78.2 per cent felt that there was no possibility for 'people like me' to influence the actions of government; and finally,
(iv)   79.9 per cent noted how Russian politicians today only thought about lining their own pockets.

The majority of young people in Russia believe that the responsibility for carrying out the reforms lies with the President. If in April 1993, 54 per cent supported Yeltsin and 46.1 per cent his socio-economic policies, then by late 1994, only 26.7 per cent planned to vote for him and only 26.4 per cent to support his reforms. This might have implications in the forthcoming 1995-96 elections. Young people constitute a large proportion of those disillusioned with politics. Changes in the political orientation of young people in Russia are documented in table 8.1 below:

Table 8.1
Social and political attitudes of young people in Russia,
1990-94 (median of a 6 to 9 point scale)

Support for	1990		1994	
	a	b	a	c
Strong leader	1	7.45	2	5.83
'Every man for himself'	2	6.80	5	5.43
Free enterprise	3	6.70	3	5.70
Strong state	4	5.42	4	5.53
Traditional democratic principles	5	6.25	1	5.91
National patriotism	6	6.21	-	-
'Closed society'	7-8	5.69	7	5.15
Sovereignty	7-8	9.69	8	4.84
Parliamentary Republic	9	5.64	6	5.19
Communism (of conversative variety)	10	4.64	9	4.61
Radical and democratic ideas	11	2.83	10	4.08

Key:
a   ranking
b   ranked on a 9 point scale
c   ranked on a 7 point scale

Source: 'Social development of youth surveys', Russia 1990-94.

It is evident that young people see a strong leader as essential to solve all the difficulties facing Russia today. At the same time however, support for democratic principles has climbed from fifth to first place, although the notion of this entailing a parliamentary system of government has declined from sixth place in 1990 to ninth place by 1994. All in all, although a belief in communism remains low, the same situation applies to radical and democratic ideas which occupy last place. It is difficult to predict which will eventually win out.

Although it is true to say that the number of young people represented in various democratically elected institutions is higher than in management positions, the proportion of Russian youth elected to the former is declining: for example, in 1990, 40.7 per cent of young people surveyed were members of various elected bodies, but two years later this total had declined by 40 per cent. Part of the explanation for this lies with the collapse of the largely discredited Komsomol which has not been replaced by any other 'affirmative action' for youngsters.[6] Fewer and fewer young people are taking an interest in current affairs, as the results from our surveys of Voronezh in 1990-92 in table 8.2 below demonstrate:

Table 8.2
Changing attitude of current events among Voronezh youth,
1990-92 (in per cent)

How much do you follow current events?:	1990	1992
Closely	20.5	13.8
Superficially	49.1	44.6
Sporadically	11.2	17.7
Not at all	7.4	14.3
Hard to say	11.8	9.6

Source: 'Social development of youth surveys', Russia 1990-94.

As a consequence, by 1994, only 16.7 per cent of Russian youth affiliated themselves with a particular political party and only 6.3 per cent belonged to the so-called informal groups (*neformal'nye*).

Over the last four years then we have seen the growing alienation of youth, greater anarchy in the country as a whole and a growing tendency towards authoritarianism in the senior echelons of the Russian power structure.

Social mobility[7]

The social mobility of Russian youth is being adversely affected by the acute crisis in Russian society which is changing their social status and position in the social structure. More and more young people are living below the poverty line as real incomes fall and prices sky-rocket. However, there are marked differences in the scale of differentiation in youth living standards according to region. Our research demonstrates that the living standards of youth are considerably higher in the capital and regional centres of the Russian Federation than in remote, peripheral, rural areas. Furthermore, the proportion of those who can be described as 'well off' is higher among young intelligentsia and students who receive substantial financial assistance from their families in comparison to young people from poorer working-class and peasant backgrounds. Of this group, most find their situation normal and regard it as acceptable. This probably reflects underdevelopment or flaws in the education system/socialisation process. For decades under communism, young people had been educated in the spirit of self denial, unpaid labour, scorn of materialism and the priority of societal interests over individual needs. This system of values rejected competition - as it was a Western bourgeois concept - as a stimulant for development. As a result, nowadays many, though not all, young people regard competing for success too much of a burden. Despite the fact that only one in ten young people view their situation as worse than that of others, they do not think they are poor because everyone else is in the same boat. Although at present the downward mobility of youth is unlikely to act as a catalyst for change, current trends suggest that this is only a temporary respite because the increasing gap between rich and poor, documented above and in chapters 6 and 7, is certain to breed discontent among young people in the not too distant future. On top of these difficulties in climbing up the status ladder, there are also as we saw earlier inequalities in educational and job opportunities according to social group. Those coming from proletarian backgrounds are worse off than offspring of the professional classes. But this is not just a class issue. For many young bright men and women in Russia today access to higher education is also limited by the shortage of places in dormitories, incompatibility of school and university programmes, bribery and other forms of corruption. Our surveys between 1990-94 show that 40.6 per cent of Russian youth feel that education should be universal and free, with only 26.5 per cent accepting partial fees and 17.4 per cent recognising the legitimacy of paying for education in the new Russia.

All in all, our research shows that most young people want a strong hand at the helm. Like society in general, young people are tired of lawlessness, unfounded populism, unchecked chaos and the false promises of former communists turned democrats. The large majority of young people in Russia today have no faith in a corrupt leadership which, led by Yeltsin, seems incapable of leading the country out of the crisis. Despite the fact that transition has proved to be a painful process for Russian youth,[8] the overwhelming majority have thus far towed the conformist line. But among a small minority, their anomie has expressed itself in deviant behaviour - involvement in anti-social activity, conflict with the law, rising youth crime etc.[9] These issues will be dealt with in chapters 9 and 14.

Integration into society or not?

As we saw above, the position of young people in Russia is a precarious one. Thus the number of low income students has increased from 9 per cent in 1990 to 19 per cent of those surveyed by 1994, with half of all students having an average per-capita income of 50,000 roubles per month to live on. 80.6 per cent of students in Russia today do not receive any grants. Of this group 66.2 per cent receive help from their parents on a regular and 20.2 per cent on a periodical basis. All in all one in three students cannot make ends meet. Despite their plight, students are passive and unwilling to defend their rights. Our surveys show that by 1994, 79.2 per cent of students would be unwilling to engage in strike activity or other acts of civil disobedience. Thus despite the disintegration of Russian society, Russian youth is still being conformist. But is conformist the right word? In our opinion, pragmatic is a more accurate term because apathy, pessimism and a tendency to dwell on their own problems are the main characteristics of young people's behaviour in the New Russia of the 1990s.

The danger of disintegration

Clearly the fact that young people in Russia today are showing little interest in the process of political democratisation and the transition to a market economy is a major area of concern to youth workers, politicians and the Yeltsin government. However, the present situation cannot be resolved by resorting to repressive methods. It is no use continuing to see youth as a social problem for society.[9] It is time for the government to restore young people's faith in their ability to put Russia back on the road to progress. Although the future looks bleak in relation to economic recovery and political stability, there is nevertheless room for optimism. The main reason for this is that a third of all young people we surveyed between 1990-94 still believed in mankind. In addition, 41 per cent thought globally when looking at specific problems and seeking ways and means of solving them. True 14-18 year olds are more flexible in their thinking than those older than 18 years because the latter came under the influence of the Cold War. But at a time when nationalism is rearing its ugly head, it is encouraging to discover that many young people recognise the need for the consolidation of progressive forces inside Russia and desire the integration of Russia, and its young people, into the new world order. However, the tendency to think globally or more in one's own national interest varies according to the ethnic status of youth. Generally speaking, we found that in the conditions of instability generated by the transition to new political and economic systems, a sense of identity with one's ethnic community contributed to a feeling of individual security in the face of external dangers - the break-up of the USSR and the rise of newly independent states, on the one hand, and possible threat from the West, on the other. The highest degree of ethnic status development occurred among youth in Tatarstan whereas the status of dispersed ethnic groups - for example, Ukrainian youth living in Russia - was much lower. On the whole, however, Russian youth tended to identify itself with the multi-ethnic population of the Russian Federation rather than with fellow Russians.

The position of rural youth[10]

Above we dealt with the position of urban youth. But how has the collapse of communism and the transition to the market economy affected young people in rural areas? Nowadays, in capitals, key regions, cities and districts as well as major rural areas, 60-80 per cent of young people are businessmen. However, when we turn to consider the position of rural youth we find it is in a far more precarious situation. Of the more than 30 per cent of the rural population capable of working, only 7 per cent of rural youth is actually working, largely on farms. But this percentage is falling year by year. For instance, in the period 1990-93, it fell by half. The large majority of young people living in the countryside have either joined the rural exodus to the towns or drifted away from the farms into the service sector - 40-60 per cent were employed in this way by 1994. Others are gainfully employed in private enterprises. Part of the problem has been providing rural youth with the necessary training to meet the demands of the market.

Between 1991-93, we carried out research with the assistance of V. Staroverov and I.V. Popov among rural youth. We interviewed 663 young experts as well as 252 senior and 332 junior school and college students. Finally, we interviewed 164 students from Kostoma pedagogical Institute. Of this number, 247 were from rural areas. We discovered that rural youth, like its urban counterparts, possessed firm beliefs in individualism (and above all 'self'), the value of good health, a successful marriage, independence etc. Notions of 'collectivism' and 'comradeship' have long since been abandoned. Thus only 3.6 per cent replied that they worked hard for society as opposed to 34.6 per cent who said they did it for personal rewards. In order to maximise the latter, 26.1 per cent of our respondents said you needed a 'good head for business'. Rural youth said they were willing to be flexible, hard-working and resourceful in order to avoid the threat of unemployment. 42.8 per cent of our interviewees argued that 'ability to adapt' was essential in order to survive and 23.8 per cent declared that these were the qualities necessary for a 'good career'. Our findings indicate that rural youth were quickly adapting themselves to the new market conditions. A third of junior school students said that they intended to get jobs which guaranteed high incomes whereas nearly two-thirds of senior students wanted a career in commerce. As for desired goals, our research revealed the following results: 22.1 per cent wanted 'to live in comfort' (31 per cent of men and 18.1 per cent of women); 38 per cent 'satisfactory pay' (51.7 per cent of men and 30.9 per cent of women) and finally 33.3 per cent 'enough to live on and not to want for anything' (37.9 per cent of men and 30.9 per cent of women).

We then went on to investigate rural youth's attitudes towards a range of issues. Our findings are presented in table 8.3 below. It is clear that a large proportion of young people believe their peers have no interest in politics - 33.7 per cent - or are prejudiced towards other nationalities - 31.3 per cent. Nevertheless, despite today's difficulties, 48.2 per cent of those surveyed still have a strong desire to study. Part of the problem, as young people see it, was their supposed love of drink - 54.8 per cent or drugs - 17.5 per cent. Perhaps in order to survive, 32 per cent of our sample thought that many young people resorted to prostitution. In line with the introduction of the market, 43.4 per cent had strong materialistic values. Finally, 58.4 per cent of young people thought their peers were rude or violent to others. As for their future careers, 19.3 per cent wanted a job with law firms, 47.6 per cent other profession, 65 per cent to enter the army and 5.4 per cent to pursue a career in religion. On the question of young persons' attitudes towards other nationalities over a third were hostile - 34.8 per cent - and a further 30.8 per cent said other nationalities simply caused trouble. Furthermore 40.3 per cent said they were willing to participate in any international conflicts should they arise. Finally, we found that 90 per cent of our sample of rural inhabitants were relying upon their families for financial support. They were most fearful about hunger, crime and unemployment. Most saw their future in the big city, only 8.7 per cent of those surveyed intended to stay in the countryside and engage in agricultural related activities.

On the whole, rural youth are the victims of the demise of Russian agriculture. The reforms undertaken over the last decade have ripped the heart out of the Russian village. The rural exodus has hindered matters further because the brain drain has largely involved the most talented young inhabitants.

Table 8.3
**Answers to the question 'To what extent, in your opinion, are
these phenomena widespread among rural youth?'
1990-94 (in per cent)**

'To what extent, in your opinion, are these phenomena widespread among rural youth?'	a	b	c
Lack of interest in politics	33.7	53.0	13.3
Prejudice towards other nationalities	31.3	54.2	14.5
Desire to study	48.2	44.5	7.2
Weakness for alcohol	54.8	37.3	11.4
Prostitution	32.0	53.6	14.4
Materialistic	43.4	45.2	11.4
Take drugs	17.5	53.0	29.5
Violence, rudeness	58.4	36.1	5.5

Key:

a   Widespread
b   Less widespread
c   Not widespread

Source: 'Social development of youth surveys', Russia 1990-94.

Conclusion

Russian youth is increasingly susceptible to the pressures of the transition period. Its resources for survival are presently being used to the full. Although today's youth is more capable, more individualistic and more enterprising than their parents, the pressures of the market might nevertheless be too strong for numerous young people. There is a danger, therefore, that a proportion of the young will reject the world of market relations. Assuming that we want such a transition to take place, then a new, innovative youth policy and a new vision of youth in the society of the future is required. In this respect, Coles' policy recommendations, such as a Ministry for Youth and the development of a Charter for Young People's Rights, might prove to be a useful starting point.[11] As Riordan, Williams and Ilynsky point out, though, there is still a long way to go before this happens.[12]   Nevertheless, our research indicates that there are considerable integration processes already at work. These may be grouped into the following categories: normative, cultural, communicative and functional.

The *normative aspects of integration* are determined by the degree of institutionalisation of modern norms in youth relations. These are already signs of this in Russian youth's support for democratisation and the broadening of rights and freedoms throughout the Russian Federation. Although young people are in favour of democracy, it is not yet a norm in Russia and events since 1993 indicate that it might be gradually giving way to new totalitarian tendencies.

The *cultural aspects* reflect emerging tendencies towards strengthening the level of co-ordination between standards and behaviour patterns, mostly with regard to youth subculture.[13] Integration tendencies are also evident in the spheres of music, leisure and youth fashion. This is partly the outcome of the strengthening and dissemination of Western mass culture patterns among Russian youth. Western ways of life as well as behaviour, work, consumption patterns and communicative norms are becoming more marked.

The *communicative* basis of integration is characterised by a variety of social ties, information exchanges and widening contacts among the young. In this respect, international networking is playing an increasingly important role.

Finally, there is the *functional aspect* of youth integration in contemporary Russia. This reflects the role, or lack of it, which young people play in the organised activity of the state, public and youth structures, including international ones.

It is too early to tell as yet whether the integration forces will outweigh the disintegration ones, but if the latter forces gain the upper hand this will have profound implications for Russia society and its transition to democracy in 1996 and beyond.

Notes

1. See V.I. Chuprov, *Sotsial'noe razvitie molodezhi: teoreticheskie i prikladnye problemy,* Moscow Izd. instituta molodezhi 'Sotsium', 1994, pp. 21-47.

2. On this point see V.I. Chuprov, 'Molodezh' Rossii: kharakteristika integratsionnykh protsessov', in I.I. Il'inskii et al., (eds.), *Tsennostnyi mir sovremennoi molodezhi: na puti k mirovoi integratsii,* Moscow 1994, pp. 33-41. Professor Vladimir Chuprov, Julia Zubok and Christopher Williams have embarked upon a Nuffield Foundation sponsored project on *Russian youth in transition, 1990-96.* The goal is to examine the following issues: the nature of the Communist legacy; youth and the market; the plight of rural youth; educational inequalities and the rise of a new youth elite; the process of youth marginalisation; youth attitudes towards political institutions, leaders and the key political parties; youth values concerning the role of the individual, human life; religion, culture, money and wealth, family, nation etc.; youth people's attitudes concerning outside help for Russia, the European Union; European integration and so forth and finally ways and means of resolving the problems of transition and their negative impact on the position of Russian youth in the post-communist phase. The results of our research will be completed in late 1996 and published in 1997.

3. Bob Coles, *Youth and Social policy: Youth citizenship and youth careers,* University College London Press, London 1995, p. 8.

4. On these general issues see I.I. Il'inskii et al. (eds.), *Tsennostnyi mir sovremennoi molodezhi: na puti k mirovoi integratsii,* Moscow 1994, as well as J. Riordan, C. Williams and I. Ilynsky (eds.), *Young people in post-communist Russia and Eastern Europe,* Dartmouth, Aldershot 1995.

5.   On this see chapter 3 as well as C. Williams, 'Abortion and women's health in contemporary Russia' in R. Marsh (ed.), *Women in Russia and the Ukraine,* Cambridge University Press, 1996.

6.   For a more detailed discussion here see J. Riordan, 'The Rise and Fall of a Youth Elite in Russia', in Riordan et al., 1995 op cit., pp. 81-95.

7.   The authors would like to acknowledge the help of Michael Fedorovich Chernish, co-author with Vladimir Chuprov of *Motivatsionnaia sfera sozdaniia molodezhi: Sostoianie i tendentsii razvitiia,* Moscow, Institut molodezhi/Institut sotsial'no-politicheskikh issledovanii, 1993, for his assistance with this part of our work.

8.   See Ilinskii 1994 op cit.; Riordan et al. 1995 op cit., as well as Deborah Adelman's two volume work: *The 'Children of Perestroika: Moscow teenagers talk about their lives and future,* M.E. Sharpe, New York 1991, and her *The 'Children of Perestroika' Come of Age: Young people of Moscow talk about life in the New Russia,* M.E. Sharpe, New York 1994.

9.   For a useful overview here see C. Williams, "Respectable fears' versus 'Moral panics': Youth as a social problem in Russia and Britain', in Riordan et al. 1995 ibid, pp. 29-50.

10.   This section draws on the work of our colleague Professor Vladimir Staroverov.

11.   See Appendix in Cole 1995 op cit., pp. 211-218.

12.   Riordan et al. 1995 op cit.

13.   On this see H. Pilkington, *Russian youth and its culture: A Nation's constructors and constructed,* London, Routledge 1994, especially Parts II and III.

9 Young people, politics and youth policy

ANDREI SHARONOV* AND BORIS RUCHKIN

Introduction

On 28 April 1994 an Agreement on Social Harmony (*Dogovor ob obshchestvennom soglasii*) was signed at the Kremlin by 245 out of 248 members of the Russian Federal Assembly. Following this, approximately 1,000 parties, social groups, organisations, trade unions and the heads of all regions added their support. Boris Yeltsin responded in a Presidential press conference by concluding that: 'it is not just some agreement signed by those in power, it is part of the new social climate which is developing in our country'.[1] But politics can only be politics when millions of people are included in the process. In politics anything less than this does not count. This is why the agreement of political parties and groups, although significant in itself, does not automatically guarantee the support of the entire population. The process of polarisation of society has become ingrained. The main problems and the foundations of serious political difficulties and crises in the state will continue for at least the time being. The resolution of these problems requires a realistic and concrete approach to the analysis of reality, life and the plight of the people, well beyond mere statistics. Such a process must include youth as a major social force. Russian youth will be crucial to the building of Russia's future. This chapter addresses two key questions: firstly, to what extent are young people in Russia today likely to support such an agreement? and secondly, if not, what are the consequences likely to be for young people in general and Russia's future in particular? Historical experience has shown that reconciliation of national interests and the rejection of violence indicates the presence of certain values and ideals concerning human nature.[2] This leads us nicely onto a series of other related questions namely: who will lead youth and what values will hold its attention?

Youth and social harmony

Russian youth, it must be stated at the outset, is not a unified force which can simultaneously halt or change the process of current socio-economic and political reforms. How on earth can young businessmen, employees, military personnel, school-children, students, Cossacks and so on act as one? They are too diverse to be able to act in a united way. In any case, *each category of youth will judge for themselves the degree of fairness or injustice of the existing system.* This is as much true of the capital as the provinces, of the city as well as the countryside.

The extent to which harmony will be achieved to a large extent depends upon the current social and economic situation. However, present predictions are rather bleak. In relation to Russian youth a recent report concluded that each and every generation of young people is worse off than the previous generation in terms of health, intellectual and spiritual development and so on.[3] With the exception of young businessmen all quality of life indicators are negative. Although there are marked variations according to region, thus inhabitants of large cities, such as Moscow, St. Petersburg and Ekaterinburg, believe that their health status is better than that of their counterparts living in small to medium sized towns or villages, it was nevertheless still the case that 45 per cent of young people surveyed in 1994 said that they did not think their lives would improve over the next two years.

The need to adapt to market conditions

Our analyses show that a considerable number of young people are progressively adapting to market conditions by using a variety of supplementary sources of income. The barely adequate economic situation in the country is affecting their standard of living. Thus the number of young people receiving minimum incomes increased 250 per cent among workers and 420 per cent among university and technical university students between 1990-94. Not surprisingly only 50 per cent of young people consider their economic situation as 'good'. As a rule, though, youth perceptions of the future are negative and pessimistic: 29 per cent of 15-22 year olds consider the current situation 'worrying'; 47 per cent argue we are in 'crisis'; 17 per cent state that the current position is catastrophic and only 6 per cent consider it to be normal. The corresponding figures for 22-29 year olds are: 24 per cent; 38 per cent; 29 per cent and 4 per cent respectively. In other words, young people in post-communist Russia worry above all about problems of concern to everyone, not just themselves.

The primary concerns of today's youth are crime (45 per cent), poverty (36 per cent), rising unemployment (29 per cent), the collapse of Russia (18 per cent) and the possibility of the outbreak of civil war, not only in Chechnya but in other regions too (24 per cent). These factors are all influential in determining whether or not young people will support the harmony agreement. However, whilst the input of young people's ideas as part of this process of reform and transformation must not be forgotten, ultimately it is the character of our social and economic policies and the nature of our power structures which will be the decisive factors at all levels - local, regional and national.

Changing the direction of social and youth policy

Our current social policy needs to be revised in order to take into account the general needs of youth as well as the desires of different social and age groups. On the whole, though, social policy geared towards youth needs to be reoriented in another direction. This new framework should include the following elements.

Greater social support for the needy sections of the younger generation

Lets consider an example. There are 200,000 homeless, 200,000 deaf and 13,000 blind children in Russia. Under communism, they were given protection and certain guarantees. But since 1991, egalitarianism has been replaced by the dictat of the market which determines the allocation of resources. Nowadays it is profit versus need and the former wins virtually every time. As a result, homeless, deaf and blind children and their parents constantly fight for survival. Such vulnerable groups in society need protection from the harsh realities of the market.

Encouraging the more able sections of the young generation

Here those able to survive and encourage others under the new conditions need all the support they can get. Our surveys show that 22 per cent of young people actually work in enterprises but 47 per cent are willing to do so. The difference of 25 per cent needs to be eradicated by providing young people with appropriate support to achieve their goals in life. This is especially true of those young businessmen under 35 years. At the moment they are junior or middle-level managers - 41 per cent are employed in small businesses and 42 per cent in medium sized ones - but to make it to the next rung up, they need help - training, education, promotion prospects etc. which currently don't exist. One of the priorities of labour policy must be the creation of the necessary legal and economic conditions for these changes to take place (see chapter 11). In addition, innovation and a greater role in policy and decision-making must be encouraged. In this way they will provide not only for the well-being of themselves but prosperity for all of our society. Some steps have already been taken. For example, in April 1994 a Young people's Business Society (*Molodezhnyi soiuz predprinimatelia*) was set up, or the April League (*Liga Aprel'*) for short. Its aim is to provide small businessmen, the large majority of its membership, with financial, legal and other types of moral support. Part of the difficulty here is that the salary of young people is 56-65 per cent less than other older professionals. As a result, approximately 50 per cent of young people aged 15-29 years old surveyed in Voronezh oblast between 1992-94 relied on their parents for material support. But money is not the only obstacle. The low professional status of youth which reflects their qualifications, experience etc. is also an area of concern and the reason why the April League and similar organisations were set up.

Developing free enterprise and a well-motivated youth

The problems of the development of free enterprise culture are well-known, but it is necessary, as mentioned above, to create opportunities for young people in Russia, so that they can open up their own businesses. This situation partly reflects the current economic climate - high risk for low reward - but it also reflects the work attitudes of youth today - only 20 per cent of those young people surveyed between 1992-94 were found to be highly motivated.

In our opinion, it is necessary to implement policies which encourage a new work ethic, which fight economic crime, which encourage honesty and respect for work and above all which do not simply promote materialism.

A major difficulty here is the poor state of our education system (see chapter 13). This means that many young people in Russia leave school, college or university ill-prepared for the world of work. This problem is being compounded by the fact that only 15 per cent of young people between 1992-94 wanted to continue their education after school. Sadly the gap between educational training and occupational need is growing. This has resulted in a highly paradoxical situation developing: 50 per cent of highly educated young people are working in jobs below their level of education whilst the remaining 50 per cent are employed in jobs for which they are not properly qualified. Unfortunately, many young people are unemployed. In St. Petersburg, for instance, half the young people on the unemployment register failed to be placed in appropriate jobs in 1994. The corresponding figure in Svedlovsk was a third and in Russia as a whole a staggering 50 per cent and more. Therefore reform of the education system is essential if we are to develop an appropriate state youth policy.

Remedying economic and political instability

There is growing dissatisfaction in all sections of society, especially among the young, about the pace and direction of the present reform programmes. We asked, after the events of October 1993 (i.e. the Storming of the White House), are present politicians capable of solving the country's most serious problems? We received the following answers listed in table 9.1 below:

Table 9.1
Answers to the question: 'Are present politicians in Russia capable of solving the country's most serious problems?'
Survey of 11 regions of Russian Federation, 1993-94
(n = 1,700)

Group	Answer		
	Yes	No	Don't Know
Young people aged 18-24 years	20.5%	56.0%	23.5%
People aged 30-34 years	21.0%	61.0%	18.0%
Farmers	30.0%	58.0%	12.0%
Businessmen	28.0%	59.0%	13.0%
Students	20.0%	60.0%	14.0%

It is evident that in the overwhelming majority of cases, young people alongside a range of other groups have little trust in the current ruling politicians' ability to put Russia's problems right. According to a March 1994 opinion poll, young people ranked incompetent politicians second after crime as their major area of concern.

Finding solutions to the systemic crisis

Here we are in the realm of the political beliefs of Russian youth. According to our survey: 26 per cent were *democratic* in orientation; 18 per cent *nationalist*; 15 per cent were in favour of a firm dictatorship and less than 5 per cent were of *socialist* orientation. Almost a third had no association with any political party or leader and the rest gave no clear indication either way. All in all, only 23 per cent supported a particular party or leader. It is hardly surprising under these circumstances to discover that the support base of well known leaders and parties is dwindling fast. This confirms the findings outlined earlier in chapter 1. Russian youngsters are, however, unclear which socio-political group might provide them and their country with a better future. They support the wide spectrum of political groups from liberals to traditionalists through to those favouring a strong state. But the large majority of respondents - 66 per cent - were apolitical and bewildered as to who could get Russia back on the right road again.

Defining and creating a new society

In order to generate harmony we must not only resolve current difficulties but also be concerned about where we are going. It is much easier to know where we have been than to predict what our future new society might consist of. Russian youth in the main rejects both the course pursued by the Communist Party of the Soviet Union (CPSU) and the policies which Yeltsin has introduced since 1992. 56 per cent of young people want a new course in economics and more specifically a third are in favour of a social market in which the state provides minimum guarantees without placing restrictions on high achievers. Such a position explains why Russian youth places so much stress on jobs in enterprises and entrepreneurial activity in general. For this to happen, 40.2 per cent of Moscow and 36.5 per cent of St. Petersburg students want a democratic form of government to be introduced. For 21 per cent this is a Presidential system of government and for a further 12.5 per cent a parliamentary democracy. In both instances, 76.7 per cent of students were in favour of a separation of powers between the executive, legislature and the judiciary. The only exception to this liberal democratic approach was among cadets of military establishments and more right-wing students: 49.8 per cent of the former and 14.6 per cent of the latter were in favour of a military dictatorship.

Resorting to the use of violence

Our survey shows that in the event that their lives are threatened or a civil war occurs young people in Russia stated that they were willing to use violence. On the whole, though, young people said that they would support a vote of no confidence (14 per cent on average, 22.9 per cent among students) in government, use political parties and trade unions to apply pressure (12.9 per cent and 18.4 per cent respectively) and/or go on strike (5.7 per cent and 5.6 per cent) to try and influence the course of policy and government attitudes. Only 8.1 per cent of young people and 5 per cent of students - a narrow minority - said they were willing to use revolutionary means to bring about change. Such a 'Barricade mentality' was most widespread amongst supporters of nationalist forces. This is why it is perhaps necessary to talk about *harmony with opposition*. However, groups of all political persuasions have signed the agreement. This includes the 'whites' (*belye*), with the exception of the Yavlinsky faction, but it does not include the 'reds' (*krasnye*), such as communists, agrarians, the majority of 'patriots' and followers of Zhirinovsky.

Harmony requires a new system of youth upbringing

Our research demonstrates that in order to achieve greater harmony in Russian society, economics and politics, a new system for the upbringing of youth will be required. The most characteristic thing about the present generation (15-25 years) is that it is 'de-ideologised' or non-ideological (*deideologizirovannost'*). The old ideas have been buried and not replaced by new ones.[4] However, now that this generation of young people has freedom of choice - in the social, economic, political and spiritual sense - it is rejecting all notions of going back to the past. For the current generation of Russian youth *there is no going back*. This is the most positive outcome of a decade of radical reforms. However, in our opinion, the present type of freedom is of the unsatisfying, pre-capitalist variety. The second key point we would like to emphasise is that the new generation gained this freedom without major struggle, virtually for nothing. That is why for certain groups of youngsters, this *freedom has no value at all*. For instance in 1992, 33-40 per cent of different groups of youth from Orenberg admitted that political and economic freedom was the main achievement of democracy and the collapse of communism, but by 1994, only 11 per cent held this opinion. The main conclusion coming from our research is that the new generation might come to *rely upon non-freedom*.[5]

Although the family must continue to be an important institution for socialising the next generation, it is, as we showed earlier in chapter 3, in a state of crisis. Russia's youth policy must start to offer greater support for the family, including measures for protecting mothers, children and young people as well as other policies designed to generate credits, additional opportunities for employment and so forth.

Youth can become one of the key determinants of stability in Russian society if it is given an appropriate system of upbringing and is influenced by the right people. Young people need clear ideologies and moral codes. Money, profit and the market are not the correct ideals for today's youth. It is difficult to distinguish between those who are genuinely interested in Russia's future and those who are simply 'jumping on the bandwagon'.

Conclusions

Sociological research shows that for this upbringing to happen, we need *a strong state capable of caring.*[6] In our opinion, one of the main criteria of upbringing must be not simply a young person serving him/herself and his/her close relatives but also his/her country. The idea of patriotic service of Russia, according to researchers attached to the Scientific Research Centre of the Institute of Youth in Moscow, must constitute a core element in state and social upbringing, otherwise Russia's transition will be endangered. The absence of duty to one's country as well as oneself and one's family creates ambiguity and uncertainty and ultimately leads to an unstable social order. In this context, the family, school, army, church and other agencies responsible for socialisation must be strengthened. Unfortunately at present, there are no mechanisms providing stability so that such a socialisation role can be performed properly and effectively. The Agreement signed in late April 1994 is geared towards creating harmony, less polarisation and greater unity between different social and political groups. If harmony is not achieved, the current discord will continue until crisis turns into catastrophe. If the latter course is to be avoided, harmony must not be restricted to top political circles, but evident in all sections of society, especially youth as the bearers of Russia's future. This required some give and take on both sides. On the part of the government a respectful, socially-oriented youth policy[7] must be implemented and in return young people must show a more positive attitude towards the reform process, their country and a greater respect for others. However, recent research by the Committee on youth affairs revealed that by the time young people have fully matured (27-30 years) the overwhelming majority have negative attitudes towards our government and are disappointed that they are excluded from the decision-making process. This situation largely reflects the level of gerontocracy in the Soviet period in which access to the political elite was closed and in which strict hierarchical trends operated. But it also stems from a failure to overcome these difficulties in the post communist period. Neither of these goals will be easy to achieve in the transition period especially given the fact that youth is not yet a priority area of contemporary Russian politics. Until we create suitable conditions for the present and future generations, conflict and crisis will continue. One possible step forward here might be the introduction of 'positive discrimination' in order to accelerate the entry of young people into positions of authority. These sorts of measures are currently being proposed. They include the provision of better education facilities, special government training programmes and increased government support for youth organisations and their ideas.

The evolution and development of a means of raising youth consciousness and public awareness of youth issues is compounded by a number of problems and contradictions at the present time. For instance, the high level of dissatisfaction with low standards of living, conflicts in the low level of work requirements and the relatively high value placed upon knowledge is in direct contrast to the low prestige of young people and so forth. At the moment, Russian youth feels neglected. They are becoming accustomed to a situation in which no one appears to care about their plight. As a result, many now lack spiritual or moral fibre and are turning to crime. This 'dehumanisation' of our society as a whole, and our young people in particular, is likely to have a significant impact on Russian's democratic transition. In order to reverse this trend, greater attention needs to be devoted to family, church, youth and education. But time is running out as Russia heads towards her second parliamentary election and her first presidential election since the collapse of the USSR in late 1991.

Notes

*   The views expressed in this chapter are those of the author, not necessarily those of the State Committee on Youth Affairs.

1.   Cited in *Rossiiskaia Gazeta* 11 June 1994.
2.   See *Al'ternativy voine ot antichnosti do kontsa vtoroi mirovoi voiny: Antologiia,* Moscow 1993.
3.   This conclusion and the following discussion is based upon a survey of 1,700 young people in 11 regions of the Russian Federation carried out in 1993-94. For more information see *Tekyshchii arkhiv NiTS pri Institut Molodezhi,* Moscow April 1994.
4.   For a useful discussion here see A. Yakovlev, *The Fate of Marxism in Russia,* Yale University Press, London 1993.
5.   Reliance on non-freedom (*nesvoboda*) does have historical analogies. Beneto Mussolini once declared: 'People are tired of freedom. For anxious and resolute young people, coming into life in the morning darkness of a new history, there are different words which carry much greater appeal: order, hierarchy, discipline'.
6.   This need became evident when a member of the gang in Belgorod who had committed 13 murders was interviewed. This young person stated:

> 'Youth values have been turned upside down. Freedom has been given but young people have not been shown how to use it. What is valuable? Cars, hard currency and drugs. Why should I bother working: 9 out of 10 of our friends if offered a thousand bucks to get rid of a man would not refuse because you cannot earn this money honestly. And for the work you are doing, you cannot even buy decent clothes'.

Research shows the disappearance of a belief not only in human beings but also in one's motherland. The new generation 'does not acknowledge Russia as their home'. It is clear that the new Russia as well as its flag and national anthem must earn the respect, trust and admiration of the new generation of young people.
7.   For more on this see I.I. Il'inskii et al. (eds.), *Tsennostnyi mir sovremennoi molodezhi: na puti k mirovoi integratsii,* Moscow 1994, as well as J. Riordan, C. Williams and I. Ilynsky (eds.), *Young people in post-communist Russia and Eastern Europe,* Dartmouth 1995.

PART III

A SECTORAL ANALYSIS

10   Social policy in Russia

FAINA KOSYGINA AND SOLOMON KRAPIVENSKII

Introduction

Much of the existing literature on developments in post-communist Russia has focused on political and economic change to the detriment of social change. The aim of this chapter is to examine whether or not there is sufficient political will to tackle Russia's major social ills. Particular emphasis is placed upon the impact which the current recession, on the one hand, and uneven political developments in Russia, on the other, are having on the social reorientation of our country. It is argued that political and economic reform go hand in hand with social change and that unless the adverse effects of the transition from authoritarianism to liberal democracy and the move from planned to market economy in Russia are taken into account, it will not be possible for Russia to reverse the downturn in its education and health care system, housing, social welfare and the environment in the 1990s.

Our main contention is that the question of social protection in Russia is one of the most serious issues in the current political climate and poses one of the most fundamental theoretical problems for social scientists. Social protection for the population as a whole is a key indicator of the level of modernisation in our society as well as a measure of how far democracy has become entrenched. Social measures are important in another sense too, in that they involve a number of aspects: economic, politics, ideology and so forth.

Pre-perestroika

In the pre-perestroika period, social protection was not problem-free but certain egalitarian principles were nevertheless put in place, as shown by the fact that education and medical care were free of charge and unemployment virtually non-existent. Let us illustrate this point by choosing a few case studies.

Housing

The Bolsheviks and successive Soviet governments promised decent housing, but on the whole this goal was not met. There is insufficient housing stock; growth failed to keep pace with the high birth rate and increased rural-urban migration and high expectations from the 1920s to the 1960s. Shortages, lack of investment and the absence of building materials, resulted in extremely long waiting lists. Much of the Soviet housing stock was of poor quality with a lack of running water, indoor lavatories, bathrooms and central heating. Furthermore, there was no incentive to maintain the quality of the property. All in all, the housing stock gradually deteriorated from the 1960s onwards and was characterised by sloppy workmanship, inadequate maintenance etc.

Education

Likewise the education system suffered during the communist era. Teaching was distorted through censorship and the need to adhere strictly to Marxism-Leninism. There were tremendous shortcomings in structure and content as well as in the physical condition of Soviet educational establishments. Although tuition was free at Higher Education level, the system was highly centralised and the expansion of places slow. Despite the use of extra credits for weaker entrants (such as those of manual worker or peasant origin), the education system still failed miserably to reduce inequalities of opportunity.

Social welfare benefit system

Finally social welfare benefits for anything ranging from maternity to old-age were distributed through the Soviet social insurance system. Benefits were largely, though not exclusively paid through the state budget in the period from Lenin to Gorbachev. A wide range of benefits were offered including: retirement, invalidity, maternity, family/child allowance, OAP etc. Despite these various schemes, the prolonged economic crisis, which was at its worst in the 1960s and 1970s, reduced the overall standard of living of the population. The number of people forced to live in poverty under communism was hidden, but under glasnost in the mid-late 1980s, it was quickly discovered that the elderly, disabled, single-parent families, those with large number of children and students were the groups most adversely affected by these trends. Thus, as one English specialist, Mervyn Matthews points out, Russia was characterised by 'frequent food shortages, scarce low quality consumer goods, high prices, long queues, inadequate housing etc.'[1]

Although a welfare state and other major social measures were implemented, democracy was absent in the political sphere and personal freedom did not exist.

Gorbachev to Yeltsin

Over the last decade, Russia has undergone fundamental reform. This strategy was supposed to create a developed Russian, former Soviet, society.[2] But what price have we paid? How far have we progressed since the mid-1980s? Has the transition from the old Soviet system to a new one based on capitalist virtues been beneficial or detrimental?

The transition to the market economy has resulted in a growing number of closures, redundancies and increased unemployment especially in state industry. Such a situation has placed the old system of social protection under great pressure. In effect, the welfare state as previously constituted has largely disintegrated alongside the USSR. This brings into question the 'cost of revolution' and the costs incurred by 'structural reform'. The latter has not been a gradual but very rapid process, without the necessary social measures in place to cushion the population from the adverse effects of the market. The old system of social protection in education, health care, housing, social welfare etc. has collapsed but it has not been replaced by a fully operational alternative system.

The main reasons for the lack of development of a new system of social protection are two-fold. On the *subjective side*, this has arisen because of the lack of socio-political will. Social measures have continued to be a low government priority and the introduction of new education, health, housing and other policies has therefore been slow. This occurred because of problems of finance as well as conflict between different interest groups over which types of policies were the most beneficial in each case. By contrast on the *objective side*, we need to take into account the complete breakdown of Russian society and the values upon which it was based for most of this century.

For the last 10 years, Russia's education system, health-care provision, housing and social welfare has significantly deteriorated. Trends in social policy have been totally undermined by the transition to the market, especially the move from collectivism to individualism. Let us consider two examples.

Ecology

For most of the communist period, the state as well as individual Russian citizens aggressively exploited nature for their own ends. However, such exploitation led to environmental degradation in the regions of Chernobyl, Semipalatinsk, Chelyabinsk and so on. The environment was destroyed for the sake of economic growth. In the socialist period, the state pursued these goals in the interests of 'socialism'. But unfortunately, Russia's economic growth declined from the late 1960s onwards. Nowadays, the new Russian state and private sector continue to exploit our environment in order to facilitate the transition to capitalism and a fully fledged market economy. However, this policy has back-fired, it has only had adverse effects upon many areas and regions of Russia. In other words, the rate of exploitation of the environment has continued in the post-communist phase. Old negative attitudes towards the use of land, water and other resources still prevail. A lack of respect for the environment among senior Russian politicians is still a major problem. Until our political culture changes, our ecological base will be destroyed and before long we will be unable to avert a serious ecological disaster of worse proportions than Chernobyl.[3]

Poverty and the demise of the welfare state

Absolute poverty refers to minimum needs below which people are regarded as being poor whereas relative poverty can be defined in terms of personal disposable income per-capita.[4]   In Russia we have traditionally defined 'poverty' as the equivalent to national assistance benefit.[5]   Our research shows that the 'relative deprivation' of the urban and rural poor was especially acute in the Stalinist era, but eased under Khrushchev and Brezhnev as the needs of the consumer in the Russian economy were given greater state priority. However, until Gorbachev's *glasnost*, poverty was virtually a taboo subject in Russia. But by the late 1980s, it was estimated by Soviet economists that 43 million people in the ex-USSR lived below the official poverty line (set at 75 roubles per month). Two years later, *Goskomstat* estimated that 90 million people, or more than 30 per cent of the population were in receipt of incomes below the poverty line. Both Western and Russian economists, such as Rimashevskaya, argue, however, that these official figures probably underestimate actual poverty levels due to the difficulties of utilising household budget analysis and the way Soviet statisticians calculate per-capita incomes.[6]

During the communist period, the Soviet state was given primary responsibility for providing the essentials of life - food, shelter etc. - at affordable prices in order to prevent poverty. This was encapsulated in the notion of egalitarianism which prevailed from the October 1917 Revolution onwards. The state also played a major role in meeting any deficits in 'social need' by establishing the appropriate mechanisms capable of eradicating such deficiencies. The main objective of the Russian state was to provide a minimum standard of living for all; to ensure financial security in times of individual and family crisis and to make a range of essential services - health care, education, safety and security etc. - available to the entire population, irrespective of age, sex, ethnic group and so forth. The goal was to create a more equal society in line with the idea of communism. However, even though the official ideology of Marxism-Leninism stressed our commitment to the welfare state, the latter was a low priority sector starved of funds and the structural position of the Ministries of Public Health and Labour compared with agriculture, industry and defence were rather weak.

Whereas in tsarist times, there was a reliance on voluntary organisations to meet the needs of the poor, after 1917 the Soviet state took a more active role by providing financial assistance via the social security system to those who were poverty stricken. Benefits were wage related and differentiated according to industrial and agricultural labour forces, but pension levels were not index linked and were woefully inadequate by Western standards.

Mikhail Gorbachev's tenure (1985-91) not only revealed the extent but also tried to address the causes of poverty in the former Soviet Union. In the period 1985-90, benefits for OAPs, the disabled, and for collective farm and state employees were revised upwards to take account of hidden inflation. The aim was firstly to eradicate past shortcomings and secondly to provide a **safety-net** during the transition to a market economy. These changes were followed in April and August 1990 by the introduction of indexed linked family allowances and the elimination of the birth grant allowance and its replacement with a one-off birth grant totalling three times the minimum wage. This move was geared towards modernising the social security/insurance system, on the one hand, and alleviating poverty among families with children, on the other. However, the smooth implementation of these reforms was hampered by the disintegration of the Union in December 1991. Nevertheless, Soviet and Western sources indicate that the percentage of persons living below the official Soviet poverty line fell from 53 per cent in 1967 to 17.9 per cent in 1985 before reaching 14.5 per cent in 1988.[7] Despite such significant improvements, hardened attitudes towards the poor were beginning to make themselves felt by the late 1980s-early 1990s. Thus Russian public opinion poll data from December 1990 indicated, for example, that while 82 per cent of those surveyed wished to 'help the poor', a further 4 per cent wished to liquidate and an additional 3 per cent isolate them from society. As regards specific groups within this 'poor' category, 46 per cent wanted to assist the homeless or social dregs (*bicha*) but 10 per cent wished to liquidate and 23 per cent isolate them from society.[8]

Following the collapse of the Union in 1991, *besprizornost'* (homelessness) became more widespread. By the early 1990s, for example, there were an estimated 30-100,000 homeless in Moscow alone.[9] This has happened for two main reasons: firstly, there is no strong welfare state in place and secondly, although the safety nets established in the Gorbachev era remain in place, current income maintenance programmes are barely adequate as existing state benefits are constantly eroded by inflation. People from all walks of life, therefore, now find themselves caught up in a vicious poverty trap.

The problem since 1992 has been that social policy matters have not been high on the post-communist agenda. As a result of this rejection of egalitarianism and exposure to the harshness of the market mechanism, one report submitted to President Yeltsin by a leading group of economists (including Stanislav Shatalin, Leonid Abalkin and Nikolai Petrokov) in the first half of February 1994, suggested that a third of the population of Russia - 49 million people - are currently living below subsistence level and a further 15 million people or a tenth of the population below 'starvation wages'. This is hardly surprising given that in 1990 food bills represented 30 per cent of average incomes while today a Russian family spends 60-70 per cent of its income on food. The comparable figure for pensioners is 83 per cent of earnings, with a staggering 90 per cent of this group living below the poverty line. Clearly the current four-year long shock therapy programme is taking its toll on Russia, as indicated by the growing proportion of people facing poverty.

Aggressive individualism

A more aggressive individualistic attitude has made itself felt in a number of spheres including:

The economy

In the last few years we have witnessed the reckless exploitation of national wealth; adherence to short rather than long-term strategic planning; speculation; a belief that resources are infinite, when in fact they are scarce; a failure to halt the rapid rise in unemployment; to eradicate poverty or to improve our poorly developed transport network.

Management

The government has failed to appreciate the necessity of a more active role in running the country. Instead, in the last decade, the government has left things to the 'invisible hand' of the market. This has led, as we saw earlier, to a decline in living standards and greater impoverishment. Despite so-called 'democracy', the people have had less and less say in how the country is run. The government and our rapidly expanding bureaucracy are preventing concrete day to day problems from being resolved, such as rising crime[10] (see chapter 14), extremism, fascism, the *mafiya* and so forth.

Education

The transition to market principles has severely weakened the education system. The quality of its work - its staff base, resources and the quality of our students - has plummeted in many respects over the last decade. This has led to two significant developments: firstly, a decline in socialisation resulting in poor upbringing. As a consequence many youngsters do not understand the difference between right and wrong. Secondly, our graduates are often ill-prepared for the demands of today's labour market (see chapters 8, 11 and 13). This applies at all levels of the education system from school through to the university sector. As a result of the aforementioned trends, today's youth is of a different psychological make-up to those of earlier historical periods, in that they have less respect for their fellow human beings and are more reluctant to study or work hard (see chapters 8-9).

Public health

This is the subject of chapter 12, so suffice it to say here that health care in the state sector is woefully inadequate and of poor quality. Nowadays, many of the best medical staff are leaving the profession in search of better paid jobs elsewhere, leaving those lower qualified behind. There are also widespread shortages of supplies, medical facilities, such as polyclinics and hospitals, as well as beds except for those in a position to pay. Diseases which everyone thought had been eradicated, such as TB, are now on the increase. New diseases such as AIDS are placing our disintegrating health service under increased strain. The state sector simply does not have the staff and resources to cope with the mounting health crisis and overall decline in health conditions outlined in chapter 12. As we saw in chapter 3, this situation is having an adverse effect upon demographic trends - a falling birth rate and an increasing death rate.

Why then is social policy such a low priority? How can we reverse the current situation, so that the population becomes less pessimistic and more optimistic about future levels of social protection? What steps can be taken to make Russian social policy more effective? and finally, and perhaps most importantly, how can we avert a national catastrophe in all the aforementioned areas?

Systemic crisis

There is, at present, a systemic crisis in the field of social protection which is making itself felt at a macro as well as micro level.

Macro

At the macro level, the key aspects are the organisation and financing of various social measures as well as who should have overall responsibility and the main co-ordinating role - the state, the private sector or a mixture of the above. Although each relevant Ministry has control in its own sphere of interest - such as education, health care etc. - there is, in the current economic recession, fierce competition between them for scarce resources. In addition, each Ministry is influenced by various outside interest groups as well as the relevant professions.

Micro

At a micro level, we move away from the way in which various social policy measures are devised, implemented and financed to consider the impact which the existing social protection measures have had on individual citizens at a local or regional level. Our research demonstrates that since the mid-1980s, the quality of provision has declined. Earlier egalitarian policies have long since been abandoned by the state and other agencies in the interest of offering fee-paying services. Access to education, health care, housing and social welfare is becoming more and more restricted every day. The best quality education is obtained in private schools or in a restricted group of universities; health care is of higher quality in the embryonic private rather than state sector and so on. This is partly because the older legislation no longer applies and has only gradually been replaced by new laws based on market principles.[11]

As a result of this situation, the per-capita consumption of most groups has fallen and standards of living have plummeted in the last decade, with the pace rapidly increasing in the post-communist phase. Sadly, officialdom has been found wanting. Our government has only been able to offer minimum guarantees. Provision in most cases, however, remains pitifully inadequate, with most of the population struggling to give their children a good education or to provide their families with adequate housing, health care and social services. Thus in overall terms the transition to the market economy has not been beneficial but largely disadvantageous to most sections of the population. This applies as much to workers and managers as it does to students, housewives, families and OAPs. The social measures currently in place have failed to shield anyone, except the *ex-nomenklatura* and the 'New Russians', from the adverse effects of the new social conditions brought about by the process of economic reform.

State versus private sector

One of the key events since the collapse of communism has been a reduced state role in social policy provision and greater intervention by the private sector. However, this process of transfer of responsibility for social measures is so far incomplete and unco-ordinated. There is as yet no unified system of social measures. One can only hope that this situation will not prevail for a long time. For this to be the case, greater co-operation between government, private sector, trade unions and social organisations will be essential. They must devise and implement a realistic programme of social measures together. This in turn will require the development of a civil society. Unfortunately, at present, neither of these pre-conditions for change exist (see chapter 15).

In 1994, attempts were made to try and halt the fragmentation of social policy. This occurred when a new draft social policy was discussed. This document included a call for a more active state role and the development of a European-style social policy. In essence, this new social policy included the following aspects:

(i)   equality before the law;
(ii)   better quality medical care;
(iii)   improved provision for the unemployed; and finally
(iv)   the government was to act as trustee of education, culture etc.[12]

This marked a step in the right direction towards re-thinking current social policy measures. If such a policy was elaborated upon further, this might signal two things: firstly, the re-emergence of a 'socially oriented' government and secondly, attempts to create a solid system of social measures in an uncertain, politically unstable Russia.

Unfortunately, such a policy has failed to materialise over the last two years or so. This was because of tension between government and civil organisations, on the one hand, and the failure to make a transition to a civil society, on the other. Economic difficulties and political divisions at the apex of the political system hindered matters still further. In order to break the deadlock, we must make social policy our first priority.

Priority 'number one': social policy measures

To put social policy on a different footing the following important steps must be followed:

(i)   examining sources of finance;
(ii)   ensuring that we have an effective and efficiently functioning economy;
(iii)   curtailing the bureaucracy
(iv)   encouraging government and public organisations to work and co-operage together;
(v)   guaranteeing a minimum standard of living;
(vi)   eradicating current shortcomings in education, health, housing, social welfare and so on
(vii)   targeting specific groups which are in need of immediate assistance such as vagrants (*bomzhi*), the homeless (*bezdomnyi*), the poor (*nishchii*), invalids, the unemployed, OAPs, students and large families etc.;
(viii) paying greater attention to the environment;

(ix) clamping-down on crime;
(x) strengthening our education and health care systems; and finally
(xi) restoring Russian culture and ensuring that it does not fall in the hands of the barbarians

In relation to the above 11 point programme, which is not exhaustive, due attention must also be devoted to the difficulties facing different age groups, sexes, occupations and nationalities.

Problems and solutions

Unfortunately any such programme will remain a fiction until a democratic mechanism is created and implemented by all groups. While this process will undoubtedly take a long time, it is nevertheless still true that certain business groupings have expressed support for and interest in developing a new post-communist social policy.[13] However, it will take the development of a different kind of political culture for this mythical policy to become a reality. For this new social policy to be introduced, a significant number of influential Russian politicians would have to back it. As we saw in chapter 1, we possess neither a good President (*khoroshii Prezident*) or government (*khoroshoe pravitel'stvo*) capable or lending their considerable weight to its success. The same is also true of the political parties which are involved in an on-going political struggle within and between themselves. The passivity of the population, and its lack of interest in politics generally, is exacerbating matters further because citizens are failing to put pressure on the major political actors and institutions. Until all the parties concerned - President, government, representatives in key Republics and regions, economic interest groups, independent trade unions throughout the Federation, the parliament main political parties and the general population work in unison and fight for a new social policy, it has little chance of materialising. Current trends suggest that this policy has been blocked because of rivalry and plotting by various enemies against one another (*poiski vragov*). This has inevitably led to alienation (*otchuzhdenie*) of the population, who lack faith in the current government because it is not sufficiently 'socially oriented' and is not committed to the idea of creating a civil society.

The relevance of Marx's theory of alienation

How then can we eliminate this feeling of alienation? This phenomenon has been analysed by Karl Marx in his **Economic and Philosophical Manuscripts of 1844**, which are generally referred to as his 'Paris Manuscripts'. In essence, his theory of alienation attempts to show how people have become stripped of their finer qualities by an inhumane economic system. Capitalism was said to deprive the workers of a means to express themselves through their work, and in doing so, wo/man's main character and social relations have become contaminated. For Marx, alienation could not be abolished at the level of consciousness, for consciousness does not determine one's social being, but was determined by it. It was therefore necessary to change society. Marx regarded the individual as both unique (concerned with *self-affirmation*) and as a social being (a socially moulded creature whose activities have an impact upon others). He therefore concluded that it was wrong to draw a distinction between the individual and society, because the individual was a social being. According to Marx, wo/man is what his/her activity determined, and it was through labour that the worker 'reproduces him/herself' in society. As human control of the world has developed, and the methods of production became more advanced, raw materials, tools and production were gradually owned by the few. This reached its height under Capitalism, where the bourgeoisie owned the 'means of production' and the proletariat sold their labour for wages. Because capitalism used large-scale factory production, involving intense specialisation, this process separated the worker from the product of his/her labour. But since work is central to life, alienation is not confined merely to production, it affects all aspects of life and all members of society.

Nearly a century and a half after Marx, alienation supposedly ended when the October 1917 Revolution led to the introduction of communal ownership which thereby supplanted private ownership of the means of production. Since the collapse of communism and the introduction of capitalism, alienation has resurfaced again - the Russian worker of the 1990s, as in the pre-revolutionary period, is alienated from the work process and from his/her fellow-workers. This is destroying the very fabric of Russian society as Marx predicted. The conditions are being created in which our citizens are becoming de-humanised. This is not the fault of the individual capitalist, who only exists largely in embryonic form, but is the consequence of the introduction of the market which determines what the capitalist sells.

Alienation affects all strata of society. But in contemporary Russia, the worker in not simply divorced from the labour process, s/he is also alienated from the government as a whole. There are many reasons for this, but one of them is the abandonment of former egalitarian principles and the failure to introduce *realistic social measures*. In order for the latter to be implemented, and alienation overcome, we urgently need to eliminate the objective and subjective obstacles outlined earlier. Another essential pre-requisite for the success of the social measures programme detailed above, is an effective strategy for economic reform. This would mean a significant change of direction, as the present reforms have merely had adverse effects since the mid-1980s, increasing alienation even further.

Conclusion

We have reviewed certain areas of social policy in general terms and shown that under present conditions it has not been feasible to implement a new strategy to replace the old one which largely fizzled out with the collapse of communism at the end of 1991. The basic character of this new policy was outlined. Thus far the obstacles to the implementation of such a policy - shortage of finance, lack of consensus, no political will, poor theoretical and organisational frameworks - have far outweighed the factors promoting a reorientation of Russian social policy. Unless major groups at the apex of the Russian political system, as well as broad sections of society, begin to back fundamental change, social policy will remain woefully inadequate and ineffective as we head towards the 21st century.

Notes

1.   M. Matthews, *Poverty in the Soviet Union: The lifestyles of the underprivileged in recent years*, Cambridge University Press: Cambridge 1986, p. 10.
2.   On this see S.Ye Krapivenskii, *Paradoksy sotsial'nykh revolutysii*, Voronezh 1992.
3.   *Pravda* 13 January 1989.
4.   OECD, *Public expenditure on Income programmes*, OECD: Paris 1976, p. 76; T.M. Smeeding et al., *Poverty, inequality and income distribution in Comparative perspective,* Harvester Wheatsheaf, New York 1990.
5.   V. George and N. Rimashevskaya, 'Poverty in Russia', *International social security review*, Vol. 46, No. 1, 1993, pp. 67-72.
6.   H. Flakierski, *Income inequalities in the former Soviet Union and its Republics,* M.E. Sharpe, London 1993, pp. 57-58.
7.   V. George, 'Social security in the USSR', *International social security review,* Vol. 44 No. 4, 1991, pp. 47-65.
8.   VTsIOM, *Obshchestvennoe mnenie v tsifrakh* , 1990, No. 2.
9.   V. George and N. Rimashevskaya, 'Poverty in Russia', *International social security review*, Vol. 46, No. 1, 1993, p. 75.
10.   See V. Kabo, 'Subkul'tura lagaeria i arkhetipy sozdaniia', *Sovetskaia Etnografiia* 1990, No. 1 and G. Levintin, 'Naskol'ko 'pervobytna' ugolovnaia subkult'tura', *Sovetskaia Etnografiia* 1990, No. 2.
11.   See O.V. Romashov, 'Sotsial'naia zashchita trudiashchikhsia: problemy puti resheniia', *Sotsiologicheskie issledovaniia* 1993, No. 1.
12.   For more on this see T. Alekseeva, 'Tsentristskii proekt dlia Rossii', *Sovremennaia mysl'* 1994 No. 4, p. 10.
13.   *Delovoi Mir* 1 October 1994.

11 Labour policy

YEVGENII KATUL'SKII*

Introduction

We saw earlier in chapter 3 that the prospects for the development of Russia's population until the end of this century look rather bleak - a declining birth rate, reduced fertility, increased mortality from various diseases and falling life expectancy. It seems unlikely therefore that the population of Russia will reach 150 million by the turn of the 21st century. Because of all these factors, the demographic aspects of manpower will undergo radical changes over the next few years in both quantitative and qualitative as well as in geographical terms. Russia has witnessed a transition from a situation in which there were excess labour supplies and virtually no unemployment to one of relative labour scarcity, especially in the regions, and a contradictory situation of rising unemployment. Although the transition to the market sought to eliminate poorly utilised labour, increase the level of mechanisation and exert greater control over the labour market, with the aim of increasing labour productivity and averting a decline in output, these goals were only partly achieved by the end of the communist period.

On top of this, the reduction in the size of the population of able bodied age coupled with mass migration has seriously affected Russia's labour supply. Furthermore, Russia has lost much of its former market in the Commonwealth of Independent States and in Central and Eastern Europe. This has been accompanied by increasing foreign debts of c. US$30 billion, rising budget deficits, enterprise closures and the introduction of Western oriented economic policies involving substantial changes in the industrial, agricultural and trade sectors as well as in monetary and fiscal policy. But what impact has Russia's economic transformation had on employment and unemployment trends? What labour policy measures have been introduced to try and remedy rising unemployment? and finally what problems are likely to arise if these challenges are not met by the time of the Presidential elections? Before addressing these important issues, we need to have some appreciation of the difficulties encountered when one is trying to assess labour market trends in Russia.

Methodology and data problems

As with earlier periods, contemporary Russian unemployment data suffer from a number of defects. In the 1920s, population censuses, Ministry of Labour *(Narkomtrud)* labour exchange data and trade union information were all used to estimate the extent of unemployment in Russia. However, the coverage was not extensive, labour exchanges only existed in medium and large-scale towns, regulations for registering as 'unemployed' were frequently altered (excluding for instance new arrivals from the countryside) and finally, some people sought jobs via non-official channels.[1] As a result, the number of registered unemployed recorded in official statistics was well below its true level.

Similar problems exist today. Figures on the number of unemployed in post-communist Russia are supplied by the Federal Employment Service (*Federal'naia Sluzhba Zaniatosti*, hereafter simply FES) which collects monthly data from local employment offices. Three categories are used: first, the number of registered job seekers; second, the number of registered unemployed and finally, the number of people in receipt of unemployment benefit.[2] The problem, however, is that FES data are not accurate measures of unemployment because they only refer to the number of registered unemployed job seekers defined as 'officially unemployed'.[3] An additional difficulty is that many of the unemployed do not in fact register with the FES agencies.[4] As a consequence, the Ministry of Labour estimated in April 1993 that the number of unemployed was 4.5-5 million or four to five times the number of registered job seekers (751,000).

One clear fact emerges from the aforementioned analysis namely that there is a clear contradiction between the relatively low unemployment figures (see below) and the rapid decline in output levels, enterprise closures and the intense process of economic restructuring over the last decade. Pointing to a possible reason for the inconsistent evidence on unemployment, Oxenstierna notes that unemployment is defined in different ways by different agencies and officials. The term 'unemployment' has been used firstly to refer to the number of unemployed; second, to denote those leaving the state sector as unemployed, third to mean the estimated stock of unemployed, fourthly, to refer to those eligible for unemployment benefits and finally to denote a certain proportion of the non-employed population, especially in regional analyses and discussions.[5] We shall see below that although there is now greater consistency in Russian usage of the terms 'employed' and 'unemployed', which refer to those participating in the labour force and those not active in the labour market respectively, the matter is still complicated by individuals who enter and re-enter the labourforce, on the one hand, and by the changing nature of the public/private sector and their relationship to one another, on the other.

Russian Employment Trends

Table 11.1 below provides details of Russian employment patterns since 1990. This enables us to compare trends in the late communist period with those in the post-communist phase. It is clear that state sector employment has declined. Under perestroika for instance, the number of employees in the Soviet state sector fell from 118.5 million in 1986 to 112.8 million by early 1991.[6] This constitutes a fall of over one million a year and 5.7 million overall during this five year period. This trend continued after 1991, as table 11.1 shows:

Table 11.1
Trends in Russian employment, 1990-95 (in millions)

Sector of Economy	1990	1991	1992	1993	1994	Nov 1995
Industry	22.8	22.4	21.3	20.8	19.2	17.3
Agriculture & Timber	9.9	10.0	10.4	10.3	10.3	9.8
Construction	9.0	8.5	7.9	7.2	7.0	6.5
Transportation	5.8	5.7	5.6	5.4	5.3	5.3
Trade	5.9	5.6	5.7	6.4	6.4	5.9
Housing	3.2	3.1	3.0	3.0	3.0	na
Public Health[a]	4.2	4.3	4.2	4.2	4.2	]
Education[a]	7.2	7.2	7.5	7.2	7.2	]14.4
Science[a]	3.1	3.1	2.3	2.2	2.0	]
Credit, finance & insurance[b]	402	439	494	581	630	na
State Administration	1.8	1.7	1.5	1.6	1.4	na
Other	1.8	1.6	2.1	1.8	2.4	na
TOTAL	75.3	73.8	72.1	70.8	69.3	na

Key:
a   denotes unified category
b   thousands
na   equals data not available

Sources: *Rossiia v Tsifrakh*, 1995 (Goskomstat, Moscow 1995) p. 44 and 'Zaniatosti v Rossii', *Ekonomicheskie Novosti*, No. 21, November 1995, p. 12.

Thus state sector employment in Russia fell from 75.3 million in 1990 to 69.3 million in 1994, the last year for which data is available. This constitutes an overall decline of 6 million or over 1 million a year since 1990. All in all, the growth of employment in general and state sector employment in particular has slowed down over the last decade.

The *productive sector*[7] has lost a great deal of its employees. For instance, industrial employment fell from 22.8 million in 1990 to 17.3 million by November 1995; employment in the agriculture and trade sectors remained constant; the transportation sector lost half a million employees while the construction industry lost a staggering 2.5

million workers in the period 1990-95. Employment in the *non-productive sector*[8] has also fallen from 17.7 million in 1990 to 14.4 million by November 1995. This has been coupled by a reduction in the size of the state bureaucracy by a fifth since 1990.

This reduction in state sector employment has been partly offset by a rise in the size of private sector. This has partly been promoted by a massive privatisation drive over the last few years. Thus while those employed in the state sector fell by 30 million or 48 per cent between 1990-94, the number of people working in the private sector rose from 9.4 million in 1990 to 22.1 million in 1994. This constitutes a growth rate of 235 per cent or nearly 13 million.[9] One area which has clearly benefited is the service sector. As table 11.1 shows the number of people working in credit, finance and insurance has increased 1.6 times from 402,000 in 1990 to 630,000 by the end of 1994.

But why has there been a change in employment patterns over the last decade or so? Part of the explanation lies in the changing demographic situation. Demand for and the supply of labour varies throughout the Russian Federation. The demographic and migration trends depicted in chapter 3 hint at the underlying problem; a shortage of able bodied workers. Thus even though the proportion of able bodied people of working age rose by 200,00 between 1992-94, a significant proportion migrated elsewhere, leaving Russia with an ageing working population. Hence in the same two year period, 1.2 million able bodied workers were middle aged or older.[10] The 'brain drain' during the post-communist era has seen 300,000 of the most highly skilled and qualified specialists emigrate to the 'Near abroad' or the West. Of this group, a quarter were well or extremely highly qualified.[11] But demographic factors are not sufficient explanations on their own. As state employers have become subject to tightening budget constraints, they have been forced to lay-off more and more workers. Thus in the post-communist period, the number of state sector employees losing their jobs totalled 41 million between 1992-94, with another 3.2 million being added to this figure in the first half of 1995, bringing the overall total up to 44.2 million. 37.2 million others have so far managed to hold onto their jobs. But many, and this especially applies to women, are only employed for a few days a week or in some cases a few days each month.[12] For example, by March 1995, 4.2 million or 6 per cent of the labour force were employed on a part-time basis.[13]

The evolution of a new labour policy

During the communist period, labour was administered and allocated using the centralised planning system. Wage levels were set according to output levels, hours worked, regional coefficients and so forth. All able-bodied people were obliged to work and those who failed to do so were branded as 'parasites'. In order to meet the requirements of the Russian state, graduates were assigned on a mandatory basis for up to three years to regions where their skills were in greatest demand. Finally, the state controlled the process of migration, using a system of internal passports or residence permits. In return for these restrictions, workers received job security, regular wages and employment related benefits. However, although labour participation was high, labour productivity was relatively low. This partly reflected a situation in which wages were determined centrally and not related to productivity rates. Finally, unemployment was officially denied, but in reality 'hidden' unemployment existed and those in this predicament received no state support.

Since the collapse of communism, many of these old guarantees and norms have been abandoned, often with dire consequences. Thus whereas the Soviet authorities sought to broaden the labour participation rate, which was highest among women, women have been the first to lose their jobs since 1991. Similarly, no attempt is now being made to conserve potential labour resources, such as pensioners. Many OAPs are no longer being retained on factory and other pay-rolls. In addition, former restrictions on migration have now been lifted, so international migration is feasible. This has facilitated greater labour mobility but exacerbated regional labour shortages throughout the Russian Federation. Furthermore, although greater attention has been paid to workers' rights since 1985, and trade unions are now independent of state control, state wage controls are still in place. It has also been extremely difficult to break the old attitudes of employers, many of whom still retain workers whose skills have been overtaken by technological advances. This has only stalled the inevitable - reduced labour productivity, falling output and rising enterprise deficits culminating eventually in closure. To try and avoid debts and closure, many enterprise managers have cut corners, especially in the areas of labour saving devices and health and safety. This has increased waste and inefficiency and also put workers' lives at risk. Thus the number of occupational diseases in Russia has risen 2.4 times in the last four years.[14] But in the end as enterprises fail to compete, the Russian government has had no choice but to withdraw its subsidies. Hence more and more loss-making enterprises are going bankrupt, forcing thousands, perhaps millions, onto the Russian dole-queue. This has led to the emergence of a society consisting of the 'haves' and 'have-nots' and as we saw earlier in chapters 6-7 is a source of social tension.

Regional aspects

These problems are particularly acute at local and regional level, as table 11.2 below shows. These difficulties have been exacerbated by price rises, wage variations and differences in taxation rules. Aware that wages are greatest in the capital and other large cities, and also of the fact that shortages in consumer goods are less common, most highly qualified workers prefer to settle in Moscow and St. Petersburg. Thus in June 1995, incomes in Moscow were three times greater than the average for Russia as a whole and 4.6 times greater than the minimum living wage. Elsewhere, the situation was very different. In Krasnoyarsk krai, for example, wages were only 2.5 times the minimum necessary for survival while in Tyumen, wages were 2.6-2.7 times the *prozhitochnyi minimum*.[15] Against this background, it is hardly surprising to find that 65 per cent of those with higher specialist training now reside in Moscow and St. Petersburg, leading to acute labour supply shortages elsewhere as table 11.2 shows.[16] Regional variations in labour supplies, coupled with mass migration, has made it extremely difficult for the Russian government to replenish its labour resources and resolve regional imbalances. Whereas prior to 1991, it was possible to assign graduates to areas of need throughout Russia, nowadays the number of students with the appropriate skills, training and experience is dwindling, as we shall see in chapter 13. In any case it is no longer politics but economics (via the market) which determines the distribution of labour. As a result of the aforementioned problem, there is currently a major mis-match between labour supplies and requirements in many parts of the Russian Federation.

Table 11.2
Unemployment by region of the Russian Federation, June 1995

Region of Russia	Number of unemployed registered at FES agencies
Northern	142,196
North West	135,817
Central	384,468
Volga-Briatsk	181,852
Central-Black Earth	71,022
Volga	178,877
North Caucasus	203,996
Urals	294,273
Western Siberia	156,237
Eastern Siberia	98,361
Far East	124,337
Kalingrad oblast	21,921
Total	1,994,903

Source: *Statbiulleten' Gosudarstvennaia sluzhba zaniatosti*, No. 6, Moscow 1995, pp. 6-7.

At present, Russia is faced with a contradictory situation: on the one hand over 70 per cent of migrants from the Russian Federation are of working age while on the other the number of registered unemployed has risen from 17 per cent in 1992 to 33 per cent by the first half of 1995. This situation is due to the fact that labour policy is being dictated by the market, the power of individual industrialists and the clout of certain groups of workers who are able to put pressure on the government and local/regional politicians.

The impact of the market

Has the transition to a market economy since the mid-1980s had a positive or negative impact on labour policy and labour relations in contemporary Russia? In order to answer this question, I would like to examine several aspects of the current labour situation, namely wage arrears and poverty.

Wage arrears

One of the most serious issues threatening to undermine labour relations between the

Russian government, employers and workers is that of wage arrears. Goskomstat data shows for instance that wage arrears as a percentage of the monthly wage bill have increased from 8 per cent in January 1993 to 45 per cent by April 1995. In real terms, this constitutes an increase from 45 billion roubles (in December 1992 prices) to 125 billion roubles by 1995.[17] This is a major cause of conflict between management and workers.

Combating poverty

Despite an overall reduction in the rate of inflation and the fact that income is growing faster than prices, the rate of poverty will only gradually fall. Thus although the number of people living below the poverty line has decreased, the current total of 29.4 per cent of the Russian population is still far too high. The large majority of those defined as 'poor' (*bednyi*) are workers employed in the state sector. But the 'poor' also include many young families as well as middle-aged workers. Future school-leavers will also swell the aforementioned figure.

The main priorities in the development of Russian social policy (see chapter 10) as well as labour policy should be combating poverty and providing jobs. In my opinion a *National Programme for combating poverty* must be worked out. Given the fact that many employees are listed among the 'poor', it is necessary to increase basic wage levels in order to motivate labour. This would involve a change in income and fiscal policy and act as a guarantee not just of minimum wages but of wages high enough to survive on. This is the key to any genuine restructuring of the Russian economy. Such a change in direction is not only essential for economic reasons, it also has a deeper social meaning. As we saw earlier in chapters 6-7, growing poverty is alienating the population and engendering class conflict. This must be avoided at all costs and the gap between rich, who have access to food, nice houses, a decent education, private health care and all the trappings of a Western market oriented society, and the poor who spend 80 per cent of their income on food and other basic essentials, must be reduced to more acceptable levels. Unfortunately, the Russian government has been unsuccessful on all counts.

Real incomes have increased 6.2 times since 1992. But this increase in income has only been achieved at the expense of falling consumption. Moreover, as a consequence of the deepening economic recession, real GDP is declining (see table 1.1) and is likely to continue doing so in the near future by approximately 20 per cent. This will mean that recent increases in incomes might not be sustained in 1996. Current income and consumption levels will only be maintained if the slump in production is halted, if normal economic relations are restored and if the economic performance of several sectors, most notably industry, of the Russian economy improves. None of these scenarios are likely.

As a result of the above, the economically active population will again be asked to support a growing number of dependents. Such a situation is inherently unstable and economically inefficient. Unfortunately, the overall decline in wages in real terms, means reduced revenues from taxes. Thus recent announcements regarding the 1996 budget are very ambitious indeed and are unlikely to be fulfilled, especially as expenditure was based on low inflation projections. It is probable, therefore, that the rich will get richer and be able to purchase shares, securities, currency etc. while the poor will get poorer. Current estimates suggest that the ratio between the incomes of the richest 10 per cent of the population and the poorest 10 per cent is 8:1.

Financing social and labour policy through taxation

We urgently need to address this issue by introducing a system which facilitates the more even distribution of social expenditure. This will probably entail the development of a more effective tax system. It is high time that the wealthier sections of society paid higher taxes. This is particularly important in view of the demise of the welfare state and the lack of a safety net (see chapter 10). Thus higher pensions, better unemployment benefit, improved health care, higher maternity and sick pay could all be financed through taxation if the political will to do so existed.[18] Any residual monies could be used to alleviate poverty and thereby reduce the proportion of families living below the poverty line (*prozhitochnyi minimum*). So far this has failed to happen, so over 40 million Russians are living in poverty.

Prioritising social policy measures

As for the socially unprotected strata of Russian society who are not in a position to fend for themselves, it is necessary to implement additional social measures, judged on an individual basis, to give everyone adequate social support. Such attempts to aid the 'poor' might in the short-term lead to distortions in the composition and level of people's incomes. Thus any sharp increases in the range of benefits and other compensating payments for the needy might in part undermine the incentive function of wages and work-related pensions. This situation might in turn promote conflict between different groups in Russian society. Despite these problems, more aid for the poor and a reorientation of current social and labour policy is nevertheless essential. After all it would be a clear indication of the development of democracy in Russia today and signal to the people that the Russian government does care about its people.

In order to successfully resolve current social and labour problems and to eradicate potential social conflict, it is important to have a greater awareness of the nature of the social processes currently underway in Russia. This goal can be achieved by monitoring socio-economic changes including living conditions, labour activity, employment trends, income and expenditure, consumption, consumer demand, social policy, migration and so forth. Many of these issues have been examined in this volume.

Limited success

Despite the growing number of poverty stricken and rising wage arrears, some successes have occurred. Since 1993, for example, Russia has managed to prevent the mass exodus of the workforce out of the productive sphere and also to preserve a 'core' of cadres essential for the functioning of the Russian economy. However, this core is dwindling all the time.

On the whole, however, the labour market situation remains fragile and extremely complicated. The number of people employed in most branches of the economy is declining. Thus table 11.1 shows that the number of workers in manufacturing has fallen by 7.3 per cent and those in science and technology by 13.8 per cent since 1993. This is the consequence of a tough fiscal policy, based on a monetarist philosophy, which has resulted in restrictions on public spending and a fall in production due to declining demand. However, we must be careful not to exaggerate the extent of the decline. In other instances, such as health care, education and social services, staffing levels have remained constant while those employed in insurance, taxation and legal services have expanded (see table 11.1). On balance, though, as we shall now see, such limited successes have been largely offset by rising unemployment.

The past legacy: unemployment trends in Russia, 1917-1991

After the October 1917 Revolution, unemployment in Russia gradually increased from 160,000 on 1 January 1922 to 335,000 by 1 October 1930. Although this constituted a doubling overall, unemployment levels were way down on the peak of 1.7 million of 1 April 1929.[19] The end of mass unemployment was declared in 1931.[20] From 1931 until the rise of Gorbachev registered unemployment did not officially exist in Russia.[21] However, open unregistered unemployment did not in fact disappear because of the perennial problems of the Russian economy, namely high labour turnover. As a consequence, labour exchanges (*biuro trudoustroistva*) which were originally abolished in the early 1930s, were in fact re-established as early as 1967.[22]

Early on in the Gorbachev era, one Soviet scholar, Nikolai Shmelev, declared that unemployment (*bezrabota*) stood at about 3 per cent.[23] As a result on 22 December 1987, a Central Committee of the CPSU, USSR Council of Ministers and All-Union Central Council of Trade Unions resolution was passed calling for a more 'effective employment of the population', together with 'a perfecting of the job placement scheme' and a strengthening of the 'social guarantees of workers'.[24] The goal of this decree was to rationalise over-manning estimated to be between 13-19 million.[25]

Table 11.3
Unemployment in Russia, 1990-95

Year	Working population	Unemployed
1990	na	1.30
1991	na	2.10
1992	75.6	3.59
1993	74.9	4.12
1994	74.6	5.24
1995	74.1	5.50

Key: NA data not available.

Sources: *Rossiia v Tsifrakh*, 1995 (Goskomstat, Moscow 1995), p. 44 and *Rossiia pered vyborom*, ('Obozrevatel' ', Moscow 1995), p. 35.

Although some scholars argued in 1989 that 20 million workers would lose their jobs because of technical modernisation and the streamlining of the Russian bureaucracy,26 such predictions of a dramatic rise in unemployment as a result of Gorbachev's economic reforms failed to materialise in the late communist period. However, since the collapse of communism in 1991 unemployment has steadily increased as we can see from table 11.3 above. Thus since 1990 there has been a four fold increase in the number of unemployed in Russia. The reasons for this trend will be explored below.

The post-communist phase

Taking into account the communist legacy, this section examines: the types of unemployment existing in Russia today; who are the employed; unemployment legislation and policies - active and passive; the nature of the social partnership and the obstacles to the development of a more effective labour policy.

Types of unemployment

Unemployment refers to the existence of a section of the labour-force able and willing to work, but unable to find suitable employment. Four distinct causes of unemployment can be distinguished:

(i)   *frictional unemployment* which is caused by people being between jobs or looking for one;
(ii)   *classical unemployment* which is caused by excessively high wages;
(iii)   *structural unemployment* refers to a mismatch of job vacancies with the supply of labour available. This is caused by shifts in the structure of the economy;
(iv)   *Keynesian unemployment* results from the existence of a deficiency of aggregate demand which is simply not great enough to support full employment; and finally,
(v)   *Monetarists* argue that all unemployment is either classical or voluntary. In their view, unemployment either exists because wages are artificially held too high or else, unemployed people have not chosen to take a job at the going wage rate.

In Russia's case, the main types of unemployment are *structural*, as Russia makes a transition from military to civilian production and gears herself up to meet the demands of a global market, and *frictional*.

Why has this occurred? Firstly, Russian unemployment is the result of a decade or so of macroeconomic destabilisation, reduced demand and the collapse of the command economy and second, rising unemployment reflects sectoral imbalances, exposure to world markets, the introduction of modern technology and the development of new Western style forms of management practice.

The unemployed

Who are the main victims of the aforementioned changes? As table 11.4 below shows most of the unemployed are women (who outnumber men by two to one) and those aged between 30-49 years (half of men and women). At present, the average age of the unemployed is 34 years, but a third of those without jobs are the young (those aged 16-29 years) and nearly 40 per cent are graduates.

Table 11.4
Age and sex of unemployed in Russia, March 1995

Unemployed	Males (%)	Females (%)
As a whole	37.7	62.3
of which aged:		
Less than 20 years	9.2	12.4
20-24 years	17.3	15.7
25-29 years	11.6	11.2
30-49 years	49.3	50.4
50-54 years	4.9	4.6
55-59 years	5.8	3.5
Older than 60 years	1.9	2.2
Middle aged	34.7	34.0

Source: *Statisticheskoe obozrenie*, No. 9, 1995, p. 68.

Unemployment legislation

Two pieces of legislation have been passed so far. The first came in 1988, at the height of perestroika, and talked about the right to work and the need to improve efficiency.[27] By contrast, 1991 Labour legislation stressed the freedom to choose one's job, the need for retraining, assistance for those seeking jobs and finally, the right to be protected from job discrimination. The most significant change in these three years was in the area of the 'right to work' - jobs were no longer guaranteed and work was now voluntary. Thus earlier references to those out of work as 'parasites' were now dropped and it was acknowledged that some people might be unemployed through no fault of their own.[28] Other legislation is forthcoming (see below).

Unemployment policy

Following Fretwell and Jackman, it is possible to argue that unemployment policies fall into two categories: *active* or *passive*. The first strategy refers to measures geared towards helping the unemployed return to work. This includes job counselling; training schemes and the provision of temporary work to gain enough experience for a permanent job later. *Passive measures*, on the other hand, include the payment of unemployment benefit (hereafter simply UB). The latter is seen to be counterproductive in so far as it encourages fraudulent claims or idleness because benefits might be set too high and therefore act as a deterrent to those looking for work. UB is also costly to administer.[29] What type of measures are in place in Russia?

Unemployment benefits

Since July 1991, UB have been payable in the event of loss of employment. At present, UB is payable for a maximum of 12 months and is phased in three stages as follows: the first phase lasts three months when UB constitutes 75 per cent of previous earnings, but excludes bonuses and extra payments, a substantial part of earnings. The second phase lasts for the next four months when UB is reduced to 60 per cent of previous earnings and the final stage, makes up the last five months when UB totals only 45 per cent of previous earnings.[30] The number of registered unemployed in receipt of UB in Russia has steadily risen from 64 per cent in 1991 to 84 per cent by the end of 1994.[31] By June 1995, this amounted to 2.35 million people.[32] Unfortunately, there is a six month lag between registration with an FES agency and payment of any UB. When it is eventually paid out UB is abysmally low: only 13 per cent of the average wage by the third quarter of 1994.[33] This situation is a product of the severe financial constraints currently operating. Although eligibility rules are being tightened, those defined as 'unemployed', include mainly those unable to find 'suitable work'. The latter term refers to a job that matches people's education, but in most instances age, relevant work experience and the distance required to travel to work are also taken into account.[34]

Job creation

Employment exchanges (*biuro trudoustroistva*) and career advisory centres (*proforientatsionny tsentry*) have been established to help the unemployed find work.[35] Unfortunately, the number of unemployed per job vacancy has steadily increased from 11.2 in 1992 to 16.3 by the end of 1994.[36] Why? In the main this stems from the reluctance of many employers, especially of large scale enterprises, to use such employment services.[37] As a consequence it has been extremely difficult to create new jobs. Thus the 5.5 million unemployed in Russia today are left struggling for fewer and fewer job vacancies. According to Goskomstat data there were only 549,000 vacancies by mid 1995, down 84,000 or 10 people per job vacancy. By the summer of 1995, most vacancies were for workers in the oil, metallurgy, chemical, machine building, electroenergy, science, credit and financial sectors. Clearly not every unemployed person possesses the skills, qualifications and experience necessary to meet current demand.[38]

Involuntary leave, short and part-time work

Over the last few years we have also seen a growing number of workers placed on involuntary leave, short and part-time work in Russia. For example, one Goskomstat publication recently noted that those on compulsory unpaid leave or part-time work totalled 4.8 million or 6 per cent of the labour force.[39] The average duration of involuntary leave was 25 days in the first half of 1995.[40] Ministry of Labour surveys indicate that 40-60 per cent of Russian employees have now moved onto short or part-time work. This is especially true in textiles, the electrotechnical industry and in the tractor and agricultural machinery sector. Thus even though Russian unemployment appears to be low (see table 11.3), such an impression can be misleading, as many people do not register as 'unemployed' or else they are on involuntary leave, short and part-time work. However, whilst part-time work is less desirable than regular full-time permanent employment, it is nevertheless true that temporary or part-time jobs have helped to avoid serious social problems in towns and regions with only one main employer.

Insolvent enterprises

In cases where major employers have gone bankrupt, this affects the morale of not only unskilled and uncompetitive workers, but also the more qualified workers, including technicians, metal craftsmen, fitters, welders, machine-tool setters and many others. Because of the dire consequences for entire communities, the implementation of the March 1993 insolvency procedures have been delayed for as long as possible. As a result, few cases of bankruptcy have so far reached the courts. To date approximately 1,400 enterprises employing two million workers and with debts totalling 14 trillion roubles have gone bust.[41] However, this is a drop in the ocean as the actual number of companies who already have or will soon go bankrupt is nearer 4,500. If the fall in output continues, the ranks of the unemployed are likely to swell in 1996 and beyond.

Devising an alternative labour strategy

In order to resolve the above problems, the following measures are necessary:

(i)   a more flexible labour market;
(ii)   a job creation programme;
(iii)   anti-employment measures;
(iv)   greater support for profitable enterprises;
(v)   further social guarantees for workers;
(vi)   support for managers to enable them to expand production and hire more workers using tax incentives and other benefits;
(vii)   greater power for local authorities in determining manpower policy;
(viii)   the creation of more joint-stock companies;
(ix)   the gradual elimination of the State monopoly;
(x)   a re-evaluation of the role of trade unions in the labour process; and
(xi)   the extension of the social partnership (*Sotsial'noe partnerstvo*).

All of these issues have been the subject of intense debates since 1992 involving the Presidential Administration, the Russian government, the Ministry of Labour, Russian industrialists and other interested parties. A New Labour Code is currently under review. This involves not only strengthening existing guarantees but also introducing new ones relating to social protection for redundant workers. But what chances is there of success? The possible scenarios will become clearer if we examine the nature of the social partnership more closely.

The fragile social partnership

The social partnership dates back to November 1991 but the aftermath of the August coup d'etat and the collapse of the USSR in December 1991 disrupted progress so this issue was not taken up by Yeltsin until 1992. Since 1992 the aim has been to develop a corporate strategy based on greater co-operation between government, business and labour.[42] This change of heart was deemed necessary in order to resolve head on collisions between employers (who resorted to dismissals) and workers (who went on strike). Thus far it appears to have worked. For instance, the number of enterprises involved in strike activity in Russia has fallen from a peak of 6,273 in 1992 to only 514 by 1994. Moreover, fewer workers are now willing to strike. Thus the number of strikes has fallen from 357,600 in 1992 to only 155,300 by the end of 1994. All in all this has meant fewer lost working days which have declined from 2.3 million in 1991 to 755,100 by 1994.[43] On top of these successes, wage settlements have also been resolved quickly with minimal conflict. A general Agreement and 46 branch agreements on wage tariffs were concluded in 1994 and various regional agreements followed in 1995.

However despite such progress, the social partnership is still not operating efficiently enough to provide a balance between the interests of various social groups, hired workers, employees etc. Why is this the case? It seems that the government still wants to have the final say on the wage negotiation process. In addition, the trade unions have been slow to modify their behaviour to suit the changing economic context, namely no plan but a market. To a large extent, both the government and labour organisations are firmly anchored in the past. For instance, Russian trade union leaders still have a tendency to approach government rather than employers during collective bargaining whilst employers have consistently failed to negotiate with workers' representatives at branch or regional level. New incentives, laws and other norms need to be introduced to break the deadlock and give the main participants in individual or collective bargaining greater decision-making powers.

Other obstacles to an effective labour policy

In addition to the above problems pertaining to the social partnership, other more serious obstacles hindering an effective post-communist labour policy include: budget deficits and financial destabilisation; a declining GDP, especially in industry; relatively high inflation and a declining demographic situation. In order to limit the damage done by the first three of these problems there is a need for a shift from monetarism to Keynesianism in economic policy. As regards the fourth, greater attention needs to be paid to health provision in general and for labour in particular. Closer attention must also be paid to migration policy. A number of options are available here including tighter restrictions on migrants and refugees moving for non-job related reasons, on the one hand, as well as better incentives - higher incomes, housing provision, job permits - for those relocating to regions with acute labour shortages, on the other.[44] The Ministry of Labour has urged the government to act quickly and decisively on these matters, because by April 1995, the difference between the 10 per cent highest paid workers and the lowest 10 per cent was 21 times in industry, 24 times in agriculture and 25 times in construction,[45] but to no avail. Such a situation cannot prevail for much longer without major social unrest. As we saw in the recent December 1995 parliamentary elections people's patience is running out and this might ultimately lead to Yeltsin's downfall in June 1996.

Finding a way forward

I hinted at what was required to solve Russia's labour problems earlier, but in order to alleviate the labour crisis and stabilise living standards a number of other measures are essential. The Russian government must:

(i)   guarantee a minimum wage, pensions and other related measures;
(ii)   regulate the cost of goods and services;
(iii)   implement measures to ensure economic and financial stabilisation; and
(iv)   introduce a modern taxation system.

The above strategies must be implemented throughout the Russian Federation and take into account regional variations.[46]

Unemployment and social conflict

Increased joblessness among many sections of Russian society will undoubtedly prove to be a source of social conflict in the near future. The longer a person is without a job, the more likely s/he is to become involved in political protest. This happened in December 1993 and it might well happen again two years later unless something urgent is done to restore the confidence of the unemployed in the Russian government and above all its President. But what can be done? Above all, we must reorientate our general economic, budgetary and credit policy along new lines. Investment programmes need to take into account the issue of 'releasing' or 'freeing-up' of workers, especially young people. Regional policies must be devised to combat unemployment before many areas become like 'ghost-towns'. The occupational training of prospective job-seekers must be improved to enable them to meet market demands. (For more on this problem see chapter 13). This applies as much to school and university students as it does to middle-aged workers made redundant. Retraining programmes must be put in place now.[47] In seeking to generate new jobs, the scope of the existing public works programme must be extended and finally, it is crucial to encourage both workers and employers to use labour exchanges, career advisory services and other appropriate agencies in order to meet their needs.[48]

Conclusion

Over the last decade Russia has undergone major economic transformation. This has led to a decline in state sector employment and the rise of the private sector. Changes in the demographic situation and the rate of inflation coupled with a decline in real wages and the introduction of tax and insolvency laws, has led to alterations in the demand and supply of labour. Although official statistics suggest relatively low levels of unemployment, the lack of a safety net has resulted in widespread poverty and growing social discontent. Unless this situation is addressed quickly, it might ultimately undermine an already fragile social partnership. Unfortunately changes in labour policy have been slow and no sustained action has been taken on poverty, unemployment and other serious social issues. It is now evident that this might well have dire consequences for Russia's political landscape and ultimately hamper her transition to liberal democracy for many years to come.

Notes

*   The views expressed in this essay are those of the author, not necessarily those of the Russian Federation, Ministry of Labour.

1.   R.W. Davies and S.G. Wheatcroft, 'A note on the sources of unemployment statistics', in D. Lane (ed.), *Labour & Employment in the USSR*, Harvester Press, Brighton 1986, pp. 36-37.

2.   For a more detailed discussion see Sheila Marnie, 'Who and where are the Russian unemployed', RFE/RL Research Report, Vol. 2 (33), 20 August 1993, pp. 37-38.

3.   Ibid, p. 37.

4.   In the summer of 1993, Fedor Prokopov, head of the FES, noted that only 20-25 per cent of the unemployed actually registered with labour employment services (*Rossiiskaia Gazeta* 15 June 1993).

5.   Susanne Oxenstierna, 'Trends in Employment and Unemployment', in A. Åslund (ed.), *The post-Soviet Economy: Soviet and Western Perspectives*, Pinter Publishers, London, 1992, pp. 39-40.

6.   Ibid, table 3.1, p. 42.

7.   According to Russian economists this comprises industry construction, transport, agriculture, trade and communications.

8.   This refers to education, health care, housing and other public services, science, state and local administration, finance, banking, art and culture.

9.   *Rossiia v tsifrakh 1995*, Goskomstat, Moscow 1995, p. 49.

10.   V. Vososel'skii, *Sostoianie rynka truda Rossii v 1992-1994 goda i pervoi polovine 1995 goda*, Russian Ministry of Labour Report dated 15 June 1995, p. 1.

11.   Ibid, p. 2.

12.   Ibid.

13.   Ibid, p. 3.

14. *Rabochnaia Tribuna* 7 February 1995.
15. V.F. Kolbanov, 'Vystuplenie pered predstaviteliami i mestnykh organov po trudu, obuchaiushchimisiia v IPK', unpublished Russian Federation, Ministry of Labour report, October 1995, p. 11.
16. V. Vososel'skii, *Sostoianie rynka truda Rossii v 1992-1994 goda i pervoi polovine 1995 goda*, Russian Ministry of Labour Report dated 15 June 1995, p. 2.
17. OECD Economic Surveys, *The Russian Federation 1995*, OECD 1995, figure 19, p. 114.
18. See ibid, table 22, p. 127 for a detailed breakdown of the way in which each of these social policies can be funded via taxation.
19. R.W. Davies and S.G. Wheatcroft, 'A note on the sources of unemployment statistics', in D. Lane (ed.), *Labour & Employment in the USSR*, Harvester Press, Brighton 1986, table 3.5, p. 44 and J.L. Porket, *Work, Employment and Unemployment in the Soviet Union*, St. Antony's/Macmillan, London 1989, table 3.1, p. 47.
20. R.W. Davies, 'The end of mass unemployment in the USSR', in D. Lane (ed.), *Labour & Employment in the USSR*, Harvester Press, Brighton 1986, p. 31.
21. J.L. Porket, *Work, Employment and Unemployment in the Soviet Union*, St. Antony's/Macmillan, London 1989, pp. 88-89.
22. Ibid, pp. 93, 99.
23. Nikolai Shmelev, 'Avansy i dolgi', *Novyi Mir* No. 6, June 1987, pp. 148-49.
24. Cited in J.L. Porket, *Work, Employment and Unemployment in the Soviet Union*, St. Antony's/Macmillan, London 1989, p. 195.
25. Ibid, p. 197.
26. Ibid.
27. *Pravda* 19 January 1988, pp. 1-2.
28. *Sovetskaia Rossiia* 25 January 1991, p. 1.
29. David Fretwell and Richard Jackman, 'Labor markets: Unemployment', in N. Barr (ed.), *Labor markets and Social Policy in Central and Eastern Europe*, L.S.E./World Bank, Oxford University Press, Washington D.C. 1994, p. 160.
30. United Nations, Economic Commission for Europe, *Economic Survey of Europe in 1994-95*, New York & Geneva 1995, table 3.4.9, p. 118.
31. Ibid.
32. *Statbiulleten' Gosudarstvennaia sluzhba zaniatosti*, No. 6, Moscow 1995, p. 3.
33. United Nations, Economic Commission for Europe, *Economic Survey of Europe in 1994-95*, New York & Geneva 1995, table 3.4.9, p. 118.
34. *Sovetskaia Rossiia* 25 January 1991, p. 1.
35. For more on the work of these exchanges see G. Gendler and M. Gildingersh, 'Labor exchanges in St. Petersburg', RFE/RL Research Report 20 August 1993, pp. 43-48 and more recently O. Ivanov et al., 'Klinenty sluzhby zaniatosti naseleniia Sankt-Peterburga: Kto on?', Informatsionno-analiticheskii biulleten' *Monitoring: Sotsial'no-ekonomicheskoi situatsii i sostoianiia rynka truda S.-Peterburga*, No. 1, 1995, pp. 43-48.
36. United Nations, Economic Commission for Europe, *Economic Survey of Europe in 1994-95*, New York & Geneva 1995, table 3.4.8, p. 117.

37.   Guy Standing, 'Recruitment, training and human resource management in Russian industry', paper presented to a conference on *Employment Restructuring in Russia*, Moscow & St. Petersburg, 21-29 October 1992.

38.   V. Vososel'skii, *Sostoianie rynka truda Rossii v 1992-1994 goda i pervoi polovine 1995 goda*, Russian Ministry of Labour Report dated 15 June 1995, pp. 4-5.

39.   *Sotsial'no-ekonomicheskoe polozhenii Rossii 1994g*, Moscow, Goskomstat January 1995, pp. 135-36.

40.   OECD Economic Surveys, *The Russian Federation 1995*, OECD 1995, footnote 198, p. 165.

41.   Ibid, p. 97.

42.   On the original social partnership agreement of November 1991 see *Rossiiskaia Gazeta* 19 November 1991, p. 2 while on trends since see E. Teague, 'Russian government seeks "social partnership"', RFE/RL Research Report 16 June 1992, pp. 16-23.

43.   *Rossiia v Tsifrakh 1995,* Goskomstat, Moscow 1995, p. 58.

44.   See V.F. Kolbanov, 'Vystuplenie pered predstaviteliami i mestnykh organov po trudu, obuchaiushchimisiia v IPK', unpublished Russian Federation, Ministry of Labour report, October 1995, pp. 5-6.

45.   Ibid, p. 13.

46.   Ibid, pp. 14-15.

47.   Ibid, p. 18. On the range of unemployment policies available see C. Williams, 'Unemployment in Britain, Europe and Russia: A Comparative analysis', Paper presented to a conference on *The transformation of social structure in post-Soviet society: Trends and prospects*, Vologda, 4-6 October 1995.

48.   V.F. Kolbanov, 'Vystuplenie pered predstaviteliami i mestnykh organov po trudu, obuchaiushchimisiia v IPK', unpublished Russian Federation, Ministry of Labour report, October 1995, pp. 18-19.

12 Russian health care in transition

CHRISTOPHER WILLIAMS

Introduction

This chapter seeks to explore the changes which have swept health care since the collapse of the USSR in December 1991 and will examine the main challenges facing the health service four years on. However, in order to understand current events, we need first of all to be aware of the nature of the communist legacy.

The communist legacy

Throughout the period from the October Revolution of 1917 to the emergence of Gorbachev in the mid-1980s, the main characteristic of Russian social policy was the key role played by the state in determining social need and in establishing the means (i.e. bureaucratic mechanisms) to implement social policy decisions. This monopoly role was particularly evident in the Stalinist period (1928-53) when the primacy of heavy industry and defence were emphasised to the detriment of consumer industry and social services. As a result, the latter developed in an ad hoc, fragmented and often unplanned way and although quantitative achievements were impressive, quality was sacrificed. All in all trends in the health sector were subordinated to economic policy directives.[1] Chronic shortages, low pay and a rapid deterioration in the level of health care offered and in the health status of the Russian population were common. This was the case for several reasons: alarming levels of pollution; poor working and living conditions; inadequate diet (due to food production and distribution difficulties); excessive use of tobacco and alcohol and low levels of personal hygiene. This trend continued in the post-Stalin period. From the mid-1960s to the mid-1980s, people in Russia worked longer hours, suffered from increased journey time due to the deterioration of public transport and had to spend more time queuing to secure basic necessities. This situation was in turn reflected in a number of adverse trends: declining life expectancy; increased mortality for all age groups, but especially males (as a result of cardiovascular diseases, accidents and poisoning, cancer); a rise in the number of working days lost etc.[2]

The Soviet health service which was charged with combating this deterioration in health conditions was itself facing many problems: chronic underfunding and under-investment; deterioration of plant, especially hospitals; inadequate facilities; widespread shortages of medical services, drugs and equipment; overcrowding; high turnover of staff (who were poorly paid; forced to take on extra jobs; tired and demoralised) and so forth. As a consequence, doctor-patient relationships became difficult, but patients had little opportunity to chose their doctor. Queuing meant that visits to a Russian GP were very time consuming. Undoubtedly without the use of *blat* (influence) to get on the books of another doctor or the substantial black market in pharmaceuticals, the health of Russian citizens would have deteriorated further. Thus although in theory the health care system was run on egalitarian principles - free of charge, widely available etc. - in reality, major inequalities existed.[3]

The structure of the health service during the Soviet period is shown in figure 12.1 below:

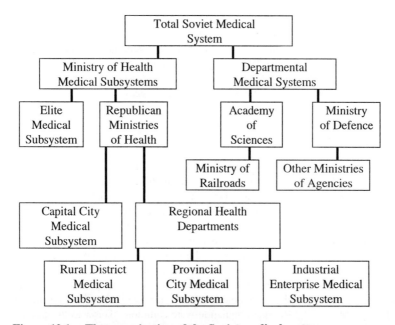

Figure 12.1   The organisation of the Soviet medical system

Source: C.M. Davis, 'The organisation and performance of the contemporary Soviet health service', in G.W. Lapius and G.E. Swanson (eds.), *State and welfare USA/USSR*, (Berkeley, Institute of International Studies, 1988), p. 117.

The above figure indicates that the Ministry of Health (*Minzdrav*) was responsible for the overall co-ordination of Russian health care which was split into several sub-systems - 15 Republican ministries (now full blown Ministries of health for the new fledgling democracies of the former Soviet Union) - which themselves were sub-divided into capital city (Moscow, Kiev, Vilnius etc.), industrial (St. Petersburg, Urals etc.), provincial city and rural health care systems.[4] Although it appears that resources were allocated on the basis of need, in actual fact the distribution of health care reflected the economic and political priorities of the Soviet state. Thus if one region was more important than another, it received and was able to provide better quality medical care. The sharp disparity in health services is highlighted by the existence of **elite** medical facilities. These were either available to the Soviet political elite in the form of the 4th Administration or to important Ministries, such as Foreign Trade, Finance, Defence, State Security, Internal Affairs etc. as well as the military in all its forms and the railroads, waterways and civil aviation.[5]

Up to 1991 *Minzdrav* and the 15 Republican Ministries administered the large majority of medical establishments. *Minzdrav* itself was run by a Minister and 20 senior officials. The national Ministry concentrated upon policy formulation; foreign liaison; planning (on a five-year basis); budget allocation etc. while the management of the medical system was left to the 15 Republican ministries.[6]

Some indication of the level of medical facilities in the period from Stalin to Gorbachev are shown in table 12.1 below:

Table 12.1
Soviet medical system resources and expenditure, 1950-85

Indicator	1950	1955	1960	1965	1970	1975	1980	1985
Doctors	14.6	na	20.0	23.9	27.4	32.7	37.5	42.0
Paramedics	39.6	na	64.2	72.8	87.2	98.5	105.7	113.5
Hospital Beds	55.7	65.1	80.4	95.8	109.4	117.9	124.9	129.6
Hospitals	18.2	24.4	26.7	26.3	26.2	24.3	23.1	23.3
Expenditure	10.5	20.8	14.6	5.1	5.8	5.5	5.4	4.6

Key:
NA denotes data not available.
All figures in column 1 refer to numbers per 10,000 population except data on hospitals (which are in thousands) and health expenditure (which is expressed as a per cent of total state budget).

Sources: *Narodnoe khozyiastvo* (Moscow 1970g - 1989g) and *Gosudarstvennyi budzhet SSSR: Budzheti soiuznykh respublikhakh* (Moscow 1966g and 1982g).

In the period up to 1985, the Russian medical system operated according to a five-year plan system in which the state through *Gosplan* (the State Planning Committee) set the targets for the entire health sector - numbers of doctors, beds, out-patient visits etc. In the post-Stalin period, most plans were modest, involving steady increases of inputs and medical service outputs. Health budgets were then allocated to finance these activities. Table 12.1 illustrates Russia's emphasis on the quantitative development of inputs. Thus the number of doctors increased three-fold from 14.2 per 10,000 in 1950 to 42.0 per 10,000 by 1985 and a similar rate of growth occurred among paramedical personnel. The number of hospital beds doubled while the number of hospitals rose by just over 5,000 or 144 hospitals a year. All this was achieved on a declining proportion of the state budget allocated to health which fell by 50 per cent between 1950 and 1985 from 10.5 per cent to only 4.6 per cent of overall budget expenditure. By 1985, the Soviet medical system employed about 7 million people or 6 per cent of the total labour force. Table 12.1 demonstrates therefore that most health care inputs increased in the post-Stalin period.

Table 12.2
Distribution of medical facilities in the former USSR, 1950-82

Republic	a		b		c		d	
	1950	1982	1950	1982	1950	1982	1950	1982
Russian Federation	15.6	39.2	43.8	117.8	59.2	132.1	54.8%	53.0%
Ukraine	13.9	38.9	36.6	106.7	52.2	128.0	16.3%	16.6%
Belarus	9.3	35.3	31.3	102.5	41.2	127.0	2.9%	3.4%
Uzbekistan	10.2	30.7	23.2	86.7	49.7	117.4	2.8%	4.7%
Kazakhstan	9.5	33.6	30.7	104.1	52.1	131.4	2.7%	5.1%
Georgia	26.7	50.9	46.5	114.8	54.6	107.5	2.1%	1.8%
Azerbaidzhan	22.0	35.0	46.9	87.8	57.8	97.2	1.7%	1.5%
Lithuania	10.7	40.7	22.6	113.9	42.1	121.4	0.8%	1.4%
Moldavia	10.3	34.0	32.6	110.6	45.1	121.8	1.0%	1.3%
Latvia	15.1	45.7	33.0	119.9	71.7	138.0	1.0%	1.1%
Kirghizia	9.9	30.9	27.0	90.0	40.3	120.4	0.6%	1.1%
Tadzhikistan	8.4	25.1	21.9	66.9	43.9	100.9	0.6%	1.0%
Armenia	18.9	35.9	33.5	86.4	47.6	84.3	0.7%	1.0%
Turkmenistan	13.4	29.1	43.8	81.7	61.3	106.1	0.7%	0.9%
Estonia	13.5	23.9	35.7	111.4	66.1	126.4	0.7%	0.6%

Key:

a   Doctors per 10,000 population
b   Paramedical staff per 10,000 population
c   Hospital beds per 10,000 population
d   Health service expenditure as a percentage of USSR state budget

Source: *Narodnoe khozyiastvo* (Moscow 1970g - 1989g) and *Gosudarstvennyi budzhet SSSR: Budzheti soiuznykh respublikhakh* (Moscow 1966g and 1982g).

However, these official statistics ignore two key variables: the quality of and inefficiency with which resources were used. They also fail to indicate regional variations in distribution. Data on this aspect are shown in table 12.2 above which illustrates that there were high levels of inequality in the distribution of medical care throughout the former Soviet Union under communism. This is an important but extremely difficult issue to assess. However, in terms of the four indicators chosen - doctors, paramedics, hospital beds and Republican health care expenditure allocations - significant inequalities existed between ex-Soviet Republics from 1950s to the early 1980s.

The ex-Soviet economy in the period to 1985 is best described as a 'shortage economy' in which financial constraints were widespread; shortages of inputs common and the quality of medical care poor. It was also difficult to attract good quality staff because the average wage in the health sector only increased from 48.6 roubles in 1950 to 134.9 roubles a month by 1986. Despite this 3-fold increase, medical workers' wages declined from 75.7 per cent of the national average in 1950 to 69 per cent by 1986. This situation had a number of adverse effects: firstly, low wages reduced the quality of entrants to medical and nursing schools; secondly, the health sector became dominated by women; thirdly, there were high levels of turnover, especially among middle-ranking personnel; and finally, as wages were not linked to performance, there were few incentives for higher productivity etc. The declining state budget allocations to health care also made it extremely difficult for *Minzdrav* and its Republican counterparts to keep hospitals and other medical establishments in good condition and for the health sector to purchase essential pharmaceutical goods and medical equipment. As we shall now see, this situation had a detrimental impact on health conditions.

Health conditions

Health conditions in Russia showed a great improvement in the two decades after the Second World War. For instance, life expectancy at birth rose from 47 years in 1938-39 to 70 years in 1965-66. Although improvements in the fields of housing, diet and income distribution assisted in the attainment of targets for mortality reduction, the medical system was given most credit for the evident progress.[7] However, over the next two decades this trend was reversed - the death rate increased from 7.1 in 1964-65 to 9.4 per 1,000 in 1975-76; similar increases also took place in the infant mortality rate (IMR). These trends were partly offset by a rise in the birth rate from 17.4 in 1970 to 19.8 per 1,000 population in 1983. However, in overall terms, life expectancy at birth fell from 62 years for males and 73 years for females by 1982. As a consequence, the party and state authorities became increasingly critical of the health sector in the early-mid-1980s.

The Gorbachev era, 1985-91

Unfortunately any real attempts at rectifying these difficulties did not occur until Gorbachev's rise to power from March 1985 onwards. In 1986, in the early stages of perestroika (restructuring), Gorbachev emphasised the need to place **utmost importance** upon the maintenance and strengthening of people's health. He aimed to achieve this goal by providing a 'high-quality curative, preventive' medical service. But before this was possible, he stressed the need to 'tackle many urgent scientific, organisational and cadre problems'.[9] Among the goals set by Gorbachev were:

(i)   increasing the effectiveness of public health policies;
(ii)   introducing an anti-alcohol campaign;[10]
(iii)   implementing a comprehensive screening programme of the entire population for diseases;
(iv)   improving levels of public sanitation and reducing environmental pollution;
(v)   improving the quality of medical care;
(vi)   promoting efficiency; and finally,
(vii)   improving the performance of supporting health sector institutions.[11]

In order to achieve these objectives, Gorbachev set about transforming the health sector. This necessitated: first, removing ineffectual senior health manager. For instance, 165 heads of medical establishments were replaced between 1985-87. These included the Minister of the Medical Industry, Melnichenko (replaced by Bykov); the USSR Minister of Health, Burenkov and the Head of Planning-Finance, Golovteev;[12] second, increasing the pay of medical staff; third, expanding the network of fee-paying polyclinics; fourth, cracking down on second economy activity; fifth, setting new health plan fulfilment priorities, for instance, on contracts for the building and repair of medical facilities; sixth, improving the supply and distribution of medicines and medical equipment; seventh, accelerating the level of technological progress; eighth, placing greater emphasis on biomedical R & D; and finally, reforming the nature of medical foreign trade e.g. structures and mechanisms. Some indication of the degree of success in achieving these aims is shown in table 12.3 below which illustrates in great detail various aspects of health sector development in the late Communist period. A number of trends are evident:

(i)   An increase in the level of medical inputs, finance and output of the medical system (table 12.3, sections A-C);
(ii)   A modest growth in the facilities, personnel and output of the medical supply system (table 12.3, section D);
(iii)   Although certain indicators increased, such as the output of pharmaceuticals, vitamins and medical equipment by the medical industry (table 12.3, section E), it was still nevertheless true that Russian domestic industries were unable to meet demand. The situation in fact worsened. For example, only 38 per cent of demand was met domestically in 1991, compared to 52.1 per cent in 1985 (table 12.3, section E); and finally,
(iv)   The situation was especially acute in relation to medicines, so deficits were met using imports - 90 per cent of which came from the socialist countries. The amount spent on medicines totalled one billion foreign trade roubles (table 12.3, section F).

Table 12.3
Soviet medical system resources and expenditure, 1985-91

Section A: Soviet medical facilities and personnel

Indicator	1985	1986	1987	1988	1989	1990	1991
Hospitals (000s)	23.3	23.5	23.6	23.5	23.7	24.1	24.3
Outpatient clinics (000s)	39.1	40.1	40.8	41.3	42.8	43.9	44.4
Hospital beds (000s)	3,607.7	3,659.8	3,711.8	3,762.6	3,822.3	3,832.1	3,837.0
Hospital beds (per 10,000 pop)	129.9	130.1	130.6	131.3	132.9	132.6	132.3
Doctors (000s)	1,170.4	1,201.7	1,231.2	1,255.7	1,278.3	1,279.2	1,279.7
Doctors (per 10,000 pop)	42.0	42.7	43.3	43.8	44.4	44.2	44.1
Middle medical personnel (000s)	3,158.9	3,226.9	3,288.6	3,351.7	3,386.0	3,420.2	3,437.3
Scientific workers in medical science & pharmacology (000s)	77.3	78.6	80.2	81.4	84.5	86.0	86.8

Section B: Soviet medical system finance

Indicator	1985	1986	1987	1988	1989	1990	1991
State health budget (billion roubles)	17.5	17.9	19.3	21.7	24.4	28.3	36.6
Health share of total state budget (%)	4.6	4.3	4.5	4.8	5.1	5.6	5.4
Total health expenditure (billion roubles)	22.5	23.5	25.3	28.9	33.6	36.0	46.3
Annual rate of growth of health expenditure (%)	NA	4.4	7.7	14.2	16.3	7.1	28.6
Real total health expenditure (billion 1985 roubles)	22.5	22.8	23.7	26.0	28.7	28.1	24.1
Health expenditure per capita (roubles)	81.4	84.3	89.8	101.6	117.2	124.7	159.6

Indicator	1985	1986	1987	1988	1989	1990	1991
Health expenditure share of national income utilized (%)	4.0	4.1	4.3	4.7	5.1	5.1	5.0
Health expenditure share of gross national product (%)	2.9	2.9	3.1	3.3	3.6	3.6	3.5
Medical wage as a % of whole economy wage	0.70	0.69	0.71	0.69	0.68	0.68	0.66

Section C: Outputs of medical services in the USSR

Indicator	1985	1986	1987	1988	1989	1990	1991
Outpatient visits plus Doctor home visits (million)	3,168.4	3,200.1	3,231.8	3,063.9	2,896.0	2,867.0	2,838.4
Preventive screenings (million)	123.2	125.0	127.9	124.7	121.9	118.9	116.0
Hospital bed days (million)	1,172.5	1,164.9	1,156.2	1,146.8	1,139.0	1,116.3	1,106.6
Hospitalisations (million)	69.6	71.9	73.4	73.5	70.3	70.3	69.6
First aid delivered on outpatient basis or by emergency services (million cases)	94.9	95.4	95.9	100.5	98.3	98.4	97.4
Hospital bed utilisation per year (days)	325.0	318.3	311.5	304.8	298.0	291.3	288.4
Operations carried out in hospitals (million)	11.0	11.4	11.6	11.6	11.6	11.8	11.6

Section D: The Soviet medical supply system

Indicator	1985	1986	1987	1988	1989	1990	1991
Pharmacies (000s)	29.5	29.7	30.2	30.2	30.3	30.5	30.6
Pharmacists (000s)	271.3	280.0	285.5	291.0	307.6	318.0	232.7

Indicator	1985	1986	1987	1988	1989	1990	1991
Total sales turnover (million roubles)	4,385.3	4,547.2	4,811.0	5,203.4	5,666.88	6,228.8	2,757.9
Retail sales (million roubles)	2,411.9	2,513.2	2,618.8	2,728.7	2,887.0	3,008.3	3,832.6
Wholesale sales (million roubles)	1,973.4	2,034.0	2,192.2	2,474.4	2,779.8	3,220.5	2,925.3
Total sales turnover (million 1985 roubles)	4,385.3	4,410.8	4,504.5	4,677.4	4,841.9	4,868.5	4,397.9
Medicine sales per capita (roubles)	12.5	12.9	13.5	14.4	15.6	17.0	15.4
Satisfaction of requirements for medicines by domestic production and imports (%)	86.0	83.0	81.5	78.0	86.0	72.0	60.0

Section E: The Soviet medical industry

Indicator	1985	1986	1987	1988	1989	1990	1991
Output of total medical industry (million roubles)	4,698.0	5,071.3	5,386.3	5,710.8	6,105.9	6,559.7	9,977.3
Index of medical industry output (1985 = 100)	100.0	108.0	114.7	121.6	130.0	139.6	212.4
Annual rate of growth of medical industry output (%)	NA	8.0	6.2	6.0	6.9	7.4	52.1
Output of the pharmaceutical industry (million roubles)	2,878.0	3,118.0	3,321.0	3,482.0	3,687.0	3,911.0	5,948.6
Index of output of the pharmaceutical industry (1985 = 100)	100.0	108.0	115.0	121.0	130.0	138.0	206.7
Annual rate of growth of pharmaceutical industry output (%)	7.6	8.3	6.5	4.9	5.9	6.1	52.1
Output of the vitamin industry (million roubles)	923.0	996.8	1,061.5	1,116.8	1,199.9	1,273.7	1,937.3

Indicator	1985	1986	1987	1988	1989	1990	1991
Output of the medical equipment industry (million roubles)	897.0	956.5	1,003.8	1,112.0	1,219.0	1,375.0	2,091.4
Output of total medical industry (million 1985 roubles)	4,698.0	4,921.3	5,044.8	5,131.9	5,214.9	5,124.2	4,611.8
Satisfaction of requirements for medicines by domestic industry (%)	52.1	50.8	49.4	48.1	46.7	39.1	36.0

Section F: Soviet foreign trade in medical products

Indicator	1985	1986	1987	1988	1989	1990	1991
Imports of pharmaceuticals (million foreign trade roubles)	1,165.5	1,232.0	1,249.4	1,316.9	1,847.4	2,273.2	1,295.7
Exports of pharmaceuticals (million foreign trade roubles)	104.8	102.6	107.6	107.8	100.2	89.2	44.6
Pharmaceuticals share of total imports (%)	1.7	2.0	2.1	2.0	2.6	3.2	3.2
Annual rate of growth of pharmaceutical imports (%)	5.0	6.1	1.4	5.4	40.3	23.1	-43.0
Pharmaceutical exports as a share of pharmaceutical imports (%)	9.0	8.3	8.6	8.2	5.4	3.9	3.4
Share of pharmaceutical imports from socialist countries (%)	89.6	92.5	93.6	92.7	83.8	78.1	68.5
Import of medical equipment and instruments (million foreign trade roubles)	362.3	349.1	343.2	396.6	462.8	904.1	515.3

Section G: Health output indicators in the USSR

Indicator	1985	1986	1987	1988	1989	1990	1991
First diagnoses of cancer, age adjusted (cases per 100,000 pop)	263.0	270.0	273.0	274.0	268.0	266.0	264.0
Salmonellosis morbidity (cases per 100,000 pop)	27.5	27.3	34.0	46.8	54.6	56.0	57.6
Temporary work incapacity (cases per 100 workers)	101.0	103.0	94.5	106.3	102.3	101.7	104.0
Infant mortality rate (deaths per 1,000 live births)	26.0	25.4	25.4	24.7	22.7	21.8	21.4
Crude death rate (deaths per 1,000 pop)	10.6	9.8	9.9	10.1	10.0	10.3	10.6
Life expectancy at birth (years)	68.4	69.6	69.8	69.5	69.5	69.5	69.0
First diagnoses of tuberculosis (per 100,000 pop)	45.7	44.8	43.7	42.0	40.0	36.9	35.9
Accidents in production (per 10,000 workers)	56.0	56.0	55.0	54.0	55.0	57.0	59.0

Source: C.M. Davies, 'The health sector in the Soviet and Russian economies: From reform to fragmentation to transition', in: *The former Soviet Union in Transition*, Vol. 2, JEC, US Congress, Washington 1993, pp. 855-58.

Health status

Table 12.3 section G above shows that despite these attempts to rectify the chronic shortages of medical equipment, reduce the levels of queuing etc., the medical system was unable to prevent a deterioration in health conditions during perestroika. As a result in the period 1985-91, life expectancy at birth remained stagnant while the death rate continued to be high. There are several factors which can be cited by way of explanation. The main ones include: shortages of food; increased consumption of tobacco and alcohol; a reduction in housing construction; a deterioration in sanitary conditions, especially in public establishments; pollution; a rise in the number of infectious and degenerative diseases; intensifying problems with capital stock, labour and supplies in the health sector (for example, according to a 1990 survey, 9 per cent of hospitals were said to be in a dangerous condition; 14 per cent needed major reconstruction; 15 per cent had no water supply; 49 per cent no hot water and 24 per cent no sewer system[13]) and the fragmentation of the health sector, against the backdrop of demands for devolution of power and the crumbling of the Russian Empire.

All in all, by the end of the Gorbachev era, the Russian economy, and the health sector within it, were facing enormous difficulties. On the economic front, by the end of 1991, the USSR had a budget deficit of 200 billion roubles (20 per cent of GDP) and was close to defaulting on its $58 billion hard currency debt. On the health front: the birth rate in 1990 stood at 13.4 per 1,000 while the death rate totalled 11.2 per 1,000. The age-standardised death rate was 12.0 per 1,000; the IMR stood at 17.4 and life expectancy was 69.3 years on average (but 63.8 for men and 74.4 for women), a slight decline since 1986. The level of abortions had reached 4 million by 1990 (195 per 1,000 births) and maternal mortality was high (54 per 100,000 live births). Mortality from diseases of the circulatory system, especially heart disease, from malignant neoplasms (cancer of the trachea, bronchus and lung), from suicide and self-infected injuries and from road traffic accidents all increased between 1986-90. Only diseases of the respiratory system and of infectious and parasitic origins were showing systematic declines.[14]

The extent of health service provision and trends in health conditions varied throughout the former Soviet Union. By 1990 only Russia and the Ukraine really possessed sufficient medical facilities and support networks to be reasonably self-sufficient in the increasingly likely event of Union collapse.[15]

From mid-1989 onwards growing demands were made for the devolution of power away from the All-Union Ministry of Health. As a result by 1991, the USSR Ministry of Health had agreed to reduce its size, narrow its role to largely strategic issues and hence to pass on most tasks relating to operational management to the then Republican Ministries. In the post-August 1991 coup d'etat period, discussions were already underway in various Republics on the creation of health services independent of Moscow (for instance as early as November 1991 in the case of Estonia). After the collapse of the USSR at the end of December 1991, the old USSR Health Ministry gradually disintegrated and health care fragmented.[16] In 1992-93, new Ministries of Health were created in the fledgling democracies of the ex-USSR, including Russia.

The post-communist phase, 1992-95

We saw earlier that the problems inherited from the communist regime were immense. With the collapse of communism in late 1991, society's expectations of substantial socio-economic improvements were high. As we saw in chapter 1, over the last five years, Russia has continued with her market reforms and the first competitive parliamentary elections took place in December 1993 and the second in December 1995.

However, because Russia is still in the process of transition, there are few new and relatively stable institutions and processes of decision-making. The conflicts between President Yeltsin, his cabinet and the Duma documented in chapter 1, have meant that social policy has been ad hoc, with only very general promises made. The government has no real vision of what post-communist social policy might be and the absence of a set of concrete, coherent social policies has resulted in social policy issues being assigned less priority than economic or political reform.

A substantial health reform programme 'On safeguarding the health of citizens' was started in 1991, but progress was interrupted by the abolition of the USSR Ministry of Health in November that year and the subsequent transfer of staff, resources and subordinate units to the newly independent states. In the first half of 1992, the health reform process was resumed. Under 'shock therapy', the following aspects were emphasised: preventive medicine; a reduced state role in health care; the introduction of national medical insurance; the need to put health care on a more commercial basis; and finally a greater involvement of foreign firms in the development of the Russian health sector.

In order to implement the above strategy, the old Ministry of Health was split into two: the **State Committee for Sanitary and Epidemiological Surveillance** and the **Ministry of Health of the Russian Federation**. Similar changes were made elsewhere. Thus a new **Union of Health Workers** was set up and the medical supply system, medical industry and medical foreign trade sectors were all reorganised. Finally in line with the new capitalist value system, restrictions were no longer placed on private practice; doctors were able to charge fees to individual patients and state medical equipment was available for rent.[17]

Russia's 'shock therapy' had an adverse effect upon the organisation of health care leading to the duplication of health facilities, empire building, institutional rivalry between the State Committee for Sanitary and Epidemiological Surveillance and the Ministry of Health of the Russian Federation[18] and also impacted upon health conditions in the post-communist phase, as table 12.4 below shows.

The decline in health status in the last few years was due to falling food consumption; inadequate funds to promote environmental protection; tight budget constraints (thus 35 billion roubles were required to implement the health reform programme but only 18 billion were received); declining health expenditure (in real terms by 1993, it was still at 1990 levels) etc. This led to continued shortages of staff, capital and supplies (drugs, instruments, bandages, linen, X-ray film etc.). Not surprisingly, the general public and medical staff became increasingly dissatisfied. One indication of this were the strikes by medical staff in January and April 1992 and again in August 1993.[19]

Table 12.4
Health status in the Russian Federation, 1992-94

Indicator	1992	1993	1994
Birthrate (births per 1,000)	10.7	9.4	9.6
Salmonellosis (cases per 100,000)	80.1	68.3	70.1
Diphtheria (cases per 100,000)	2.6	10.3	27.0
Whooping cough (cases per 100,000)	16.2	26.6	33.1
Measles (cases per 100,000)	12.5	50.3	19.5
Cancer (first diagnoses per 100,000)	271.8	276.3	280.2
Tuberculosis (first diagnoses per 100,000)	35.8	42.9	48.2
Hospital beds (per 10,000)	130.8	129.4	127.5
Doctors (per 10,000	44.7	45.2	45.7
Invalids from childhood (per 10,000 children up to age 16)	80.9	99.9	115.5
Infant mortality (per 1,000 live births)	18.0	19.9	18.6
Maternal mortality (per 100,000 births)	50.8	51.6	52.1
Mortality of males aged 40-44 (deaths per 1,000 in group)	8.8	11.1	11.7
Crude death rate (deaths per 1,000)	12.2	14.5	15.7
Life expectancy (years at birth)	68.6	68.0	65.0

Source: *Zdravookhranenie v Rossiiskoi Federatsii: Statisticheskii sbornik* (Goskomstat, Moscow 1995), pp. 6, 13, 15, 24, 29, 66, 68, 80. G.V. Osipov, *Sotsial'naia i sotsial'no-politicheskaia situatsiia v Rossii: analiz i prognoz (pervoe polugodie 1995 goda)*, (Moscow 'Academia' 1995), p. 46.

Unfortunately these deficiencies could no longer be rectified by the state or the embryonic private sector. Thus, economic recession resulted in many state enterprises going bankrupt. Those firms which survived were forced to move to self-financing and cost-accounting. This often resulted in cost-cutting exercises, for instance, in relation to workplace social provision - health care and social service facilities etc. Thus whereas 39 per cent of a sample of 2,000 in 13 regions of the Russian Federation received housing as part of their job; 50 per cent medical care and 51 per cent kindergarden facilities in January-February 1992; by June-July 1993, of a similar group of 2,000 from 15 regions of Russia, only 21 per cent received housing benefits; 31 per cent medical care and 31 per cent child-care facilities as part of their jobs.[20]

From crisis to catastrophe?

Between 1992-94, the health sector failed to keep pace with the transformation of the Russian economy as we can see from table 12.5 below.

Table 12.5
The health sector in post-communist Russia, 1992-94

Indicator	1992	1993	1994
Section A: Medical facilities and personnel			
Hospitals (000s)	12.6	12.5	12.3
Outpatient clinics (000s)	1,940	1,915	1,872
Hospital beds (000s/ per 10,000 pop)	130.8	129.4	127.6
Doctors (000s)	662.6	668.5	672.0
Middle medical personnel (000s)	1,684	1,647	1,607
Section B: Medical system finance			
State health budget (billion roubles)	33.8	37.8	35.7
Health share of total state budget (%)	9.8	9.4	8.4
Total health expenditure (billion roubles)	467.8	5,414.6	19,706.9
Health expenditure per capita (roubles)	160.0	180.0	190.0
Section C: Outputs of medical services			
Outpatient visits plus doctor home visits (million)	3,341.7	3,404.9	3,443.7
Hospital bed days (million)	1,058.5	1,098.7	1,109.6
First aid/emergency services (million cases)	90.3	88.9	89.1
Hospital bed utilisation per annum (days)	290	301	304
Operations carried out in hospitals (million)	14.0	13.8	13.8
Hospitalisations	67.8	69.4	69.4

Sources: *Zdravookhranenie v Rossiiskoi Federatsii* (Moscow Goskomstat 1995),
pp. 6, 13, 15, 29, 62, 68, 70, 74-5, 79-81, 85 and G.V. Osipov,
*Sotsial'naia i sotsial'no-politicheskaia situatsiia v Rossii: analiz i
prognoz (pervoe polugodie 1995 goda)*, (Moscow 1995), p. 46.

These problems stemmed from the failure to eradicate the dysfunctions of the old social services and health care systems, as table 12.6 illustrates:

It quickly became evident in the early stages of transition that the Yeltsin Administration was finding it increasingly difficult to retain past levels of social service provision and welfare benefits amid the deepening recession. Thus when the New Russia Barometer team carried out 2,106 interviews with respondents from 13 regions of the Russian Federation between 26 January - 25 February 1992, they discovered that 19 per cent were having to use connections to see a doctor; 53 per cent to obtain medicines and 10 per cent for hospital places. 86 per cent of the same sample believed that the post-communist government was not in a position to provide 'good social services' as against 13 per cent who thought this was possible. Pessimistically, half this sample also stated that conditions would not improve over the next five years. Amazingly, however, only 8 per cent said the government should prioritise health care; 12 per cent stressed the need to address care for the poor and sick and a mere 8 per cent emphasised the necessity to combat environmental pollution.[21]

Table 12.6
Data on shortages of basic necessities and social welfare provision
(12 regions of the Russian Federation, March-April 1994, sample 3,535)
Which of the following have you had to do without in the past year?
(Answers in per cent)

Category	a	b	c	d
Heating and electricity	91	6	2	1
Food	43	35	21	1
Medical treatment	68	18	9	4
Clothing	22	37	34	7
Petrol	76	7	6	11
House repairs	29	22	23	26

Key:

a   never
b   rarely
c   often
d   constantly

Source: Richard Rose, 'Getting by without government: Everyday life in a stressful society', *Studies in Public Policy* No. 227, CSPP, University of Strathclyde, 1994, p. 14.

Table 12.6 above shows that this situation had worsened by early 1994, with 13 per cent of respondents left without medical treatment at any one moment in time. This problem was further exacerbated by frequent shortages of food and clothing and a deterioration in housing. Meanwhile elite medical services - 4th Administration, Botkin hospital and facilities for the old KGB and MVD etc. - were largely unaffected by the fragmentation.

Although Dr Christopher Davis has argued that by 1993 Russia's health system was one of the best in the ex-USSR,[22] a year later, Russia was ranked 68th in the world in terms of health care. Several variables have contributed to this decline in health status by the mid-1990s, the main ones being:

(i)   30 per cent of Russia's water supply is not up to WHO standards;
(ii)   diets contain only a quarter of the required proteins; a half of vitamin C and a fifth of vitamin B requirements;
(iii)   life expectancy is rapidly declining (e.g. 65 years on average (but 59 for men and 72 for women));
(iv)   most diseases are rising (e.g. measles in 1993 was up 300+ per cent over 1992; mumps by 28 per cent; diphtheria by 26 per cent; whooping cough by 64 per cent; scarlet fever by 20 per cent; TB by 26 per cent; VD by 152 per cent;

gonorrhea by 35 per cent and so on);[23]

(v)   despite the collection of massive sums of money through the new health insurance scheme - 1.1 trillion roubles in 1993; 650 billion in the first half of 1994 - only 40 per cent of these funds were used for their intended purpose;[24]

(vi)   the death rate exceeds the birth rate. For instance, in the period 1988-92 the death-rate rose by 15 per cent, but in 1993 this difference increased to 18 per cent. It is generally agreed by Russian scholars that the birth-rate is insufficient to guarantee reproduction of the population[25] (see chapter 3);

(vii)   Russia is suffering from an ageing population - 11 per cent are in the 65+ group and 20 per cent are pensioners;[26]

(viii)   Population decline is generating a demographic crisis which is further compounded by the growing number of refugees entering. This situation is placing the health sector and other welfare facilities under great pressure;

(ix)   One in three Russians live below the poverty line (45 million by September 1995); the income of the richest 20 per cent has increased by 30 per cent since 1992; while that of the poorest 30 million has fallen by 3-5 per cent. In overall terms the gap between rich and poor has risen 17-20 times in general and in wage terms 27 times;[27] and finally;

(x)   Morale is low among health service workers. This is hardly surprising as in the period January-June 1994, the average wage was 166,000 roubles a month. Unfortunately, medical workers are 29-42 per cent below this average.[28]

Against this background, it is hardly surprising that 57 per cent of a sample of 3,535 respondents from 12 regions of the Russian Federation concluded in mid-March to early-April 1994, that health care must be **prioritised**. A further 47 per cent said the same about ecological pollution and 49 per cent about pensions. 18 per cent of the same sample regarded 'poor medical services' as a major area of concern.[29] The West too has recognised that the situation is serious. In 1992-93, the WHO/UNICEF allocated $418m to assist the FSU in meeting many of the acute challenges mentioned above in the areas of public health, nutrition, the environment etc. In a similar vein, but for economic and political reasons too - the desire to see the market reforms and political democratisation processes succeed - the IMF has provided Russia with $2.5 billion since 1992. By the end of 1994, Russia owed the Paris club of Western creditor nations $80 billion. In March 1994, the IMF extended a further $1.5 billion loan and in June 94, Russia's debt to the Paris club was rescheduled over 15 years, with nothing due for the next 3 years.

Despite such investment, Russia's health crisis has continued throughout 1995. Current estimates suggest that two-thirds of Russians live in regions where air pollution has reached dangerously high levels; the number of alcoholics reached 2.4 million in 1994, of which 13.2 per 1,000 population died from alcoholic poisoning and finally cancer and heart disease still remain major killers.[30] As a result of these trends the number of deaths exceeded the number of births again. This is now the fourth year in a row (see table 3.1). Unfortunately, health service workers are leaving the profession because their wages are still below the national level at 76.8 per cent in 1994.[31] The Yeltsin Administration seems unable to reverse this trend of declining health conditions and a collapsing health service as only 2-3 per cent of GDP was spent on health care in

1994, a drop in the ocean given inflation levels of 8-18 per cent in the first half of 1995.[32]

Difficult choices lie ahead

As we saw earlier in chapter 1, Russia took an economic U-turn (*povorot*) in Easter 1994. This situation has resulted in minimal financial support being given over to social welfare, education etc. Furthermore, the 1995 budget led to significant cuts in expenditure to get the economy back on the rails. The current war with Chechnya will generate additional financial strain in the coming months. This will clearly have a detrimental impact on social policy trends over the next 12-18 months. In late October 1995, the Russian government began considering a world bank/IMF proposal for health reform. If it is approved it will take many years to implement and will either lead to improvements or exacerbate an already bad situation. Only time will tell.[33]

Conclusion

All in all, President Yeltsin, the parliament and the political parties in Russia are very weak, so the current political situation is highly unstable. This coupled with the economic recession means that the ingredients exist for a possible crisis and breakdown in the near future. This situation is already having a negative impact on health service developments and health conditions and has meant effectively stalling the debate on health reform. Whether or not these issues will be put back on the agenda will depend on developments up to the June 1996 Presidential elections. The difficulty at present is that no one seems capable of putting health reform on the political agenda. Until this stalemate is resolved the acute crisis in the health sector is likely to continue and this unfortunately means that income and consumption levels in Russia will remain low by Western standards while the ranks of the low paid, OAPs, the incapacitated and dependent persons, single persons and the unemployed as well as others in the poverty trap will dramatically increase. The question is how long can this situation, alongside the other problems outlined in previous chapters, continue before confrontation between the Russian state and its citizens occurs.

Notes

1.   C. Williams, 'Soviet Public health: A case study of Leningrad, 1917-32', unpublished PhD in History, University of Essex 1990 and C. Williams, 'The Revolution from above in Soviet medicine, Leningrad 1928-32', *Journal of urban history*, Vol. 20, No. 4, August 1994a, pp. 512-540.
2.   J.C. Dutton , 'Causes of Soviet adult mortality increases', *Soviet Studies*, Vol. 33 (4), October 1981, pp. 548-559.
3.   C. Davis, 'The economics of the Soviet health service: An analytical and

historical study, 1921-78', unpublished PhD in Economics, Cambridge University 1979; M. Ryan, *The Organisation of Soviet Medical Care,* Martin Robertson, London 1978.

4.   C. Davis, 'The organisation and performance of the contemporary Soviet health system', in: G. Lapidus and G.E. Swanson (eds.), *State and Welfare USA/USSR,* Berkeley, Institute of International Studies 1988, pp. 115-120.

5.   C. Davis, 'The economics of the Soviet health service: An analytical and historical study, 1921-78', unpublished PhD in Economics, Cambridge University 1979.

6.   C. Davis, 'The organisation and performance of the contemporary Soviet health system', in G. Lapidus and G.E. Swanson (eds.), *State and Welfare USA/USSR,* Berkeley, Institute of International Studies 1988, pp. 116-118.

7.   W. Ward Kingkade, 'Demographic prospects in the republics of the former Soviet Union', in R.F. Kaufman and J.P. Hardt (eds.), *The former Soviet Union in Transition,* M.E. Sharpe, New York 1993, pp. 805-807.

8.   C. Davis, 'The economics of the Soviet health system' in: US Congress, JEC, *Soviet economy in the 1980s: Problems and prospects,* Washington D.C., 1983.

9.   *XXVIII S'ezd Kommunisticheskoi partii Sovetskogo Soiuza: Stenograficheskii Otchet,* Moscow 1986.

10.   C. Williams, 'Old habits die hard: Alcoholism in Leningrad under NEP and some lessons for the Gorbachev administration', *Irish Slavonic Studies,* 1991, No. 12, pp. 69-96.

11.   C. Davis, 'Developments in the Soviet health sector, 1970-90' in: US Congress, JEC, *Gorbachev's Economic Problems,* Washington D.C. 1987, pp. 326-332.

12.   Ibid, pp. 327-28.

13.   Cited in M. Feshbach, 'Continuing negative health trends in the former USSR', in R.F. Kaufman and J.P. Hardt (eds.), *The former Soviet Union in Transition,* M.E. Sharpe, New York 1993, pp. 848-49.

14.   C. Davis, 'The health sector in the Soviet and Russian economies: From reform to fragmentation to transition', in US Congress, JEC, *The former Soviet Union in Transition,* Vol. 2, Washington D.C. 1993a, p. 862; C. Davis, 'Health crisis: The former Soviet Union', *RFE/RL Research Report,* Vol. 2, No. 40, 8 October 1993b, pp. 35-43; J. Dunlop et al. (1993), 'Profiles of the newly independent states: economic, social and demographic conditions', in R.F. Kaufman and J.P. Hardt (eds.), *The former Soviet Union in Transition,* M.E. Sharpe, New York, pp. 1021-1187 and M. Ryan, *Contemporary Soviet society: A handbook,* Edward Elgar: Aldershot 1990, pp. 37, 50.

15.   Davis 1993a ibid, pp. 860-62.

16.   Ibid, p. 862 and C. Davis, "Health crisis: The former Soviet Union', *RFE/RL Research Report,* Vol. 2, No. 40, 8 October 1993b, pp. 37-39.

17.   Davis 1993 ibid, pp. 863-64; C. Williams, *AIDS in post-communist Russia and its successor states,* Avebury: Aldershot, 1995, chapter 3.

18.   Williams 1995 ibid.

19.   C. Davis, 'The health sector in the Soviet and Russian economies: From reform to fragmentation to transition', in: US Congress, JEC, *The former Soviet Union in*

Transition, Vol. 2, Washington D.C. 1993a, p. 864-66.

20.   I. Boeva and V. Shironin, *Russians between state and market: The generations compared*, Studies in Public policy, No. 205, CSPP, University of Stathclyde 1992, p. 10; R. Rose, I. Boeva and V. Shironin, *How the Russians are coping with transition: New Russia Barometer II*, Studies in Public Policy, No. 228, CSPP, University of Strathcylde 1993, p. 16.

21.   Boeva and Shironin 1992 ibid, pp. 16, 26, 32-33.

22.   C.M. Davies, 'Health care crisis: The former Soviet Union'. *RFE/RL Research Report*, 8 October 1993, pp. 40-41.

23.   *Nezavisimaia Gazeta* 16 July 1994.

24.   *Literaturnaia Gazeta* 21 September 1994.

25.   *Pravda* 16 July 1994; *Literaturnaia Gazeta* 16 July 1994.

26.   *Izvestia* 11 August 1994.

27.   *Trud* 19 August 1994 and *Pravda* 2 September 1995, p. 2. For more on this see C. Williams, 'Shock therapy and its impact on poverty in Contemporary Russia', Paper presented to the Politics of Social security in East European session of 22nd ECPR workshop, Madrid 17-22 April 1994b.

28.   *Sevodnya* 11 August 1994.

29.   R. Rose and C. Haerpfer, *New Russian Barometer III: The Results*, Studies in Public Policy, CSPP, University of Strathclyde 1994, p. 22.

30.   G.V. Osipov, *Sotsial'naia i sotsial'no-politicheskaia situatsiia v Rossii: analiz i prognoz (pervoe polugodie 1995 goda)*, Moscow 'Academia' 1995, pp. 14, 39-40 and L.M. Filimonov, *'Zdravookhranenie v Rossii: ot krizisa k neobkhodimomu razvitiiu'*, in *Reformy v Rossii s pozitsii kontseptsii ustroichivogo razvitiia*, Novosibirsk 1995, p. 45.

31.   Osipov 1995, ibid, p. 34.

32.   Ibid, pp. 21, 43 and I.E. Ivanova, *'O zdorov'e naseleniia Rossiyan'*, in *Sovremennaia sotsial'no - demograficheskaia situatsiia i zaniatost' naseleniia Rossii*, Moscow 1994, pp. 44-48.

33.   A. Vogonov, 'Bol'naia natsiia kak istochnik pribyli', *Nezavisimaia Gazeta*, 28 October 1995, p. 1.

13 An education system in crisis: meeting the demands of the market

VLADIMIR CHUPROV AND JULIA ZUBOK

Introduction

During the Soviet period, the education system was recast to break the ruling-class monopoly over education and culture; to generate fewer inequalities in access and to create new social groups devoted to the new socialist regime. However, although these changes lead to an expansion in the education system, reduced illiteracy and increased social mobility, especially for those from peasant and working-class backgrounds, research shows that during the late Khrushchev and especially the Brezhnev period a young person's educational attainment depended upon their parents' socio-occupational status and educational level; income; place of residence; degree of parental encouragement; the child's own academic performance; the type of school attended and finally, success depended upon the child's own educational and occupational aspirations. Although in theory the USSR was supposed to be superior to the West, in practice inequalities of access to education were just as pronounced in Russia. As a result, bribery and *blat* (the use of contacts) were common in order to gain access to the most prestigious universities and institutes. All in all, by the end of the 1980s, we had a situation in which there were widespread contradictions between the USSR's commitment to equality and its commitment to the economic and political goals of the state. Greatest stress was placed upon the need to create the conditions necessary for the building of communism and the creation of the New Soviet Man and Women, rather than on removing obstacles to educational inequality. The goal of the educational system prior to 1991, therefore, was to encourage loyalty and support for the existing communist system; to ensure that the population adhered to the basic principles of

Marxism-Leninism; to create a new type of individual who was law-abiding and dedicated to society and to ensure that graduates from institutes, colleges and universities were equipped to meet the needs of an expanding Soviet economy. As we now know, Russia was only partially successful in meeting these goals. There was a widespread rejection of socialist legality; the continued adherence to old values; increasing dissent; growing cases of delinquency and above all the USSR lagged behind the West in certain fields of expertise. These difficulties paved the way for Gorbachev's policies of perestroika and glasnost in 1985. This chapter seeks to examine changes in the education system over the last decade and assess whether the demands of the market have put the education system under too much pressure.

From fragmentation to crisis

The reforms begun under Gorbachev and continued under Yeltsin have lead to a review of the educational curriculum, democratisation of the tertiary sector, the development of mass and elitist education, the introduction of a greater variety of teaching methods, a general improvement in the quality of education, significant levels of autonomy for universities and finally, we have seen the introduction of independent sources of finance for institute and university sectors. These are some of the positive trends which have occurred as a result of the reform of the Russian education system over the last decade.[1]

Increasing numbers and over-stretched resources

On balance, however, it has become increasingly evident since 1992 that the restructuring of the education system along similar lines to the market economies of Western Europe and the United States has produced a major crisis; a fall in the number of students as well as a decline in the number of specialists working in the state education sector. This is clear from the information contained in table 13.1.

As we can see the number of primary and secondary schools has only marginally increased (by 880 schools or a mere 1.4 per cent) since 1980, a time of tremendous economic change. Similarly, the number of pupils in these schools have risen from 18.5 million to 21.1 million or by 13.6 per cent over the same period. Thus the growth in schools has failed to keep pace with demand and hence classes are becoming more and more overcrowded. A comparable situation prevails in relation to staff. The number of teachers in the primary-secondary school sector rose from 1.2 million in 1980 to 1.7 million in 1994/95 or by 33 per cent. Despite this increase, there is still a shortage of teachers - over a third of a million by July 1995. This is hardly surprising as teachers are poorly paid, over-worked and not adequately appreciated by society at large. By July 1995, the average monthly salary in the education sector was 276,500 roubles or less than half of that in industry and just over a third in comparison to those working in finance, banking and insurance.[2] More importantly, this salary was less than the minimum wage of 293,400 roubles in July 1994.[3]

Table 13.1
The development of Russia's education system, 1980-95

Category	Academic year(s)					
	1980/1-'1989/90	1990/1	1991/2	1992/3	1993/4	1994/5
Number of primary & secondary schools	67,320	67,571	6,891	68,270	68,113	68,200
Number of pupils in primary & secondary schools (millions)	18.5	20.3	20.4	20.5	20.6	21.1
Number of primary & secondary school teachers (000s)	1,188	1,442	1,497	1,561	1,624	1,682
Number of teacher vacancies (000s)	520	515	396	303	296	335
Number of universities	503	514	519	535	549	553
Number of university students (000s)	2,953	2,825	2,763	2,638	2,543	2,500
Students per 10,000 pop	206	190	186	178	171	166
Number of specialists (000s)	460.8	401.1	406.8	425.3	443.6	407.0
Number of specialists (per 10,000 population)	32.1	27.0	29.0	29.0	30.1	27.0
Number of postgraduates	66,642	67,626	63,156	50,126	na	na

Key: na denotes data not available

Sources: *Rossiia pered vyborom* (Moscow 'Obozrevatel' 1995), pp. 53-54, 157 *Molodezh' Rossii: Vospitanie zhiznesposobynkh pokolenii (Doklad komiteta Rossiiskoi Federatsii po delam molodezhi)*, (Moscow 1995), p. 79 and *Rossiia v tsifrakh 1995* (Goskomstat Moscow 1995), pp. 83, 87.

The crisis in higher education

This crisis is not confined simply to the pre-university sector, it is also widespread in tertiary education. Thus despite an expansion in the number of universities from 503 in 1980-81 to 553 in 1994-95 (or 9 per cent), the number of students studying at university has fallen rapidly from 2.9 million in 1980-81 to 2.5 million in 1994-95 or from 206 to 171 students per 10,000 population (i.e. by 20 per cent) (see table 13.1). In Russia today, students are neglecting their education in favour of well-paid jobs. While this might suffice in the short-term, what will it mean for students and above all Russia's educational base in the future?

The brain drain

There has also been a 'brain drain' among university specialists. Their number has declined from 4.6 million in 1980-81 to 4 million in 1994-95 or from 32.1 to 27.0 per 10,000 population, an overall decline of 15 per cent. Sadly, it is the most talented, research active individuals who are deserting education for a more profitable salary and better working conditions elsewhere in the private sector.

Declining numbers of post-graduates

One clear indication of the health of an education system is its ability to replenish its ranks in the future. We are, of course, talking about the size of the post-graduate population. However, in Russia's case, as table 13.1 illustrates, the number of post-graduates has declined by 25 per cent from 66,642 in 1980 to 50,126 in 1992-93. Similar reasons apply here. Post-graduate grants are virtually non-existent and if they do exist then they are pitifully low. Only the most well-motivated individuals are now undertaking research; most stop upon graduation. As a result, the number of newly qualifies staff in universities and institutes with higher degrees is falling, while the average age of Professors in senior positions is increasing. In a few years time when the current group of Professors retire, we will have difficulties replacing them with suitably qualified candidates of similar academic standing.

The attitude of Rectors

A number of recent surveys have evaluated the attitude of Rectors to these trends in the tertiary sector. For instance, in October 1993, 5 per cent of Rectors described the situation as normal; 66 per cent as hard and 29 per cent as catastrophic. However, by March 1994, their opinions had changed dramatically because 69 per cent said the situation was hard and 31 per cent catastrophic. No one referred to the situation as normal.[4] Two of the main reasons for this feeling of impending doom are declining salaries and the brain drain. Salaries of staff in Russia's education system were four times greater than those in industry in 1960 but by 1990, teachers earned, only 2.6 times more than industrial workers. However, by 1995, teachers' salaries were only half that of those working in industry, itself a crisis sector. One consequence of declining salaries in real terms has been the loss of 15 per cent of Professors and 10 per cent of Senior Lecturers/Readers since 1992.[5] Rectors of universities, institutes and research centres are therefore struggling to retain highly qualified staff with MPhil or PhD degrees. Unfortunately they are not always successful, as many of the most talented staff have already gone into the private and commercial sector.

This is by no means an even process. Although the number of university students stood at 2.5 million in the academic year 1994-95 or 98 per cent of its 1993 level and 95 per cent of its 1991 level, the fall in numbers is more pronounced in some fields than others. The situation is particularly dire in technical subjects, such as transport and agriculture as well as in leisure, such as physical education and sport. However, in other instances, namely economics, trade, law, art and cinematography, demand is higher. Thus in 1994, for example, there were three people for every place on university law degrees and two for every place on economics courses. Furthermore, the overall loss of good staff is especially acute in the provinces and regions outside of Moscow and St. Petersburg. All in all, whereas in 1989, 15.8 per cent of Russia's education system was said to be in a 'crisis state', by 1995, this figure is put at an astonishing 70 per cent.[6]

Meeting the challenge of the market

The problems outlined earlier may have made themselves felt in the last decade, but their origins date back to at least the 1960s. In the past, the state played a major role in financing the education system, determining educational policies and priorities and therefore in ensuring that Russia's intellectual potential was retained. However, as the legitimacy of the communist state was brought into question the flaws in past educational policy began to emerge. Throughout the late 1980s, the flaws in the communist educational system got bigger and bigger. As a consequence, one newspaper article estimated that at the start of the 1990s, the quality of Russia's education and science provision was two to three times less than that of the United States.[7] This situation has deteriorated even further in the last five years.

Generally speaking, the fall in the number of students and the declining quality of Russian education is a symbol of the overall turmoil evident in Russian society today. Insufficient attention is being devoted to education. Moreover, changes in the value system has meant that many students have lost their motivation to study and prefer instead a highly paid job which does not necessarily demand a first or higher degree. In many instances, of course, such jobs only exist in the criminal sections of our society. This reorientation of the value system of Russian youth is likely to be a source of social conflict way into the next century. Drawing upon longitudinal sociological research carried out since 1990, we would like to explore this issue in greater depth.

The legislative basis of Russian education

Our Constitution guarantees everyone an education up to the end of secondary school. Beyond this level it is a matter of personal choice, educational opportunities and a number of other factors, including income levels of parents etc. When we carried our project concerning 'The social development of youth' in 12 regions of the Russian Federation,[8] we discovered that 34 per cent of the 10,412 young people surveyed aged between 15-29 years in 1990 placed a high value on education. A follow-up survey in 1994 among 2,612 young people in the same age group revealed that 44.1 per cent thought education was important and that knowledge was not only an end in itself but also very valuable in obtaining jobs in a highly competitive labour market. However at the same time, whereas only 14.7 per cent of our 1990 sample thought education was not important, four years later this figure had jumped to 32.9 per cent. Thus despite a 1992 'Law on Education' and Constitutional guarantees of an education up to 9th form level, it is clear that education is losing its significance for many young people in Russia today. Why?

This situation reflects several things: the changing nature of our society; the poor economic situation of youth; the emergence of different value systems among Russian youth and the crisis in Russian education, which is a consequence of the current government's failure to meet its Constitutional obligations. The transition to the market has led to a total rethink on the part of youth regarding their future career - formerly very prestigious jobs are now less well thought of because they are poorly paid. Employment in the state sector is now severely limited, so young people are moving into the business and commercial sector. However, despite educational reforms which were supposed to guarantee improved training and a greater ability to meet the demands of the market,[9] the reality is rather different. Many students in Russia now receive poor quality education which does not prepare them for their future careers. Government statistics put the number receiving less than adequate training and preparation for market conditions at 1.7 million out of 21.1 million (or 8 per cent) in 1994-95. Students often discover this for themselves very early in their university studies and drop out. Very soon word spreads and the spell of the market - a good job with an attractive salary - seems more attractive than the prospect of continuing with one's education. Our surveys between 1992-94 demonstrate that 15 per cent of young people had no desire to continue with their education after school. Although in the short-term this may not seem harmful, there is a distinct possibility that the long-term career prospects of many people will be restricted by their limited educational qualifications, especially once all the best jobs have been filled by the most talented, and most likely best qualified candidates. Thus short term gains may well turn out to produce long term disaster and an overall lack of occupational mobility for large sections of the Russian population by the end of the 1990s and into the 21st century. The government needs to step in quickly to rectify this situation before it is too late. This is essential because a good education system provides an excellent foundation for the development of democracy in Russia. Educational policy therefore needs to be revised in order to attract highly qualified staff, increase student numbers (which would be greatly facilitated by higher grants) and above all to enable 'new blood' to enter the profession and revitalise it.

Education and the labour market

It might appear at first sight that the educational reforms introduced under perestroika and largely maintained by Yeltsin have met the needs of the market. It is clearly true that we have witnessed greater decentralisation; the emergence of a variety of new schools and greater flexibility over admissions policies, curriculum design etc. One prominent aspect of the changes since 1991 is the rise of private educational establishments.[10] Although this change was justified by reference to 'freedom', 'greater educational choice' etc., in reality only the most well-off in society or those with connections have gained access to these schools. As in the past, but perhaps more obviously so today, there are still immense differences in educational opportunities. Those people who were previously prioritised by social origin, locality and so forth have now been forgotten. It is the New Russians who are able to provide their children with the best education in the best schools, institutes and universities because they have sufficient financial resources. The rest are left to rot in the state sector. As a consequence, despite the demands of the market, only 50 per cent of students in one

1994 survey felt prepared for their future careers while 38 per cent said they had had inadequate training.[11] Of course, this trend varied according to specialism, reflecting current market demands and the ability of different disciplines to meet the challenges of the market. Thus some, though not all, subjects and educational establishments are in a position to invite foreign Professors to give guest lectures and seminars, or to have exchanges of teachers and students. Similarly the degree to which textbooks or other materials have been translated into Russian also varies markedly. Thus in one 1994 survey, 69 per cent of economics graduates and 64 per cent of medical graduates felt prepared for the world beyond university compared to only 36 per cent of agricultural science specialists.[12] This situation reflects the greater level of international co-operation in economics and medicine as well as the flooding of the Russian market with translated editions of the classics of Western economics etc. By contrast agricultural science continues to be taught in old fashioned ways, with fewer changes in curricula and the retention of old rather than completely revised textbooks containing the latest information on advances in agricultural science and technology in the West.

Young people and their careers

Recent research carried out among students and graduates in five higher educational establishments in Moscow in 1994-95 revealed just how much educational reforms since 1985, and especially since 1991, have affected the nature of their studies and future job prospects.[13]

Table 13.2
Nature of training at various higher educational establishments
in Moscow, 1994 (in per cent)

Institution	Classes	Enterprise placement	Independent Study	Other methods
Chemical & Mechanical Engineering Academy (MGAKhM)	25.9	16.5	52.9	4.7
Moscow State Construction University (MGSU)	7.4	7.4	80.0	5.2
The Russian Economics Academy (REA)	-	2.7	95.5	1.8
Moscow Pedagogical University (MPU)	15.0	12.5	62.5	10.0
Moscow State Pedagogical University (MGPU)	4.3	19.3	75.5	0.9
All (average)	9.7	11.2	74.8	4.3

Source: T.V. Gerasimova et al., 'Vypuskniki Moskovskikh vuzov na rynke truda', in V.I. Staroverov et al. (eds.), *Rossiia nakanune XXI veka, Vypusk II* (Moscow 1995), p. 496.

Professor Gerasimova and her colleagues carried out research among 500 final year students from the Chemical and Mechanical Engineering Academy (MGAKhM); Moscow State Construction University (MGSU); The Russian Economics Academy (REA); Moscow Pedagogical University (MPU) and finally, Moscow State Pedagogical University (MGPU). They discovered that whereas in the past, prior to the introduction of the market, the state laid down the curriculum, nowadays there is more room for independent study and placements, as table 13.2 above shows.

In the sense of opening up the curriculum and introducing greater flexibility in modes of study, the educational reforms introduced since 1992 are beginning to have a positive impact.

Myths versus reality

But just how successful are Russian graduates in getting jobs? Gerasimova et al. also examined the *desired career paths* of these 500 students studying in five Moscow higher education establishments. Their findings are presented in table 13.3 below:

Table 13.3
Desired career path of 500 Moscow final year
undergraduates, 1994 (in per cent)

Desired place of work	a	b	c	d	e
Government enterprise/organisation	48.8	26.5	12.7	48.0	45.7
Foreign firms	8.6	10.3	15.1	11.0	9.9
Private enterprise	7.3	17.1	25.4	12.0	18.5
Own business	1.2	6.8	6.3	4.0	6.2
Work abroad	2.4	11.1	4.0	2.0	3.7
Other	31.7	28.2	36.5	23.0	16.0

Key:
a   Chemical and Mechanical Engineering Academy (MGAKhM)
b   Moscow State Construction University (MGSU)
c   The Russian Economics Academy (REA)
d   Moscow State Pedagogical University (MGPU)
e   Moscow Pedagogical University (MPU)

Source: T.V. Gerasimova et al., 'Vypuskniki Moskovskikh vuzov na rynke truda', in V.I. Staroverov et al. (eds.), *Rossiia nakanune XXI veka, Vypusk II* (Moscow 1995), p. 500.

The above table indicates that, with the exception of future graduates in economics, many of the other students of chemical and mechanical engineering and construction still possessed a strong desire to work in state firms. This ranged from as low as 12.7 per cent in the case of REA students to as high as 48.8 per cent among MGAKhM students. The key issue is these students' understanding of the real job market. It is possible, as Kitaev argues, that some young university students in Russia still believe that state-run industries offer guaranteed social benefits and a stable and predictable work pattern whereas the newer firms which have emerged within the last decade offer a more unstable and unpredictable future.[14] The reality today is the frequent closure of both types of firms, state or private, although, more private sector firms are springing up all the time. Perhaps in recognition of this unstable economic climate, 9-15 per cent of Gerasimova's sample wanted to work for foreign firms; 7-25 per cent in private enterprise and only 1-7 per cent to set up their own business. Surprisingly few wanted to work abroad - as low as 2 per cent of MGPU students to as high as 11.1 per cent of MGSU students were so inclined. On the whole, half of these 500 Moscow students wanted, if possible, to work in their own specialism; 16 per cent had no desire to do so and over a third were as yet undecided.[15]

When Gerasimova et al. traced the job patterns of these students after graduation, they discovered that on average a third (33.2 per cent) had managed to find permanent jobs (this was as low as 19.8 per cent in the case of chemical and mechanical engineers to as high as 48.2 per cent among economists); 39.2 per cent only worked from time to time and over a quarter (27.6 per cent) were unemployed.[16]

Table 13.4
Job patterns of Moscow graduates from 5 higher educational establishments, 1995
(in per cent)

Type of work	a	b	c	d	e	f
Own specialism	24.6	25.8	15.7	49.0	38.8	31.2
Production	6.2	4.3	4.5	-	4.7	3.8
Shop, cafe, kiosk	9.2	7.5	10.1	5.3	7.1	7.7
Broker	4.6	5.4	4.5	2.1	9.4	5.2
Trade	15.4	11.8	5.6	3.2	12.9	9.4
Service industry	13.8	7.5	7.9	3.2	5.9	7.3
Coach	3.1	1.1	3.4	14.9	7.1	6.1
Private sector	7.7	21.5	6.7	5.3	4.7	9.4
Other work	15.4	15.1	41.6	17.0	9.4	19.9

Key:

a   Chemical and Mechanical Engineering Academy (MGAKhM)
b   Moscow State Construction University (MGSU)
c   The Russian Economics Academy (REA)
d   Moscow State Pedagogical University (MGPU)
e   Moscow Pedagogical University (MPU)
f   Average

Source: T.V. Gerasimova et al., 'Vypuskniki Moskovskikh vuzov na rynke truda', in V.I. Staroverov et al. (eds.), *Rossiia nakanune XXI veka, Vypusk II* (Moscow 1995), p. 505.

On closer inspection, Gerasimova found that few had obtained their 'desired job' in 1995. Therefore table 13.4 above shows that between 15.7 per cent (of REA) - 49 per cent (of MGPU) of these 500 graduates ended up in jobs related to their own specialism. Unfortunately most ended up being employed in a range of jobs suited either to any university graduate - production, trade, service industry etc. - or else employed in dead end jobs as a sports coach, cafe or kiosk employee, a waste of training and talent. In the latter cases, Russian graduates had already begun to experience the realities of the market economy. When jobs are few and far between, it is necessary to take what you can until something better comes along.

What is also interesting is the attitude of these graduates towards 'work'. Between 28.4-48.1 per cent of Gerasimova's sample thought work was 'essential'; between a quarter and a third thought work was important but not the 'driving force' in their lives and 2.1-7.5 per cent said work was important to them, but unfortunately they were still unemployed.   Although it is common nowadays to think of Russian youth in stereotypical terms as wanting success and wealth and hence they are perceived as being willing to take risks and even get involved in illegal activities in order to achieve these goals in the shortest time possible,[17] Gerasimova discovered that 11-26 per cent of her sample thought it was more important to find a job that was interesting and fulfilling rather than one that simply paid well.[18] Nevertheless, as we shall show below, there are some students who retain a strong belief in education and the value of knowledge, but they are gradually being replaced by those who, against the backdrop of falling educational standards, feel that there is no need for a degree or post-school qualifications in order to get a job.

Our research findings over a much longer period and in a greater number of regions of Russia support the conclusions reached by Gerasimova. We discovered that of the 13,000 students surveyed between 1990-94, 25 per cent had graduated from Vocational training schools (PTUs); 22.2 per cent from specialised secondary schools/institutes (*tekhnikum*) and 28.1 per cent from University (VUZ). However, whereas in 1990 very few of these graduates came from science and technology - 7.5 per cent in machine building; 11.7 per cent in light industry; 11 per cent in construction and 14.2 per cent in transport - four years later, and rather surprisingly, more students had taken technical subjects. For example, by 1994, 63 per cent of our sample were graduates in construction and light industry related subjects. Of course, such a shifting balance between subjects might reflect the demands of the market and in any case graduates in all disciplines are essential for the technological development of all countries, especially Russia.

From the point of view of this chapter, however, there is a very worrying trend developing, namely the fact that few graduates wish to enter the teaching profession - only 4 per cent of those we surveyed between 1990-94. This will do nothing to relieve the current 'brain drain' and to alleviate the symptoms of crisis described earlier. This trend is by no means restricted just to education. Our research shows that as low as 30 per cent of Russian youngsters in 1990 planned to enter the professions. Instead they preferred to work in occupations which required fewer qualifications, such as being a barman, waiter, hairdresser, taxi driver etc. By 1994, almost 50 per cent of our sample fell into this category. This trend has continued on into 1995. Thus research carried out among 2,000 students in secondary schools, PTUs, tekhnikums and VUZy in Stavropol Krai and Kirov, Novosibirsk and Ivanov Oblasts revealed that 10.8 per cent had no wish to be employed in jobs compatible with their educational qualifications.

The higher education crisis - rising numbers of drop-outs

In chapter 8, as well as earlier on, we dealt with the transition from school/university to work and the difficulties facing the Russian education system in the 1990s in trying to prepare students for the outside world.   However, not all students in Russia today are fortunate enough to complete their education.   We will confine our comments to higher education only.   Widespread inflation has eroded the value of student grants (*stipendii*) over the last few years.   According to data collected by the Committee on Youth Affairs, the average student grant in Russia is spent as follows: 30 per cent on food; 17 per cent on clothes; 27 per cent on training and books; 23 per cent on leisure and entertainment and 3 per cent on other items.[19]   However in the present harsh economic climate, many students are turning to crime in order to survive.   Thus whereas 1.2 per 10,000 students were registered as criminals in 1985; by 1994, this figure had jumped to 15.9 per 10,000, an increase of   over 1,300 times.[20]   Sociological surveys show that 48 per cent of students drink on a regular basis; between 7-10 per cent are thieves and an estimated 8-12 per cent act as prostitutes.[21]

One major consequence of this situation has been the rapid rise in the number of expulsions from university (*otchisteny iz vuzov*).   Thus whereas in 1985, 17 per 10,000 students were expelled for amoral behaviour and one per 10,000 for criminal activity; by 1991, these figures had increased to eight per 10,000 and two per 10,000 respectively. Three years later, eight students per 10,000 were being expelled for amoral behaviour and an amazing 18 per 10,000 students for criminal activity.[22]   Because of the difficulties encountered above, more and more students are failing to progress from one year to the next, leading to an increasing number of drop-outs or a longer period of study combined with work.   Data is hard to access, but Committee on Youth Affairs researchers believe that the number of students failing to progress in their studies has risen from 325 per 10,000 students in 1985 to 515 per 10,000 by 1994. This constitutes a rise of 158 per cent.[23]   Clearly urgent action is required.

University staff, students and the government

Because the Russian government has failed to respond quickly and effectively to remedy the aforementioned problems, there is a growing lack of faith in the Yeltsin Administration amongst university staff and students.   One recent Committee on Youth Affairs report notes that in 1993 only 13 per cent of the student body thought the government was acting in their interests.   As a consequence, during Russia's first democratic elections of December 1993, only 41 per cent of students voted and of this group 18 per cent supported the government opposition.[24]   Nowadays research demonstrates that 57 per cent of students and 44 per cent of teachers view the situation in Russia as one of 'crisis' while 17 per cent and 25 per cent respectively see Russia as heading towards the abyss.[25]

One study carried out in Voronezh between December 1993 - March 1994 confirms these pessimistic findings.[26]   Professor Glukhova surveyed 650 Professors, 108 Research Associates, 112 scientists and laboratory personnel and 640 students. She discovered that 65.3 per cent viewed the situation in higher education as 'tense' and 17.3 per cent as one of 'acute conflict'. In overall terms, 81.8 per cent of her sample had a negative attitude towards the government. This view was evident among 89.7 per cent of Research Associates; 90.8 per cent of staff in technical and 92.6 per cent in social science departments and among 72.7 per cent of students. Evaluating changes over time, Glukhova concluded that whereas in 1992, 54 per cent disagreed with the course of government reforms, especially in education, by 1994, this figure had risen to a staggering 89.7 per cent.[27] This viewpoint is not confined just to Voronezh, it is typical of many parts of Russia in the mid-1990s. Hence, one recent Committee on Youth Affairs report concluded that three-quarters of students possess a negative view of Yeltsin and his government. After only 4-5 years of reform 'scepticism' prevails among 87.3 per cent of students; a further 82.5 per cent are 'cynical'; 71.2 per cent feel 'cheated' and 74.6 per cent express a strong sense of 'disappointment'.[28] All the danger signs are already in place. In the December 1995 parliamentary elections, 60-80 per cent of young people failed to vote. Of those who did so, most were in favour of the LDPR.

Although in the 1980s, 60-70 per cent of Russian education was considered to be of 'good quality', this figure had already dropped to 30-40 per cent by 1995 according to official figures.[29] The government needs to act quickly to restore the faith of staff and students at all levels of the education system from school through to university. So far a firm response has not been forthcoming. Prognoses of the future on the part of teachers and students are far from encouraging. In Glukhova's survey of Voronezh between December 1993 - March 1994, 4 per cent of a sample of 1,510 predicted *democracy*; 17.5 per cent *authoritarian rule*; 26.9 per cent a variation on *anti-democratic/authoritarian tendencies* and 35.3 per cent *pure anarchy*.[30] Thus far, only anarchy has prevailed. However, this situation has had a detrimental effect on trends in Russian education and on the plight of students and staff alike. The situation is especially acute in the provinces. Current estimates suggest that the number of specialists working in regions outside the capital has declined 2-2.5 times since 1991. This 'rural exodus' has meant that it is four times more difficult to gain a higher education in rural as opposed to urban areas. This is generating further educational inequalities across the urban-rural divide and is bound in the long-term to create conflict not only between the towns and the countryside but also between the centre and the periphery.

A way forward - reversing the loss of intellectual potential in Russia

Finding remedies to the above problems, which have become ingrained over the last three decades and more, and which emerged in full sight during the transition to the market after 1985, is an extremely difficult task. One 1994 survey analysed the ability of school pupils to adapt to the new market conditions. Researchers found that 55 per cent favoured the reassertion of discipline; 21 per cent wanted a better education; 16 per cent better staff and finally 11 per cent wanted greater attention to be devoted to the pupils themselves.[31]   One thing is clear, unless we address the crisis in Russian education now, there will be a major lag in educational provision between Russia and the rest of the world way into the next century. In our opinion, there is an urgent need to rethink current educational policies and reforms. Any new educational strategy, if it is to benefit Russia, its teachers and students, must contain some, preferably, all of the following elements:

(i)   higher priority in government policy given to education - greater resources, finance etc.;

(ii)   greater balance between state (73.5 per cent) and private (26.5 per cent) education;

(iii)   closer attention to the link between educational provision and the market, so that students are better prepared for an ever-changing labour market;

(iv)   greater assistance to students in the form of higher grants and stricter control over access to education. This is necessary in order to ensure that access to the best facilities is not restricted just to those with wealth and contacts but is also open to the most able students irrespective of their family position;

(v)   there is an urgent need to introduce some form of credit system for education which is partly state, partly private sector financed. Both sectors should be encouraged to sponsor individual or groups of students in full or in part. This would act as a stimulus to students and encourage higher performance levels. It might also foster closer links between education and the economy;

(vi)   we should seriously consider reviving the old system of funding which encouraged talented young people through olympiads, competitions, grants etc.;

(vii)   greater recognition should be given to the role which the education system plays in socialising the next generation. This is especially important in view of the fact that the family in contemporary Russia is in crisis (see chapter 3) and because of the crisis in values brought about by the transition from collectivism to individualism; and finally,

(viii) higher priority must be given to all sections of the educational system from school to university level. Particular attention needs to be devoted to the educational infrastructure in the provinces and regions.

If all these and other policies can be put in place in the not too distant future, then we might just be able to save a valuable resource for creating a New Russia - education.

Notes

1.   On these changes see A. Jones (ed.), *Education and Society in the New Russia*, M E Sharpe, New York 1994 and S. Sting and C. Wulf (eds.), *Education in a period of social upheaval*, Waxman Munster/New York 1994, pp. 9-25, 119-31.

2.   *Statisticheskoe Obozrenie* No. 9, 1995, p. 61.

3.   Ibid, p. 63.

4.   *Molodezh' Rossii: Vospitanie zhiznesposobnykh pokolenii (Doklad komiteta*

Rossiiskoi Federatsii po delam molodezhi), Moscow 1995, p. 78.

5. Ibid, pp. 78-79.
6. Ibid, p. 62.
7. *Izvestiia* 22 January 1991, p. 3.
8. For a description of the methodological and theoretical framework underpinning this research see V.I. Chuprov, *Sotsial'noe razvitie molodezhi: teoreticheskie i prikladnye problemy,* Moscow Izd. instituta molodezhi 'Sotsium', 1994, pp. 21-47.
9. H.D. Balzer, 'Plans to reform Russian Higher Education', in A. Jones (ed.), *Education and Society in the New Russia,* M.E. Sharpe, New York 1994, p. 31.
10. For an interesting discussion here see M.A. Westbrook et al., 'The independent schools of St. Petersburg: Diversification of schooling in post-communist Russia', in A. Jones (ed.), *Education and Society in the New Russia,* M.E. Sharpe, New York 1994, pp. 103-119.
11. *Molodezh' Rossii: Vospitanie zhiznesposobnykh pokolenii (Doklad komiteta Rossiiskoi Federatsii po delam molodezhi)*, Moscow 1995, p. 81.
12. Ibid.
13. This section draws on the following sources: A.Ia. Glukhova, 'Sotsial'no-politicheskaia situatsiia v Rossii v otsenke Vuzovskoi intelligentsii' and T.V. Gerasimova et al., 'Vypuskniki Moskovskikh vuzov na rynke truda', in V.I. Staroverov et al. (eds.), *Rossiia nakanune XXI veka, Vypusk II* (Moscow 1995), pp. 76-86 and 495-509 respectively.
14. I.V. Kitaev, 'The labor market and education in the post-Soviet era', in A. Jones (ed.), *Education and Society in the New Russia,* M.E. Sharpe, New York 1994, p. 315.
15. T.V. Gerasimova et al., 'Vypuskniki Moskovskikh vuzov na rynke truda', in V.I. Staroverov et al. (eds), *Rossiia nakanune XXI veka, Vypusk II,* Moscow 1995, p. 501.
16. Ibid, p. 503.
17. See, for example, I.V. Kitaev, 'The labor market and education in the post-Soviet era', in A. Jones (ed.), *Education and Society in the New Russia,* M.E. Sharpe, New York 1994, table 14.3, p. 321.
18. T.V. Gerasimova et al, 'Vypuskniki Moskovskikh vuzov na rynke truda', in V.I. Staroverov et al. (eds.), *Rossiia nakanune XXI veka, Vypusk II,* Moscow 1995, p. 502.
19. *Molodezh' Rossii: Vospitanie zhiznesposobnykh pokolenii (Doklad komiteta Rossiiskoi Federatsii po delam molodezhi)*, Moscow 1995, p. 81.
20. Ibid.
21. Ibid, p. 2.
22. Ibid.
23. Ibid.
24. Ibid, p. 83.
25. Ibid.
26. A.Ia. Glukhova, 'Sotsial'no-politicheskaia situatsiia v Rossii v otsenke Vuzovskoi intelligentsii' , in V.I. Staroverov et al. (eds.), *Rossiia nakanune XXI veka, Vypusk II,* Moscow 1995, pp. 76-86.

27.   Ibid, pp. 78-79.
28.   *Molodezh' Rossii: Vospitanie zhiznesposobnykh pokolenii (Doklad komiteta Rossiiskoi Federatsii po delam molodezhi)*, Moscow 1995, p. 84.
29.   Ibid, p. 85.
30.   A.Ia. Glukhova, 'Sotsial'no-politicheskaia situatsiia v Rossii v otsenke Vuzovskoi intelligentsii' , in V.I. Staroverov et al. (eds.), *Rossiia nakanune XXI veka, Vypusk II,* Moscow 1995, p. 84.
31.   Cited in *Molodezh' Rossii: Vospitanie zhiznesposobnykh pokolenii (Doklad komiteta Rossiiskoi Federatsii po delam molodezhi),* Moscow 1995, p. 68.

14　Law and order

IGOR ILYNSKY

Introduction

In the communist period, Western scholars faced a number of problems in analysing crime in Russia. The primary difficulty was statistical evidence of crime. Although prior to Gorbachev, statistics were widely distributed on economic and political trends, with an overall low level of secrecy, the reverse was true of criminology.[1] The second problem was one of interpretation. Lists of crimes - divided according to specific categories and largely reflecting 'conviction rates' - were often dubious and ambiguous. The unreliability of statistics also hampered systematic analysis and in some instances prohibited publication. Finally, and perhaps most importantly of all, admitting the existence of crime went against the portrayal of a harmonious socialist society. The desire not to contradict this picture led to the manipulation of statistics by local police and party-state officials seeking to understate certain categories of crime.

However by analysing the speeches of officials involved in the policy-making process as well as the mass media, a number of studies have made it clear that although there was a fall in crime in the post-war period, crime was on the increase again by the 1960s and 1970s, especially among juveniles.[2] The situation in which Soviet society was deemed to be 'crime free' gradually began to be contradicted. Until Gorbachev, Soviet theorists explained away flaws by referring to survivals of capitalist mentality which in the long-term would disappear. Thus from Khrushchev to Gorbachev stress was placed upon malfunctioning in the family and the education system as the primary causes of crime. As a result, many government officials and specialists called for the further strengthening of these agencies of socialisation.

Under glasnost, Gorbachev smashed any illusions the West and Soviet citizens had about crime. This topic was no longer taboo and was covered on a regular basis in newspapers as well as on television from the mid-late 1980s onwards. Furthermore, criminal statistics were now declassified and Soviet explanations of crime began to converge with Western thought on origins.[3] For example, in 1986 nearly two million crimes were reported but by 1988 the crime rate was beginning to escalate and this was said to be due to enhanced freedom and overstretched law-enforcement agencies trying to cope with a rapidly changing society.[4] By the late communist period crime was increasing each year: for example by 32 per cent between 1988-89; by 33 per cent in 1990 and by 22 per cent in 1991.

For most of the communist period, the residents of Russia were proud of the fact that they could walk through the streets, even at night, without fear for their lives. Of course, as we saw earlier, crime existed and its scope was substantial, but it was just one problem among many. However in the last four to five years, crime has become the number one problem. It is turning into a national disaster. Public opinion polls show that the fear of being attacked or robbed as well as for one's safety and life stands above all other concerns including poverty and unemployment.[5] Millions of people have installed metal doors, put steel bars on their windows and started to arm themselves. Of course, to a certain extent the situation is being overdramatised by TV and press reports, such as *Kriminal' naia khronika or Dorozhnyi putrol'* which are highly sensationalist and include photos of terrible crimes. However, if it were only the press that was to blame for the situation, it would be easy to put things right. Unfortunately the mass media do not make things up.   Cold statistics show that crime in Russia (the consequence of ideological, political, economic, social, spiritual, moral and psychological shocks) is rapidly increasing, picking up speed all the time. There is little hope that this pace will slacken in the near future.

General assessment of the state and dynamics of crime

As we can see from table 14.1, the general level of crime increased from 1.5 million or 992.4 per 100,000 population in 1983 to an estimated 2.9 million or 1,987.5 per 100,000 by 1995. The number of cases of serious physical injuries increased from 28,381 in 1985 to 69,060 in 1995 or by 2.5 times, whilst the number of murders rose from 12,160 to 48,000 or nearly four times during the same period (see table 14.2 below). According to public opinion poll data, 90 per cent of citizens are extremely anxious about their safety and for 50 per cent their security is a source of constant worry.   Social differentiation, rising prices and low incomes are forcing people to turn to crime. Criminal elements in Russian society are becoming more and more professional all the time. The overall situation has worsened because of the growing number of organised bandit groups specialising in robbery and protection rackets.[6] As we shall see below there is a web of corruption between politicians, bureaucrats, the Mafia and the militia in Russia.

Crimes against banks, finance departments of different enterprises, institutions and agencies and on debt collectors, with the aim of seizing large sums of money, are quite common. In addition, drug trafficking and corruption is enabling the extension and consolidation of criminal groups, the expansion of the scope of their influence and a manifold growth in monies they earn illegally.

Table 14.1
The level of crime in Russia, 1983-95

Year	Number of Crimes	
	Millions	**per 100,000 population**
1983	1.40	992.4
1984	1.41	987.0
1985	1.42	989.8
1986	1.34	929.8
1987	1.19	816.9
1988	1.22	833.9
1989	1.62	1,089.5
1990	1.84	1,242.5
1991	2.17	1,463.2
1992	2.76	1,855.5
1993	2.80	1,887.8
1994	2.63	1,770.5
1995 (estimate)	2.93	1,987.5

Sources: Ia. Gilinskii, 'Prestupnost' bezopasnost' naseleniia v Rossii i Sankt-Peterburge', *Informatsionno-analiticheskii biulleten' Monitoring*, No. 1, September 1995, p. 66 and G.V. Osipov et al., *Sotsial'naia i sotsial'no - politicheskaia situatsiia v Rossii: Analiz i prognoz* (Moscow 'Academia' 1995), p. 38.

Organised criminals are becoming very important and starting to lay claims on leadership in politics and the economy. Some former criminals, relying on the power of money, are advancing their candidatures for mayors of cities etc. Law enforcement agencies are powerless stop them. If they try, the police themselves are subjected to violence. For example, in 1992, over 1,300 attacks were made on the militia. In one-third of such instances firearms were used resulting in 313 policemen being killed and 586 wounded in the line of duty. An extremely tense atmosphere continues to exist in public places, particularly in the streets of large cities and the provinces. In 1992 compared to 1990, street crimes increased by 23.7 per cent, up to 303,600 offences. Serious criminal offences are increasing at a very rapid pace. Their number has risen by 36.3 per cent reaching 137,300. The trend of rising crime has continued in recent years too. In 1993, it rose by 30 per cent and in 1994 by 43 per cent. Thus anxieties remain high. For instance, public opinion surveys carried out in June 1993 revealed that 36 per cent said hooliganism was very likely and 52 per cent thought it could happen. The corresponding figures for theft and robbery were 32 per cent and 51 per cent and those for organised crime 13 per cent and 31 per cent respectively. A further 25 per cent of those surveyed felt that underground wheeler-dealers or the *mafiya* were in control of the *raion* or *gorod*.[7]

Table 14.2
Different categories of crime in Russia, 1985-95

Year	Murder		Grievous Bodily Harm		Theft of personal property		Robbery		Violent attacks	
	a	b	a	b	a	b	a	b	a	b
1985	12,160	8.5	28,381	19.9	319,143	223.3	42,794	29.9	8,264	5.8
1986	9,437	6.6	21,185	14.7	272,376	189.2	31,441	21.8	6,018	4.2
1987	9,199	6.3	20,100	13.9	268,285	184.8	30,414	21.0	5,656	3.9
1988	10,572	7.2	26,639	18.2	359,464	245.6	43,822	29.9	8,118	5.5
1989	13,543	9.2	36,872	25.0	558,959	379.2	75,220	51.0	14,551	9.9
1990	15,566	10.5	40,962	27.7	648,496	438.1	83,306	56.3	16,514	11.2
1991	16,122	10.9	41,195	27.8	839,880	566.9	101,956	68.8	18,311	12.4
1992	27,006	15.5	53,873	36.2	1,096,882	737.6	164,895	110.9	30,407	20.4
1993	29,213	19.6	66,902	45.1	1,063,829	717.3	184,410	124.3	40,180	27.0
1994	32,286	21.7	67,706	45.6	NA	NA	148,540	100.0	37,904	25.5
1995	48,000	33.2	69,060	46.6	1,558,509	1051.6	155,967	105.3	47,115	31.8

(estimate)

Key:
a   absolute number of crimes   b   rate per 100,000 population
NA   data not available

Sources: Ia. Gilinskii, 'Prestupnost' bezopasnost' naseleniia v Rossii i Sankt-Peterburge', *Informatsionno-analiticheskii biulleten' Monitoring*, No. 1, September 1995, p. 66 and G.V. Osipov et al., *Sotsial'naia i sotsial'no - politicheskaia situatsiia v Rossii: Analiz i prognoz*, (Moscow 1995), p. 38.

This situation is hardly surprising, as in 1994, according to the Russian Ministry of Justice, the courts handled over 5.2 million crimes. Of the 925,000 people arrested in 1994: 21,300 were murderers; 80,300 had inflicted various types of grievous bodily harm; 11,200 had committed rape; 85,000 had assaulted their victims during robberies or extortion; 25,400 had stolen weapons and used them in crimes and 25,400 were involved in the illegal drugs trade.[8]

Unfortunately, fewer criminals are being arrested and more crimes left unsolved. For example, between 1986-88 the number of people arrested and detained fell from 749,000 to 402,000.[9] Whereas in 1988, 64 per cent of crimes were solved, this figure had dropped to 49 per cent by 1990. Between 1990-92, the number of unsolved crimes increased by 19 per cent to 194,700.

This trend has continued in the last few years. In 1994, for instance, of the 925,000 people arrested for crimes in Russia - 40 per cent were sent to prison; 18 per cent received a suspended sentence, 10 per cent were fined and the remaining 32 per cent were released due to lack of evidence or illegal arrest.[10] MVD data suggest that only 75 per cent of crimes were solved in 1994,[11] other estimates put the figure nearer to 34 per cent.[12]

As we can see from table 14.3, the number of crimes in Russia's two biggest cities - Moscow and St. Petersburg - increased dramatically between 1989-93. It is hardly surprising, therefore, that citizens in contemporary Russia view law and order as extremely important.

Table 14.3
The level and type of crime in Moscow and St. Petersburg 1989-93

Type of crime	Level of Crime (per 100,000)			
	Moscow		St. Petersburg	
	1989	1993	1989	1993
Murder	4.7	15.9	4.9	17.7
Grievous bodily harm	10.5	22.0	16.5	43.5
Violent attacks	12.8	37.2	15.3	64.5
Robbery	32.6	63.6	61.1	285.3
Theft of personal property	230.5	351.0	401.0	887.7
Assault with a deadly weapon	4.2	4.4	5.3	6.5
Group crimes	74.4	90.8	103.9	617.8
Crimes among 14-17 year olds	1208.9	1335.2	1732.4	2114.8

Sources: Ia. Gilinskii, 'Prestupnost' bezopasnost' naseleniia v Rossii in Sankt-Peterburge', *Informatsionno-analiticheskii biulleten' Monitoring*, No. 1, September 1995, p. 70.

Organised crime

> 'During the process of economic reform mafiya type relations have become dominant in our country and infiltrated key spheres of society' (Leonid Paidiev, *Nezavisimaya Gazeta* 24 December 1994, p. 1)

The most dreadful thing happening in Russian society today is the emergence of a criminal class or profession. Criminal organisations with their own 'code of honour' operating within a strict and disciplined framework, with access to modern weapons, communications systems and transport, are emerging. They can best be described as the Russian or red (*krasnaia*) *mafiya*.[13]

A series of Western studies show that organised crime is the product of the society in which it emerges. But this is not just a one-way process. Organised crime also influences society. Western analysts, such as Paddy Rawlinson, have questioned the validity of the term *mafiya* arguing that the Russian variety is not the same as its Western counterparts - in particular the Sicilian mafia - with a strong basis in society. She believes therefore that if we simply adopt Western models we are ignoring the specific Russian context.[14] By contrast, Stephen Handelman has argued that organised crime exists in many parts of the ex-USSR. Flaws in the old system - political corruption, the second economy - as well as various legislative acts under Gorbachev, such as those on labour activity in 1986, Joint-Ventures in 1987 and the law on Co-operatives on 1988, enabled numerous criminal elements to penetrate the Russian business sector. They subsequently became fronts for their illegal activities in drugs, prostitution and money laundering.[15] As a consequence organised crime was in full view in Russia from 1988 onwards. The research which I am about to outline tends to support the second of these two perspectives and shows:

(i)   that there is a *mafiya* in Russia;
(ii)   that the legislative action taken to try and curb it is woefully inadequate;
(iii)   that some sections of society and the law enforcement agencies actually support organised criminals, and finally,
(iv)   that the *mafiya* is to a certain extent linked to the current economic and political system.

At the outset, it is useful to note that gangs, which vary in size, have their own spheres of influence and separate 'business' activities. The number of organised criminal groups has steadily increased throughout the 1990s: 785 in 1990; 952 in 1991; 4,352 in 1992; 5,691 in 1993 and 8,053 in 1994. Of these groups, the number with international connections has decreased from 75 (or 10 per cent) to 467 (or 6 per cent) over the same period but the number with connections or corrupt officials has increased from 5 to 13 per cent between 1990-94. The number of registered crimes they committed also increased from 3,515 in 1990 to 19,422 in 1994.[16] 25 per cent of gangs have inter-regional contacts, for example there were 264 organised gangs in St. Petersburg led by 1,025 key figures.[17] The areas which they control include arms sales, stolen cars, casinos, misappropriation of funds, drugs, the export of raw materials, energy resources, rare and non-ferrous metals and finally organised criminals also steal and export historical and cultural treasures.

Via these activities many criminal organisations have accumulated enormous amounts of money. But as it is illegal earnings (or 'dirty money'), money laundering is developing in Russia. This money is often invested in the economy. As a result we have witnessed the strengthening of *criminal diktat* in the sphere of production, distribution of commodities as well as the use of uncivilised forms of competition and pressure on rivals to increase the price of all goods and services in order to maximise profits. Since the late 1980s, and more so in recent years, we estimate that criminal groups invest about 80 per cent of their money in legitimate businesses. Despite outward appearances, one in three enterprises are under *mafiya* control.

Law enforcement

In the period 1990-92, criminal proceedings were instigated against 2,700 criminal groups, with members being charged with the perpetration of 10,700 dangerous crimes. Of these 2,700 groups only 1,700 were investigated and their bosses taken to court. In the end, money and goods to the tune of 3.1 billion roubles and US$9.7 million dollars were confiscated, together with 648 cars and over 4,500 weapons. This represents a very small part (perhaps 1 per cent) of the wealth of those who were caught red-handed, taken to court and convicted. Part of the reason for the poor success rate is long-standing corruption in the KVD and MVD.[18] But the efficiency of militia activity and the intensification of efforts against organised crime are also impeded by low pay, making staff susceptible to bribes (see below), inadequate legislation, poor information, a lack of material and technical support, poor methods of conducting investigations and above all by the scale of organised crime operations. The state and law enforcement agencies are simply not ready for this struggle. As a consequence, many leaders and a significant proportion of mafiosi remain in the shadows. Corruption in the militia, the procurator's office and various judicial offices does not help the supposed clamp-down either.[19] The response is so weak that in 12 regions of Russia (including St. Petersburg), not a single leader of a criminal group has ever been prosecuted and one in five criminal prosecutions are dismissed. If this situation persists it will not only damage Russia's economic recovery - by discouraging Western investment - but also endanger our democratic transition. Unfortunately, Russian surveys show that an estimated 25 per cent of the major banks are under *mafiya* control whilst former Vice-President Rutskoi went as far as to argue that 90 per cent of officials are on the take. One Western scholar, Charles Rudkin, noted recently that organised crime has reached the top of the Russian state - 40 per cent of GNP and 2,000 major enterprises were said to be under the control of organised criminals.[20] Steps have already been taken to combat this problem. Government attempts to clamp down on organised criminal groups date back to the early mid-1950s. Laws were passed for example in 1953, 1955 and 1958.[21] In the 1970s the government was trying to round-up the bigwigs (*tuz*), especially in the field of gambling. Activities centred in Moscow and the Black Sea around Sochi. Despite these activities, the *mafiya* was still active at the start of the 1980s. As a result Brezhnev passed a law in 1982 on organised criminal operations. However by this time organised crime was so widespread that laws were largely ineffective. For example, thieving rackets totalled between 700-2,000 by 1983.[22] By 1988, things were getting out of hand. Numerous mafia groups had cornered different sections of the Russian economy. The 'Basova' group for instance centred on robbery and theft from government premises. In 1988, they stole 210,000 roubles worth of equipment. Meanwhile the Barabashev group which operated in 11 regions had 50 swindling operations going in the 'lottery ticket' field. They earned an estimated 500,000 roubles in the same year. Finally, the Sverchkav gang earned 2,157,000 roubles from intimidation and violence. These are only a few examples of the activities of the many groups spread throughout Russia's territory.

In 1985-86, Gorbachov issued several decrees designed to clamp down on organised crime and increase the size of facilities available to the MVD. Other decrees followed in 1988.[23] By the late 1980s, there were 144 specialists and 1,200 assistants in the MVD dealing just with the mafia.[23] Another decree of May 1990 facilitated inter-regional co-operation on organised crime.[25] However, as the MVD was increasingly unable to combat organised crime responsibility for this was passed onto the KGB from August 1990 onwards.[26] Nevertheless, the MVD was still co-operating with Interpol and with its German and Polish counterparts.[27] However, such work was hindered by the gradual break-up of the USSR. By the early 1990s the *mafiya* was not confined just to Russia but also active in the Ukraine, Moldavia, Central Asia and so on.[28]

In the post-communist period numerous other decrees have been added to this list including a 1992 decree on 'The fight against organised crime'. This culminated in the setting up in October 1992 of a special inter-departmental commission on combating crime and corruption. Alongside the Security Council, the role of this commission was to co-ordinate the work of the Ministry of Internal Affairs and the Ministry of Security. This was followed in 1994 by the introduction of a new law on 'Banditism and organised crime'. This decree created a new tax police with extensive powers to root out those laundering money as well as clamp down on criminal usage of legitimate businesses. However given the difficulties described earlier these laws have been of little use. Now a number of other steps are required. According to Leonid Paidiev of the newspaper *Nezavisimaya Gazeta*, the Russian President and government must take the following steps if they wish to eradicate organised crime:

(i)   Strengthen the legal justice system;
(ii)   create a well-organised police force capable of crushing the *mafiya;*
(iii)   introduce incentives for policemen and police-forces;
(iv)   improve the intelligence network; and
(v)   introduce the death penalty for 'gangsters'.

These measures are geared towards increasing the success rate in solving crimes. But they can only work in the short-term; in the long-term a solution to Russia's crime problem lies in a successful market transition and rapid economic development.[29]

On 29 September 1995, the International Fund 'Reform' sponsored a Round-Table on Organised Crime in Russia. The key participants included: Procurator General, Oleg Gaidanov; first Deputy Minister of the MVD, Vladimir Kolesnikov; Yuri Kozlov, Moscow University expert on organised crime; Leonid Abaklin, First Vice President of the International Fund 'Reform'; Svetlana Marasanov, First Deputy President of the Tax Police and others. Among the main conclusions drawn by this panel of experts was that there exists certain 'political sympathies' with organised crime and so there is a lack of political will to introduce concrete policy measures to combat organised crime. It was pointed out that despite appeals by senior MVD staff to President Yeltsin on 25 August 1995, very little has been done. The President and Russian government recognise that the problem of organised crime exists, but laws drawn up remain fiction not fact - they largely exist on paper and have not been properly implemented. As a result, few major in-roads have been made. For example, in the first half of 1994, the operational bases of 300 key Moscow criminals were searched and the bandits rounded up. But this is a drop in the ocean. There are one, two, three, maybe 500 others waiting to replace them.[30] Conflict between organised criminals remains rife.[31] This Round Table concluded that: 'organised crime must become the number one government priority in the 1990s'.[32] But why has this not been the case?

Corruption[33]

Corruption in the main organs of power and management serve as a reliable cover for criminals. Corruption and bribery have reached an unprecedented scale, as figure 14.1 below shows:

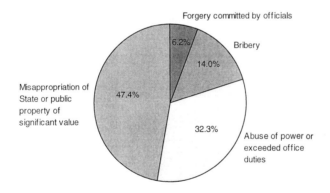

Figure 14.1   Offences committed by public officials in Russia, 1990-94

According to the data at our disposal, one in six criminal groupings use corrupt officials to achieve their objectives and nearly two-thirds of enterprise managers are corrupt. Russia has a long, well-established history of corruption in trade, transport, taxation, foreign trade, licensing and privatisation.[34] High prices are charged for re-registering commercial activities, discharge from military service, assistance with customs violations and other illegal activities.

Corruption is a serious threat to our democracy. Let's consider an example of the recent land reforms.[35] The credit and financial system is under increasing strain and being misused constantly. Between 1990-92 for instance, 541 cases of misappropriation and 76 cases of bribery were exposed. Granting credits has been made extremely difficult, but at the same time banks charge extremely high interest on loans. Bribery is often used to overcome these difficulties. Corruption has also penetrated the law enforcement agencies. In 1992 bribery in the MVD increased 1.8 fold while in 1993, 283 officials were charged with corruption - 97 per cent of them from the Ministry of Internal Affairs.

The distinction between public and private interest is becoming rather blurred. Many territories and regions of Russia have managers who suppress competition and enterprise and also award themselves unjustified privileges. Similarly, many government officials are also corrupt. For example, in the period 1990-92, 2,000 prosecutions were brought against corrupt public figures. 600 were dismissed or made accountable in some other way. The difficulty which the Yeltsin government faces is that because the rules of the game are unclear or else strict rules are not yet in place, successes have been few and far between. Thus in 1992-93, 980 bribery cases were taken to court in Russia but 50 per cent of them were dismissed, 10 per cent more than in 1991. The main reason for this is nepotism, clientelism and the dominance of private over public interests. This partly stems from the de-legitimation of the old elites and political system, but the transition to the market has also facilitated greater opportunities for corruption - economic change has in fact increased profits, allowed unsavoury elements access to influence the new *nomenklatura* etc. As this situation gives the Russian government little room for manoeuvre, Gavril Popov, the former Mayor of Moscow, has argued that Russia has no choice but to legalise bribery by turning it into a payment for intermediary services or such like.[36] This is a recognition of the fact that it is extremely difficult nowadays to distinguish between business and politics. This leads us nicely into the topic of economic crime, which I would like to distinguish from organised crime.

Economic crime

Criminal groups operating in the economy have drawn a substantial number of businessmen into illegal activity - large-scale bank frauds, illegal currency operations and tax evasion.[37] For example, in the period 1986-88, 200,000 cases of embezzlement were registered together with 15,500 cases of bribery resulting in losses of 353 million roubles.[38] Over 127,000 crimes of this kind were exposed between 1990-92, with losses amounting to 2.3 billion roubles. In the period 1993-94 such losses increased to 23 billion roubles.[39] The real figure is ten, perhaps a hundred times, this official one. This mass penetration of crime into the economic sphere has been highly detrimental to Russian economic growth and recovery. Multi-million dollar fortunes are gained through criminal transactions involving the draining of raw materials and other resources from state to private enterprises with the aim of misappropriating and then reselling them. In enterprises, owned by the Russian state, the Russian private sector or Western investors, many managers have turned a blind eye to bribery and corruption. It is extremely common for Western businesses to use fixers (*tolkacha*). Russian investors also pay protection money whenever required to do so. A breakdown of misappropriations and embezzlements by section of the economy in 1992 is given in figure 14.2 below:

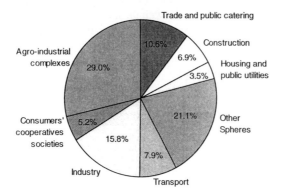

Figure 14.2   Misappropriation and embezzlement according to sector of the Russian economy, 1992 (in per cent)

Our research shows that economic crimes are being committed by groups rather than individuals. The proportion of crimes committed by groups increased from 20 per cent in 1990 to 34.6 per cent in 1992. Of these groups, 40.2 per cent had been in existence from one to three years and 10 per cent for more than three years; the rest had been in existence for less than a year. Nearly half of the well-established groups boasted of inter-state relations within a CIS framework. A third of groups committing economic crimes were co-operating or united with members operating in different establishments and on different territories. They are clearly quite pervasive and very well organised. By the mid-1990s, nearly two-thirds of criminal groups involved in economic crimes had corrupted different legal bodies including the credit and financial apparatus (16 per cent), law enforcement agencies (15 per cent) and government and management personnel (23 per cent).

The theft of raw materials and finished products out of Russia through illegal channels, particularly energy resources, non-ferrous and rare metals, has become widespread. Between 1990-92, 6,600 offences of this type were discovered in relation to the exporting of vital strategic products alone. They were worth a staggering 759.3 million roubles and US$112 million dollars. In operation 'Trawl' carried out in 1992, the illegal export of 900,000 tons of oil, 35,000 tons of metals and 54,000 cm^2 of timber and other products, worth 37 billion roubles, was prevented. With raising fuel prices, the number of crimes connected to oil and oil products is increasing. For instance, between 1990-92, 769 large-scale misappropriations and thefts were committed in the oil production and petro-chemical enterprises.

Finally, one of the greatest areas of concern is the expansion in the number of counterfeiters. In the period 1990-92, the number of cases of manufacture and sale of counterfeit money and securities increased 2.4 times. False banknotes to the value of 1,000 and 5,000 roubles as well as foreign banknotes are being manufactured using xeroxing techniques or the production of special plates. Up to 1992, attempts by criminals to steal 250 million roubles with the help of counterfeit bank documents were averted. Recent legislation allows the appropriate authorities to search the offices of any persons suspected of committing an economic crime and to confiscate relevant documents. But heavy-handed tactics and false arrests, such as the famous Vainberg case, only serves to alienate the business community.

Drug related crime

Drug taking and the crime connected with it have reached a socially dangerous level. The number of registered drug and toxic substance abusers increased from 2.5 per 100,000 in 1985 to 4.8 per 100,000 by 1989.[40] Since the collapse of the Soviet state in late 1991, the full extent of the problem has emerged. Official statistics show almost a three-fold increase in the number of drug users in Russia, from 14,000 in 1985 to 38,000 in 1994.[41] However in 1991, specialists estimated that there were 1.5 million persons in Russia using drugs for non-medical reasons. Two-thirds of these drug addicts were juveniles and young people. By 1993, this total had increased to between 5.5 - 7.5 million people.[42] In St. Petersburg, for example, the number of drug addicts rose from 16.4 per 100,000 in 1983 to 36.4 per 100,000 by 1994. In 1990, of this group, 46.6 per cent were using opium; 1.2 per cent cocaine; 0.9 per cent amphetamines; 2.4 per cent morphine; 21.3 per cent cannabis and 25.8 per cent were multiple drug addicts.[43] Part of the reason for the increase in drug usage in Russia in general and St. Petersburg in particular, where the rates are higher than the national average, is the growing production of synthetic drugs. But there are problems. Some people in St. Petersburg, for example, are making extremely impure substances from raw toxic vegetable matter extracted from crops affected by the Chernobyl disaster which is extremely hazardous to health.[44] Illegal drug trafficking is mostly under organised crime control. Income from drugs totals an estimated 50-60 billion roubles a year.[45] Over one-third of the drugs sold in Russia come from the 'near abroad'. Up to 80 per cent of confiscated drugs comes from the states of Central Asia, Kazakhstan, Azerbaijan and the Ukraine. New transfer routes are being set up in the Baltics and Belarus. This increases the likelihood that drug abuse in Russia will expand rapidly in the near future.

The process of integration of the *drug mafiya*, which is operating throughout the CIS, into the international drugs market is gaining strength. Throughout the Russian Federation contraband routes for the transfer of drugs now exist to Western Europe, Scandinavia and even the United States. Today dirty money from the drugs trade or *narcodollars* as it is known is being used to establish joint-ventures and to set up enterprises in a variety of spheres of activity. The investigation and search of criminal associations dealing in drugs has been permissible since 1992. As a consequence up to 1993 nearly 22,000 tons of narcotics were removed from circulation and 13,500 drug sowing areas destroyed. Between 1984-94, the quantity of confiscated drugs in Russia has increased 30 times.[46] Although many drug barons escaped, their workforce - chemists, doctors, scientific and technical personnel, distribution staff and lower level *mafiya* leaders - were caught. This clamp-down resulted in the closure of 151 underground narcotics laboratories.

The number of drug related crimes has also risen from 30,000 in 1985 to 115,100 in 1994 or by nearly four times, as we can see from table 14.4 below:

Table 14.4
The number of drug-related crimes in Russia, 1985-94

Year	Level
1985	30,000
1986	40,800
1987	32,000
1988	23,800
1989	13,500
1990	16,250
1991	19,350
1992	29,800
1993	80,500
1994	115,100

Source: *Prestupnost' v Rossii v deviannostykh godakh i nekotorye aspekty zakonnost, bor'by s nei,* (Moscow 1995), p. 76.

Of those committing drug related crimes 45.7 per cent were unemployed; 27.9 per cent had a previous criminal record; 8.7 per cent were minors and 17.7 per cent persons from other backgrounds. The large majority of pickpockets in big cities as well as those breaking into flats or medical establishments are junkies trying to earn money to pay for their habit.[47] The number of registered cases of theft of narcotic substances from hospitals increased from 24 per 100,000 in 1990 to 43 per 100,000 in 1994. This is only the tip of the iceberg. The problem is that despite increasing use of cocaine and hashish, and rising drug-related crimes, anti-drugs campaigns and facilities are grossly inadequate. In St. Petersburg, a city where the drug problem in the 1990s is becoming acute, no municipal anti-drugs programme is in place. The work of relevant departments and social organisations is unco-ordinated and the level of medical facilities for drug users has rapidly declined in recent years. For example, the number of dispensaries in Russia for drug users fell from 100 in 1990 to 70 by 1994; the number of hospitals from 100 to 65 and the number of beds for drug users from 100 to 50 per 100,000 population.[48] Modern medical assistance for drug addicts is scarce, especially the use of methadone as a 'cold turkey' treatment. Thus in St. Petersburg there are only three drug and alcohol clinics serving drug users, including one municipal clinic with 40 beds for adults and 25 beds for teenagers. Negative public and government attitudes towards drug users has resulted in only 270-350 people using these facilities annually. Nowadays private clinics - there are 10 non-state medical centres offering anonymous treatment or self help groups such as 'Drug Addicts Anonymous', 'Return' (with a membership of 20 people) and 'Pilgrims' (around 30 people, offering aid to 150) are trying hard to rehabilitate drug addicts and produce anti-drugs information. On the whole, though, past and present policies of prohibition and punishment have failed to yield good results often pushing junkies into the hands of hardened criminals.[49] If St. Petersburg is anything to go by - it had 3,200 drug users according to official figures in 1994, but according to medical specialists the real total is nearer 360,000[50] - then something urgently needs to be done otherwise the crime rate will continue to soar, especially as recent MVD forecasts suggest that the number of drug users in Russia could reach 20 million by the year 2000.[51]

Violent crime

Violence has become one of the principal means of committing crime. In the list of 'criminal services', assassination and other forms of criminal terrorism have now appeared. In some regions of the Russian Federation, the proportion of first degree murders committed for mercenary motives totals 60-70 per cent, while murders committed by hired assassins constitutes 13-15 per cent. Violent crime is especially common among organised criminal groups. Armed violence between such groups with the aim of eliminating their competitors frequently takes place on the streets of Moscow, St. Petersburg and Ekaterinburg. These shoot-outs are often the result of differences between those involved in racketeering and extortion or else gangs are settling old scores. In other cases explosives have been used. For instance in Moscow, St. Petersburg and Ekaterinburg between 1990-92, there were 185 gun fights and explosions in which 31 people were killed and 144 injured. Since 1992 the number of contract killings has increased each year: 102 in 1992; 289 in 1993 and 564 in 1994. Most of the victims were fellow criminals or businessmen.[52] According to Vladimir Kolesnikov, Director of the Russian Federation MVD Chief Criminal Investigation Division, the typical hired killer - from a sample of 50 caught - was a male under 30 years old, who was a war veteran but who is now unemployed. Most also had previous criminal convictions.[53]

Even when mafiosi are caught it is hard to convict them because victims and witnesses are intimidated to pursuade them to give false evidence or to retract earlier statements.

Clamping down on the use of firearms has proven to be an extremely difficult goal to achieve. Although 86,800 weapons were withdrawn from circulation between 1990-92 as a result of large-scale police operations, a substantial number of guns remain in illegal hands. In the first quarter of 1992, for instance, 1,600 offences were committed using firearms; in the second quarter - 2,100 crimes; in the third 2,200 and finally by the end of 1992, firearm use in Russian crimes was up 75 per cent over 1991. As law and order declines, more and more people are thinking of arming themselves. Thus whereas in July 1992, 16.9 per cent were in favour of using firearms and 30.7 per cent in favour with some reservations of obtaining firearms; 64 per cent of men, 39 per cent of women and 70 per cent of youth displayed a readiness to arm themselves by June 1993.[54] In 1994, of 32,000 murders, killers used firearms in 386 cases and explosives in another 143 instances to do away with their victims.[55]

Table 14.3 above shows that in Moscow and St. Petersburg assault using a deadly weapon still exists.

Crimes against individuals, including grievous bodily harm (GBH), continue to increase. Table 14.2 indicates that there were 28,381 cases of GBH in 1985 but a decade later this figure had risen to 69,060. Meanwhile in Moscow, cases of GBH increased by over 100 per cent between 1989-93 while in St. Petersburg, GBH rose by 250 per cent over the same period (table 14.3). Jealousy, quarrels and other reasons were the primary cause in 50 per cent of all murders and 80 per cent of GBH cases in Russia. Crime against individual persons also resulted from hooliganism. Finally two-thirds of murders and serious cases of GBH were committed and inflicted whilst in a state of intoxication and, nearly 2,300 murders and cases of GBH together with 1,900 instances of hooliganism between 1990-92 were committed using firearms.

Property offences

There has also been a rise in the number of crimes against the property of both companies and individuals, as shown in tables 14.2 and 14.3 above. In this category of crime, thefts prevail, making up about 60 per cent of the overall total. Between 1985-95, there was a two fold increase in the number of thefts from individuals. The chaotic state of the Russian economy, and confusion and a lack of total control at enterprise level has created favourable conditions for mass pilfering from factories, enterprises and other state and public properties. By 1992, such crimes had reached 533,200 (a 40 per cent increase since 1990). Twice as many thefts from shops, warehouses and other trading units (129,900) were committed between 1990-92.

Crimes against artistic, cultural and/or historical establishments are also increasing in frequency. In the period 1990-92, these offences rose two-fold up to 4,200. The same is true of theft from people's rooms which increased from 16,842 in 1990 to 35,720 in 1994. Similarly thefts from private flats and houses also rose from 74,156 to 99,014 in the same four-year period. More than 25,000 items - stolen pictures, sculptures, icons, jewellery and other valuables - are said to be improperly protected. Furthermore, only 60 per cent of museums and 35 per cent of cultural establishments have centralised security arrangements. Sadly the appearance of security guards on the door of large firms and shops is becoming increasingly common in Russia nowadays.

In addition to the above, freight, carried largely by rail, continues to be a major area of criminal activity. 61,600 cases of theft from railways were registered between 1990-92. Over 42 per cent of those committing these crimes were railway workers. Even when valuable goods are in transit, they are accompanied by military guards in only 25 per cent of instances.

The area of biggest concern, alongside crimes against the person, is theft from private property. 2.6 million such cases were recorded by 1990-92. This is 50 per cent higher than in the period 1985-90. 14.9 billion roubles worth of damage was caused. In the last three years, this trend has continued (table 14.2).

Car theft is also rising. High car prices as well as the rising cost of car parts has made this an extremely lucrative business for the criminal fraternity. In Moscow 60 cars are declared 'stolen' every day. The number of private cars stolen increased by two-thirds between 1990-92 rising to 35,000 while the number of cars belonging to the state which were stolen increased 2.3 times in the same two-year period. All in all, in 1992, approximate 157,000 cars and motorcycles were registered as stolen.

Many of these cases of crime against property - private or business - are accompanied by the use of violence. One in ten property offences was accompanied by threats or the use of violence. Between 1990-92, 195,300 burglaries and armed attacks were committed, an overall increase of 1.6 times. As table 14.2 shows, the number of violent attacks has risen from 8,264 in 1985 to 47,115 by 1995 or by nearly six-fold.

Juvenile crime

In the past, juvenile delinquency was attributed to malfunctions in the family, education system or in adolescent psychology. But there is no use trying to explain juvenile delinquency away by referring to ideology as it now surpasses that of adult crime. Thus one Western specialist declared a decade and a half ago that: 'One of the most alarming crime trends in the Soviet Union today is the increasing percentage of offences committed by juveniles'.[56] Nowadays 57 per cent of all crimes are committed by 14-29 year olds. In overall terms, juvenile crime in the last few years has surpassed the rate of growth in crime by a staggering 15 times. In the period 1981-91, for example, juvenile crimes increased by 60 per cent from 100,000 to 159,500 while the number of offenders rose by 4 per cent from 919,00 to 956,000. Of the latter, those in the 14-17 year old age range increased by 8 per cent (from 7.7 to 8.3 million). Among those minors committing crimes by 1992 - 21 per cent were school-children; 22 per cent came from technical vocational schools; 22 per cent were young workers and 23 per cent were unemployed young people. The 16-17 year olds are particularly prone to crime committing three times more offences than 14-15 year olds. Table 14.3 above shows that the proportion of crimes committed by juveniles increased by 10 per cent in Moscow and 22 per cent in St. Petersburg between 1989-93.

Past research shows that most juvenile delinquents come from troubled homes, where violence is common. This is now making itself felt in the nature of crimes themselves which are more violent. Sadly in Russia today those who rape or who commit attempted rape are often under-age juveniles. This group are also twice as likely to steal cars than adult offenders and three times more likely to commit murders and inflict serious injuries. Thus in 1988, according to official statistics, 56.6 per cent of embezzlements in the Former Soviet Union (hereafter FSU); 33.4 per cent of thefts of state property; 41.2 per cent of premeditated murders; 41 per cent of grievous bodily harm cases; 86.7 per cent of rapes; 77.2 per cent of crimes against personal property; 33.6 per cent of speculation; 77 per cent of cases of hooliganism (which is much broader than disorderly conduct); 62.7 per cent of drug offences and 53.1 per cent of public transport and motoring offences were committed by persons under the age of 30 years.

Other important facts have also emerged from studies by Russian experts. Volkov and Lysov noted for instance how young offenders in the FSU were committing crimes in groups in conjunction with seasoned adult criminals.[57] Our research shows, for example, that one in three racketeers in the period 1987-91 had juveniles in their ranks. By the end of 1991, over 55,000 minors belonging to 15,000 groups were registered with the militia because of 'anti-social tendencies'. These 15,000 groups were headed by so-called 'thieves-in-law', 78 of whom were imprisoned between 1990-92. However, it is also true that these hardened criminals tend to reproduce their behaviour while in prison, influencing others in the process. In prisons, 2,500 such groups have formed ready to unleash themselves on an unsuspecting world once they are released from prison.

The number of offences committed by girls and women is also rising. Between 1990-92, for instance, there was a two-fold increase in such crimes among girls from 6,000 to 12,000. In 1991, 34,000 female juveniles were registered with the MVD. Annually over 12,000 girls are sent to borstals. Over 60 per cent of female offenders drank spirits at school and were promiscuous, having many sexual partners. As a result many became prostitutes. Research currently indicates that every second or third prostitute in Russia is a minor.[58] However despite this fact prosecution is low. Afanasayev and Skorobogatov argue, for example, that between 1987, when a campaign against prostitution began, and 1990, by which time it had petered out, only 5,000 women in the entire USSR had been arrested for soliciting.[59] Although a change in policy occurred in mid-1993 when a special unit to combat pornography and prostitution was set up by the Russian Home Office, leading to a clamp-down on brothel keepers,[60] this has done little to curb the use of young girls on the game from being used to set somebody up or act as 'look-outs' or accomplices in thefts, robberies, rackets and even murders. Thus an estimated two-thirds of those in borstals are there because of property offences and crimes against the individual while a further 39 per cent of young women are doing time for 'narcotics' and 40 per cent for hooliganism.[61]

Drunkards and alcoholics account for a substantial proportion of young criminals. Every third or fourth juvenile commits an offence while he or she is in a state of intoxication. This is so in 90 per cent of hooliganism cases and 60 per cent of rape cases. In 1991 alone, despite the anti-alcohol campaign,[62] 116,500 minors broke the anti-alcohol law. 18.1 per cent of those involved were school students. Most of those minors who were drunk were discovered on the streets - 52.600 in 1991 - and over 50 per cent of these were under 17 years old and already registered with the authorities for similar offences.

Trends in the post-communist period have been far from encouraging. According to one *Komsomolskaia Pravda* commentator, 200,000 crimes were committed by young people by early 1993. 100,000 of these offenders were under the age of 14 at the time. All in all, according to Karmaza, between 1987-93, the number of criminals aged 14-15 years rose by 50 per cent. As in the communist period, most of these criminals (one in three) came from 'troubled families' in which many already had criminal records.[63]

The corrective and retraining system is faced with serious problems. There were 60 borstals in the Russian Federation up to 1992. They are located in 47 regions and accommodate 21,300 convicted minors. A further 40 new special schools capable of housing 8,500 inmates were established in early 1993 in an attempt to cope with the growing number of juvenile delinquents. But research shows that over 10 per cent of those convicted had already been to borstals, whilst 30-50 per cent of those who are released from these institutions commit crimes again.[64] Part of the problem given Russia's current transition is that the number of minors who are not studying or working has increased by 20 per cent since 1991. Thus it is an uphill struggle fighting juvenile crime (see chapters 8, 9, 13).

Some conclusions: looking ahead to the future

In view of the fact that Russia's economy, political system and society are in a state of crisis, which in the coming months, perhaps years, will probably not be fully resolved, crime in 1996 and the next few years will probably go on increasing. The reason for this is that the factors producing crime - inflation, the sharp decline in living standards, property differentiation, open and disguised unemployment, mass migration and the generally unfavourable psychological situation brought about by economic difficulties and other unsolved problems - will take a while to disappear.

Added to this is the question of market transition and the weakness of legal mechanisms to control business and competition. Nowadays economic relations are regulated not by the law but with the help of criminal methods. The increasing link between crime and business will continue to make itself felt in the number of first degree murders, cases of grievous bodily harm, deliberate destruction of property via arson, bribery and blackmail, illegal trafficking in arms, drugs, prostitution etc. These practices are having a detrimental impact in our banking, finance and accounting sectors. Furthermore high rates of inflation and our underdeveloped banking system encourage businessmen from putting their money in bank accounts. Instead many keep huge sums of money in offices and homes encouraging theft, robbery and murder. The constant issuing of money and new notes is also encouraging the growth of counterfeiting and forgery of banknotes and securities.

At times of crisis and uncertainty, individual and group psychology undergoes significant change. More and more people are tolerating crime and criminals. Furthermore, aggressiveness and cruelty, including that of the unmotivated kind, continues to grow. Such cruelty is affecting children particularly badly. There are about half a million orphaned children in Russia today.[65] Many of these children have been turfed out on to the streets by alcoholic parents. As a consequence many minors have to beg to survive.[66] If this tactic does not work then they frequently turn to crime.

Finally, various mafiya groups are likely to go on competing with one another for a larger share of the loot. Throughout the rest of the 1990s, therefore, we will witness increased smuggling and trafficking in drugs, weapons and nuclear materials; greater prostitution, more racketeering and extortion and an increase in financial and 'computer' assisted crimes.[67]

Law enforcement agencies are central in any attempt to combat crime. But they are seriously under-resourced. The MVD is in disarray, the best law enforcement specialists are leaving in droves and conditions of work are becoming more and more difficult. The net result today is that less than half the number of registered crimes are solved.

The loss of authority and a lack of confidence in the police among members of the general public is leading to suspicion on both sides. The public are not reporting crime and law enforcement officers - despite being relatively highly qualified - are adopting a negative view of the Russian general public. The overall impact of this situation is that criminals are getting away with crime. This 'climate of impunity' is stimulating the level of crime.

From the point of view of this book, rising crime and corruption is threatening to derail Russia's reform programme. At a recent conference on 'Reforms in Russia: Entrenched interests and Practical Alternatives' held in Moscow between 13-16 April

1995, Sergei Glazyev concluded that the absence of 'legal institutions, mechanisms for fulfilling economic goals, a system of norms, standards and rules of behaviour' as well as a judicial system, has resulted in a number of adverse trends: bankruptcy; racketeering; rampant theft; corruption; the rise of organised criminals and so forth. All of these negative forces, according to Glazyev, are draining the Russian economy - between 1992-95, GDP has declined by half; industrial production by two-thirds; capital investment by three-quarters etc.[68] Although some delegates blamed this situation on Yeltsin and his government, Sergei Vasilev rightly pointed out that the problem was not simply one of economic strategy it was also a 'matter of the seizure of a number of state institutions by the mafiya'. In the absence of a clear direction and political will, Vasilev suggested that, the mafiya had successfully stepped into the vacuum left by hopelessly divided politicians.[69]

In my opinion, however, providing the socio-economic and political situation in Russia stabilises by the end of this century, and this assumption is predicated on: the full establishment of market relations; the emergence of a corresponding new infrastructure and on better relations between Russia and the newly independent states, on the one hand, and the West, on the other, then it is possible that the crime rate will fall. For the moment, though, crime is likely to go on increasing in line with the overall high level of anxiety and tension in society which is accompanying the current economic recession and political instability. Current projections for 1996 suggest that the crime rate will rise by 44-48 per cent while 1997 estimates suggest a 55 per cent increase in crime. Given the weakening of the family and social control over the behaviour of children, it is probable that juvenile crime will account for a significant proportion of these increases - 20 per cent in 1996 and 28 per cent in 1997. Sadly there are likely to be more murders, cases of grievous bodily harm, theft and attacks, especially robberies and burglaries, in the future. This is hardly surprising in conditions of continued crisis. Unless our economic and political problems are resolved, the crime rate will remain unacceptably high. In such circumstances the strengthening of the State's role as guarantor of law and order takes on major significance. This will involve the creation of a strong legal base and a means of clamping down on crime, including the consolidation of law enforcement bodies, tougher action on illegal activities and the restoration of the public's trust in the ability of the police and the government to maintain law and order.

Notes

1. Peter H. Juliver, *Revolutionary law and order,* Free Press, New York 1976.
2. V. Chalizde, *Criminal Russia,* Random House, New York 1977; W. Connor, *Deviance in Soviet Society,* Columbia University Press, New York 1972; *Lichnost' prestupnika,* Moscow 1971; A.M. Iakovlev, *Teoriia kriminologii i sotsial'naia praktika,* Moscow 'Nauka' 1985; V.Y. Kalmykov, *Khuliganstvo i mery bor'by s nim,* Minsk, Belarus 1979 and *Kurs Sovetskoi kriminologii,* Moscow 'Iuridicheskaia literatura' 1985.
3. L. Shelley, 'Crime in the Soviet Union' in A. Jones, W.D. Connor and D.E. Powell (eds.), *Soviet social problems,* Westview Press, Boulder Colorado 1991, p. 256.

4. V. Luneev, 'Prestupnost' v SSSR za 1988g: statistika i kommentarii kriminologa', *Sovetskoe Gosudarstva i Pravo* 1989, No. 8, p. 85.
5. Thus Alexandr Golov of the Centre for Public Opinion Research (VTsIOM) in Moscow stated in July 1993 that: 'For the majority of our country's population, the most pressing problem right now is crime', *Izvestiia* 23 July 1993, p. 4.
6. For an example in the food trade see *Moskovskii komsomolets* 21 February 1989. One journalist recently discovered that small businesses were having to pay up to $50,000 a month in order to trade. (Mikhail Giblov, 'Bandity ob'iavili na menya rozysk', *Argumenty i fakty* No. 41, October 1995, p. 12).
7. *Izvestiia* 23 July 1993, p. 4.
8. *Izvestiia* 14 April 1995, p. 4.
9. O. Kipman, 'O kompetentnosti i professionalizme', *Sovetskaia militsiia* 1990, No. 4, p. 22.
10. *Izvestiia* 14 April 1995, p. 4.
11. *Nezavisimaya Gazeta* 11 April 1995, p. 1.
12. Vladimir Kolesnikov, MGU expert on crime cited in V. Bakatin, 'Organizovannaia prestupnost' kak spasti ot nee obshchestvo', *Moskovskaia Pravda* supplement 11 October 1995, p. 8.
13. On this topic see A. Gurov, *Organizatsiia prestupnost' - Ne mif, a real'nost',* Moscow 'Znanie' 1992 and A. Vaksberg, *The Soviet Mafia,* Weidenfeld and Nicolson, London 1991. The term 'Red mafia' is taken from A. Gurov, *Krasnaia Mafiya,* Moscow 'Kommercheskii Vestnik' 1995.
14. P. Rawlinson 'Organised crime in Russia', paper presented to the BASEES Annual conference, Fitzwilliam College, Cambridge March 1995.
15. See S. Handelman, *Comrade Criminal: The Theft of the Second Russian Revolution,* Michael Joseph, London 1994.
16. *Prestupnotst' v Rossii v devianostyikh godakh i nekotorye aspekty zakonnosti bor'by k nei,* Moscow 'Kriminologickeskaia Assotsiatsiia' 1995, p. 14.
17. Ia. Gilinskii, 'Prestupnost' bezopasnost', naseleniia v Rossii i Sankt-Peterburge, *Informatsionno-analiticheskii biulleten' Monitoring,* No. 1, September 1995, p. 70.
18. This is not a new problem, it dates back to the Communist period see for example Konstantin Simis, *USSR: Secrets of a corrupt society,* J.M. Dent & Sons Ltd, London 1982, pp. 67-88.
19. Ibid, chapter 9.
20. Charles Rudkin, 'Is there really a link between Russian business and organised crime? Problems of methodology', paper presented to the BASEES Annual conference, Fitzwilliam College, Cambridge March 1995.
21. A. Gurov, *Krasnaia Mafiya,* Moscow 'Kommercheskii Vestnik' 1995, pp. 113-119.
22. Ibid, p. 153.
23. Ibic, pp. 211-218.
24. Ibid, p. 220.
25. Ibid, p 283.
26. Ibid, p. 230.
27. Ibid, pp. 228-30.

28. Ibid, pp.251-52.
29. *Nezavisimaia Gazeta* 24 December 1994, p. 2.
30. V. Balatin, 'Organizannaia prestupnost' kak spasti ot nee obshechestvo?' *Moskovskaia Pravda* supplement, 11 October 1995, p. 8.
31. See *Kriminal'naia Khronika* or more specifically, V. Fedorov, 'Banditizm krepchaet', *Moskovskaia Pravada*, 13 October 1995, p. 1 and Ye. Kiseleva and D. Bratskii, 'Moskva zakhleb nulas' krov'iu: gangsterskie voiny vyplesnulis' na ulitsy goroda', *Moskovskaia Pravda*, 11 October 1995, p. 1.
32. V. Balatin, 'Organizannaia prestupnost' kak spasti ot nee obshechestvo?' *Moskovskaia Pravda* supplement, 11 October 1995, p. 8.
33. Corruption in the upper echelons of Russia's power structures has a long history see Simis 1982 op cit., chapter 2.
34. On this general issue see R. Frydman, A. Rapaczynski and J.S. Earle et al. (eds.), *The Privatisation Process in Russia, Ukraine and the Batic States,* CEU/Privatisation Report, Vol. 2: Oxford University Press/CEU, Oxford 1993, Part I and S. Clarke et al., 'The privatisation of industrial enterprises in Russia: Four case-studies', *Europe-Asia Studies* Vol. 46 (2), 1994, pp. 179-215.
35. For a discussion of the background to these changes see R.F. Miller, 'Reforming Russian Agriculture: Privatisation in Comparative Perspective', in A. Saikal and W. Maley (eds.), *Russia in search of its future,* Cambridge University Press, Cambridge 1995, pp. 66-84.
36. *Argumenty i fakty* No. 14, April 1992.
37. On earlier trends under communism see Simis 1982 op cit., chapters 4-5.
38. A. Gurov, *Krasnaia Mafiya,* Moscow, 'Kommercheskii Vestnik 1995, p. 26.
39. *Prestupnost' v Rossii v deviannostykh godakh i nekotorye aspekty zakonnost, bor'by s nei,* Moscow 1995, p. 31.
40. I. Kirillov, 'Potreblennie alkogolia i sotsial'nye posledstviia p'ianstva i alkogolizma', *Vestnik Statistiki* 1991, No. 6, p. 65.
41. Y. Gilinsky, V. Podkolzin and E. Kochetkov, 'The drug problem in St. Petersburg', in N Chaika, *HIV/AIDS, STDs, Drug use and prostitution in St. Petersburg and Russia,* St. Petersburg Pasteur Institute, St. Petersburg 1995, figure 1, p. 19.
42. *Komsomol'skaia Pravda* 23 April 1993, p. 2.
43   Ibid, tables 1 - 2, pp. 14 - 15.
44. Ibid, p. 16.
45. *Moskovskii Novosti* 11 November 1992 and *Moskovskii Novosti* 11 May 1993.
46. *Sankt Petersburgskii Vedomosti* 19 May 1994.
47. Y. Gilinsky, V. Podkolzin and E. Kochetkov, 'The drug problem in St. Petersburg', in N Chaika, *HIV/AIDS, STDs, Drug use and prostitution in St. Petersburg and Russia,* St. Petersburg Pasteur Institute, St. Petersburg 1995, figure 1, p. 19.
48. Ibid, figure 6, p. 21.
49. Ibid, p. 17.
50. Ibid, figure 9, p. 24.
51. *Argumenty i fakty,* No. 35, August 1995, p. 8.
52. See for example *Izvestiia* 12 February 1993, p. 5 and *Izvestiia* 23 July 1993, p. 4.

53.   *Nezavisimaia Gazeta* 11 April 1995, p. 1.
54.   Cited in ibid.
55.   *Nezavisimaia Gazeta* 11 April 1995, p. 1.
56.   Connor 1972 op cit.
57.   Cited in L.I. Shelley, 'Crime and Delinquency in the Soviet Union', In J.G. Pankhurst and M.P. Sacks (eds.), *Contemporary Soviet Society: Sociological perspectives,* New York: Praeger 1980, p. 220.
58.   For more on this see C. Williams, 'Victim, villain or symbol of capitalism? Whores in Russian history', *Irish Slavonic Studies,* forthcoming No. 15 1995, and V. Afanasayev and S. Skorbogatov, 'Prostitution in St. Petersburg', in N. Chaika, *HIV/AIDS, STDs, Drug use and prostitution in St. Petersburg and Russia,* St. Petersburg Pasteur Institute, St. Petersburg 1995, pp. 26-29.
59.   Afanasayev and Skorbogatov 1995 ibid, p. 26.
60.   Ibid, pp. 26-27.
61.   *Moskovskie novosti* 21 February 1993, p. 11.
62.   See C. Williams, 'Old habits die hard: Alcoholism in Leningrad under NEP and some lessons for the Gorbachev administration', *Irish Slavonic Studies*, No. 12, 1991, pp. 69-96.
63.   *Komsomolskaia Pravda* 13 April 1993, p. 8.
64.   *Nezavisimaia Gazeta* 31 March 1993, p. 6.
65.   *Rossiiskie Vesti* 14 April 1995, p. 1.
66.   F.N. Il'iasov and O.A. Plotnikova, 'Nishchie v Moskve letom 1993 goda', *Sotsiologicheskie zhurnal* 1994, No. 1, pp. 150-56. In this survey of Moscow carried out in June-July 1993, 5.9 per cent were children, ibid, table p. 154.
67.   *Nezavisimaia Gazeta* 24 December 1994, p. 2.
68.   Cited by Mikhail Leontiev in *Sevodnya* 22 April 1995, p. 3.
69.   Cited in ibid.

15   Civil society in Russia

VLADIMIR RUKAVISHNIKOV, TATIANA
RUKAVISHNIKOV, ANATOLII DMITRIEV AND
LARISA ROMANENKO*

Introduction

Key elements in the evolution of contemporary Russia are the transitions to democracy
and a market-type economy. The success of the latter depends in a large measure on
political stability and the development of a civil society. At present we are faced
simultaneously with an acute economic crisis, permanent political conflict, high levels
of social tension and major changes in attitudes. All of these aspects have been
addressed in previous chapters. In this chapter we shall assess the general characteristics
of the evolution of a civil society in Russia using public opinion surveys for the period
1988-94 as well as the results of the December 1993-95 national elections.

The importance of civil society

The concept of civil society is an important element in sociological theories of
democracy and modernisation.[1]   The radical character, complexity and inherent
difficulties of the process of Russian economic, and especially political transformation,
raises the question as to whether 'civil society' as a concept is a useful explanatory
framework or whether one must search for new theories and concepts to explain political
trends in ex-communist states such as Russia. Professor Stephen Cohen has argued that
the concept of 'civil society' has no validity in relation to Russia's transition from
totalitarianism to liberal democracy. Speaking in 1992 about the new myths concerning
Russia, Cohen declared:

> 'Myths may not be entirely false ... Take, for example, the current notion
> that a 'civil society', eager for a democratic market system, has emerged as
> the driving force in Russian political life, even after defeating the coup last

August.   For many observers of Russia..... this has become a new orthodoxy.   'Civil society' isn't a very meaningful concept in this context. Borrowed from the history of Western democratic theory, it's another attempt to squeeze Russia's traditions and realities into our ideological constructs.   Opinion polls tell us that a great many Russians don't understand or don't want markets or democracy..... Russian sociologists worry that much of their country is akin to a '*lumpen* society', the opposite of civil society.   Anyway, to explain everything in terms of a surging civil society is bad analysis and history.   Several thousand Russians may have actively opposed the (1991) coup; the rest were passive or silent'.[2]

Our intention here is not to take issue with Cohen as such or to criticise his interpretation of the attempted August 1991 coup,[3] instead we shall confine our comments to an assessment of the usefulness of the concept of 'civil society' as an analytical tool for examining the political dynamics of Russia from the end of the 1980s onwards.

Our theoretical framework

There are, as Miller points out, several different theoretical approaches to the concept of 'civil society'.[4]   This term was coined to analyse Western socio-economic and political systems and cannot be applied to 'actual socialism' or post-communist states without modification.   Both Janita Frentzel-Zagorska and Marcia A. Weigle have used the term in its neo-Gramscian sense to refer to the desire for a network of independent social organisations and channels of communication, distinct from, but acting within and exercising pressure upon the state.[5]   According to this approach, the 'political system' is part of 'civil society' in so far as it attempts to influence state power either directly or through channels of political representation.   The 'political system' is both a part of civil society and a mediator that realises its aim of linking state goals with those of independent population groups through different mechanisms of mediation.[6]   The roots of 'politics' are in 'civil society' and therefore the strength or weakness of our political system depends upon its level of support within society and its maturity (including movements, political parties, interest groups and their impact upon state activity).

The above interpretation of 'civil society' differs from that of Hegel as outlined in his *Philosophy of Right and Law* (1821) in which he drew a distinction between the realms of 'private life and the state'.   Because 'civil society could not function without the state and the state could not realise its full potential without a properly constituted and functioning civil society', according to Hegel,[7] it is clear that this Hegelian interpretation only applied to some of the so-called 'socialist countries'.   As regards the post-communist situation Kusio points out that: 'While civil society requires the state (or government) be limited in the scope of its activities, at the same time the state is expected to protect civil society and its necessary liberties'.[8]   Kusio is therefore using the term in its traditional sense but in a slightly modified way to take into account trends since the collapse of communism.

This brief discussion illustrates that the concept of 'civil society' is used in a number of different ways by a variety of scholars. Most definitions of 'civil society' following Marx emphasise the idea of peoples' interdependence rooted in mutual obligations and individual private interests; but some, with Durkheim in mind, point to the notions of *organic solidarity* or *collective consciousness* based upon mutually shared basic values. In our opinion, civil society refers to a system in which the hegemonic cultural and political **values** of the entire society become part of the consciousness of individuals who shared them. This set of values, orientations, ways of thinking and modes of behaviour can be variously labelled 'liberal', 'democratic', 'Western' or even 'progressive'. In our research on the development of the Russian political system and the emergence of civil society, we have adopted all of the aforementioned approaches.

The emergence of civil society and a political system in Russia

As is well known, from 1917 onwards Russia set out on a different road in trying to build a socialist society in a largely capitalist world. Although the individual was placed at the centre of this new society, it did not lead to substantial freedoms or the creation of a civil society. This question was, for reasons to do with the nature of the development of our political system and our political culture, as well as bureaucratisation and centralisation, not put back on the political agenda for nearly 70 years.

Trends during perestroika

The creation of a civil society was one of the primary goals of Gorbachev's perestroika. At that time the term 'civil society' was used as an antonym to such notions as 'totalitarian society' or 'the dictatorship'. Gorbachev and his advisors used the term 'civil society' in its general sense to refer to the opening up of the political system, but offered no systematic discussion or analysis of it despite glasnost'.[9] In our opinion, adherents of perestroika who spoke of the need to transform Soviet society into a civil society were merely using the idea as a means of eradicating the stranglehold which the CPSU had over society and the private lives of citizens. They favoured pluralism and the elimination of censorship, individual initiatives in the private as well as co-operative sector and the introduction of private property. All these were primary goals. All the evidence from the period suggests that in the leader's eyes the basis for a political system was created but not the preconditions for a civil society. However, one must remember that in a Russian context, there is **no real distinction between a civil society and a political system** because all independent activity has always been politicised given its threat to the legitimacy of the CPSU. Thus if a political system was created, it emerged as part of a newly constituted civil society.[10] Although in reality this new political system and the notion of civil society were extremely fragile during perestroika, in so far as Russia's new political formations between 1989-91 were largely unable to transform general public and specific social group interests and demands into policy before the August 1991 coup, it is still nevertheless true that the changes which occurred under Gorbachev paved the way for more recent trends. A key event here was the deletion in 1990 of Article 6 of the Russian Constitution removing the CPSU's monopoly of power. This was a major factor in the subsequent dismantling of the USSR in late 1991.

The post-communist period

The two years following the abortive August 1991 coup d'etat were characterised by an intense struggle between various political actors, in particular Boris Yeltsin and the Supreme Soviet. This confrontation ended in bloodshed in Moscow in October 1993 when the 'Storming of the White House' occurred. A New Constitution was adopted and in December 1993 a new parliament was freely elected. Thus the Russian political system was transformed from a single party monopoly to a multi-party system. It has often been argued that if a society possesses well-developed institutions, is pluralistic in nature and has a great array of interest groups, then it is easier to constrain authoritarianism and to develop the inter-group competition necessary to sustain a liberal democracy system. As we saw earlier in chapter 1, the parties and political system of post-communist Russia are not yet in a position to fulfil this rule. Instead apathy and mistrust in politics are widespread. As a result, the roots of a political system and with it a civil society are still very weak. The danger at present is that only the narrow interests of a small elite will be represented, rather than the common interests of broader, specific groups. As Weigel put it in 1992: 'This could lead to a dangerous form of nationalist populism and open the doors for authoritarianism which seeks to capture the imagination of the disillusioned masses by direct interaction with a charismatic leader'.[11] Russians neither under- or overestimate this possibility as a real threat.

Chapter 1 illustrated that there are a number of different political parties of all political persuasions, but they tend to be small, with the large majority operating in a particular city or region. Although some parties have attempted to locate a specific social base e.g. entrepreneurs (the *Party of Economic Freedom*); farmers, intellectuals or broadly defined working people (*United Front of Workers, Russian Workers Movement*) etc., this search for a strong electoral base is only in its infancy. In the long-term it is linked with the process of building political consciousness of autonomous social groups with their own sets of ideas and interests. Research shows, however, that less than 1 per cent of adults in Russia identify with political parties, with the large majority poorly informed about political party programmes.[12] While we agree that the December 1993-95 elections represent the emergence of distinct and already formed new social groups with their own interests, to a large extent they also reflect the pessimistic mood of the people, the ideological crisis of the electorate and the high level of social discontent currently prevailing. It must also be borne in mind that a significant number of people failed to vote in 1993 and 1995. Nearly a third in the recent December 1995 parliamentary elections.

Another important point in relation to post-communist Russia is that there is a fairly large group of socially and politically relevant independent organisations representing the interests of businessmen, trade unions, youth, veterans, women and so forth. Unfortunately the flowering of such independent activism has yet to have a significant impact on the content and pace of reforms. Our research shows that Russians do not consider the aforementioned groups as influential or powerful. For example, one May 1993 survey of 1,172 respondents in Russia carried out under the auspices of Vladimir Rukavishnikov showed that 30 per cent of respondents thought no organisation could protect the interests of ordinary citizens, 17 per cent put their faith in the media, 16 per cent the courts, 12 per cent trade unions and 1 per cent the executive. All in all, we believe that **contrary to the development of a civil society, economic, political and social indicators suggest that a process of elite-directed modernisation is currently underway.**

Public opinion polls for the period 1992-94 indicate that the gap between mass expectations, hopes for a better life and higher living standards, which many thought would materialise after the downfall of the old communist regime, is now increasing causing growing frustration and dissatisfaction. As tables 15.1-15.3 below show, public opinion is now split regarding the content, course and pace of economic reforms of the Yeltsin Administration. Such differences reflect opposing ideological values as well as varying social, educational and age groups.[13]

Table 15.1
Retrospective evaluations of reform under perestroika
Question: 'What was your attitude towards perestroika
in the mind-1980s?' (in per cent)

Answer	May 1993	May 1994
Too young to say	10%	11%
Positive	66%	63%
Negative	16%	19%
I don't remember	9%	7%

Although these results are influenced by individual perceptions of changes in Russia in 1993-94 as well as by the personal life of respondents, it is clear from table 15.1 that although a high proportion of respondents still look back on perestroika favourably - 63 per cent in May 1994; it is nevertheless still the case that fewer would have supported perestroika even if they could have predicted the present unfavourable economic climate - 30 per cent in May 1994 as opposed to 40 per cent in February 1991 (table 15.2).

Table 15.2
Attitudes towards perestroika in the light of present-day reforms
Question: 'If in 1985 you had known about the nature of 1990s reforms would you
have supported perestroika more or not? (in per cent)

Year	Yes	No	Not Sure
February 1991	40%	35%	25%
April 1992	36%	46%	18%
May 1993	40%	42%	18%
May 1994	30%	53%	17%

Note: Sample sizes were as follows: 1991 = 873; 1992 = 1,126; 1993 = 1,172; 1994 = 1,657. Most respondents came from urban parts of Russia.

The results presented in table 15.3 below must be interpreted in the light of the fact that Russia's transition to a market economy has led to high inflation, rising crime, a drop in living standards and a deterioration in a feeling of personal security as we saw in the previous chapter. Thus people who initially greeted the collapse of communism with enthusiasm now have mixed feelings about what followed in the light of the enormous economic and social costs of modernisation. Thus only slightly more on average favour the market as opposed to the plan as a means of allocation of resources. Similarly although most of our respondents are now positively disposed towards private entrepreneurs, they have reservations about the desirability of privatisation. Older workers as opposed to younger private businessmen feel they have more to lose than gain.

Our research shows, in line with table 15.3, that it is mainly well-educated, younger age groups who are the most energetic supporters of reform - ranging from between a third and two-thirds - set against the less educated, middle to old age groups with traditional values and attitudes who are still conservative in their thinking and therefore less supportive of radical change.[14] These trends were confirmed in the December 1995 election results, as outlined in chapter 1.

What does all this mean for our discussion of civil society? Broadly speaking democrat reformists in Russia see the development of a civil society as a key political goal, whereas opponents of the government tend to play down its importance. So how crucial is the concept of civil society in trying to understand Russia's transformation? In seeking to answer this question in the affirmative, we would like to utilise modernisation theory.

The relevance of modernisation theory

For modernisation theorists, a modern society is characterised, amongst other things, by the following: significant levels of industrialisation; sustainable economic development; widespread use of energy resources; a commitment to scientific rationality (taking into account environmental concerns); abundant food and material goods; bureaucratic and political structures run in an impersonal and meritocratic way, a large middle class and so forth. Such theorists also believe that attitudinal and value changes are essential pre-requisites in the creation of a modern society. Thus a willingness to change, openness towards new experiences, a belief in the efficacy of science and medicine, an ability to make independent choices regarding individual destiny, self-assertiveness, a strong interest in politics, major ambitions for oneself and one's children etc. are among the main characteristics of 'modern wo/man'.[15] Many features of Russian wo/man differ from those of their Western counterpart. Among the most important are a reduced interest in politics, collectivism and so forth. Russians are currently in the process of changing their way of life, traditional systems of values, moral norms etc. Russia is struggling to come to terms with imported Western, especially American, cultural patterns. Thus 'Westernisation' has severely challenged long-standing cultural traditions in Russia. If we fail to adapt, then Russia will not be able to integrate herself into the Western system of ideas and values, laws and rules of behaviour. For some this would spell disaster; for others, a narrow escape. In our opinion, the benefits of closer integration for Russia will be substantial; but in the short-term the social costs and cultural erosion implicit in Westernisation are also considerable. For many Russians, the present transition has undermined the image of the 'Golden West', which has now lost its attractiveness.

Table 15.3

Russian views regarding economic reform, June 1993 - February 1994

Sample n = 3,998 (in per cent)

Aspect	a	b	c	d	e	f
1. **Attitudes towards the free market**						
Q: *Which is better the plan or the market?*						
A: Plan	34.2	30.1	15.0	19.6	31.5	51.2
A: Market	41.2	41.7	14.1			
2. **Attitudes towards private enterpreneurship**						
Q: *What is your attitude towards the development of private entrepreneurship?*						
A: Positive	54.4	60.3	84.1	74.5	56.3	33.6
A: Negative	28.4	24.8	6.5	15.8	26.3	43.2
3. **Attitudes towards privatisation**						
Q: *Do you think privatisation is helping Russia out of her economic crisis or aggravating it?*						
A: Helping recovery	28.4	31.8	51.4	41.1	30.2	14.3
A: Aggravating crisis	25.1	22.2	12.1	16.8	22.2	37.2
4. **Degree of personal gain/loss**						
Q: *Do you think you will personally gain or lose as a result of the privatisation of state property?*						
A: Gain	17.4	19.3	37.4	29.6	16.3	8.7
A: Lose	27.6	27.1	12.1	20.4	27.3	34.2

Key:	Q = Question		A = Answer
a	General population	b	Source of income: wages
c	Source of income: private business	d	Less than 29 years old
e	Between 30-54 years old	f	55 years old and over

However, despite growing scepticism concerning the Yeltsin Administration, increased alienation from politics and constant rebelliousness against the so-called 'colonial behaviour' of the West, the large majority of Russians still believe in the notion of a democracy. Current debates centre around the alternatives i.e. the best means of achieving this goal. In our opinion, despite the tremendous difficulties outlined in this book, a return to old ways appears unlikely. Only a small proportion of the population support the restoration of the old communist regime and a system of centralised planning, with even less believing in Gorbachev's dream of a 'socialist market economy and society.

Constructing a civil society in post-communist Russia

Although most of the features of the old system have been destroyed, not all pillars of the new one are in place. As a result we have a 'hybrid' - part old, part new. How then can we make the final leap from one to the other? Or to put it another way, how can we continue our progress towards the formation of a civil society?

How bad is the current situation?

Whilst one might be tempted to conclude that little which is positive has occurred since the fall of the old regime, a recent survey of public opinion between 1989-94 in the newspaper *Sevodnya* revealed some very interesting results. VTsIOM carried out two surveys: one in 1989 among a sample of 2,957 in various regions of Russia; the other in November 1994 among a similar group totalling 1,325. The results are presented in tables 15.4 and 15.5 below.

Table 15.4
Assessment of various periods in Russian development according to November 1994 survey
(n = 2,957)

Event	Viewpoint (in per cent)			
	a	b	c	d
Time of 1917 Revolution	27	38	7	28
Stalin era	18	57	5	20
Khrushchev period	33	14	33	21
Brezhnev era	36	16	33	16
Perestroika	16	47	17	20

Key:

a	Made things better	b	Made things worse
c	Nothing special	d	Hard to tell

Source: VTsIOM Survey cited in *Sevodnya* 24 January 1995, p. 10.

These tables show that the 1917 Revolutions, the Stalin era and perestroika are seen in a negative light by most respondents, but by and large most of the changes in the last decade are perceived positively.

VTsIOM researchers also investigated what Russians thought were the most important issues in 1989 and 1994; among the top three in 1989 were material prosperity (cited by 40 per cent), fairness without special privilege (30 per cent) and a revival of the countryside (3 per cent) compared with the desire for law and order (20 per cent), stability (16 per cent) and a dignified life (10 per cent) in 1994.[16]

Table 15.5
Assessment of specific changes in Russian development according to November 1994 survey (n = 2,957)

Nature of changes	Viewpoint (in per cent)	
	a	b
Freedom of speech/press	53	23
Rapprochement to West	47	19
Right to leave the country	45	23
Free enterprise	44	28
Multi-party elections	29	33
Right to strike	23	36
Break up of USSR	8	75

Key:

a   Brought Russia more good   b   Brought Russia more harm

Source: VTsIOM Survey cited in *Sevodnya* 24 January 1995, p. 10.

The VTsIOM 1989-94 surveys also pointed to the obstacles on an individual level when trying to create a civil society. The results are given in table 15.6 above. Among the main difficulties are a lack of culture and good upbringing, a lack of political rights and an absence of moral fibre and self-confidence. All these factors are likely to hinder a closer relationship between different individuals, let alone that between state and society.

Table 15.6
In your opinion what does a person in Russia most lack today?
(per cent of those surveyed)

Answers	1989a	1994b
Material prosperity	51	54
Culture & good upbringing	41	25
Industriousness	35	13
Moral principles	15	12
Self-confidence	15	26
Political rights	11	6
Respect for the past	6	13
Opportunity to relax	6	7

Key:

a   1989 sample totalled 2,700   b   1994 sample was 2,957

Source: VTsIOM Survey cited in *Sevodnya* 24 January 1995, p. 10.

Thus if the transformation of Russia's ex-socialist culture into a 'Westernised culture' is to succeed, the slow and painful process of collective learning will require a long-term perspective since norms are not formed through indoctrination but via socialisation across generation, formal education etc.

Conclusion

Looking back on the question posed earlier on in this chapter, we think that the term 'civil society' can be used in relation to post-communist Russia but it needs to be modified to take into account the specifics of transition from a state run economy to one based on the market as well as from a one party dictatorship to liberal democracy. Although this process can be analysed in terms of modernisation theory, modernisation in the contemporary ex-socialist world is not simply a mere repetition of other countries experiences. This is the case in Russia for at least two reasons: first because of the uniqueness of the cultural area involved and second because of the uniqueness of the revolutionary circumstances in which this process of change started. Former communist states at the beginning of their radical economic and political reforms differ greatly in terms of their level of economic development, ranging from the status of developing nations in the case of the ex-Soviet Central Asian states to highly industrialised nations such as Russia. Each is faced with very different sets of tasks and challenges, but they share one thing: a communist past. Using the notion of a 'civil society' we can therefore begin to explore in a more serious fashion Russia's chances of building and then consolidating a civil and political society and the influence which its success or failure is likely to have on Russia's transition from totalitarianism to freedom and pluralist democracy. In seeking to analyse such changes, however, the modernisation of Russia cannot simply be analysed using North American or West European models in an uncritical fashion. If we ignore this fact then there is also a possibility that excessive Western involvement in Russia's transformation will seriously deform the development of our 'civil society' into a new 'government' form (*grazhdanskoe obshchestvo-gosudarstvo*).

So what chance does Russia have of developing a civil society? According to the criteria laid down by Bollen[17] the following factors are key indicators of the development of a civil society: a free press, free opposition, pluralism, popular sovereignty, open elections and the rule of law. By these criteria, Russia still has a long way to go.

Notes

*   The first three authors wish to thank the Russian Fund for Fundamental Research for grant No. 93-06-10280 which facilitated the research on which part of this chapter is based.

1.   For a useful discussion see Ye.N. Gurenko and O.I. Skaratan, 'Ot etatizma k stanovleniiu grazhdanskogo obshchestva', *Rabochii klass i sovremennyi mire*

1990, No. 3; I.I. Kravchenko, 'Kontseptsii grazhdanskogo obshestva v filosofskom razvitii', *Polis* 1991, No. 56; Iu. Krasin and A. Galkia, 'Grazhdanskoe obshchestvao: put' k stabil'nosti' *Dialog* 1992, No. 3; *Politologiia Kurs lektsii Tema 9: Grazhdanskoe obshchestvo,* Moscow 1993 and Robert F. Miller (ed.), *The developments of civil society in communist systems,* Allen & Unwin, Sydney 1992.

2.   S. Cohen, 'What's really happening in Russia', *The Nation* 2 March 1992, pp. 259-64 cited in *Svobodnaia Mysl'* Number 8.

3.   However, we would like to mention in passing that in our opinion, Cohen's interpretation of mass behaviour during the 1991 coup is incorrect. Polls conducted in the period 1989-91 suggested a desire for both the market and democracy. Furthermore, the growing economic crisis and the erosion of the ideological basis of the communist regime had already undermined the legitimacy of the communist regime.

4.   R.F. Miller, 'Civil society in communist systems: An introduction' in Robert F. Miller (ed.), *The developments of civil society in communist systems,* Allen & Unwin, Sydney 1992, pp. 1-10.

5.   See for example J. Frentzel-Zagorska, 'Civil society in Poland and Hungary', *Soviet Studies,* Vol. 42 (4) 1990 and her 'Two phases of transition from communism to democracy in Poland and Hungary', *Sistphus, Sociological Studies,* Vol. 7, Warsaw 1991, pp. 95-114 as well as M.A. Weigel, 'The consolidation of civil and political society in post-communist regimes: Central Europe and Russia', paper delivered to the Annual meeting of the Midwest Political Association, Chicago, Illinois, 9-11 April 1992.

6.   For a more detailed discussion of this process see A. Arato, 'Social movements and civil society in the Soviet Union', in J. Sediatis and J. Butterfield (eds.), *Perestroika from below: Social movements in the Soviet Union,* Westview, Boulder 1991, pp. 197-214.

7.   Cited in Robert F. Miller (ed.), *The developments of civil society in communist systems,* Allen & Unwin, Sydney 1992, p. 4.

8.   T. Kusio, 'The multi-party system in the Ukraine on the eve of the elections: Identity problems, conflicts and solutions', *Government and Opposition,* Vol. 29 (1), 1994, pp. 109-27.

9.   See also T.H. Rigby, 'The USSR: End of a long, dark night?', in Robert F. Miller (ed.), *The developments of civil society in communist systems,* Allen & Unwin, Sydney 1992, pp. 19-23.

10.   A similar point was made by M.A. Weigel, 'The consolidation of civil and political society in post-communist regimes: Central Europe and Russia', paper delivered to the Annual meeting of the Midwest Political Association, Chicago, Illinois, 9-11 April 1992, p. 6.

11.   Ibid, p. 45.

12.   See *Rossisskaia Federatsiia* 1994, No. 1.

13.   On this see V. Rukavishnikov, 'A split society: Political crisis and popular support for transition to a free market and democracy in Russia', *Sociale Wetenschapen* 1994, No. 2.

14.   Ibid.

15.   A.L. Allahar, *Sociology and the periphery,* University of Toronto Press, 1989.
16.   VTsIOM Survey cited in *Sevodnya* 24 January 1995, p. 10.
17.   K. Bollen, 'Issues in the comparative measure of Political democracy', *American Sociological Review* 1988, Vol. 53 (1).

16 The ethnic question

VILEN IVANOV

Introduction

In contemporary Russia, many things depend upon the nature of the relations between nations. The people of different national groups, who had lived together without any major conflicts for a century, are all of a sudden experiencing distrust, even hostility, towards each other. Increasing tension between nations means that conflict has become a reality in many regions. What factors are playing the decisive role in causing such conflict and what can be done to prevent ethnic tension?

These questions are being addressed in current sociological research. My research shows that whereas in the pre-perestroika and perestroika periods ethnic conflict was the product of failure to create 'developed socialism'; in the post-communist period ethnic tensions have increased because of the demise of socialism and the introduction of capitalism.

The process of transformation has exerted a strong influence not only over the economy and the political system, but also over the relationship between and within different nations. Of course, these variables are inter-related. For example, the erroneous policy of radical economic reform, based on monetarism (i.e. shock therapy) has merely brought about serious failures - a massive and continuing decline in production, reduced investment, loss of scientific and technical potential, falling living standards, inflation, enterprise closures etc. These failures have generated adverse trends in the social sphere - increased social polarisation, crime and the marginalisation of society as we saw in earlier chapters. This situation has only served to increase social discontent and with it the likelihood of social conflict produced by a loss of social status, an inability to adjust to the new conditions, loss of property and less power to make the situation more stable.

In fact in today's Russia, a peculiar type of potential ethnic conflict has developed, it will ultimately determine the expression of social discontent and this will in turn take different forms in different spheres.

Of course, it would be a gross over-simplification to imply that potential conflict is caused only by economic failure; it is also the product of rising **social atomisation** (*sotsial'noi atomizatsii*), which helps create a competitive environment in which it is a case of dog eat dog, with only the strongest managing to survive. Today, it has become increasingly obvious that this is a strange notion in a Russian context - after all our past was dominated by a belief in collectivism and egalitarianism not individualism, egoism and materialism. Thus the emergence of ethnic conflict nowadays is also the outcome of contradictions in the value system, which inevitably finds reflection in group conflict.

All the aforementioned factors - economic failure; social atomisation; contradictions in the system of values - have, as we saw in chapter 1, already produced significant conflict between the legislature and the executive in Russia. But the conflict has not stopped there. It has also spilled over into conflict between different ethnic groupings and in some cases led to civil war - Chechnya is a case in point. Unless we find a rapid solution to the aforementioned problems, social conflicts will go on increasing and involve a significant part of the population.

The potential for ethnic conflict

It would certainly be wrong to consider ethnic conflict as only arising out of socio-economic and political contradictions. My research shows that the primary factor influencing ethic tension and conflict is a growth in interest in national culture, history, language and nation state formation among the nations that made up the former USSR. However, although in overall terms this process of increased national consciousness is usually a progressive process, occasionally it has drawbacks.

From nationalism to separatism

Under perestroika attempts were made to eradicate past errors, but this merely produced rising nationalism which eventually transformed into separatism. This was the outcome of two inter-related processes: the rejection of socialist ideology, on the one hand, and rising nationalist feelings encouraged by local elites in the fight for power and determination to break-away from Moscow, on the other. In addition to new nationalistic political elites, the church, the intelligentsia and the mass media were in favour of this shift from nationalism to separatism.

Nationalism was also promoted by some national movements. For example the *Ittifakh Party* from Tatarstan believes in Turk unity and speaks out in favour of its territorial claims to its neighbours regions; the Bashkir national centre *Ural* defends its special status, the radical wing of the *Dzhamagat* society of Karavaevo-Cherkassy, and the Karelian Movement in Karelia etc. are all pursuing their own nationalist objectives. Although different *mafiya* and extremists often use these groups for their own ends, increased national consciousness on the part of such groups of their own national culture, history, language and sense of nation state formation brings them into conflict with their respective regimes and increases the degree of ethnic tension and conflict. In other cases, it has led to national isolation and separation.

Russia's linch-pin role

Economic, historical and social factors have promoted the need for ethnic consolidation. But by and large despite the collapse of the Union little has changed in some respects. Thus, Russia is still the largest nation in the former Soviet Union. Historically Russia has played and still plays a key co-ordinating role, determining the relationship between itself and other nations as well as between other nations, to some extent, in the Commonwealth of Independent States (CIS).

However, Russia's position has declined in the last few years. It is less and less able to fulfil this linch-pin role. This role has to a certain degree been replaced by an anxiety on the part of Russia's population of its own national consciousness, as well as about the plight of Russians living in the 'near abroad'. More and more Russians are sympathising with their fellow Russians abroad who are encountering increasing discrimination. As a consequence, as we saw in chapter 3, an increasing number of Russians are being forced to migrate elsewhere or else serve as hostages in political struggles of various types. For example when staff from the Sociology of Ethnic Relations division of the Institute of Socio-Political Research carried out research into this question in 1993, they found that most of the respondents gave a very low evaluation of the ability of the Russian authorities to protect the interests and rights of Russians living in the 'Near abroad'. Thus only 2 per cent of Moscow residents said our government's policies were 'adequate' in this regard, whereas 71 per cent declared that they were 'totally inadequate', with 27 per cent giving no answer at all. In Stavropol 2 per cent, 79 per cent and 18 per cent of our sample gave the same responses.[1]

The plight of Russians living in the 'Near abroad' to a large extent depends upon their political behaviour and their political loyalties, aims and motivations. According to surveys carried out in Kazakhstan and the Ukraine by staff from the Centres of Conflict Regulation and the Association of Nationalities Research at the Universities of Stanford and Berkeley, California, under the auspices of the MacArthur Fund, there are technically speaking no material divergencies between Russians and the local population. Western researchers discovered that Russians usually do not participate in political in-fighting at a local level. Our research shows that the majority of Russians express agreement with the main policies of the countries in which they live in. In Kazakhstan, for example, up to 40 per cent of Russians do not intend leaving this Republic whereas in the Ukraine, this figure is twice as high at 80 per cent.[2]

However, the position of Russians resident abroad cannot be considered in such single-issue terms. In addition to the variables mentioned earlier, the policies of the ex-Soviet Republics are also highly significant. The latter also determine the fate of Russians living in 'Near abroad' countries.

The place of Russians in the new world order

Some scholars are trying to prove that on the whole Russians do not fit into trends in the late 20th century and hence major problems are building up for the next century. Others say that some but not all Russians fit into the New World Order. A new term 'New Russians' has been invented to describe those Russians who fit into the current situation.

They have proven their ability not only to survive but to prosper. We should not rule out the possibility, however, of these so-called 'New Russians' developing a strong sense of patriotism and nationalist feelings in the not too distant future. Thus according to Professor Nikolai Keizerov: 'Democrats did not take into consideration that patriotic feelings and wounded national consciousness cannot be violated and offended with impunity'. They therefore run the risk, Keizerov adds, of ignoring the fact that 'Humiliation produces a strong reaction'.[3] In my opinion it is not possible to ignore Russian's legitimate demands anymore. But the reaction to these demands must be measured too. Of course, there are also extremists who make unreasonable demands.

Sovereignty versus independence

The solutions offered to this situation vary. Some, out of concern about Russia's lack of prosperity, wish to create a unified Russian state, so that Russians can feel some sense of independence and sovereignty (*suverennost'*). Sovereignty was declared a long time ago and entailed the Russian Federation having control over its territory, resources and over the right to entry/exit from Russia. For many decades, Russia and the USSR meant one and the same thing. After the break-up of the Union, sovereignty from Russia was demanded by all of the former Soviet Republics. Even within the Russian Federation, many smaller states demanded independence and sovereignty.

Despite the fact that a New Constitution has now been adopted, this does not mean that the question of Russia's sovereignty has been resolved; far from it. The break-up of the New Russia cannot be ruled out. Many Republics lend their support to the notion of sovereignty. For example in an interview in *Nezavisimaia Gazeta*, the President of Tatarstan, Mintimer Shaimiev, stated that: 'In Tatarstan, the idea of sovereignty is deeply rooted in the consciousness of the people'. Shaimiev went on to add that this idea was shared not only by the Tartars, but by other groups living in this Republic. A similar situation was said to prevail in Karelia, Yakutia, Bashkortastan and so forth.[4]

Russian sovereignty in a comparative perspective

It is necessary to examine Russia's sovereignty problem more carefully by taking into consideration the experience of other countries as well as the peculiarities of Russian history.

First of all, let us look at some historical background. According to the 1989 census, 81 per cent of the population of the RSFSR were Russians. At present, this percentage is steadily increasing due to forced migration. By the end of 1994 it stood at 83 per cent. The micro population census of 1994 revealed the changing composition of national groups living in Russia today. As table 16.1 shows, since 1989 the number of Russians (2 per cent), Armenians (34 per cent), Avars (11 per cent), Ossetins (15 per cent), Buryats (8 per cent), Yakuts (16 per cent), Lezgins (15 per cent) and Ingushi (18 per cent) have all increased, whereas the number of Ukrainians (21 per cent), Belorussians (19 per cent), Germans (6 per cent) and Kazakhs (10 per cent) among others have fallen. How does this situation compare with other countries? In France, 82 per cent of the population are French, in England, 77 per cent are English and in Spain 70 per cent of the population are Spanish.

Table 16.1
National composition of Russia according to 1994 micro-census data

Nationality	1989	1994	% change 1989-94
Russians	81529	82950	+2.0
Tatars	3763	3773	+0.3
Ukranians	2967	2345	-21.0
Chuvash	1206	1172	-3.0
Bashkirs	915	936	+2.0
Belarussians	820	662	-19.0
Mardvas	730	636	-13.0
Germans	573	536	-6.0
Udmurts	486	485	-0.2
Armenians	362	485	+34.0
Avars	370	411	+11.0
Kazakhs	432	387	-10.0
Ossetins	274	315	+15.0
Buryats	284	308	+8.0
Yakuts	259	300	+16.0
Jews	365	268	-17.0
Komi	229	244	+7.0
Lezgins	175	201	+15.0
Ingush	146	172	+18.0

Sources: *Osnovye itogi mikroperepisi naseleniia* (Moscow 1994), pp. 5-6 and *Rossiia v tsifrakh 1995*, (Goskomstat, Moscow 1995), p. 31.

Secondly, let us look at the position of the non-Russian proportion of Russia's population. 36 per cent of non-Russians are peoples of the former USSR's other Republics, such as Ukrainians, Belorussians, Armenians, Azerbaijanis etc. or of far off countries, namely Germany, Greece, Poland and so forth. For these groups, there is no problem regarding sovereignty. About another third of non-Russians (28.5 per cent) do not live within the borders of the Russian Federation and therefore do not have powerful aspirations regarding sovereignty. Finally, of the remaining group (35.5 per cent) of non-Russians living within their own national formations most have strong desires for their own sovereignty. It is the latter who tend to reside in Tatarstan, Bashkortostan, Chechnya, Saha, Mordovia etc.

In any West European country, no one would give into the demands for sovereignty on the part of such a small proportion of the population. Illustrative examples here include British policy towards Northern Ireland prior to the recent Peace Talks and the

Spanish government's attitude towards the Basques. In other countries, even though large populations reside there, they have never demanded sovereignty. This includes the 5 million Germans resident in the USA as well as the 536,000 Germans in the Russian Federation.[5]

Third, it is clear from the aforementioned discussion that the situation in Russia is markedly different to that in Western Europe. Despite this fact, there is a temptation to follow the Western path. There have even been attempts to adhere to it. But we should strongly resist such temptations. Russian mentality has always been different, making it difficult for us to associate with the hopes and expectations of other nations. To abide with the latter would have serious consequences and possibly lead to major conflicts. As G. Fedorov, an outstanding Russian philosopher declared:

> 'Russia is not Rus, but the union of the peoples, united around Russia, these peoples are not speechless anymore, but they aspire to drown each other with the noise of their discordant voices. For many of us, the present situation is still unusual, we cannot reconcile ourselves to it. If we do not reconcile ourselves to it.... then we will stay only in Great Russia i.e. Russia will not exist'.[6]

Rejecting coercion

In solving national problems, we must refuse to dictate and avoid coercion. The latter only creates the appearance of resolution, when in fact the particular problem still survives underneath the surface. Violence is dangerous in any form especially as it produces a violent reaction, bringing us back to square one. Chechnya is a good example. Despite the death of an estimated 32,000 in the Chechen conflict and the need for 5.4 billion roubles to rebuild the war-torn Chechen economy,[7] the war escalated of late. Violence on both sides makes the Caucasus region like a time bomb waiting to go off. In the end the conflict may spread elsewhere.[8]

No matter how attractive the national idea is, Russia cannot pursue the same path that the other ex-Soviet Republics are pursuing, even to a lesser, let alone a greater degree.

For today's multi-national Russia, the most important point is not a sense of national belonging, but a sense of belonging to and identifying with a more unified state. Here a correct analogy would be with the situation in America. As the famous American historian Arthur Schlesinger noted: 'The majority of the minority group members born in the USA, blacks as well as whites, consider themselves Americans and only then as members of a certain ethnic group'.[9] Russians have historical and other reasons for sympathising with this statement. To fail to understand this might have tragic consequences.

Ethnicity and politics

Russia has to become a democratic Federation of subjects with equal rights, with a high degree of independence and a strong sense of self-government. But these gains are counterbalanced by restrictions upon the **freedom to enter and exit from the Russian Federation**. Today there are sufficient grounds to conclude that the process of regional (as well as national) consciousness is on-going. We must take this into account when drawing up any policies to address the *National Question*. Attempts to create new Republics support such a statement.

Asymmetrical developments

In order to prevent ethnic conflict, we have to reconcile ourselves to a situation in which in a few years time, the Russian Federation will be 'asymmetrical' (*asimmetrichnyi*) in its character. And this asymmetry will be connected to the genuine relations that will exist between centre and periphery. We will also witness the creation of a situation in which all subjects are equal before the law, although their relationship to the central authorities might differ slightly. The Centre will also adopt a paternalistic policy towards some regions in which certain nationalities are grouped according to ecological or other criteria, or as a result of coercion. In such cases, it is preferable that a Special fund for regional support be created, with the appropriate legislation being introduced wherever necessary to facilitate such support.

The Centre not only has responsibilities towards certain ethnic groups and regions where they reside, it also has a duty to support large population groups deployed for specific tasks, such as those in military industrial complexes (MIC) or the defence industry. These groups have served the nation well but are now suffering as firms close and their employees are made redundant. As the MICs tend to be located in specific regions, this might also be a sphere worthy of support from the Special funds mentioned above. The Centre can also offer financial support for local projects or else embark upon projects of Federal importance in areas where former MICs/defence industries were located.[10]

Some asymmetry is also inevitable in Russia's relations with the 'Near abroad' nations. Some of them will be in the same rouble zone as Russia, others will participate in the realisation of mutually advantageous projects while the rest will mostly decide to resolve defence issues together. The 'variety' of such scenarios will only serve firstly, to increase **integration tendencies**; secondly, to restore multi-dimensional connections and finally, to overcome national mistrust and separation.

The introduction of the necessary pre-requisites for the prevention of ethnic conflicts must take higher priority than demands for greater mass consciousness. As two American scholars Roger Fisher and William Urry aptly noted: 'the reason for conflict is not the objective reality, but what is going on in people's minds'.[11] In my opinion, it is impossible to prevent ethnic conflicts from arising without understanding the nature of mass consciousness prior to the emergence of ethnic tension.

The national/ethnic question in the post-communist period

How can we characterise mass consciousness concerning ethnic relations today? What perceptions and forecasts currently prevail? The Socio-Political Research Institute of the Russian Academy of Sciences (ISPI, RAN) together with the Sociology of Ethnic

Relations Centre (TsSMO) carried out significant inter-regional social research into the problem of the normalisation of ethnic relations in the Russian Federation during the period 1991-94. I would like to discuss our findings in order to throw some light on the nature of the national/ethnic question in the post-communist period.

In each of these years, a representative sample of 7,000 adults from different population groups and different cities - Petrozavodsk, Moscow, Orenburg, Ufa, Stavropol, Cherkessk, Nal'chik, Makhachkal, Ulan-Ude and Yakudsk - were surveyed. In other instances, such as North-West Russia, respondents from Leningrad, Novogorod and Pskov regions (*oblasti*) as well as those in the city of St. Petersburg were only surveyed once in 1991.[12]

1994 survey results

The surveys conducted in 1994 generally confirmed earlier trends which were as follows:

(i)   increased tension existed between nations according to 45.9 per cent of our Moscow respondents in 1994 compared with 33.9 per cent in 1992;

(ii)   22 per cent of those surveyed in 1994 admitted there was obvious ethnic tension in Moscow, as compared to 17 per cent two years earlier. Jews[13] followed by Ukrainians and Russians were most concerned about it;

(iii)   Even the smallest of regions were experiencing ethnic tension. For instance in Cherkessk in 1994, 47 per cent of respondents admitted the existence of such tension and 21 per cent the possibility of future conflict; and finally we found that

(iv)   Greatest concern about ethnic tension and conflict was expressed by Russians, 15 per cent of whom consider conflicts on national grounds possible. At the same time, our research revealed that 7 per cent of Abazins, 6 per cent of Cherkessians, 5 per cent of Nogais and 3 per cent of Karachais shared these fears. However in the case of respondents from Stavropol, 47 per cent admitted ethnic conflicts already existed and 15 per cent said they were likely in future.

From the above evidence, we can conclude that there are negative public attitudes towards the National Question. Although this partly stems from **negative national stereotypes**, it also arises from a genuine fear of ethnic conflict.

Degree of hostility

In order to determine the degree of hostility towards other ethnic groups than ones own, we posed the question: 'Are there any nationalities that you feel hostility towards?' In 1994, 37 per cent of those surveyed answered 'yes'; 47 per cent 'no' and 16 per cent 'don't know'. More specifically among the different ethnic groups resident in the capital Moscow, highest levels of prejudice towards other nationalities was expressed by Ukrainians, Russians and Jews in that order. It is interesting that **the lowest degree of prejudice in all ethnic groups was among persons of an older age.** Thus, we found that 69 per cent of those under 20 years old held hostile views towards other nationalities than their own, compared to only 25 per cent of those in the 50-60 year old age range.

Among the national groupings towards which there was hostility, Armenians, Azerbaijanis and Georgians figured prominently. Furthermore, as the question was vague and left open ended, some respondents simply replied 'people from the Caucasus' when describing which groups they felt hostility towards.

Our research also demonstrates that it is young people who express the highest degree of hostility towards different nationalities. Thus when we asked young people the same question as before, namely 'Are there any nationalities that you feel hostility towards?', 20-40 per cent said 'yes'. This negative attitude towards others was especially pronounced among students who tended to be less tolerant of different nationalities, only interested in their own wealth and prosperity and who also tended to ignore differences, norms of living, or culture, and do not display a sense of historical values.

Explaining prejudice

Despite the obvious differences according to age, most of the aforementioned hostility towards different nationalities stems from a sense of us and them: thus one nationality feels that the 'other' nationality has a higher standard of living. In Moscow, for instance, 55 per cent of those surveyed in 1994 thought in this way. Among those deemed to be more 'prosperous' (*blagopoluchnyi*) were people coming from the Caucasus (34 per cent of those surveyed) and the Jews (5 per cent). Russians and Ukrainians were only mentioned by 0.5 per cent of those interviewed.

Infringement of national rights

We also discovered a lack of awareness concerning infringement of the rights of different ethnic groups. Of those surveyed 22.9 per cent of Jews, 14.9 per cent of Ukrainians and 14.7 per cent of Russians were totally ignorant about the extent of and how their national interests could be protected. Most of those surveyed freely admitted that their rights were often violated in the course of their everyday lives. Therefore they possessed little sense of national pride, were constantly discriminated against and were frequently abused on nationalist grounds. Those who occupied first place in the hostility stakes among Moscow respondents were those from the ex-Soviet Republics selling goods on the streets of the capital (44 per cent) or those seeking permanent jobs and residence in Moscow (21 per cent).

A question of rights

Our respondents' replies regarding the degree of priority to be assigned to different national titular and non-titular groups' rights also proved to be extremely fascinating. 67 per cent of our respondents in the city of Nal'chik expressed their disagreement with the assertion that the indigenous population/nationality should have greater benefits than 'non-natives'. Only 14 per cent of those surveyed concurred with this viewpoint. However, among representatives of 'titular nationalities', a higher percentage of respondents agreed with this view - 39 per cent of Karbardians and 26 per cent of Balkars. In addition, we also discovered that 50 per cent of Balkars and 47 per cent of Karbardians believe that their local authorities partly take into consideration their interests while 5 per cent and 9 per cent respectively think that their interests are completely ignored in the policy/decision-making process. By contrast, 11 per cent of those in Stavropol thought their interests were taken into account; 24 per cent only partially adhered to and finally, 15 per cent of those surveyed from Stavropol thought the local authorities ignored the views of the community. The extent to which the latter prevailed among specific nationalities varied from 24 per cent among Ukrainians to 26 per cent among Armenians.

Why does national tension exist?

Our research indicates that in the hierarchy of factors causing ethnic tension and conflict, primary emphasis was placed upon a deterioration in the economic situation. In addition to this, the migration of non-indigenous nationalities was also a cause of concern. This was as true of Moscow as it was of the North Caucasus (the area where the Chechen conflict is centred). For instance in Cherkessk, political instability and a worsening of the economic situation were cited as the main reasons for ethnic tension amongst 60 per cent of our respondents.

Harmonising ethnic relations

Our surveys show that few respondents are prepared to accept or tolerate others. Instead in a number of regions 'extremism' is on the increase. Thus in 1993 in Moscow we posed the question: In what ways can we improve ethnic relations and reduce tension? 39 per cent of our sample replied clear Moscow of 'visitors'. When we went on to ask how can this goal be achieved, most respondents called for 'ethnic cleansing'. We must reject such extremist views and think of the long-term consequences of such actions, not only in terms of the impact of 'ethnic cleansing' on non-Russians residing in Russia, but also on Russians living in countries whose citizens are subject to such policies. Retaliation is always a strong possibility. Such a response would not improve ethnic relations and reduce tension but have the opposite effect in increasing ethnic conflict between different nationalities. However, not everyone favoured 'ethnic cleansing' as a solution to ethnic tension. 33 per cent of those surveyed called for improvements in the social situation and the restoration of order; 15 per cent said an improvement in the economic situation of Moscovites might help and 2-8 per cent of those surveyed pointed to the need to create national schools, cultural societies, newspapers, magazines and TV programmes to promote different languages and cultures. The solutions offered varied according to region. In the capital of Kabardino-Balkaria, Nal'chik, the paramount measures, in order of preference, to stabilise ethnic relations were as follows: 52 per cent strengthen the fight against displays of nationalism and chauvinism; 33 per cent provide genuine economic sovereignty and 15 per cent provide clearer definitions ol things such as 'political status'. Other solutions offered included creating national-cultural centres and solving the problem of migration. Such differences in approach reflect regional factors and as such should be included in Russia's policy on the *National Question*.

Preserving Russia's wholeness

Respondents' answers to questions relating to the need to preserve the wholeness of Russia proved extremely interesting too. Table 16.2 presents our research findings on this issue:

Table 16.2
Attitudes towards the preservation of Russia, 1994
Question: Do you agree that the wholeness of Russia should be preserved at any cost?

Town/Region	Answer (in per cent)		
	Agree	Disagree	Unable to say
Rostov on Don	62.8	18.7	19.1
Chelyabinsk	55.0	14.2	18.4
Penza	56.7	16.4	26.9
Chita	74.4	13.2	12.5
Abakan	60.2	19.7	19.3

In Russia as a whole, 57 per cent of those surveyed in 1994 agreed that the wholeness of Russia should be preserved. As we can see from table 16.2, those in Chelyabinsk and Penza were on a par with national attitudes, but in Rostov, Chita and Abakan, attitudes were stronger and more people agreed with such a sentiment. By comparison, as table 16.3 below shows, our respondents from the five regions selected were divided over what the future holds for Russia.

Table 16.3
Attitudes towards Russia's future, 1994
Question: What future do you think Russia has?

Town/Region	Answer (in per cent)		
	a	b	c
Rostov on Don	17.8	12.7	17.0
Chelyabinsk	14.2	16.3	17.7
Penza	8.2	19.6	21.8
Chita	14.1	10.2	17.0
Abakan	18.1	11.3	19.5

Key:

a   Liable to disintegrate further
b   Will exist in present borders
c   People will eventually unite around Russia

As low as 8.2 per cent in Penza and as high as 18.1 per cent in Abakan thought further disintegration was likely; between 10-20 per cent according to region believed Russia would retain its existing borders and finally, 17-22 per cent thought that sooner or later a process will begin in which various peoples will eventually united around Russia. Our research points therefore to greater optimism rather than pessimism about Russia's future, excluding public discontent over Chechnya. On the whole, given the right circumstances, our surveys illustrate a desire towards integration and the unity of all peoples living in Russia.

National policy during the transition period

Russia's complex ethnic situation, mass migration, as we saw earlier in chapter 3, coupled with ethnic conflicts and wars at and within its borders, are posing a serious threat to the very nature of the Russian state. This highly unstable political climate makes the problem of working out a nationality policy for the 1990s a very difficult task. This problem is compounded further by the many contradictions inside Russia, especially in the Northern Caucasus with the Chechen crisis, as well as growing problems along the Volga river (*Povol'zhia*) and in the 'Near abroad' countries. The present uncertain 'ethnic climate' is throwing into question the nature of what constitutes the Russian state. As in the late Gorbachev era, so in the mid-1990s, the key issue is over which areas the Russian government can exert its authority. This issue first emerged on the political agenda a decade ago and culminated in the emergence of a range of sovereign independent states of the ex-USSR in the period 1989-91. Given the short time scale since the collapse of the USSR, we are still in the process of dismantling the old state and are only just beginning to start the process of state building. The latter is signified by the recent declaration 'Concerning Nationality policy' which was adopted in 1993 after the New Constitution was approved. According to the New Constitution Russia has 21 Republics, 6 krais and 49 oblasts.[14] The aim of this declaration was as follows: firstly, to clarify the purposes and tasks of the state in relation to the Ethnic Question; second, to draw up concrete measures in different areas of social practice designed to led to a national renaissance and the development of all Russian peoples; third, to unite all these peoples together and finally, the aim is to prevent the further dismantling of the Russian state by pursuing policies which foster co-operation between Russia and the CIS countries on mutually beneficial grounds.[15]

Finding a way forward

Unfortunately what this declaration failed to do was provide the theoretical basis for the development of a new ethnopolitical strategy to suit the post-communist era. In my opinion, such a policy must bear in mind the fact that **national policy is an integral part of an overall strategy geared towards the renaissance and renewal of Russia.** The main purpose of nationality policy in the current transition period should be the creation of favourable conditions for the development of **the spiritual and material culture of all peoples living within Russia** as well as the **harmonisation of their relations on the basis of equal rights, freedoms and legal status.** In this regard,

Russia must abide by United Nations principles and also ensure that **the Union of the 21 Republics, 6 krais and 49 oblasts is guaranteed by the constitution**. We must not simply declare that Russia is a multi-ethnic state, but also devise a proper Federal government structure suited to the new conditions of the late 1990s. The difficulties which we are currently experiencing in Chechnya and other regions of the Russian Federation[16] has called into question the validity of the national policy devised a few years ago and illustrated that certain areas of Russia want their independence from Moscow. In our view while the preservation of the wholeness and unity of the Russian state is a highly desirable goal, this objective must not be achieved on the basis of the Centre's superiority. Although Chechnya's demands for independence are referred in government quarters as 'separatist' and as such 'unconstitutional', the rights of such Republics should be protected and extended and their sovereignty maintained **providing this does not lead to demands for succession and providing Chechnya and the likes abides by the Constitution**. However this cuts two ways. Neither the Centre nor its subjects must ignore the Constitution, otherwise sanctions might have to be enforced. It is preferable therefore that the Centre and the periphery act in unison and that de-centralisation be placed on the reform agenda. Furthermore, the protection of individual rights - irrespective of whether a citizen belongs to the national majority or minority - must be given greater priority. Mere reference to 'historical claims' must be declared inadmissible. If Russia is to continue to exist in its present form and to retain its existing borders then we must seek to create the conditions in which **a free union of equal nations flourishes**. Not a Union, as in the past based upon coercion, but one based upon **voluntary unity**. Only the latter will guarantee political stability, economic growth and the protection of Russia's national security in future.

Giving the regions greater priority

The Centre must assign higher priority to the regions so that they can carry out reforms, introduce local self-government and ensure that their local economy, society and cultures survive. Russia has two opportunities open to her: she can look to Western experience and/or examine her own past e.g. zemstvos of the late 19th century. Steps have already been taken in this direction. In the period 1990-92 local self-administration (*mestnoe samupravlenie*) was reformed. The laws enacted meant that local government had greater autonomy; in principle there was to be a separation of powers between the President and Soviets; the roles of 'executives' and 'representatives' were separated and hence as a result in large cities such as Moscow and St. Petersburg, mayors wielded significant political power.[17] This partly explains Yeltsin's ability to come back from oblivion under Gorbachev to raise again to become President. However, in October 1993 these structures and the new system of checks and balances were effectively abandoned. Now all chief executives were responsible to Yeltsin. According to Vladimir Gel'man, from late October 1993 regional chief executives had the power to confirm the regional budget, to veto all decisions of regional representatives and to be independent of deputies.[18] Although in theory this created a new system of regional power, in practice regional executives had to work within the confines of the new constitution and be loyal to Yeltsin in order to remain in power.[19] Thus despite the collapse of communism, the regions and their political institutions remain subordinated to the Centre. This applies to policy-making procedure, the legal system, the mass media as well as political parties. All are under the Yeltsin Administration's control because the centre controls the purse strings.[20] To rectify these problems and extend the power of the regions over their own geographical area, a number of steps must be taken: the main ones include a redistribution of finance and other resources away from the centre to other political actors and institutions in the localities and a clearer division of responsibilities between centre and periphery.

The idea of creating new national regions also deserves support. For example in Krasnodar, such a demand was made by the Congress of the Shapsug people. Special measures must be introduced which will give the peoples of tiny minorities the possibility of influencing decision-making connected with their way of life, economy or culture in their own region or Republic. The latter policy is, of course, based upon the assumption that different native peoples will wield different powers and degrees of influence upon the centre or their regional/Republican authorities depending upon the economic and cultural significance of their area and peoples. The same fate awaits Russian communities in a number of ex-Soviet Republics.

Conclusion

The Federal and local authorities in Russia should lend their support to the notion of the unity of all Russia's regions on the basis of national agreement and ethnic consolidation. This is necessary in order to prevent an on-going struggle against different forms of nationalism and separatism.[21] The Centre and the periphery should also actively support inter-regional economic unions and establishments as well as cultural exchanges. Further rapprochement with the CIS countries is an essential aspect of Russia's domestic and foreign policy. Examples of good practice here include the closer economic and military ties between Russia and Belarus, Kazakhstan and the Central Asian nations. In my opinion, the opportunity of recreating a Union of a new kind is a distinct possibility. Steps must therefore be taken to draw up a series of bilateral agreements to foster this goal. One of the greatest obstacles to this process of creating a New Union is, as we saw in chapter 3, the refugee and migration issue. In the short-term agreements on dual citizenship, bilingualism, education in one's native language and equal access to the mass media will also need to be resolved as quickly as possible. This requires joint action by the Russian authorities in co-operation with their counterparts in other countries of the ex-USSR. Such a process will be extremely difficult and expensive. Thus research in the first half of 1995 revealed that in Moscow and Ufa hostility towards other nationalities had increased from 27 per cent in 1994 to 41 per cent by 1995; furthermore 42 per cent and 48 per cent respectively of those surveyed wanted local government institutions to represent their national interests.[22] However in the long-term the aforementioned policy will pay dividends. Above all it will ensure the economic regeneration of Russia because the influx of Russian speaking migrants from the 'Near abroad' will help rebuild Russia. Whether or not this becomes a reality very much depends upon the implementation of a clearly defined nationalities policy suited to the new conditions of the 1990s and beyond. Although the creation of a New strong Russia should be its core element, we must also ensure that the rights and security of all

Russia's inhabitants are protected. At the same time, however, we must not forget that consolidation and integration are better than confrontation. Hence greatest emphasis should be placed upon unity and co-operation as the guiding principles of Russia's nationality policy in the transition period.

Notes

1. *Rossiia nakanune XXI veka vypusk I,* Moscow 1994, p. 52.
2. K. Povarov, *'Gotovy stat' loial'nymi', Inostranets* 1993 No. 23, p. 17.
3. *Rossiia nakanune XXI veka, Vypusk I,* Moscow 1994, p. 53.
4. *Nezavisimaia Gazeta* 10 December 1993, pp. 1, 3.
5. *Nash Sovremennik* 1993, No. 3, p. 150.
6. Cited in *Novoe Vremia* 1992, No. 10, p. 59.
7. *Pravda,* 21 October 1995, p. 1.
8. For more on Chechnya see M.B. Broxup and M. Gammer, *The Chechen struggle for independence,* C. Hurst London 1996 and Rza Shah-Kazemi, *Crisis in Chechnya,* Islamic World Report, London 1995.
9. A. Schlesinger, *Etnicheskaia obosoblennost',* Moscow 1992, p. 13.
10. For an interesting discussion of the problems encountered during conversation see Peter Southwood, *Disarming Military Industries: Turning an outbreak of peace into an enduring legacy,* Macmillian, London 1991.
11. R. Fisher and W. Urry, *Put' k soglasiiu ili peregovory bez porazhenii,* Moscow 'Nauka' 1990, p. 38.
12. I would like to acknowledge that this research could not have been carried out without financial support from the Russian Fund for Fundamental Research.
13. On this question see R.J. Brym and A. Degtyarev, 'Anti-semitism in Moscow: Results of an October 1992 survey', *Slavic Review,* Vol. 52 (1), Spring 1993, pp. 1-12.
14. For a full listing see S. White, 'Introduction: From Communism to Democracy?', in S. White, A. Pravda and Z. Gitelman (eds.), *Developments in Russian and Post-Soviet Politics,* Macmillan, London 1994, p. 12.
15. *Rossiia nakanune XXI veka, Vypusk I,* Moscow 1994, p. 62.
16. For a more detailed discussion see *Rossiia sevodnya: Real'nyi shans,* Moscow 1994, pp. 188-204.
17. For more on the restructuring of local government see *Vedomosti S'ezda narodnykh deputatov verkhovnovo Soveta SSSR* 1990, No. 16, Article 227; *Vedomosti S"ezda narodnykh deputatov RSFSR i Verkhovnovo Soveta RSFSR* 1991, No. 29, Article 1010 and *Vedomosti S"ezda narodnykh deputatov RSFSR i Verkhovnovo Soveta RSFSR* 1992, No. 13, Article 663.
18. V. Gel'man, 'Novaia mestnaia politika', in V. Gel'man (ed.), *Ocherki Rossisskoi politiki,* Moscow IGPI 1994.
19. V. Gel'man and O. Senatova, 'Politicheskie partii v regionakh Rossii', *Politicheskii monitoring* 9/1, 1994.
20. On these problems see V. Gelman and O. Senatova, 'Political reform in the Russian provinces: Trends since October 1993', in J. Lovenduski and J Stanyer

(eds.), *Contemporary Political Studies*, Vol. 1, PSA, UK, 1995, pp. 435-444.

21.   In this context, the Ministry of Internal Affairs has already devised a draft declaration 'Concerning aggressive nationalism, racism, chauvinism, xenophobia and anti-semitism' which intends to take legal steps to combat territorial expansionism, mass deportations, ethnic cleansing and the outbreak of civil wars.

22.   G.V. Osipov, *Sotsial'naia i sotsial'no - politicheskaia situatsiia v Rossii: Analiz i prognoz (Pervoe polugodie 1995 goda)*, Moscow 1995, p. 49.

Conclusions

CHRISTOPHER WILLIAMS, VLADIMIR CHUPROV AND
VLADIMIR STAROVEROV

The main goal of this book was to examine the difficulties faced by Russians during the transition to a market economy since 1985. Using the latest sociological surveys and other empirical data, *Russian society in transition* demonstrates how the problems are mounting up - class conflict, education and health care in turmoil, growing unemployment, crime, neglect of youth and so forth. The new political system which has emerged, consisting of a combination of President, parliament and a range of political parties, including democrats, centrists and a red-brown coalition, has so far failed to address the difficulties outlined in this book. This has produced a lack of confidence of voters in the Russian government - led by Chernomyrdin - and its President - Yeltsin, as shown by the Communist Party's revival and outstanding victory in the December 1995 parliamentary elections.

Whilst most Russians acknowledge that they now have greater freedom in comparison to the communist period, this freedom has only been gained at great cost and sacrifice - rising inflation, growing income differentiation, the collapse of the welfare state, growing unemployment, increased poverty, homelessness, rising crime and an overall decline in living standards. The aforementioned negative consequences of reform have made themselves felt in the growing antagonism between East and West, as demonstrated by increased hostility towards 'outsiders', but more importantly they have also led to growing conflict between different groups, classes and strata within Russian society, as the gap between rich and poor widens.

As Russia prepares for the 1996 Presidential elections, there is little evidence that the Yeltsin Administration is in a position to address the difficulties being experienced in all sections and sectors of Russian society examined in Parts II and III of this book. Over the coming weeks, Yeltsin faces a battle for political survival both from his Presidential rivals and from his opponents in the Duma and all the major political parties of Russia. As Yeltsin's health wanes and he seems incapable of resolving the main problems of the day, as epitomised by his intransigence over Chechnya, his opponents are capitalising on the situation by criticising the failures of his reforms and their negative impact upon Russian society since the end of 1991.

Speculation is running high that Yeltsin is not strong enough to win in 1996, either in terms of his health (he has already had two heart attacks) or because his policies have been a disaster and only succeeded in alienating the people. Russian and Western political commentators concede that it is difficult to nominate an obvious successor. However, it is clear from the evidence presented in this book that those who gain power in the June 1996 Presidential elections will have to exercise their political powers in a more decisive manner than has hitherto been the case in order to deal with the numerous crises evident throughout Russian society. Particular attention will have to be devoted to the equilibrium between socio-economic policy and its impact on society. This is necessary in order to reduce the current high levels of social polarisation, to offset the possibility of social protest and to put Russia back on a 'better course'. In the various political party manifestos of December 1995, there were already signs of a recognition of some of these points: thus Zyuganov called for a strong state and greater protection of state industry; Fedulova and her *Women of Russia* Party stressed the need to protect the welfare state; Ryzhkov and Yavlinsky both emphasised moderate reform but tied closer to the social base and finally, Vladimir Sherbakov of the *Trade Unions and Industrialists of Russia* grouping stressed the need to build a better social partnership.[1]

However, Russia's President, as the experience of the last six years has already shown, cannot deal with these issues alone. The peculiarities of the Russian context and the underestimation of the degree of conflict between democracy and the market, has meant that voters remain unhappy with the hardships that they have endured since 1992 and therefore nostalgic for their communist past. Moreover the absence of a well defined 'middle class' with significant entrepreneurial acumen and the Mafia's interference in Russia's economy,[2] coupled with the existence of political parties without a party system, has merely exacerbated matters further. Although Yeltsin viewed the Presidency as a means of exerting order in a chaotic situation, he has been thwarted by various political parties and parliamentary groups, who saw it as their duty to limit the abuse of Presidential power. The voters, meanwhile, are demonstrating their dissatisfaction by voting for the opposition - communists and nationalists.

Shto delat? As a bare minimum Russia requires *transformative* reforms to rid herself of the old nomenklatura - 75 per cent of Yeltsin's aides, 66 per cent of parliament, 83 per cent of regional heads and 41 per cent of top businessmen have nomenklatura ties.[3] On top of this, Russia needs *restorative* reforms to give all the political actors and institutions a clear indication of what is required of them, and finally, Russia needs to stop the current *adaptive* reforms which are only tinkering with the old Communist machinery without fundamentally changing it - the names may have changed on the doors of all the government departments, Ministries, etc. throughout the Russian Federation, but attitudes remain largely the same. Something urgently needs to be done because polls constantly show an overall lack of interest in politics and little confidence in the government, President and parliament.

Unfortunately, no one seems capable of putting real reform on the political agenda. Russian political elites are divided; politicians have not yet demonstrated the skills needed to embark upon a course of bargaining, compromise, tolerance and accountability, and the opposition parties have only recently begun to use mounting social discontent in order to put greater pressure on Russia's government. In the meantime, the plight of Russians worsens with each passing day. One recent poll published in the newspaper *Vek* summarises just how bad the present situation is in relation to previous years. Thus whereas in 1990, 11 per cent of those surveyed described their standard of living as adequate; 65 per cent as barely sufficient and 24 per cent as very poor indeed, meaning they were living below the poverty line; by late 1995, 28 per cent lived below the poverty line; 40 per cent on it; 2 per cent just above it and only 30 per cent said their standard of living was quite good.[4] Surveys reveal greater continuity than change. For example, when a sample of 1,600 Russians were asked in 1992 whether they thought 1993 would be better than the previous year: 2 per cent said yes; 32 per cent hoped so; 25 per cent said the situation would remain the same; 45 per cent said get worse and 6 per cent failed to reply. When the same question was posed in January 1996, respondents replied as follows: 5 per cent better than 1995; 33 per cent hope so; 43 per cent the same; 12 per cent worse and 7 per cent gave no answer.[5] Very few Russians are as optimistic as they were when communism fell.

But what does the future hold? In 1995, John Miller argued that there were four possible future scenarios for Russia: firstly, *statism*, in which a strong, authoritarian, centralised state presides over society; second, *reformism* which promotes widespread political and socio-economic change; third, *nationalism*, which constitutes a violent reaction against Westernism and finally, we have *communitarianism* which refers to the notion of a stateless society.[6] All these viewpoints are evident in Russia today. The first strategy is supported by the Communists and agrarians; the second by *Our Home is Russia*, *Democratic Russia's Choice* and *Yabloko*; the third by the likes of Zhirinovsky's LDPR, and the fourth and final strategy has been a prominent feature of Russian history since the last century. In the present uncertainty, it is not clear which one of the aforementioned alternatives and the appropriate groups will win out in the summer of 1996. However, it is likely that some version of the statist tradition will continue until the end of this century.

In economic terms, as we saw earlier in chapter 1, recovery will remain slow and uneven. On the political front, Yeltsin is fighting a Presidential battle with Zyuganov, Zhirinovsky, Yavlinsky and others. By the time this book goes to press the results of the June 1996 Russian Presidential elections will be known. At the time of time of writing, 78 Presidential candidates supported by 94 initiative groups and electoral associations had registered their names with the Russian Central Election Commission (TsIK). Of the original 78, only 11 submitted petitions with the one million signatures required by the deadline of 16 April.

Most Western and Russian analysts concur that the most serious candidates for the post of President are: Gennadi Zyuganov, leader of the Communist Party of the Russian Federation; Boris Yeltsin, the current Russian President; Vladimir Zhirinovsky, leader of the Liberal-Democratic Party of Russia; Grigorii Yavlinsky, leader of Yabloko; Alexandr Lebed, former Lt. General, Duma deputy and ex-leader of the Congress of Russian Communities and Mikhail Gorbachev, former President of the USSR. The most notable absentee is the Prime Minister and leader of the Our Home is Russia party, Viktor Chernomyrdin, who has withdrawn his candidature.

Opinion polls in mid-May 1996 showed Yeltsin and Zyuganov ahead of Zhirinovsky, Lebed, Yavlinsky and Gorbachev. It is widely believed that the last four will not make it beyond the first round. If, as expected, no Presidential candidate wins 50 per cent of the vote in the first round on 16 June 1996, then a run-off between the two top candidates will be held on either 7 or 14th July 1996. Around about early-mid August 1996, the new President will take office. The two candidates tipped to compete in the second round are Boris Yeltsin and Gennadi Zyuganov. But who will win is still an open question.

Boris Yeltsin who did not officially register until 3 April declared on the same day: 'I am nervous because the fight will not be easy and my rivals are strong', but he added 'I do not intend to give up without a good fight'.[7] Polls conducted by the All-Russian Centre for Public Opinion (VTsIOM) between February-May 1996 indicate that the forthcoming Presidential election will be a closely fought contest. Thus whereas in January 1996 the gap between Yeltsin and Zyuganov was 15 per cent, by April they were virtually neck and neck, and then by mid-May 1996 Yeltsin had narrowly overtaken Zyuganov, with just over a quarter of the vote.[8] Among the main reasons for the narrowing of this gap are: first, the huge backlog of wages owed to workers by the government has now been paid off; second, increases in old-age pensions have now been promised; third, Yeltsin is setting up a home ownership programme, with favourable interest rates; fourth, a peace plan was recently introduced geared towards ending 16 months of fighting in Chechnya[9] and finally, Yeltsin has now signed a deal with the Paris Club to reschedule Russia's $US40 billion debt over 25 years. This is on top of discussions with the IMF earlier in this year regarding a US$10 billion loan up until 1999.[10] Yeltsin is also negotiating with the Chechen rebels led by Zelimkhan Yandarbiev to try and get a ceasefire after 17 months of war This may yet bear fruit.

However, although the above cosmetic changes in Yeltsin's policies together with Western backing might improve his chances of re-election, Russian public opinion surveys results have a bad track record and any prognoses should be viewed with caution for many reasons: the rapid pace of change in Russian society and politics, the potential biases of polling organisations and the growing proportion of undecided Russian voters, many of whom do not make up their minds until the last minute.

Moreover as Yegor Gaidar correctly pointed out, things are far from being clear cut because the 'democratic voter is unfortunately very pessimistic'.[11] The reasons for this have been made crystal clear throughout this book - unemployment, low wages, soaring crime, corruption, a lack of trust in the main political leaders and institutions and an unpopular war in Chechnya. These are the issues dividing voters. According to a recent Institute for Comparative Research/CNN May 1996 poll of 1,058 adults the main concerns among Yeltsin's supporters were economics (35 per cent); patriotism (2 per cent); social security (22 per cent) and fear of a new leader (10 per cent) whereas Zyuganov's supporters highlighted economics (16 per cent); patriotism (9 per cent) and social security (46 per cent).[12] On top of this, Yeltsin needs to reassure voters on other matters. When University of Strathclyde researchers asked 2,246 adults in January 1996 'What issues do you think are the most important?' 77 per cent replied 'order' and only 9 per cent 'democracy'. When this was followed with the question 'Are you interested in politics?, 35 per cent said yes, 43 per cent replied slightly and 20 per cent said no.[13] Clearly discontent about the current regime is running high.

However political indecisiveness and economic recession need not necessarily mean a swing towards Zyuganov and the Communists, despite major victories in December

1995 and the fact that they are the largest faction in the new Duma. Thus if it comes to a second round in July 1996, the eventual outcome will largely depend on who the first round losers and their voters decide to support. According to Olga Bychkova of *Moscow News*, Yeltsin has more chances of relying on support from other parties and movements than Zyuganov. However, at the same time, Russian analysts also concur that Yeltsin has fewer potential voters of his own than his communist opponent. Thus according to a Public Opinion Foundation poll of March 1996, 56 per cent of Our Home is Russia voters were pro-Yeltsin, as were 34 per cent of Russia's Democratic Choice/United Democrats, 18 per cent of Congress of Russian Communities, 16 per cent of Party of Workers Self-management, 15 per cent of Yabloko, four per cent of LDPR and one per cent of communist voters. By contrast, eight per cent of LDPR, six per cent of Congress of Russian Communities, four per cent of Our Home is Russia and 2.5 per cent of Party of Workers Self-management and Yabloko voters were said to be likely to support Zyuganov's Presidential bid. The final point of great interest to emerge from this poll was that 38 per cent of voters intended not to vote for Yeltsin or Zyuganov.[14]

Although Yavlinsky noted on 12 April that 'If a lesser evil (Yeltsin) overcomes a bigger one (Zyuganov), the former is doomed to get bigger and bigger', suggesting that neither victory will benefit Russia and its populace,[15] some Russian analysts, such as Sergei Yushenkov, have noted that 'Zhirinovsky might be Boris Yeltsin's secret weapon in so far as he might turn around at the last moment and ambush the communists by supporting Yeltsin'.[16] Nugar Betaneli, Director of the Institute of the Sociology of Parliamentarism, believes that Yeltsin might win the election if he joined forces with other democratic candidates and toned down his anti-communist rhetoric which cost his supporters dearly in December 1995. Betaneli stated: 'Yeltsin's ratings are rising but not fast enough for him to win on his own ... He must join forces with others ... His strength is that he is strong enough (to win) if he unites with Fyodorov, Lebed and Yavlinsky'.[17]

No guarantees of support from other democrats for the Presidency have yet been given. Fyodorov met President Yeltsin on 15 May to discuss the possible creation of a 'Popular trust' government which would unite around a spectrum of political opinions.[18] He then met Yavlinsky the next day in which Yavlinsky expressed his concern that 'Today, to many people, a return to the past looks like salvation for the present' referring to the fact that he thought neither Yeltsin nor himself were guaranteed victory in the first round of the Presidential elections. Yavlinsky said he was willing to consider 'tense co-operation' with Yeltsin but only on the grounds that he pledges to introduce 'a radical change of the political and socio-economic course'. His 'conditions' included: a halt to the war in Chechnya; the passing of amendments to the Constitution placing limitations on Presidential power, enabling a separation of powers and preventing too much power accumulating in one man's hands; an increase in the minimum wage; reduced taxes; decentralisation of power away from the centre to the regions; combating crime; strengthening Russia's defence capability; improving relations with the CIS (in particular the Ukraine and the Baltic states) and finally that there is a government reshuffle involving the replacement of the PM, Vice-Premier, Minister of Defence and other senior officials.[19] Obviously Yavlinsky has laid down stringent conditions upon Yeltsin. Yavlinsky might gain if Yeltsin concurs to some or all of these pre-requisites. If Yeltsin fails to meet these demands, there will be a split in the democratic vote.

Either way both are taking a gamble. As one potential Yavlinsky supporter stated recently: 'I like Yavlinsky and his economic policies, but I am not a pack of cigarettes or a bottle of vodka that he can just hand over to Yeltsin whenever he wants'.[20] According to Michael McFaul, a prominent analyst of Russian affairs, 'everything is at stake here, the entire political, economic and societal makeup of the nation'.[21]

But a possible 'third force' consisting of Yavlinsky, Lebed and Fyodorov now looks unlikely as Lebed refused on 8 May 1996 to combine forces with the others. He later noted: 'How can three people cooperate for one Presidency?'.[22] It now looks as if at least one candidate (Lebed) will run separately against Yeltsin in June 1996. This will split the democratic vote; but Yeltsin may yet strike a deal with Yavlinsky and Fyodorov and Lebed in exchange for their loyalty in the second round.[23]

Thus a mere month before the election, the Presidential race is still very open. But as the old American saying goes 'Three strikes and you're out'. Yeltsin has already had two strikes in the parliamentary elections of December 1993 and December 1995. June 1996 might well be his third and last chance. The danger for Yeltsin, like Chernomyrdin, is that he will become complacent. Chernomyrdin once stated prior to the December 1995 parliamentary elections that '43 parties want power. But we have the power'.[24] Yet he quickly lost it. Similarly Boris Yeltsin declared on 28 February that 'Democrats have no other choice but to support me. They will gradually come to realise this. There is just nobody else'.[25] Could Yeltsin suffer the same fate as Chernomrydin? According to one voter from Belgorod: 'We must use this election to get Yeltsin to change'.[26] There are already signs, as we saw above, that Yeltsin recognises this fact, but is he offering too little, too late?

Sociological research carried out in January 1996 showed that 21.5 per cent of respondents trusted Zyuganov, 18.4 per cent Zhirinovsky, 4.3 per cent Yavlinsky and 4.2 per cent Yeltsin.[27] When VTsIOM followed this up in mid-April 1996 asking respondents 'Who would you least want to see President of Russia?', 56 per cent replied Zhirinovsky, 37 per cent Yeltsin, 27 per cent Zyuganov, 9 per cent Lebed, 6 per cent Yavlinsky and 4 per cent Fyorodov.[28] Thus although many recent polls suggest that Yeltsin's rating is improving it would be foolish to draw any firm conclusions because as Bychkova aptly notes: 'Sometimes people vote completely the opposite to pre-election predictions'.[29]

The main difficulty at present is the high proportion of undecided voters. VTsIOM surveys in March 1996 indicated that 54 per cent planned to vote, 13 per cent would vote, 13 per cent intended not to, seven per cent had doubts and 13 per cent were uncertain. Thus around a third of Russian voters may not vote. If they decide to vote at a very last minute, then this might clearly tip the balance in favour of Yeltsin or Zyuganov. For Bychkova: 'success mostly depends on the ability of a candidate to catch the voters' mood and use it ... the candidate who is able to calm the people will win. Zyuganov has been able to do this so far'.[30]

The question is can Zyuganov sustain his momentum or will he be overtaken by Yeltsin? Public opinion polls up to mid-April put Zyuganov ahead, but from late April onwards Yeltsin caught up and then overtook Zyuganov meaning that by early May Yeltsin was up to 10 per cent ahead of his main rival.[31] Yeltsin now seems convinced he will win. He recently declared: 'I am sure victory will be mine'. But Zyuganov countered by pointing out that 'If we add a bit to our support in the December (parliamentary) election, we have a chance not only to do well in the Presidential election but to win in the first round'.[32] Although the latest public opinion polls show President Yeltsin with a slight lead over the communist candidate Zyuganov, one Institute of the Sociology of Parliamentarism poll on 8 May 1996 suggested that Zyuganov would win a huge 43-45 per cent with Yeltsin getting only 25 per cent in the first round in June 1996.[33]

But would Yeltsin's re-election or his replacement by the likes of Zyuganov, Yavlinsky or Zhirinovsky really made any difference to the average Russian citizen? One VTsIOM March 1996 poll asked 'How will the situation change if the election was won by candidate (x)?' and the following responses were given:

Name of Presidential candidate	Prediction of future situation (%)			
	Better	Worse	Same	No answer
Boris Yeltsin	16	31	44	9
Gennady Zyuganov	34	30	16	20
Grigorii Yavlinsky	27	31	23	35
Vladimir Zhirinovsky	14	61	8	17

According to this VTsIOM poll, the prediction is one of greater improvement under Zyuganov; whereas if Yeltsin was re-elected for a second term or replaced by the likes of Yavlinsky or Zhirinovsky, the overall feeling is one of plus ça change, plus c'est la même chose.

Whoever is elected in June 1996, the task ahead is an enormous one. If the current reform programme is maintained, greater attention will have to be paid to its adverse effect on public opinion and confidence in the government and President. Yeltsin himself realises this. He stated on 7 April 1996: 'I can tell you honestly that I am not satisfied with the job I have done during my Presidency. Nearly half the Russian population lives badly while ten per cent lives well'.[34] On the campaign trail in May 1996 in Yaroslavl Yeltsin was criticised by voters complaining of high food prices and no wages. Even he confessed later on television that 'The complaints ... (are) everywhere. They weren't just single cases. The people complained en masse'.[35] It will be extremely difficult convincing the Russian electorate that his reforms will bear fruit in the immediate future. At the end of the day however, the situation is perhaps more accurately described as follows: 'Yeltsin is no great democrat, but better the devil you know than the devil you don't'.[36]

The choice in June 1996 seems to be between more of the same or muddling through under Yeltsin for four more years or further changes to bring Russian out of recession and offer the people greater hope for the future if Zyuganov was elected President.

In a recent *Izvestiia* interview Yeltsin promised voters he would eradicate the budget deficit, improve wages, provide more housing, help the development of enterprises and entrepreneurship, create circumstances to encourage saving, improve living standards and conditions in the agricultural sector, reform the army, fight organised crime and so forth.[37] These are major promises, which he has left unfilled for nearly five years. Important changes in policy will be required in order to achieve these objectives.

Meanwhile, Zyuganov is claiming he is a social democrat in the West while adopting a more tranditional hardline approach at home. In the latter context he has pointed out that Russia owes the West $300 billion dollars, has 10 million unemployed, suffered a 50 per cent drop in production since 1992 and finally, Zyuganov has argued that Russia is facing a serious demographic crisis in which there are only eight births for every twenty deaths.[38] These assertions were backed by the sociological surveys usedin this book.   Among the remedies which Zyuganov has offered to Russia's 'national catastrophe' are the introduction of Keynesian economic policies adapted to suit 'Russia's national   interests'.[39] He has rejected the use of Marxist doctrines. Furthermore he has vowed to irradicated departmentalism, to reform the political system by making it more democratic and more party based and finally to improve relations between political parties, parliament and president. He has called for the president to be more accountable to the electorate.[40] These changes are geared towards reducing the social and economic costs of transition and ensuring greater political stability. Zyuganov has clearly started to tap into the growing anti-Western/anti-reform tendencies in Russian society.   Anti-reform parties (the CPRF, LDPR, KRO, Agrarians etc.) collected 46.1 per cent of the votes in December 1995 compared to pro-Western/pro-reform parties (such as Russia's Democratic Choice, Yabloko etc.), down nearly 20 per cent since 1993.[41]

Both scenarios put fear in the hearts of many Russians. In the West concern centres on whether or not Zyuganov's victory might mean an end to democratic reforms and mark a return to communism.

What Zyuganov has going for him, as this book aptly demonstrates, is five years of shock therapy, widespread political instability and growing social discontent. As one unemployed kolkhoz worker declared: 'In the past, we had a party that listened to us and looked after us ...'[42] while another Muscovite voter stated on 17 December 1995 that 'I am voting for the communists, I trust them. They are the only people who have not deceived us over the past 10 years'.[43] Zyuganov and his followers also know that they have a lot to lose. As one speaker at a Communist nomination meeting put it: 'Russia will have no other opportunity. I am convinced that if the elections are lost, it will be our last moment'.[44]

Although Yavlinsky has criticised both Yeltsin and Zyuganov arguing that 'Russia should not have to choose between bad and terrible',[45] it is clear that a choice will soon be made. As of mid-May 1996, Russia stands at a crossroads and the parallels with October 1917 are clear: an unpopular war, the absence of fair land reforms, ethnic conflicts, inadequate state regulation of the economy and no strong leader at the helm. However, the alternative is not simply the revival of Bolshevism or the strengthening of Yeltsin-style democracy, it is more a question, as Boris Nemtsov, governor of Nizhnyi Novgorod put it of remembering that 'if we want to protect democracy, we must find a compromise between the present democratic and left candidates'.[46] Perhaps Yavlinsky offers voters such a choice. But according to Michael McFaul: 'In Russia today both camps seek a zero-sum victory, with no consensus or commitment to the new rules of the game ...'.[47]

The key question now is how long can Yeltsin survive? Part of the answer relates to his failure to offset the negative consequences of reform. The Russian people have suffered blow after blow in the fight for change and gained very few of the spoils promised after the collapse of communism. Therefore the euphoria of 1991-92 has now given way to pessimism in 1996. But the question of Western involvement in Russia's economic recovery and her transition to liberal democracy is also vital. Whilst Russia must be careful not to become too dependent upon the West, Western aid has been viewed as necessary in order to prevent a backlash. However, Yeltsin's backers, many of whom are out of touch with Russian reality, have failed to provide Russia with the room and flexibility necessary to adapt Western policies to Russian conditions. The outcome is that Russia has been pushed closer to the abyss. Recent extensions on loan repayments on Russian debts to the West, might have come too late for Yeltsin.

Russian Society in transition shows that Russia badly needs a President capable of uniting society, of resolving the burning issues of the day, of restoring Russia's sense of national pride, of bridging the chasm between leaders and led, of making peoples lives better, of putting an end to an unpopular war, of restoring Russia's international reputation and most of all Russia needs a President who is firm, yet democratic. In late-June or early July 1996 we will know who the President is, and whether he wants to strengthen the existing system or change it. Presidential candidates must learn to pay closer attention to the public mood. By early April 1996, according to one VTsIOM poll, 41 per cent of those surveyed wanted the pre-1990 Soviet political system, 27 per cent Western style democracy and nine per cent the current political system; whereas 42 per cent of respondents were in favour of central planning; 33 per cent wanted a market economy and 25 per cent could not make up their minds. If Yeltsin ignores public opinion once again, he might lose his Presidential bid. We might therefore soon witness the start of a post-Yeltsin era.

Notes

1. *Ekonomicheskie Novosti* No.21, November 1995, pp. 6-7.
2. Thus according to Yeltsin administration officials, some 70 to 80 per cent of Russian private businesses are paying exportion fees worth 10 to 20 per cent of their retail turnover to the mafia (CIA report to US Congress cited in 'Russian mafia behind terrorism and weapons proliferation', *New Europe*, Issue 154, 5-11 May 1996, p. 48).
3. *Izvestiia* 18 May 1994, p. 2.
4. V. Boikov, 'K takomu rynku my eshche ne privykli', *Vek* No. 43, 3-9 November 1995, p. 10.
5. *Moskovskii Novosti* 1-14 January 1996, p. 15.
6. John Miller, 'Alternative Visions of the Russian Future', in A. Saikal and W. Maley (eds.) (1995), *Russia in search of its future*, Cambridge University Press, Cambridge, pp. 190-206.
7. Reuters, 3 March 1996.
8. *Analytica Politica Weekly*, 13-19 April 1996, VTsIOM poll of 12 May 1996 and *Argumenty, fakty*, 23 May 1996, p. 3.
9. Zyuganov and Yeltsin lead way in Russian electoral campaign', *New Europe* Issue 153, 28 April - 4 May 1996, p. 3.
10. Russia signs historic debt deal with creditor nations', *New Europe* Issue 154, 5-11 May 1996, p. 7.
11. *Moskovskii Novosti* interview 15-21 February 1996.

12.   Cited in Michael Kramer, 'The People choose', Special Report on Russian Elections in *Time* magazine 27 May 1996, p. 25.
13.   Cited in ibid, p. 30.
14.   O. Bychkova, 'Polls and pollsters', *Moscow News* 25 April - 1 May 1996, p. 3.
15.   *RIA Novosti*, 12 April 1996.
16.   Associated Press Report, 3 March 1996.
17.   'Russian forecasts put Yeltsin far behind Zyuganov in election poll', *New Europe* Issue 154, 5-11 May 1996, p. 5.
18.   Reuters, 15 May 1996.
19.   *Izvestiia*, 17 May 1996.
20.   Cited in the *Chicago Tribune*, 20 May 1996.
21.   Cited by Michael Kramer, 'The People choose', Special Report on Russian Elections in *Time* magazine 27 May 1996, p. 25.
22.   Cited in the *Los Angeles Times*, 20 May 1996.
23.   Reuters, 8 May 1996 and 'Russian forecasts put Yeltsin far behind Zyuganov in election poll', *New Europe* Issue 154, 5-11 May 1996, p. 5.
24.   Reuters, 4 December 1995.
25.   Reuters, 28 February 1996.
26.   *New York Times*, 7 April 1996.
27.   A. Zhilin, 'Generals divided over June election', *Moscow News* 11-17 April 1996, p. 4.
28.   Cited in *Analytica Politica Weekly*, 30 March-5 April 1996.
29.   O. Bychkova, 'Polls and pollsters', *Moscow News* 25 April - 1 May 1996, p. 3.
30.   Ibid.
31.   Institute of Comparative Research/CNN May 1996 poll cited in Michael Kramer, 'The People choose', Special Report on Russian Elections in *Time* magazine 27 May 1996, p. 25.
32.   Quoted in *New York Times*, 7 April 1996.
33.   Cited in 'Zyuganov and Yeltsin lead way in Russian electoral campaign', *New Europe* Issue 153, 28 April - 4 May 1996, p. 3.
34.   Quoted in *New York Times*, 7 April 1996.
35.   On the nature of these criticisms see *Argumenty i Fakty*, 23 May 1996, p. 6 and M. Kramer, 'The People choose', Special Report on Russian Elections in *Time* magazine 27 May 1996, p. 23.
36.   Musovite voter quoted in the *Los Angeles Times*, 28 April 1996.
37.   *Izvestiia*, 24 May 1996, pp. 1, 5.
38.   Cited in *Moskovskii Novosti*, 16 May 1996, p. 6.
39.   *Nezavisimaya Gazeta*, 25 May 1996, pp. 1, 6.
40.   *Moskovskii Novosti*, 19-26 May 1996, p. 7.
41.   P.J. Stavrakis, 'Russia after the elections: Democracy or Parliamentary Byzantium?' *Problems of Post-Communism*, March/April 1996, table 3, p 16.
42.   Quoted in the *Chicago Tribune*, 28 April 1996.
43.   Reuters, 17 December 1995.
44.   Quoted in the *Wall Street Journal*, 16 February 1996.
45.   *St. Petersburg Press*, 2 April 1996.
46.   *RIA Novosti*, 24 April 1996.

47. Cited by Michael Kramer, 'The People choose', Special Report on Russian Elections in *Time* magazine 27 May 1996, p. 24.

Bibliography

Aage, H. (1991), 'Popular attitudes and perestroika', *Soviet Studies* No. 1, pp. 3-25.

Aasland, A. (1994), 'The Russian population in Latvia: An integrated minority?', *Journal of Communist Studies and Transition Politics*, Vol. 10 (2), June, pp. 233-260.

Adelman, D. (1991), *The 'Children of Perestroika': Moscow teenagers talk about their lives and future*, M.E. Sharpe, New York.

Adelman, D. (1994), *The 'Children of Perestroika' Come of Age: Young people of Moscow talk about life in the New Russia*, M.E. Sharpe, New York.

Afanasayev, V. and Skorbogatov, S. (1995), 'Prostitution in St. Petersburg', in Chaika, N. *HIV/AIDS, STDs, Drug use and prostitution in St. Petersburg and Russia*, St. Petersburg Pasteur Institute, St. Petersburg 1995, pp. 26-30.

Alekseeva, T. (1994), 'Tsentristskii proekt dlia Rossii', *Sovremennaia mysl'* No. 4.

Allahar, A.L. (1989), *Sociology and the periphery*, University of Toronto Press, Toronto.

Al'ternativy voine ot antichnosti do kontsa vtoroi mirovoi voiny: Antologiia, (1993), Moscow.

Andreev, Ye.M. and Volkov, A.G. (1977), *Demograficheskie modeli*, Moscow.

Annual Report of the International Monetary Fund (1995), IMF, Washington D.C., 30 April.

Antonov, A.I. (1980), *Sotsiologiia rozhdaemosti*, Moscow.

Antonov, A.I. (1994), 'Depopulatsiia Rossii i problemy sem'i', in the collection *Rossiia nakanune XXI veka*, Moscow.

Arato, A. (1991), 'Social movements and civil society in the Soviet Union', in Sediatis, J. and Butterfield, J. (eds.), *Perestroika from below: Social movements in the Soviet Union*, Westview, Boulder.

Baloyra, E. (1986), 'Democratic transition in comparative perspective' in Baloyra, E. *Comparing new democracies*, Westview Press, Boulder 1986, pp. 9-52.

Balzer, H.D. (1994), 'Plans to reform Russian Higher Education', in Jones, A. (ed.), *Education and Society in the New Russia*, M.E. Sharpe, New York , pp. 27-46.

Barr, N. (ed.) (1994), *Labor Markets and Social policy in Central and Eastern Europe: The transition and beyond*,World Bank/London School of Economics, Oxford University Press, New York.

Barrington Moore, Jr. (1967), *Social origins of dictatorship and democracy*, Penguin, Harmondsworth.

Boeva, I. and Shironin, V. (1992), *Russians between state and market: The generations compared*, Studies in Public Policy, No. 205, Centre for the Study of Public Policy, University of Stathclyde/Paul Lazarseld Society, Vienna.

Boikov, V. (1995), 'K tatomu rynku my eshche ne privliki: Grakhdane Rossii otsenivaiut rezul'taty ekonomicheskikh preobrazovanii', *Vek* No. 43, 3-9 November, p. 10.

Boronoeva, A.O. (ed.) (1994), *Problemy teoreticheskoi sotsiologii*, Petropolis, St. Petersburg.

Brym, R.J. and Degtyarev, A. (1993), 'Anti-semitism in Moscow: Results of an October 1992 survey', *Slavic Review*, Vol. 52 (1), Spring, pp. 1-12.

Chalizde, V. (1977), *Criminal Russia*, Random House, New York.

Chapman, J.G. (1988), 'Gorbachev's wage reform', *Soviet Economy*, Vol. 4 (4), October-December, pp. 338-65.

Chernaev, A.S. (1993), *Shest' let s Gorbachevym*, Moscow.

Chuprov, V.I. (1994a), *Sotsial'noe razvitie molodezhi: teoreticheskie i prikladnye problemy*, Moscow Izd. instituta molodezhi 'Sotsium'.

Chuprov, V.I. (1994b), 'Molodezh' Rossii: kharakteristika integratsionnykh protsessov', in Il'inskii, I.I. et al. (eds.), *Tsennostnyi mir sovremennoi molodezhi: na puti k mirovoi integratsii*, Moscow.

Chuprov, V.I. and Chernish, M. (1993), *Motivatsionnaia sfera sozdaniia molodezhi: Sostoianie i tendentsii razvitiia*, Moscow, Institut molodezhi/Institut sotsial'no-politicheskikh issledovanii.

Clark, B. (1995), *An Empire's New Clothes: The end of Russia's Liberal dream*, Vintage, London.

Clarke, S. et al. (1994), 'The privatisation of industrial enterprises in Russia: Four case-studies', *Europe-Asia Studies*, Vol. 46 (2), pp. 179-215.

Cohen, S. (1992), 'What's really happening in Russia', *The Nation* 2 March, pp. 259-64.

Coles, B. (1995), *Youth and Social policy: Youth citizenship and youth careers*, University College London Press, London.

Connor, W. (1972), *Deviance in Soviet Society*, Columbia University Press, New York.

Daeninckx, D. and Drachline, P. (1994), *Jirinovski: Le Russe qui fait trembler le monde: Collection 'Documents'*, Le cherche midi editeur, Paris.

Dahl, R.A. (1971), *Polyarchy: Participation and Opposition*, New Haven, Yale University Press.

Davies, R.W. (1986), 'The end of mass unemployment in the USSR', in Lane, D. (ed.) (1986), *Labour & Employment in the USSR*, Harvester Press, Brighton.

Davies, R.W. and Wheatcroft, S.G. (1986), 'A note on sources of unemployment statistics', in Lane, D. (ed.) (1986), *Labour & Employment in the USSR*, Harvester Press, Brighton.

Davis, C. (1979), 'The economics of the Soviet health service: An analytical and historical study, 1921-78', unpublished PhD in Economics, Cambridge

University.

Davis, C. (1983), 'The economics of the Soviet health system' in: US Congress, JEC, *Soviet economy in the 1980s: Problems and prospects*, Washington D.C.

Davis, C. (1987), 'Developments in the Soviet health sector, 1970-90' in: US Congress, JEC, *Gorbachev's Economic Problems*, Washington D.C. 1987.

Davis, C. (1988), 'The organisation and performance of the contemporary Soviet health system', in: Lapidus, G. and Swanson, G.E. (eds.), *State and Welfare USA/USSR*, Berkeley, Institute of International Studies.

Davis, C. (1993a), 'The health sector in the Soviet and Russian economies: From reform to fragmentation to transition', in US Congress, JEC, *The former Soviet Union in Transition*, Vol. 2, Washington D.C.

Davis, C. (1993b), 'Health crisis: The former Soviet Union', *RFE/RL Research Report* Vol. 2, No. 40, 8 October, pp. 35-43.

Davydov, Y.N. (1988), 'Tekhnologiia i biurokratiia', *Sotsiologicheskie issledovanniya* No. 5.

Deacon, B. (1994), 'Global policy actors and the shaping of post-communist social policy', in de Swaan, A. (ed.), *Social policy beyond borders: The Social question in transnational perspective*, Amsterdam University Press, Amsterdam, pp. 69-91.

Diskin, I. (1995), 'Rossiiskii senator kak "chelovek bez svoistv" ', *Moskovskie Novosti* 15-22 October, p. 9.

Dunlop, J. et al. (1993), 'Profiles of the newly independent states: economic, social and demographic conditions', in: Kaufman, R.F. and Hardt, J.P. (eds.), *The former Soviet Union in Transition*, M.E. Sharpe, New York, pp. 1021-1187.

Dutton, J.C. (1981), 'Causes of Soviet adult mortality increases', *Soviet Studies*, Vol. 33 (4), October, pp. 548-559.

Dyker, D.A. (1992), *Restructuring the Soviet Economy*, Routledge, London.

Economic Survey of Europe in 1993-94 (1994), UN Economic Commission for Europe, New York and Geneva.

Economic Survey of Europe in 1994-95 (1995), UN Economic Commission for Europe, New York and Geneva.

Ekonomicheskie i sotsial'nye peremeny: monioring obshchestvennogo mneniye (1993), No. 5.

Ekonomicheskie i sotsial'nye peremeny VTsIOM Information Bulletin (1994), March-April, No. 2.

Ekonomicheskie i sotsial'nye peremeny VTsIOM Information Bulletin (1995), July-August No. 4.

Feshbach, M. (1993), 'Continuing negative health trends in the former USSR', in Kaufman, R.F. and Hardt, J.P. (eds.), *The former Soviet Union in Transition*, M.E. Sharpe, New York.

Field, M.G. (1995), 'The health crisis in the former Soviet Union: A report from the "Post-war" zone', *Social Science and Medicine*, Vol. 41 (11), pp. 1469-1478.

Fischer, S. and Gelb, A. (1991), 'The process of socialist economic transformation', *Journal of Economic perspectives*, Fall.

Fisher, G. (1964), *Science and Politics: The New sociology in the Soviet Union*, Cornell University Press.

Fisher, R. and Urry, W. (1990), *Put' k soglasiiu ili peregovory bez porazhenii*, Moscow 'Nauka'.

Fizicheskii entsiklopedicheskii slovar (1984), Moscow 'Sovetskaia Entsiklopediia'.

Flakierski, H. (1993), *Income inequalities in the former Soviet Union and its Republics*, M.E. Sharpe, London.

Fortescue, S. (1995), 'Privatisation of large-scale industry', in Saikal, A. and Maley, W. (eds.), *Russia in search of its future*, Cambridge University Press, Cambridge, pp. 85-101.

Frazer, G. and Lancelle, G. (1994), *Zhirinovskii: The Little Black book*, Penguin, Harmondsworth.

Frentzel-Zagorska, J. (1990), 'Civil society in Poland and Hungary', *Soviet Studies*, Vol. 42 (4).

Frentzel-Zagorska, J. (1991), 'Two phases of transition from communism to democracy in Poland and Hungary', *Sistphus, Sociological Studies*, Vol. 7, (Warsaw), pp. 95-114.

Fretwell, D. and Jackan, R. (1994), 'Labor markets: Unemployment', in Barr, N. (1994), *Labor markets and social policy in Central and Eastern Europe*, L.S.E./World Bank, Oxford University Press, Washington D.C.

Frydman, R. et al. (eds.) (1993), *The Privatisation Process in Russia, Ukraine and the Batic States*, CEU/Privatisation Report, Vol. 2: Oxford University Press/CEU, Oxford.

Gel'man, V. (ed.) (1994), *Ocherki Rossisskoi politiki*, Moscow IGPI.

Gel'man, V. and Senatova, O. (1994), 'Politicheskie partii v regionakh Rossii', *Politicheskii monitoring 9/1.*

Gelman, V. and Senatova, O. (1995), 'Political reform in the Russian provinces: Trends since October 1993', in Lovenduski, J. and Stanyer, J. (eds.), *Contemporary Political Studies*, Volume 1 Political Studies Association, UK, pp. 435-444.

Gendler, G. and Gildingersh, M. (1993), 'Labor exhanges in St. Petersburg', RFE/RL Research Report 20 August, pp. 43-48.

George, V. (1991), 'Social security in the USSR', *International Social Security Review* Vol. 44 (4), pp. 47-65.

George, V. and Rimashevskaya, N. (1993), 'Poverty in Russia', *International social security review*, Vol. 46 (1).

Gerasimova, T.V. et al. (1995), 'Vypuskniki Moskovskikh vuzov na rynke truda', in Staroverov, V.I. et al. (eds.) (1995), *Rossiia nakanune XXI veka, Vypusk II*, Moscow, pp. 495-509.

Gilinskii, Ia. (1995), 'Prestupnost' i bezopasnost' naseleniia: S-Petersburg na fone Rossiiskoi deistvitel'nosti', *Informatsionno-analiticheskii biulleten' MONITORING sotsial'no-ekonomicheskoi situatsii i sostoianiia rynka truda S.-Petersburga*, No.1, September.

Gilinsky, Y., Podkolzin, V. and Kochetkov, E. (1995), 'The drug problem in St. Petersburg', in Chaika, N. *HIV/AIDS, STDs, Drug use and prostitution in St. Petersburg and Russia*, St. Petersburg Pasteur Institute, St. Petersburg, pp. 13-25.

Glukhova, A.Ia. (1995), 'Sotsial'no-politicheskaia situatsiia v Rossii v otsenke Vuzovskoi intelligentsii', in Staroverov, V.I. et al. (eds.) (1995), *Rossiia nakanune XXI veka, Vypusk II*, Moscow, pp. 76-86.

Golman, S. (1991), 'The Soviet legislative branch' in Thuber, R.T. and Kelley, D.F. (eds.), *Perestroika - Era Politics*, M.E. Sharpe, London, pp. 51-75.

Goldman, M.I. (1992), *What went wrong with perestroika*, W.W. Norton, New York.

Golod, S.I. and Kletsin, A.A. (1994), *Sostoianie i perspektivy razvitiia sem'i: Teoretiko-tipologicheskii analiz. Emiricheskoe obosnovanie*, Institut sotsiologii, RAN, St. Petersburg.

'Gonka za liderom' (1995), *Moskovskie Novosti* 15-22 October, p. 7.

Gurov, A. (1992), *Organizatsiia prestupnost - Ne mif, a real'nost'*, Moscow, 'Znanie'.

Gurov, A. (1995), *Krasnaia Mafiia*, Moscow, 'Samotsvet', Miko 'Kommercheskii Vestnik'.

Handelman, S. (1994), *Comrade criminal: The theft of the Second Russian Revolution*, Michael Joseph, London.

Hill, R.J. (1994), 'Parties and party system', in White, S. et al. (eds.), *Developments in Russian and post-Soviet politics*, Macmillan, London.

Hollander, P. (1965), 'The dilemmas of Soviet sociology', *Problems of Communism*, November-December, pp. 34-46.

Iakovlev, A.M. (1985), *Teoriia kriminologii i sotsial'naia praktika*, Moscow 'Nauka'.

Il'iasov, F.N. and Plotnikova, O.A. (1994), 'Nishchie v Moskve letom 1993 goda', *Sotsiologicheskie zhurnal*, No. 1.

Il'inskii, I.I. et al., (eds.) (1994), *Tsennostnyi mir sovremennoi molodezhi: na puti k mirovoi integratsii*, Moscow.

International Monetary Fund (1995), *World Economic Outlook*, I.M.F., Washington D.C., May.

Iudina, Ye. (1995), 'Besplatno li bezplatnoe obrazovanie?', *Ogonëk* No. 44, October, p. 26.

Iur'ev, D. (1995), 'Peizakh pered bitvoi', *Sevodnya* 21 October, p. 3.

Ivanov, O. et al. (1995), 'Klienty sluzhby zaniatosti naseleniia Sankt-Peterburga: Kto on?', Informatsionno-analiticheskii biulleten' *Monitoring: Sotsial'no-ekonomicheskoi situatsii i sostoianiia rynka truda S.-Peterburga*, No. 1, 1995, pp. 43-48.

Ivanov, V.N. et al. (eds.) (1994), *Etnopolicheskaia situatsiia v regionakh Rossiiskoi Federatsii (po rezul'tatam sotsiologicheskikh issledovanii v 1994g)*, Analiticheskii tsentr gosudarstvennoi dumy Federal'nogo sobraniia RF/Institut sotsial'no-politicheskikh issledovanii RAN, Moscow.

Ivanov, V.N. (1994b), *Moskichi o gode ukhodiashchem*, Institut sotsial'no-politicheskikh issledovanii RAN, Moscow.

Ivanov, V.N. (ed.) (1995a), *Sotsial'no-politicheskaia situatsiia i mezhnatsional'nye otnosheniia v Samare v otsenkakh i predstavleniiakh massovogo sozdaniia,*

Institut sotsial'no-politicheskikh issledovanii RAN, Moscow.

Ivanov, V.N. (1995b), *Sostoianie mezhnatsional'nykh otnoshenii v g. Ufa*, Institut sotsial'no-politicheskikh issledovanii RAN, Moscow.

Ivanov, V.N. (1995c), *Sostoianie mezhnatsional'nykh otnoshenii v Orenberge v otsenkakh i predstavleniiakh massovogo sozdaniia*, Institut sotsial'no-politicheskikh issledovanii RAN, Moscow.

Ivanov, V.N. (1995d), *Problemy stabil'nosti i vnutrennei bezopasnosti Rossii (Sotsiologicheskii analiz)*, Institut sotsial'no-politicheskikh issledovanii RAN, Moscow.

Jones, A. (ed.) (1994), *Education and Society in the New Russia*, M E Sharpe, New York.

Jones, A., Connor, W.D. and Powell, D.E. (eds.) (1991), *Soviet social problems*, Westview Press, Boulder, Colorado.

Juliver, P.H. (1976), *Revolutionary law and order*, Free Press, New York.

Juliver, P.H. (1991), 'No end of a problem: *Perestroika* for the family', in: Jones, A., Connor, W.D. and Powell, D.E. (eds.) (1991), *Soviet social problems*, Westview Press, Boulder, Colorado, pp. 194-212.

Kabo, V. (1990), 'Subkul'tura lagaeria i arkhetipy sozdaniia', *Sovetskaia Etnografiia*, No. 1.

Kalmykov, V.Y. (1979), *Khuliganstvo i mery bor'by s nim*, Minsk, Belarus.

Kampfner, J. (1994), *Inside Yeltsin's Russia: Corruption, Conflict, Capitalism*, Cassell, London.

Kartsev, V. with Bludeau, T. (1995), *Zhirinovskii*, Columbia University Press, New York.

Khorev, B. (1994), 'Novye mify rezhima', *Pravda* 28 October, pp. 1-2.

Khorev, V. (1994), *Demograficheskaya tragedniia Rossii*, Moscow 'Paleia'.

Kipman, O. (1990), 'O kompetentnosti i professionalizme', *Sovetskaia militsiia*, No. 4.

Kirillov, I. (1991), 'Potreblennie alkogolia i sotsial'nye posledstviia p'ianstva i alkogolizma', *Vestnik Statistiki*, No. 6.

Kitaev, I.V. (1994), 'The labor market and education in the post-Soviet era', in Jones, A. (ed.) (1994), *Education and Society in the New Russia*, M.E. Sharpe, New York, pp. 311-332.

Kolbanov, V.F. (1995), 'Vystuplenie pered predstaviteliami i mestnykh organov po trudu, obuchaiushchimisiia v IPK', unpublished Russian Federation, Ministry of Labour report, October.

Komarov, M.S. (1994), *Vvedenie v sotsiologiiu*, Moscow 'Nauka'.

Konstitutsiia Rossiiskoi Federatsii: Priniata vsenarodnym golosovaniem 12 dekabria 1993g (1993), Moscow, 'Iuridicheskaia literatura'.

Krapivenskii, S.Ye. (1992), *Paradoksy sotsial'nykh revolutysii*, Voronezh.

Krasnika, Y. (1995), 'Vosresnik v Tsentrizbirkome', *Moskovskie Novosti* 22-29 October, p. 6.

Kryshtanovskaya, O. (1994), 'Rich and poor in post-communist Russia', *Journal of Communist Studies and Transition Politics*, Vol. 10 (1), March, pp. 3-24.

Kurs Sovetskoi kriminologii (1985), Moscow 'Iuridicheskaia literatura'.

Kusio, T. (1994), 'The multi-party system in the Ukraine on the eve of the elections: Identity problems, conflicts and solutions', *Government and Opposition*, Vol. 29 (1), 1994.

Lane, D. (1970), *Politics and Society in the USSR*, Weidenfeld & Nicolson: London.

Lane, D. (1971), *The end of inequality: Stratification under state socialism*, Penguin, Harmondsworth.

Laqueur, W. (1994), *Black Hundred: The rise of the extreme right in Russia*, HarperPerennial, New York.

Lester, J. (1994), 'Zhirinovsky's Liberal Democratic Party: Programme, Leaders and Social base', *Labour Force on Eastern Europe* No. 47, Spring, pp. 17-30.

Levashov, V.K. et al. (1995), *Kak zhivesh', Rossiia? (Rezul'taty sotsiologicheskogo monitoring - mai-iiun' 1995 god)*, Institut sotsial'no-politicheskikh issledovanii RAN, Moscow.

Levinson, A. (1995), 'Chinovniki gotovy rabotaet s kommunisticheskoi Dumoi', *Sevodnya* 17 October, p. 3.

Levintin, G. (1990), 'Naskol'ko "pervobytna" ugolovnaia subkul'tura', *Sovetskaia Etnografiia*, No. 2.

Lichnost' prestupnika (1971), Moscow.

Lipset, Seymour Martin (1970), *The Political Man*, Doubleday, New York.

Lisovskii, V.T. (ed.) *(1995)*, Sotsiologiia Molodezhi, 3 volumes, *NII Kompleksnykh sotsial'nykh issledovanii/ St. Petersburgskogo gosugarstvennogo universiteta/Institut molodezhi/ Komitet po delam Molodezhi RF*, Moscow.

Luneev, V. (1989), 'Prestupnost' v SSSR za 1988g: statistika i kommentarii kriminologa', *Sovetskoe Gosudarstva i Pravo*, No. 8.

Malevannyi, V. (1995), 'Vremya vyborov glazami Gorbacheva', *Rossiia* 1-7 November, p. 3.

Marnie, S. (1993), 'Who and where are the Russian unemployed', RFE/RL Research Report, 20 August.

Materialy sipoziuma 23 Marta 1994 (1994), *Institut sotsial'no-politicheskikh issledovanii Rossiiskoi Akademii Nauk*, Moscow.

Matthews, M. (1972), *Class and Society in Soviet Russia*, Allen Lane/Penguin Press: London.

Matthews, M. (1978), *Privilege in the Soviet Union: A study of elite lifestyles under communism*, Allen & Unwin, London.

Matthews, M. (1986), *Poverty in the Soviet Union: the lifestyles of the underprivileged in recent years*, Cambridge University Press, Cambridge.

Matthews, M. and Jones, T.A. (1978), *Soviet sociology, 1964-75: A Bibliography*, Praeger: New York.

Mau, V. (1994), *Ekonomiko-politicheskie protsessy 1994 goda i Chechenskii krizis*, unpublished Institute for the Economy in Transition report, Moscow, November.

Martynenko, A. (1995), 'Pravitel'stvo vnov' poliubilo "neotkorretirovannye" reformy', *Interfaks AiF* 16-22 October, p. 11.

McAllister, I. and White, S. (1995), 'Democracy, political parties and party formation in post-communist Russia', *Party Politics*, Vol. 1 (1), pp. 49-72.

Medvedev, V. (1994), *V komande Gorbacheva*, Moscow.

Meskov, A. (1995), 'My - za politiku "vyrashchivaniia" dokhodov', *Vek* 3-9 November, p. 3.

Meyer, A.G. 'Theories of convergence', in Chambers Johnson (ed) (1970), *Change in Communist Systems*, Stanford University Press, Stanford California, pp. 313-314.

Michels, R. (1915), *Political parties*, New York, Free Press.

Miller, J. (1993), *Mikhail Gorbachev and the End of Soviet power*, Macmillan, London.

Miller, R.F. (ed.) (1992), *The developments of civil society in communist systems*, Allen and Unwin, Sydney.

Miller, R.F. (1992), 'Civil society in communist systems: An introduction' in Miller, R.F. (ed.) (1992), *The developments of civil society in communist systems*, Allen and Unwin, Sydney, pp. 1-10.

Miller, R.F. (1995), 'Reforming Russian agriculture: Privatisation in comparative perspective', in Saikal, A. and Maley, W. (eds.) (1995), *Russia in search of its future*, Cambridge University Press, Cambridge, pp. 66-85.

Modernizatsiia: Zarubezhnyi oypt i Rossiia (1994), Rossiiskii nezavisimyi institut sotsial'nykh i natsional'nykh problem, Agentstvo infomart, Moscow.

Molodezh' Rossii: Vospitanie zhiznesposobnykh pokolenii (Doklad komiteta Rossiiskoi Federatsii po delam molodezhi) (1995), State Committee on Youth Affairs, Moscow.

Molodezh' v usloviiakh sotsial'no-ekonomicheskikh reform: Materialy mezhdunarodnoi nauchno-prakticheskoi konferentsii (1995), Vypusk I and II, Gosudarstvennyi komitet RF po vysshemu obrazovaniiu/Komitet RF po delam molodezhi, St. Petersburg.

Mosca, G. (1939), *The ruling class*, New York, McGraw-Hill.

Narodnoe khozyiastvo SSSR v 1987g (1988), Moscow.

Narodnoe khozyiastvo SSSR v 1990g (1991), Moscow.

Nazarov, M.M. (1995), *Politicheskie tsennosti i politicheskii protest*, Institut sotsial'no-politicheskikh issledovanii RAN, Moscow.

Nikonov, V. (1995), 'Vybory: neevlidova geometriia', *Moskovskie Novosti* 22-29 October, p. 5.

Obshchestvennoe mnenie v tsifrakh (1990), No. 2.

O'Donnell, G. et al. (1986), *Transitions from authoritarian rule: Comparative perspectives*, John Hopkins University Press.

OECD Economic Surveys (1995), *The Russian Federation*, OECD, Paris, September.

OECD, *Public expenditure on Income programmes* (1976), OECD, Paris.

Orlova, I. (1994), 'Migratory processes in ex-USSR under conditions of social catalysm', paper presented to the XIII World Congress of Sociology, Bielefeld, Germany 18-23 July.

Orlova, I. (1994b), *Demograficheskaia i migratsionnaia situatsiia v Rossii (Sravnitel'nyi analiz)*, Institut sotsial'no-politicheskikh issledovanii RAN, Moscow.

Osipov, G.V. (1994), 'Reformirovanie Rossii: Itogi i perspectivy' in *Rossiia nakankune XXI veka*, Moscow.

Osipov, G.V. et al. (eds.) (1994a), *Reformirovanie Rossii: Mify i real'nost' (1989-1994)*, Moscow "Academia".

Osipov, G.V. et al. (eds.) (1994b), *Sovremennaia sotsial'no-demograficheskaia situatsiia i zaniatost' naseleniia Rossii*, Institut sotsial'no-politicheskikh issledovanii RAN, Moscow.

Osipov, G.V. et al. (eds.) (1995), *Sotsial'naia i sotsial'no-politicheskaia situatsiia v Rossii: Analiz i prognoz (Pervoe polugodie 1995 goda)*, Moscow "Academia".

Oxenstierna, S. (1992), 'Trends in Employment and Unemployment', in Åslund, A. (ed.), *The post-Soviet Economy: Soviet and Western Perspectives*, Pinter Publishers, London.

Pareto, V. (1935), *The Mind and Society*, New York, Harcourt-Brace.

Parsons, T. (1965), 'An American impression of sociology in the Soviet Union', *American sociological review*, January, pp. 121-125.

Perestroika: 10 let spustiia (Otsenki Moskvichei) (1995), Institut sotsial'no-politicheskikh issledovanii RAN/Gruppa MOST Analiticheskii Tsentr, Moscow.

Perspektivy razvitiia molodoi sem'i (dannye edinovremennogo obsledovaniia) (1993), Moscow, Goskomstat, Rossiisskoi Federatsii.

Pilkington, H. (1994), *Russian youth and its culture: A Nation's constructors and constructed*, London, Routledge.

Pokrovskii, N. (1994), 'Velikii Otkaz: vozvrashchenie v feodalizm s post-modermistckim litsom', *Nezavisimaia Gazeta* 27 September.

Polozhenie detei v Rossii 1992 god (sotsial'nyi portret) (1993), Moscow.

Porket, J.L. (1989), *Work, Employment and Unemployment in the Soviet Union*, St. Antony's/Macmillan, London.

Povarov, K. (1993), *'Gotovy stat' loial'nymi'*, *Inostranets*, No. 23.

Prestupnost' v Rossii v devianostykh godakh i nekotorye aspekty zakonnosti bor'by s nei (1995), Kriminologicheskaia Assotsiatsiia, Moscow.

Pushkin, A.S. (1978), *Collected Works*, Volume VII, Leningrad 1978.

Rawlinson, P. (1995), 'Organised crime in Russia', paper presented to the BASEES Annual conference, Fitzwilliam College, Cambridge March .

Remington, T.F. (1991), 'Parliamentary government in the USSR', in Thuber, R.T. and Kelley, D.F. (eds.) (1991), *Perestroika - Era Politics*, M.E. Sharpe, London, pp. 175-205.

Remington, T.F. (1994), 'Representative power and the Russian State', in White, S. et al. (eds.) (1994), *Developments in Russian and post-Soviet politics*, Macmillan, London, pp. 57-87.

Reshetnikova, T. (1993), 'Kakuiu pobedu my prazdnuek', *Rossisskii Vestnik* 23 October.

Rigby, T.H. (1992), 'The USSR: End of a long, dark night?', in Miller, R.F. (ed.) (1992), *The developments of civil society in communist systems*, Allen and Unwin, Sydney, pp. 19-23.

Riordan, J. (ed.) (1992), *Soviet social reality in the mirror of glasnost*, Macmillan/St. Martin's Press: London/New York.

Riordan, J. (1995), 'The Rise and Fall of a Youth Elite in Russia', in Riordan, J., Williams, C. and Ilynsky, I. (eds.), *Young people in post-communist Russia and Eastern Europe*, Dartmouth, Aldershot 1995, pp. 81-95.

Riordan, J., Williams, C. and Ilynsky, I. (1995), *Young people in post-communist Russia and Eastern Europe*, Dartmouth, Aldershot.

Roberts, G.K. (1971), *A Dictionary of Political Analysis*, Longman, London.

Romashov, O.V. (1993), 'Sotsial'naia zashchita trudiashchikhsia: problemy puti resheniia', *Sotsiologicheskie issledovaniia*, No. 1.

Rose, R. (1994), 'Getting by without government: Everyday life in Russia', *Daedalus* Vol. 23, No. 1.

Rose, R. (1995), 'Mobilising demobilised voters in post-communist societies', *Party Politics*, Vol. 1 (4), pp. 549-563.

Rose, R., Boeva, I. and Shironin, V., (1993), *How the Russians are coping with transition: New Russia Barometer II*, Studies in Public Policy, No. 228, Centre for the Study of Public Policy, University of Strathcylde/Paul Lazarfeld Society, Vienna.

Rose, R. and Haerpfer, C. (1994), *New Russian Barometer III: The Results*, Studies in Public Policy, Centre for the Study of Public Policy, University of Strathclyde/Paul Lazarsfeld Society, Vienna.

Rossiia nakankune XXI (1994), Vserossiiskoe nauchnoe obshchestvo sotsiologov i demografov/Institut sotsial'no-politicheskikh issledovanii RAN, Moscow.

Rossiia pered vyborom (1995), Moscow 'Obozrevatel'.

Rossiia pered Vyborom: Sotsiologicheskii analiz obshchestvennogo mneniia elektorata (1994), *Institut sotsial'no-politicheskikh issledovanii Rossiiskoi Akademii Nauk*, Moscow.

Rossiia sevodnya: Real'nyi shans (1994), Moscow.

Rossiia v tsifrakh (1995), Goskomstat, Moscow.

'Rossiiskaia sotsiologicheskaia traditsiia shestidesiatykh godov i sovremennost' (1994), in *Materialy sipoziuma 23 Marta 1994*, *Institut sotsial'no-politicheskikh issledovanii Rossiiskoi Akademii Nauk*, Moscow.

'Rossiiskie izbirateli meniaut svoi simpatii' (1995), *Sevodnya*, 27 October, p. 2.

Ruble, B. (1978), *Soviet sociological research establishments*, Kennan Institute for Advanced Russian Studies, Washington D.C.

Rudkin, C. (1995), 'Is there really a link between Russian business and organised crime? Problems of methodology', paper presented to the BASEES Annual conference, Fitzwilliam College, Cambridge March 1995.

Rukavishnikov, V. (1994), 'A split society: Political crisis and popular support for transition to a free market and democracy in Russia', *Sociale Wetenschapen*, No. 2.

Rukavishnikov, V. et al. (1994), 'The dynamics of civil and political society in Russia', paper presented to the XIII World Congress of Sociology, Bielefeld, Germany 18-23 July.

Rutkevich, M. (1992), 'Sotsial'naia polarizatsiia', *Sotsiologicheskie issledovaniia*, No. 9.

Rutland, P. (1994), 'The economy: The rocky road to reform: From plan to market', in: White, S. et al. (eds.) (1994), *Developments in Russian and post-Soviet politics*, Macmillan, London.

Ryan, M. (1978), *The Organisation of Soviet Medical Care*, Martin Robertson, London.

Ryan, M. (1990), *Contemporary Soviet society: A handbook*, Edward Elgar, Aldershot.

Ryvkina, R. (1988), 'Reactionary traditions and revolutionary needs', *Vek XX* and *Mir 3*.

Sakwa, R. (1990), *Gorbachev and His reforms, 1985-1990*, Phillip Allan, London.

Sakwa, R. (1993a), *Russian Politics and Society*, Routledge, London.
Sakwa, R. (1993b), 'Parties and the multi-party system in Russia', RFE/RL Research Report 30 July, pp. 7-15.
Sakwa, R. (1995), 'The Russian elections of December 1993', *Europe-Asia Studies*, Vol. 47 (2), pp. 195-227.
Savel'ev, O. (1995a), 'Chetvertaia chast' rossiiskikh izbiratelei ne goveriaet nikomu iz politikov', *Sevodnya* 19 October, p. 3.
Savel'ev, O. (1995b), 'Naselenie soglasno s sotsiologami v prgnoze rezul'tatov vyborov', *Sevodnya* 3 November, p. 3.
Schlesinger, A. (1992), *Etnicheskaia obosoblennost'* , Moscow.
Schmitter, P. (1988), 'The consolidation of political democracy in Southern Europe', unpublished manuscript.
Schmitter, P.C. with Karl, T.L. (1994), 'The conceptual travels of transitologists and consolidologists: How far to the East should they attempt to go?', *Slavic Review*, Vol. 53 (1), Spring, pp. 173-85.
Shaknazarov, G. (1993), *Tsena svobody: Reformatsiia Gorbacheva glazami ego pomoshchnika*, Moscow.
Shelley, L.I. (1980), 'Crime and Delinquency in the Soviet Union', in Pankhurst, J.G and Sacks, M.P. (eds.) (1980), *Contemporary Soviet Society: Sociological perspectives*, Praeger, New York.
Shelley, L. (1991), 'Crime in the Soviet Union' in Jones, A., Connor, W.D. and Powell, D.E. (eds.), *Soviet social problems*, Westview Press, Boulder Colorado.
Shlapentokh, V. (1987), *The politics of sociology in the Soviet Union*, Westview Press, Boulder, Colorado.
Shmelev, N. (1987), 'Avansy i dolgi', *Novyi Mir* No. 6, June.
Simirenko, A. (ed.) (1966), *Soviet sociology: Historical antecedents and critical appraisals*, Quadrangle books, Chicago.
Simis, K. (1982), *USSR: Secrets of a corrupt society*, J.M. Dent and Sons Ltd, London.
Slovar' prikladnoi sotsiologii (1984), Minsk, 'Universitetskoe'.
Smeeding, T.M. et al. (1990), *Poverty, inequality and income distribution in Comparative perspective*, Harvester Wheatsheaf, New York.
Smith, S. (1994), 'Writing the History of the Russian Revolution after the fall of Communism', *Europe-Asia Studies*, Vol. 46 (4), pp. 563-578.
Sogrin, V. (1994), *Politicheskaia istoriia sovremennoi Rossii*, 'Progress - Akademiia', Moscow.
Sotsial'no-ekonomicheskoe polozhenii Rossii 1994g (1995), Moscow, Goskomstat January.
Sovremennaia zapadnaia sotsiologiia: slovar' (1990), Moscow 'Politzdat'.
Stadler, A. (1994), 'Problems of dependent modernization in East-Central Europe: A case for social democratic concern', in Waller, M. et al. (eds.) (1994), *Social democracy in post-communist Europe*, Frank Cass, London, pp. 45-65.
Standing, G. (1992), 'Recruitment, training and human resource management in Russian industry', paper presented to a conference on *Employment Restructuring in Russia*, Moscow and St. Petersburg, 21-29 October.

Staroverov, V.I. et al. (eds.) (1995), *Rossiia nakanune XXI veka, Vypusk II, Institut sotsial'no-politicheskikh issledovanii Rossiiskoi Akademii Nauk,* 'Nauka', Moscow.

Statbiulleten' Gosudarstvennaia sluzhba zaniatosti (1995), No. 6.

Statisticheskoe Obozrenie (1995), No. 9.

Sting, S. and Wulf, C. (eds.) (1994), *Education in a period of social upheaval,* Waxman Munster/New York.

Teague, E. (1992), 'Russian government seeks "social partnership" ', RFE/RL Research Report 16 June, pp. 16-23.

Tekyshchii arkhiv NiTS pri Institut Molodezhi (1994), Moscow, April.

The World in 1996 (1995), Economist Publications, London.

Tönnies, F. (1957), *Community and Society,* translated and introduced by Charles P. Loomis, Michigan State University Press, Michigan.

United Nations, Economic Commission for Europe, *Economic Survey of Europe in 1994-95* (1995), New York and Geneva.

Utechin, S.V. (1963), *Russian Political thought,* J.M. Dent and Sons, London.

Vaksberg, A. (1991), *The Soviet Mafia,* Weidenfeld and Nicolson, London.

Vasil'tsov, S. (1995), 'Kakoi zhe stsenarii primut "verkhi" ', *Sovetskaia Rossiia* No. 122, 14 October, p. 4.

Vorotnikov, V.P. et al. (eds.) (1995), *Sotsial'naia politika i predprinimatel'stvo,* Vypusk I, Institut sotsial'no-politicheskikh issledovanii RAN, Analiticheskii tsentr gruppy MOST, Moscow.

Voslenskii, M. (1984), *Nomenklatura,* Overseas Publications Interchange Ltd, London.

Vososel'skii, V. (1995), *Sostoianie rynka truda Rossii v 1992-1994 goda i pervoi polovine 1995 goda,* Russian Ministry of Labour Report dated 15 June.

VTsIOM (1990), *Obshchestvennoe mnenie v tsifrakh* No. 2.

Vybory - 1995 (1995), Moscow 'Obozrevatel'.

Walicki, A. (1969), *The controversy over Capitalism: Studies in the philosophy of the Russian Populists,* Oxford University Press, Oxford.

Walicki, A. (1975), *The Slavophile controversy: History of a Conservative Utopia in Nineteenth Century Russian Thought,* Oxford University Press, Oxford.

Walicki, A. (1980), *A History of Russian thought: From the enlightenment to Marxism,* Clarendon Press, Oxford.

Ward Kingkade, W. (1993), 'Demographic prospects in the republics of the former Soviet Union', in Kaufman, R.F. and Hardt, J.P. (eds.) (1993), *The former Soviet Union in Transition,* M.E. Sharpe, New York.

Weigel, M.A. (1992), 'The consolidation of civil and political society in post-communist regimes: Central Europe and Russia', paper delivered to the Annual meeting of the Midwest Political Association, Chicago, Illinois, 9-11 April.

Weigle, M.A. (1994), 'Political participation and party formation in Russia, 1985-92: Institutionalising democracy', *Russian Review,* April.

Weinberg, E.A. (1974), *The Development of sociology in the Soviet Union,* RKP, London.

Westbrook, M.A. et al. (1994), 'The independent schools of St. Petersburg: Diversification of schooling in post-communist Russia', in Jones, A. (ed.) (1994),

Education and Society in the New Russia, M.E. Sharpe, New York, pp. 103-117.

White, S. (1994), 'Introduction: From Communism to Democracy?', in White, S., Pravda, A. and Gitelman, Z. (eds.) (1994), *Developments in Russian and Post-Soviet Politics*, Macmillan, London.

Willerton, J.P. (1994), 'Yeltsin and the Russian Presidency', in White, S. et al. (eds.) (1994), *Developments in Russian and post-Soviet politics*, Macmillan, London, pp. 25-57.

Williams, C. (1990), 'Soviet Public health: A case study of Leningrad, 1917-32', unpublished PhD in History, University of Essex 1990.

Williams, C. (1991), 'Old habits die hard: Alcoholism in Leningrad under NEP and some lessons for the Gorbachev administration', *Irish Slavonic Studies*, No. 12, pp. 69-96.

Williams, C. (1992), 'Russian views of European integration: An historical perspective', paper delivered to a Conference on the New Europe, University of Nottingham, April.

Williams, C. (1994a), 'From the Black Hundreds to Zhirinovsky: The rise of the extreme right in Russia', Renvall Institute of Historical Research, University of Helsinki, Finland, 28 February.

Williams, C. (1994b), 'Shock therapy and its impact on poverty in Contemporary Russia', Paper presented to the Politics of Social security in East European session of 22nd ECPR workshop, Madrid 17-22 April.

Williams, C. (1994c), 'The Revolution from above in Soviet medicine, Leningrad 1928-32', *Journal of urban history*, Vol. 20, No. 4, August, pp. 512-540.

Williams, C. (1995a), *AIDS in post-communist Russia and its successor states*, Avebury, Aldershot.

Williams, C. (1995b), 'Respectable fears' versus 'Moral panics': Youth as a social problem in Russia and Britain', in Riordan, J., Williams, C. and Ilynsky, I (eds.) (1995), *Young people in post-communist Russia and Eastern Europe*, Dartmouth, Aldershot, pp. 29-50.

Williams, C. (1995c), 'Victim, villain or symbol of capitalism? Whores in Russian history', *Irish Slavonic Studies*, forthcoming No. 15.

Williams, C. (1995d), 'Abortion and women's health in contemporary Russia' in Marsh, R. (ed.), *Women in Russia and the Ukraine*, Cambridge University Press, Cambridge, forthcoming.

Williams, C. (1995e), 'Unemployment in Britain, Europe and Russia: A Comparative analysis', Paper presented to a conference on *The transformation of social structure in post-Soviet society: Trends and prospects*, Vologda, 4-6 October.

Wyman, M. et al. (1994), 'The Russian elections of December 1993', *Electoral Studies*, Vol. 13 (1), September, pp. 254-271.

Wyman, M. et al. (1995), 'The place of "Party" in post-communist Europe', *Party Politics* Vol. 1 (4), pp. 535-548.

XXVIII S'ezd Kommunisticheskoi partii Sovetskogo Soiuza: Stenograficheskii Otchet (1986), Moscow.

Yakovlev, A. (1993), *The Fate of Marxism in Russia*, Yale University Press, London.

Yanowitch, M. (1978), *Social and economic inequality in the USSR*, Martin Robertson,

London.

Zaslavskaya, T. (1987a), 'Perestroika and sociology', *Social Research* 55 (1-2), pp. 267-276.

Zaslavskaya, T. (1987b), 'Rol' sotsiologii v uskorenii razvitiya sovetskogo obshchestva', *Sotsiologicheskie issledovaniia* No. 2, pp. 3-15.

Zaslavskaya, T. (1988), 'Friends or Foes? Social forces working for or against perestroika' in Aganbegyan, A. (ed.) (1988), *Perestroika Annual*, Futura: London.

Zaslavskaya, T. (1995), *Kuda idet Rossiia?..Al'ternativy obshchestvennogo razvitiia*, 'Aspekt Press', Moscow.

Zaslavskaya, T. and Ryvkina, R.V. (eds.) (1989), *Ekonomicheskaya sotsiologiya i perestroika*, Progress, Moscow.

Zdravomyslov, A.G. (1994), 'Sotsiologiia v Rossii', *Vestnik Akademii Nauk* 64/9.

Zdravookhranenie v Rossiiskoi Federatsii: Statisticheskii sbornik (1995), Goskomstat, Moscow.

Index

Aron, R., 42
Arson, 236
Art, 206
Article 6 of Constitution, 14
Artificial abortions, 60
Asia, 52
Aspirations of Younger generation,
    chapter 8-9
Assault with a deadly weapon, Table
    14.3, 223
Associational freedoms, 29
Asymmetric interdependence, 3
Atomisation of society, Table 6.1, 94
Attitudes to perestroika, 10, 76, 219-20,
    243, 254
August 1991 coup d'etat, 1, 10, 15, 242
Authoritarianism, 2, 14, 29, 153, 214
Authority, 39
Avars, 256, Table 16.1, 257
Average wages, Table 7.2, 114
Azerbaidzhan, 69, Table 12.2, 186, 230

Balkars, 262
Baltic states, 230
Bandages, shortages of, 195
Banditism, 226
Banking, 204, 228
Banknotes, 230
Bankruptcy, 11, 112, 177
Barabeshev criminal group, 226
Barricade mentality, 148
Bashkir, 254
Bashkortostan, 257
Basques, 258
Becker, H., 98-9
Beds, Tables 12.1, 185; Table 12.2, 186;
    Table 12.3, 189; Table 12.5, 197
Beer Lovers Party, Table 1.6, 24
Belarus, 69, 186, 256, 266
Belgorod, n.6, 150
Benefits, 154
    inadequacies of, 156-7, 171-3
    unemployment, 176
Berdayev, N., 48
Berdayev, S., 42
Bermuda Triangle, view of Russia, 14

Biology, 133
Birth control, 60
Birth grant, 156
Birth rate, 3, 57, Table 3.1, 58, 58-60,
    64, 72
Black Hundreds, n.25, 33-4
Blat, 203
Blind children, 145
Bollen, K., 250
Bolsheviks, 78, 154
Borisov, V.A., 58, 72
Borstals, 235
Botkin hospital, 199
Bottlenecks, 10
Bourdieu, P., 38
Bourgeoisie, 88-9
Brain drain, 168, 208, 213
Bread, price of, 11
Brezhnev era, 248
    views of, Table 15.4, 248
Brezhnev, L., 94, 111, 225
Bribery, *see* Corruption
Budget deficit, Table 1.1, 13
Bulgakov, S., 5, 42
Bureaucracy, 88, 174, 246
    opposition to change, 10
Bureaucratic socialism, 85-6
Burglaries, Table 14.2, 222; Table 14.3,
    223, 233-5
Buryats, 256, Table 16.1, 257
Businessmen, Table 9.1, 146
Business sector, 90, 116-7

Cairo, 61
California, 255
Cancer, 184, Table 12.4, 194, 196
Capital city medical sub-system, Figure
    12.1, 184
Capitalism, 51, 116, 162
Capitalist mentality, 49
Career prospects, 129
Careers Advisory centres, 176
Car theft, 233-34
Catastrophe, 4, 197
Caucasus, 68, Table 11.2, 170, 258,
    261, 264